Music and Modernity among First Peoples of North America

Edited by Victoria Lindsay Levine
and Dylan Robinson

MUSIC AND
MODERNITY AMONG
FIRST PEOPLES
OF NORTH AMERICA

Wesleyan University Press   Middletown, Connecticut

Wesleyan University Press
Middletown CT 06459
www.wesleyan.edu/wespress
© 2019 Wesleyan University Press
Manufactured in the United States of America
Designed by Mindy Basinger Hill
Typeset in Minion Pro

In chapter 3, the lyrics to "Poem 15" (Joe 1978) are used
by permission of Rita Joe's family.

In chapter 4, the lyrics to "Bill c-31 Blues" and "Rez Sister"
by Sara Pocklington are used by permission; the lyrics to "Iskwesis"
by Sherryl Sewepagaham are used by permission.

In chapter 5, the video introductory text to *We Got This;* "Get Up,"
from *Sonic Smash;* "Papers"; and "Remember," all by
Shining Soul, lyrics by Liaizon, are used by permission.

In chapter 6, the lyrics to "Red Winter" by Drezus, the lyrics to
"Idle No More" by Rellik, and the lyrics to "Round Dance"
by Sullivan and Day are used by permission.

In chapter 7, the lyrics to "Mom's Song (Keep on Flying)," "Fresh,"
"Gotta Make Moves," and "Regals and Olds" by Emcee One, the
lyrics to "I Am My Ancestors," "I Pulled a 187 on a Mascot," "Them
Country Roads," "Fame," "California," "Oklahoma," "Superbrightstar,"
"Life So Great," "The Bird Song," "Red Zeppelin," "Radiation," "Rebel
Music," "Whiskey Bottles," and "I Resist" by Quese Imc, and the lyrics
to "Upside Down," "Guns and Roses," "405," "South Central Farm,"
"Welcome All," "Zoom," "Gravitron," "Light Up the World," "Casino
Money," and "Native Threats" by RedCloud are used by permission.

In chapter 10, the lyrics to "Timmivunga" (I am flying)
by Peand-eL are used by permission.

Library of Congress Cataloging-in-Publication Data
appear at the end of the book

5   4   3   2

CONTENTS

FIGURES

TABLES

Acknowledgments

The idea for this volume emerged in 2009 at a diner in Denver, Colorado. Exhilarated by the insights and perspectives of a new generation of Indigenous ethnomusicologists, Victoria Levine casually suggested to John-Carlos Perea and Jessica Bissett Perea that it might be time for an edited collection on contemporary Native music. A few months later Elyse Carter Vosen wrote to Vicki; Elyse had heard from another colleague that a volume was being planned, and she offered to write a chapter. Startled and mildly amused that her impromptu remark had spread, Vicki began to consider the idea in earnest. Then, in 2011, Dylan Robinson introduced himself to Vicki to propose coediting a collection, and the project coalesced. We expanded the book's theme to encompass questions surrounding what several scholars—most notably Beverley Diamond—had been theorizing as "Indigenous modernities" among First Peoples of North America. Potential contributors met in the fall of 2012 to discuss the conceptual threads that might weave the case studies together, and a year later we held a three-day writing workshop to share feedback on early drafts of each chapter. We received the finished chapters by the fall of 2016 and, despite inevitable bumps along the way, the project came to fruition.

An undertaking of this nature requires significant funding from both governmental and institutional sources, which we gratefully acknowledge. We wish to thank the Social Sciences and Humanities Research Council of Canada (SSHRC) for a generous Connections grant that enabled us to hold the 2013 writing workshop. Colorado College further supported the writing workshop through grants from the Humanities Division and the Jackson Fellows program and funded Vicki's research assistants over three successive summers through Faculty-Student Collaborative Research grants and the Christine S. Johnson Professorship in Music. Colorado College also provided a substantial subvention to support the book's publication through the National Endowment for the Humanities Distinguished Professorship. Dylan's work on the project was supported by the Banting Fellowship program and subsequently by the Canada Research Chair program.

Our project benefited from the experience and assistance of many people. Laurie Matheson, director of the University of Illinois Press, offered unstinting and enthusiastic encouragement that helped shape this volume, and we are grateful for her expertise and friendship. We appreciate the ongoing advice of our colleague and contributor Beverley Diamond, who enlightens and inspires us. At Memorial University of Newfoundland, we thank Lisa McDonald, senior administrative officer in the School of Music, for administering our SSHRC grant. At Colorado College we thank visual resources curator Meghan Rubenstein, instructional technologist Weston Taylor, music copyist Connor Rice, and research assistants Emily Kohut, Rishi Ling, and Breana Taylor for their help with manuscript preparation. We also thank Music Department administrative assistants Stormy Burns, Lisa Gregory, Andrea Schumacher, and Gina Spiers for logistical support. For their kind and careful guidance throughout the publication process, we are grateful to the staff of Wesleyan University Press (Suzanna Tamminen, director and editor in chief) and of the University Press of New England (Susan Abel, production editor; and Susan Silver, copyeditor). It was a pleasure to collaborate with each and every contributor to this volume, and we appreciate their good work and collegiality.

For friendship and encouragement throughout our work on this project, we thank Tamara Bentley, Charlotte Frisbie, Bruno Nettl, and Deborah Wong. We are grateful to the anonymous peer reviewers for their helpful suggestions. Finally, we would not have completed this project without the cheerful indulgence of our families; Vicki thanks Mark, Scott, and Elizabeth Levine; and Dylan thanks Keren Zaiontz and Chloe Robinson. We are indebted to you all.

Prologue

Pagmapak: In Modern Times

Pualanaqsiah! "Welcome, it's time to dance!" I invite readers of this volume
to consider the ideas presented here by a group of authors who have come
together from diverse backgrounds with a common cause: to discuss the idea
of music and modernity among North America's First Peoples. As an Inupiaq
musician and scholar, I invite you to partake in this book as typical traditional
and contemporary Inupiaq dance groups would invite guests to join in an opening *puala*, or invitational dance, which allows participants to get to know one
another. Inupiaq dance groups usually have between five and fifteen drummers
who play thin tambourine-type drums made with driftwood rims and walrus
stomach linings or whale liver linings for drumheads. Each drummer uses a
long, thin drumstick to hit the outer rim and drumhead from underneath the
drum. Drummers sing in unison and are joined by additional singers and dancers. Inupiaq dance gatherings often begin with *pualat*, which allow musicians to
warm up their singing voices and try out the drum tensions and give dancers a
chance to experiment with expressive movements in an improvisatory manner.
There are certain protocols for invitational dances, including gender-specific
moves for men and women: women keep their feet together, bend at the knees,
and make graceful circular arm- and hand-waving motions to the beat of the
drum, while men may stomp a foot on the floor and show off their chest muscles
by making fists and angular motions with their arms to the beat of the drum.
The leader of the drum group chooses invitational songs that have steady beat
patterns, so guests can join in dancing together with confidence. Invitational
dances are opportunities for visitors and host dance groups to share the dance
floor to get a sense of one another's skills, attitudes, prowess, and willingness to

share in celebration. Just as our traditional Inupiaq dance stems from ancient stories and practices of the past, it also grounds us in the present and helps us think about the future, as we see our youngest members of the community begin to participate and understand the importance of music as a mechanism of creating a sense of solidarity. Please join us in this publication that celebrates Native music in many forms.

The idea of juxtaposing the word *modernity* with *Indigenous* or *First Peoples* infers a sort of incongruity, as if Native peoples cannot be at once Indigenous and modern. From our Indigenous perspectives, we are always modern. In Inupiaq languages the closest expressions for "modern" are *pakmami* (*Qawiaraq* dialect), which means "now, at the present time" (R. Agloinga and Harrelson 2013, 109), or *pagmapak*, which means "now, at the present time; in modern times" (MacLean 2014, 216). Inupiaq derivatives of the word *pakmami* describe something that is modern and of the present, from a northern Alaska Native perspective, regardless of the era or point in time. We don't see ourselves as old-fashioned; rather, we exist in the present while invoking past and future generations. Bringing ideas from the past into the present is a way of "Indigenizing" just about anything, including popular and classical musics by Native composers and singer-songwriters. New music challenges listeners to rethink static images of Indigeneity through expressive media that are at once forward-looking and of the present and that embrace the past.

Indigenous musicians employ multiple processes and technologies in their compositions, and their works are Native because the artists reflect their Indigenous worldviews. Their works can be akin to contemporary Indigenous visual arts, such as those presented at the exhibition *Changing Hands: Art without Reservation*, first held at the Museum of Arts and Design in New York. In viewing this exhibit, I was struck by the visible markers that connected the past with modern or futuristic elements in materials, contents, and forms. I learned about this exhibition from my Inupiaq father, Ron Senungetuk, whose piece, titled *Columbia Glacier*, was included in the exhibit. This piece is a diptych consisting of two silver maple wood panels, into which he carved abstracted forms and tinted the wood with colorful oil stains; he used Scandinavian wood-laminating techniques combined with ideas from nineteenth-century Inupiaq graphics incised on walrus ivory. My father's works tell his own stories and often draw attention to a sense of place, but he also insists on the element of change as a constant state of being. He says, "In order for traditions to remain traditional, they must always change and adapt to present ways. Otherwise, they become part of dead cultures" (qtd. in McFadden and Taubman 2005, 116). Rather than sticking with static images of "Native art," his works challenge viewers to change with the artist. Similarly, Indigenous musicians of the current era incorporate and reflect ideas of the present and future and simultaneously recall deeply held cultural values and worldviews.

One issue presented in this volume that speaks to me as a classical violinist is the idea of sound quantum, or the idea that a certain percentage of sonic "Nativeness" is necessary for music to "qualify" as Indigenous. Who decides what constitutes sonic Nativeness in music? I've asked this question for years. As an interpreter of other artists' compositions, I am part of the collaboration and the creation of sound as art, and through this process I reveal who I am, and how I think, as a Native musician. My role as an interpretive artist depends on compositions created by others, who may or may not be Indigenous. In recent years I have played a suite of *Caprice Variations* for solo violin by the U.S. composer George Rochberg (1973). In my performances of this work, I reinterpret the titles of the movements I play, using words from Inupiaq languages in an effort to reveal my thinking processes to the audience and thus to personalize my performances. "Moderately fast, fantastico" becomes "*Niqsaaniaq* [Seal hunting]" because of the imagery that comes to my mind while I play the movement. The element of suspense created by silences followed by quick changes in tempo, combined with angular melodic lines, reminds me of stories I have heard from my elders, telling me about hunting seals on the cold winter ice, using quick, sharp motions with harpoons to secure a food source for survival. The variation "Poco Agitato ma con molto Rubato" becomes "*Ikiit, Kumait* (Bugs, Lice)" because of the agitated feeling brought on by the constant tremolo bowing throughout the movement as indicated by the composer. In Alaskan summers mosquitos can present relentless agitation, and this movement simply reminds me of the battle with bugs. I present this translation in program notes and in a verbal explanation to the audience, suggesting that they create mental imagery that connects the sounds made on the violin to ideas in Inupiaq life to gain an understanding of me as an interpretive musician. My intention is to reveal to the audience the images that inspire me to make music out of the notes provided in Rochberg's score and to make visible a process that is normally private, thus revealing my Nativeness to the audience. Quite often, as part of the violin section of a symphony orchestra, I blend in with the other players as part of a larger performing collective. While I appreciate being a part of a creative team in an orchestra, I enjoy solo performances as a way to express my inner self and the stories of the heritage I grew up with in Alaska. Our Indigenous thinking is on the inside of everything we do, even though at times it may look like some form of assimilation on the outside.

For me, the intersection of Indigenous musical expression and border politics continues to be a topic of importance. People often think of history and culture belonging to one nation or another, without realizing that regional modifications imposed by nation-states affect Indigenous peoples worldwide. In my research as a graduate student in ethnomusicology at Wesleyan University, I investigated shared musical practices in the Beringia region, which encompasses Northwest Alaska and Chukotka in the Russian Far East. The westernmost point of mainland Alaska is just over fifty miles across the ocean from mainland Chukotka, and, traditionally, Indigenous peoples traded and shared goods and cultures across the Bering Strait. During the Cold War between the United States and the former Soviet Union, all trade and cultural communications were severed between these communities for forty years. Currently, villages on both sides of the Bering Strait are showing interest in reclaiming trade networks and re-generating cultural sovereignty through music and dance, all while negotiating issues of imposed geopolitical regulations that transformed the region. In 2013 the community of Kotzebue, Alaska, was successful in bringing a group of seventeen musicians, dancers, and artists from the Chukotkan communities of Uelen and Lavrentia to participate in their biennial Qatŋut trade fair, despite much difficulty in securing expensive visas and making arrangements to meet with appropriate border agents. Decades of forced assimilation policies on either side of the border resulted in different colonial languages, but the dancers and musicians could communicate and participate together through rhythmic expressions of Indigenous performing arts. They are regenerating relationships between distant family members and creating new friendships as they share their cultural arts. This is only one example of a common predicament affecting Indigenous peoples regarding political power struggles that have an impact on musical networking and creativity.

As a Native graduate student, I appreciated being included in the process of collaboration in creating this book about modernity in music of North America's Indigenous peoples. This encouragement of emerging scholars reflects Native ways of being by including multiple generations and extended family members in educational processes. An example of this intergenerational support is the participation by parents, grandparents, and great-grandparents alongside children, grandchildren, and great-grandchildren at practice sessions for the Kingikmiut Dancers and Singers of Anchorage, a dance group with ancestral ties to the Native Village of Wales, Alaska. It takes a long time to learn the intricacies of the precise musical rhythms, song texts, and dance motions, and a single individual cannot retain and transmit an entire culture. Intergenerational participation allows for growth of the art form and inspires participants in both directions—the younger dancers and musicians learn from the elders' expertise, and the elders are encouraged by the youth to model best performance practices. The multigenerational approach in this book is important because the transfer of knowledge between generations, which is central to Indigenous epistemologies, is made "modern" when applied to academic contexts. Here the contributors provide models of scholarship for students of Indigenous studies, anthropology, and ethnomusicology, while engaging Native points of view.

Connecting with one another is another hallmark of Indigenous ways of being. In many regions of North America, Native communities have reinvigorated dance festivals in the past few decades as a way of making time to connect with one another, exchange ideas, and reaffirm larger imagined communities through shared cultural performances, languages, and foods. For example, the Native Village of Wales holds its annual Kingikmiut Dance Festival in late August or early September, creating a space for five or six regional dance troupes to come together to share their cultural heritages. This volume reflects that idea of creating a space for building alliances between Native and non-Native scholars by focusing on a theme of modernity among Indigenous performing arts. The authors demonstrate the modernity of Indigenous peoples using music through an assemblage of topics ranging from traditional and neotraditional powwow music to musical composition, Indigenizing hip-hop, gender issues, funding for music social programs, imagery in music, political power, and identity. The diversity of topics addressed in this anthology shows the depth and multiplicity of Indigenous peoples' concerns within broad geographic and cultural areas. As a collective presentation, this volume joins a small but growing body of literature in ethnomusicology that includes Native perspectives in conjunction with allies' interpretations. The book *Native American Dance: Ceremonies and Social Traditions* (1992), edited by Charlotte Heth (Cherokee), is a collection of chapters from Indigenous scholars regarding traditional forms of dance. *The Alaska Native Reader* (2009), an assemblage of chapters edited and introduced by Maria Shaa Tláa Williams (Tlingit), focuses on people of Alaska, predominantly with Alaska Native authors, but with a broader focus on their histories, cultures, and multitude of expressive art forms. *Music of the First Nations* (2009b), an anthology edited and introduced by Tara Browner (Choctaw), presents chapters by Native and non-Native authors, more specifically about regional Indigenous musics of North America. The collection of chapters in *Aboriginal Music in Contemporary Canada* (Hoefnagels and Diamond 2012) juxtaposes Native and non-Native perspectives from a wide variety of authors regarding current contemporary musical practices of Indigenous peoples of the land currently called Canada. It is our hope that *Music and Modernity among First Peoples of North America* contributes to the growing interest in Indigenous performing arts.

As an Inupiaq musician and scholar, I tend to see the issues presented in this volume in relation to Inupiaq ways of being. I welcome you to create your own alliances with the authors' ideas in their explorations of what it means to be Indigenous musicians in modern times, *pagmapak. Pualanaqsiah*!

Music and Modernity
among First Peoples
of North America

VICTORIA LINDSAY LEVINE

1. Music, Modernity, and Indigeneity

Introductory Notes

Modernity and Indigeneity have been defined in different ways at different times, often in opposition to each other. As a bundle of interrelated ideas, the concepts of modernity and Indigeneity emerged in European thought during the eighteenth and nineteenth centuries. Modernity implies industrialization, urbanization, the displacement of individuals from their communities of origin, increased mobility, technological progress, and, perhaps most importantly, a break with tradition. Indigeneity refers to peoples who originated in a particular place and who were subjugated by European settler colonists. The coimplicated concepts of modernity and Indigeneity developed in tandem, then, and represented ways of thinking used to justify European colonial expansion and the "othering" of Native peoples. For settler colonists, the term *Indigenous* conjured images of people practicing antiquated customs and rural lifestyles, removed from and out of touch with mainstream social, cultural, political, and economic trends. But Eurocentric definitions of both modernity and Indigeneity have changed, at least in academic circles. By the 1990s scholars began to develop new approaches to understanding modernity and Indigeneity that recognize modernity as a process and also recognize alternative forms of modernity (Cf. Knauft 2002). Moreover, they grasped the centrality of ancestral values, knowledge, protocols, and cognitive patterns to contemporary Indigenous peoples. Music, as a symbolic system, plays a central role in the articulation of the complexity and diversity of modern Indigenous lives—clearly illustrated in the music of twenty-first-century Indigenous individuals and communities of North America, including Native American Indians, First Nations, Inuit, and Métis peoples.

The contributors to this volume seek new ways of understanding the intersections among music, modernity, and Indigeneity in North America through individual case studies. Our twin goals are to refocus the ethnomusicology of American Indians/First Nations toward new perspectives on Indigenous modernity and to model decolonized approaches to the study of Indigenous musical cultures. The collection features the work of both established and emerging scholars in the fields of ethnomusicology and American Indian/First Nations studies and brings research on Native music into dialogue with critical Indigenous studies. As a group, we take an activist stance toward the ethnomusicology of First Peoples, and we see Indigenous musical modernity as a continuing process. We posit the existence of multiple modernities among Indigenous peoples, a multiplicity that is not reducible to a single history or set of core values. With those givens, four main themes surrounding ideologies of modernity bind these case studies together: innovative technology, identity formation and self-representation, political activism, and translocal musical exchange. The contributors also explore closely related concepts, including cosmopolitanism, hybridity, alliance studies, multilingualism or code switching, and ontologies of sound. Some chapters focus on popular music genres such as hip-hop or rock, but Native Classical, Christian, intertribal, and locally rooted styles also figure in this volume. We employ interdisciplinary methodologies, including music ethnography, history, textual analysis broadly defined, sound studies, performance studies, and media studies, alongside and informed by Indigenous ways of knowing.

The individual case studies presented here reference concepts and analytic frameworks proposed by diverse scholars, but among the most influential work for the volume as a whole is *Indians in Unexpected Places* by Philip J. Deloria. Arguing that at the turn of the twentieth century "a significant cohort of Native people engaged in the same forces of modernization that were making non-Indians reevaluate their own expectations of themselves and their society," Deloria exhorts readers to question their expectations about Native peoples to disrupt the reproduction of asymmetrical relationships often based on stereotypes, simplistic understandings, and misrepresentations (2004, 6, 4). The unexpectedness of Indigenous musical modernity creates dilemmas for American Indian/First Nations musicians, whose authenticity is repeatedly challenged or who may find themselves hovering on the margins of expected styles of expression for Native peoples as defined by the settler- and colonist-dominated music industry.

Conversely, Indigenous people have also faced challenges in relation to their home and artistic communities, who may expect them to represent tradition and speak for cultural specificity. This has sometimes made it difficult to maintain a balance between protocol and artistic innovation. Deloria documents the wide variety of venues in which Native American/First Nations artists and entertainers found opportunities to perform from the late 1800s until the middle of the twentieth century. These venues included film, opera, chamber music, jazz, ballet, and other elite and popular genres, although Native roles and presentational styles were usually shaped by white expectations and stereotypes. Yet, for Deloria, this one window of opportunity through which Native performers could exert agency in shaping mainstream modern forms of expressive culture closed by the middle of the twentieth century (2004, 14). Our case studies suggest that in the early twenty-first century, Indigenous performers are no longer confined to creating music in relation to white expectations. Unlike the earlier performers, the artists discussed here are succeeding in the marketplace on their own terms and are using music to advance Indigenous sovereignty, resurgence, and intergenerational healing in instrumental ways.

Rather than organizing the book into sections by theme, theoretical orientation, geographic area, or chronology, we chose to interweave conceptual threads from one chapter into the next. In this way we hope to suggest a circular or spiraling narrative contour that resonates with Indigenous approaches to storytelling, oration, choreography, and musical design. Heidi Aklaseaq Senungetuk explains the foundational values informing the work as a whole in her prologue. Adhering to Inupiaq ceremonial protocols, she welcomes you, the reader, to enter into our conversation.[1] Her words are celebratory, yet they remind us, especially settlers such as myself, that in North America we are all living on Indigenous lands. Her gesture of welcome asserts Indigenous sovereignty within the ethnomusicology of Native North America, while at the same time creating space for Indigenous and settler music scholars to unite in the work of transforming the often difficult history of ethnomusicology.[2] Senungetuk states our collective purposes: to engage Native perspectives, to include multiple generations in the scholarly process, and to challenge readers and listeners to join Native musicians in changing our perceptions of Indigeneity and modernity. As a classical violinist, Senungetuk describes how she Indigenizes her performances of music by non-Native composers, to "make visible a process that is normally private, thus revealing my Nativeness." She argues that "our Indigenous thinking is on the inside of everything we do, even though at times it may look like some form of assimilation on the outside." In this way, Senengetuk takes an ontological approach to music, modernity, and Indigeneity.

David W. Samuels echoes Senungetuk's call to change our perceptions of

Indigeneity and modernity in "The Oldest Songs They Remember: Frances Densmore, Mountain Chief, and Ethnomusicology's Ideologies of Modernity." Densmore published her classic work, *Teton Sioux Music and Culture*, in 1918. By then research on Native North American music had been in full swing for three decades. The non-Native Indianist composers were bringing their interpretations of Native music to public audiences, and educators were including Indigenous songs in school music books; scholars and musicians who were themselves Native also contributed to the process. At the height of this movement, the Piegan (Blackfeet) sign-language expert, Mountain Chief, posed for photographs with Densmore and an Edison cylinder recorder at the Smithsonian Institution. Samuels analyzes these iconic photos and the questions they raise about Indigeneity and modernity. He suggests that Mountain Chief and Densmore each thought of themselves as "modern" and grasped the importance of sound-recording technology in Native American music research. Yet the reception history of these photographs reveals the miscommunications inherent in Native music research. Mountain Chief, dressed in the era's new intertribal regalia, projects the image of a man living fully in the musical present and looking toward the future. By contrast, Densmore sought to record the oldest songs Native singers remembered because she and her contemporaries believed the people—and their songs—to be vanishing. The photographs, then, reveal entrenched concepts of both Indigeneity and modernity. Samuels suggests that Densmore and Mountain Chief "both... know the world is changing, and both are girded to do something about it," a portent of what was to become an ongoing discourse in the study of music, modernity, and Indigeneity.

The photographs of Mountain Chief and Densmore have been frequently reproduced and recontextualized and are therefore subject to varied interpretations. Similarly, in "Reclaiming Indigeneity: Music in Mi'kmaw Funeral Practices," Gordon E. Smith discusses the multiple narratives embedded in video images of Mi'kmaw funerals that become decontextualized through circulation on social media. But, unlike the Smithsonian photos from 1916, the funeral videos were made by Mi'kmaw people themselves to create and represent their own ethnographies. Like many First Peoples, the Mi'kmaw prioritize the preservation of language and culture in the wake of federal policies designed to disrupt tradition and force assimilation, such as removal, relocation, and Residential Schools. Mi'kmaw cultural revitalization began in the 1980s; their revival strategy involved combining historical and modern funeral practices, including components from Mi'kmaw Round Dances, Mi'kmaw Catholic rituals, intertribal powwow songs, and Cape Breton fiddling, all of which have long been part of Mi'kmaw musical life. Smith analyzes the funeral videos of Wilfrid Prosper and Sarah Denny, two leaders in the movement to reclaim Mi'kmaw culture, and demonstrates that the Mi'kmaw funeral videos not only celebrate the lives of two respected elders but also help to build the cultural revitalization process. He suggests that music is a domain through which Indigenous peoples can cross boundaries while creating contexts for social interaction and argues that "expressions of tradition are hybrid and often linked to processes of invention, innovation, and modernity." Musical modernity thus provides a cogent method of reclaiming complex Indigenous identities.

Continuing the discussion of technological production and Indigenous self-presentations of modernity, Anna Hoefnagels examines the use of technology and social media by Aboriginal women singers to advocate for women's rights. In "Indigenous Activism and Women's Voices in Canada: The Music of Asani," Hoefnagels summarizes Canadian legislation that disempowered First Nations women and created gender inequalities, which lawmakers began to address only in 1985. She then discusses the emergence of Indigenous feminism in the late twentieth century and the movement's connections to social activism. Female Aboriginal artists, such as the Alberta-based trio Asani, produce commercial recordings that are celebratory in nature and feature song lyrics "about women's rights, empowerment, and self-identification as Indigenous people [that] resonate with the current advocacy for Indigenous rights and a renewed sense of cultural pride among Indigenous people throughout Canada." In their recordings these women accompany their voices with traditional hand drums and rattles but employ stylistic elements from diverse popular music genres. They combine vocables with lyrics in English and Native languages, enabling a range of listeners to enjoy their music. Their hybrid approach to song making parallels the processes of invention and innovation discussed by Smith, but Hoefnagels explains that in this case musical modernity provides a platform for social activism within the Indigenous women's movement.

Christina Leza provides another example of Indigenous musical modernity as social activism, this time in the borderlands, in "Hip-Hop Is Resistance: Indigeneity on the U.S.-Mexico Border." The hip-hop duo Shining Soul seeks to empower and mobilize Arizona youth who have become disenfranchised because of militarization along the U.S.-Mexico border and state laws enacted in 2010 that threaten civil rights. The laws include Arizona Senate Bill 1070, requiring those suspected of being undocumented immigrants (and those who resemble

Latinos/Latinas) to present proof of citizenship to law enforcement officers, and Arizona House Bill 2281, which bans the teaching of ethnic studies in public schools. In an effort to raise consciousness about racial profiling and border-related human rights issues, the emcees Bronze Candidate (Franco Habre) and Liaizon (Alex Soto) advocate for interethnic solidarity. Habre, who identifies as Chicano, and Soto, a member of the Tohono O'odham Nation, combine their individual cultural perspectives in song poetry that recognizes the importance of collaboration and alliance among Indigenous peoples. Leza analyzes how "cultural code switching and code mixing occur at the levels of both sound and linguistic code selection" and "considers the symbolic imagery (visual and sonic) employed by Shining Soul to communicate both shared and separate sociocultural identities." She argues that hip-hop offers a musical space in which musicians based in strikingly different historical, cultural, musical, and linguistic communities can build cross-cultural alliances. Because many Indigenous artists find their voices in hip-hop, it must be considered an authentic component of Indigenous musical culture, despite its origins in African American and Latino urban block parties.

Shining Soul brings activist music to a largely self-selected audience, consisting of those who attend their live performances and beat-making workshops, watch their YouTube videos, or listen to their CDs or digital downloads. By contrast, Elyse Carter Vosen proffers a highly visible example of Indigenous music as social action in "Singing and Dancing Idle No More: Round Dances as Indigenous Activism." Focusing on Anishinaabe and Cree singers and dancers, Vosen traces the role of the Round Dance in the Idle No More movement, which began in response to Canadian legislation revoking environmental protection and social services as well as other issues of inequity described in *The Winter We Danced* (Kino-nda-Niimi Collective, 2014). She explains that the Round Dance is "uniquely suited to this historical moment of structural disruption and cultural healing because of its physical and symbolic circularity. It is multigenerational. It is conveyed solely by oral tradition and thus is highly flexible. It intersects with other artistic expression, including popular music, and moves smoothly into the realm of social media." She presents vignettes illustrating how the Round Dance animated Idle No More in singularly Indigenous ways. The vignettes center on the use of Round Dances in hip-hop videos, in a media personality's television appearance, in urban gatherings designed to draw attention to the exploitation of Indigenous women, and in political organizing on both the local and international levels. Each vignette underlines the roles of media and technology in Idle

No More, since they enable artists to combine sound and images innovatively in a display of "Indigenuity." The vignettes support Vosen's argument that "artistic expression has a unique ability to move and persuade, especially in the sometimes volatile and often entrenched setting of settler-Indigenous social relations."

The artists discussed by T. Christopher Aplin also combine sound and images in innovative ways, but their goal is to combat stereotypes of Indigeneity rather than to mobilize social action. Aplin explains that "*realness*, or perceived authenticity of identity and belonging, is among the toughest personal, political, and historical issues confronted by modern Indigenous peoples." In "Get Tribal: Cosmopolitan Worlds and Indigenous Consciousness in Hip-Hop," he explores the music and rhymes of three emcees whose work manifests the complexity of forming a personal identity for Indigenous individuals. Each of the emcees included in the case study—RedCloud, Emcee One, and Quese Imc—claims mixed Native and Latino descent but has different tribal, linguistic, and geographic roots. As Indigenous artists, they have in common the experience of marginalization and colonization, and all are highly mobile. Each traverses the rural-urban continuum as well as international borders, countering audience expectations of how Indian music should sound by sampling traditional dance songs, classic Native rock, Christian hip-hop, and country music; by invoking oral tradition and autobiography in their rhymes; and by code switching between English and tribal languages. Aplin analyzes the sonic and poetic markers in their music that communicate differently to audience members from diverse backgrounds. He argues that modern Indigenous musicians are cosmopolitans who deftly cross musical, social, and geographic borders, reminding us that First Peoples of North America have engaged in far-flung musical interaction and exchange with one another since long before the arrival of Europeans.

John-Carlos Perea further explores the challenges of identity formation among Indigenous individuals in "Native 'Noise' and the Politics of Powwow Musicking in a University Soundscape." Perea teaches intertribal powwow singing and drumming at San Francisco State University, where his ensemble rehearsals have often been perceived as unwanted noise. He analyzes the social hierarchy of the university soundscape, finding that power relationships "are in part dependent on the disciplining of unwanted . . . and loud sounds," adding that "my students become aware very quickly of what constitutes acceptable music and what constitutes noise in a university setting." He seeks explanations for the negative reception of powwow music in both Indigenous and settler-colonialist thought. For example, in a Lakȟóta interpretation of the social and spatial relationships enacted at powwows, which place the drum at the center of concentric circles, the outermost ring represents people disconnected from what is happening. He also probes the perceptions of early colonists, religious narratives, and federal Indian policy to shed light on the fear non-Native listeners may experience on hearing powwow music. Yet Perea's course in powwow musical performance empowers Native students to shape urban Indigenous identities, to build alliances with non-Native students, and to make space for the most widely recognized genre of American Indian music within the university's sonic environment. Perea continues to sound the drum in the university setting, because, for him, Indigenous modernity presupposes inclusion in the music curricula of educational institutions.

Like Perea, Byron Dueck presupposes inclusion in public institutions as one sign of a changing social order in "Powwow and Indigenous Modernities: Traditional Music, Public Education, and Child Welfare." He considers the incorporation of powwow into public organizations in Winnipeg, home to one of the largest Native populations in North America. Dueck summarizes the colonial history of removing Aboriginal children from their homes to attend residential boarding schools or to be placed in foster care with non-Native families, which formed part of the project of assimilation. Assimilationist policies began to change in the 1970s, and by the 1990s Aboriginal practices began to be included in Winnipeg's public schools and child-welfare programs through powwow clubs and culture camps. Many Aboriginal people see these activities as positive, because they are connected to broader cultural practices, they support the formation of Indigenous identities, and they contribute to the development of a "holistic concept of selfhood—comprising physical, mental, spiritual, and emotional aspects." But, for others, these activities are controversial, particularly among Native people who disagree with the kind of spirituality taught in powwow clubs or with spiritual education outside the home. Dueck points out that when powwow instruction occurs through public institutions, "Indigenous priorities may be subordinated to those of the state." He asks whether powwow is being deployed for expediency by Manitoban provincial education and child-welfare systems, concluding that cultural expediency and cultural efficacy may conjoin in institutional contexts, depending on the priorities and who establishes them.

Jessica Bissett Perea, in "Inuit Sound Worlding and Audioreelism in *Flying Wild Alaska*," circles back to the issues of authenticity, cosmopolitanism, and transnationalism raised by Leza and Aplin. Implicitly asking what it means to sound Indigenous—and who decides what that means—Bissett Perea considers the interrelated concepts of sound worlding, audible Indigeneity, and audio-reelism. She defines sound worlding as bringing the world into being through sound, asserting that Inuit musicians have always practiced this art through drumming, singing, and dancing. Audible Indigeneity refers to the stereotypical ways in which listeners determine whether or not music sounds "Native," whereas audioreelism suggests how sound-design components in popular media can express the lived realities of Indigenous peoples. She analyzes the soundtrack for *Flying Wild Alaska* (*FWA*), a reality television show, demonstrating that it uses audioreelism to portray the daily life of an Alaska Native family in the airline business. The soundtrack for *FWA* is unprecedented in its use of prerecorded music by Indigenous musicians from Alaska and the circumpolar Arctic. The featured artists set lyrics in Indigenous languages to popular musical styles such as hip-hop, rap, funk, and R&B. *FWA*'s executive producer designed the show's sound to combine local musical styles, licensed third-party music by Indigenous artists, synthesized distortion effects, and sounds such as propeller engines, aircraft alarms, and bird strikes. Bissett Perea concludes that the range of sounds heard in the score unsettle "conventional musical representations of 'The North' by European and U.S. modernist composers." Audioreelism and Native sound worlding therefore challenge settler-colonial representations of the Indigenous Arctic.

Dawn Avery echoes Jessica Bissett Perea in refusing entrenched popular notions of how Indigenous music should sound. As Avery explains in "Native Classical Music: *Non:wa* (Now)," the concept of modern "is relative to the period in which one is living. . . . It travels through time with us," and therefore "the nows of the past and future are always experienced as part of the present." Thus tradition, modernity, and Indigeneity are dynamic processes. For Avery, Native Classical music reflects the value Indigenous peoples place on the continual renewal and maintenance of creation and is central to cultural revitalization and political activism. She defines Native Classical composers by their relationship to training in Western music theory, history, and performance and by their use of some method of written music notation. Drawing on Indigenous theory and methodology, she summarizes Native creative processes and shows how they have been adapted in music by Raven Chacon, Juantio Becenti, and herself. Her analysis suggests that rather than directly quoting Native musical sources or imbuing their work with a cultural flavor, these composers strategically deploy musical hybridity, cross-cultural competency, collaboration, and audience participation to decolonize the listener's reception of Indigenous music. Avery concludes that the process of decolonization is a "constructive and healing force for Natives and non-Natives alike" and that "Native Classical composers embody this decolonizing force by presenting Indigenous worldviews and new artistic creations in performances directed at diverse audiences."

Avery advocates the use of Indigenous theory in analyzing Native Classical music, and Dylan Robinson amplifies this theme in "Speaking to Water, Singing to Stone: Peter Morin, Rebecca Belmore, and the Ontologies of Indigenous Modernity." Noting that the phrase Indigenous modernity "is seldom, if ever, used to examine the ontological or epistemological aspects of Indigenous musical practices," Robinson suggests that an Indigenous-centered approach would recognize that Indigenous cultural practices are often intended to "achieve, enact, or bring something into being." He illustrates this point through the work of two performance artists, Peter Morin (Tahltan) and Rebecca Belmore (Anishinaabekwe). Robinson discusses works by Morin that drew on structures of potlatch to support the commissioners for Canada's Truth and Reconciliation Commission in their work. In another project Morin vocalized cultural graffiti in London, speaking and singing to monuments of British colonial power as well as to Indigenous sites, which "enacts a form of Indigenous nation-to-nation contact with ancestors." Belmore constructed and installed a giant megaphone in various locations, through which people could sing or speak to particular places or waterways. Robinson refers to these performances, like John Langshaw Austin's speech acts (1962), as "song acts" or "oratory acts." As such, "they continue the work that our songs and oratory do in ceremonial contexts—they communicate with our ancestors, honor our families, and affirm sovereign rights." Works by Morin and Belmore not only represent contemporary public expressions of First Nations traditions but continue to enact Indigenous legal orders.

In "Purposefully Reflecting on Tradition and Modernity," Beverley Diamond examines the ways in which Indigenous peoples are critiquing and responding to various new theories of modernity, how their traditional practices offer challenges to static definitions of tradition, and, finally, how ethnomusicologists might learn from the active purposefulness of Indigenous tradition to further the discussion of how we might decolonize methodologies for researching and learning about Indigenous music. Diamond asks settler scholars of Indigenous music to consider what they do and what purpose their work may serve by posing a series of questions: What are the effects of transcribing Native songs, when Western staff notation is an inadequate, colonialist method of representing Indigenous music? How is learning certain repertories of Native music tied to responsibilities for the knowledge that has been shared? How has listening for complexity in our analyses of Native music sought to counter racist attitudes toward such music as lacking complexity and also been indicative of a "voracious desire to possess the knowledge of another"? What has been the impact of settler ethnomusicologists' heavy focus on hymnody to exemplify musical hybridity, while ignoring other Indigenous genres such as country, popular, and classical styles? Diamond argues that music in Indigenous tradition is action-oriented, designed to enact individual or group renewal; to enact protocols for meeting and parting, giving thanks, healing, or legitimizing social change; and to enact conflict resolution. A purposeful approach to studies of Native music, then, would consider the intentionality of Indigenous tradition, which "easily accommodates a dynamic range of practices—some innovative or adaptive, others drawing on given repertories and lifeways." In other words, Diamond suggests, the intention or purpose for Indigenous tradition, rather than what constitutes it, "is arguably more relevant to a global future than the why of modernity."

Trevor Reed brings the volume full circle, recalling Senungetuk's preface linking musical modernity to Indigenous ontologies in "*Pu' Itaaqatsit aw Tuuqayta* (Listening to Our Modern Lives)." Drawing on Bruno Latour's deconstruction of modernity (1993, 2013), Reed asks, "how can we be certain we truly understand all that is happening in modern Indigenous sonic spaces?" He describes his work to repatriate recordings of Hopi ritual songs, noting that the recordings are themselves products of Indigenous modernity. He explains that "Hopi songs originate through joint partnership with humans, other-than-humans, and environmental phenomena and become owned by all those who invest their time and energy in hearing and internalizing them." Therefore, determining song ownership complicates repatriation and runs the risk of imposing a new kind of colonialism on Indigenous peoples. Reed further proposes that audience ethnography may uncover multiple ontologies of sound in research on music, modernity, and Indigeneity.

As a whole, the contributors to this collection demonstrate that musical modernity has always been Indigenous, and Indigenous musicians have always been modern. We lay to rest the traditional/contemporary binary in research on Native American/First Nations music and encourage ethnomusicologists to develop new analytic models that privilege Indigenous theory and method. Echoing Deloria, we hope our collection reshapes non-Native expectations and inspires new ways of thinking about Indigenous music in the twenty-first century (2004, 11). More than one hundred years after the photographs of Densmore and

Mountain Chief captured a moment of transition, ethnomusicologists of the early twenty-first century are again facing a transition. Indigenous and settler scholars are navigating a path toward decolonizing our discipline, reorienting it toward resurgent and culturally specific methodologies. As the collection demonstrates, these approaches to Indigenous music foster multiple perspectives and musical idioms, regardless of how such music embraces tradition and modernity. The stakes are high for Indigenous musicians as well as for both Native and settler scholars, and we therefore hope this volume leads to new ways of doing the ethnomusicology of Native North America.

DAVID W. SAMUELS

2. The Oldest Songs They Remember

Frances Densmore, Mountain Chief, and Ethnomusicology's Ideologies of Modernity

She told us how she did it. "In my study of Indian music for the Bureau of American Ethnology," Frances Densmore wrote in 1944, "I take a recording apparatus to the Indian reservations and ask the oldest Indians to record the oldest songs they remember" (106). She did this out of her concern for tone, timbre, nuance, style — what she had earlier in her career referred to as the "Indian throat" (1915, 191). She despaired of finding a transcription practice that would capture the subtle bodily control that generated the Indian voice. "No system of the white man," she wrote in 1943, "can express, graphically, the sounds made by a typical old Indian in his singing. These sounds are an exceedingly important phase of Indian music that is disappearing and never can be 'revived.' It is one of the arts that the Indian is taking with him" (160). The phonograph was a tool of retrospection, promising listeners the ability to hear how the world used to sound. Young people in reservation communities, educated in government schools, were "seldom interested in the deeper phases of the old thought," Densmore told an interviewer. Young people "make up" songs, she said. But elders "say that all of the old songs 'came in dreams.'" Some elders would credit a particular buffalo, deer, or bear that taught them their dream song. "The song that came right from the bear or the buffalo," Densmore said, "is the song I am after" (qtd. in *Boston Globe* 1916).

Densmore's image as a preservationist is well earned, but her scientific desire to "can" the music of Native Americans before it disappeared, as many newspaper profiles of her work phrased it, has its own wrinkles (*Boston Globe* 1916). She published in the *Musical Quarterly* in 1934, and had collected as early as 1919 songs of Native American soldiers serving in World War I. Her 1918 *Teton Sioux Music* boasts a frontispiece illustration of the fully adorned Siya'ka, the singer of twenty-nine old songs. But the book also includes transcriptions and analyses of thirty-two "comparatively modern songs" (429). Densmore demonstrated statistically that newer songs had a smaller compass, more frequent use of intervallic jumps, and a more regular rhythm than "old songs." Her framing of the distinction reiterated the reason she gravitated toward working with elders: comparing the vocal style of a younger and an older Chippewa singer performing the same song, Densmore wrote, "the younger singer had slightly changed the rhythm so as to avoid the irregularity in the measure lengths," concluding that "the song had lost its native character and also its musical interest" (59).

Modernity meant change; change meant loss of character and interest. Yet when I read Densmore's outline of her methodology now, I wonder, what were the oldest songs *she* remembered? Was not her culture passing, as well—going, as they used to say, the way of the buffalo, the Albemarle pippin apple, the oompah band in the gazebo, or the morning glory Victrola? The horrific devastation of the Great War that rang the curtain down on the era of European high colonialism seemed to decide the imperatives of technological rationalism for colonizers and colonized alike. The massive organization of industry, based on the model of giant railroad conglomerates, worried social critics of all stripes. The modernity that had so convinced Native visitors to nineteenth-century Washington of the "melancholy fact" of progress (Pearce [1953] 1988) was grinding its very perpetrators under its heel. A decade after World War I, Archibald Henderson wrote of the "endless stream of humble workers, men, women, and children . . . relentlessly fed into the insatiable maws of huge factories and giant plants" (1925, 26). Stuart Chase observed that the 270,000 railroad trips in and out of New York City each day "carry New Yorkers from places where they would rather not live to places where they would rather not work and back again" (1925, 143). Conservative agrarians and Ruskinian socialists alike saw the completeness with which technological modernity threatened something older and more organic—and longed, as the Jesuit social critic Joseph Husslein put it, for "the romance of life as it can be lived at the fountain source of organic power" (1940, vii). Whose culture was dying?

THE PHOTOGRAPH

March 1916 was a turning point for Victorian anthropology—the passing, almost literally, of an era. On the twentieth of that month, Ota Benga, the Mbuti Pygmy brought to the United States to spend a portion of his adult life on display in exhibits that demonstrated the tenets of nineteenth-century cultural evolutionism, died in Lynchburg, Virginia of a self-inflicted gunshot wound to the heart (Newkirk 2015, 239). Five days later Ishi, iconic as "the last wild Indian in the United States" since the day he was found in an Oroville, California, barn (Kroeber 1912, 304), passed away of tuberculosis. The combined sense of inevitability and remorse around the eclipse and destruction of other historical and cultural practices is contained in the jump-page headline of Ishi's obituary in the *San Francisco Chronicle*: "Contact with Civilization Proved Fatal" (1916, 31).

In that same month in Washington, DC, Densmore sat for a series of photographic portraits with the Piegan (Blackfeet) leader Mountain Chief at the Smithsonian Institution. She was delivering a lecture on American Indian music to the Anthropological Society of Washington at the public library on the twenty-first of the month, and had been in the capital since December of the previous year (Jensen and Patterson 2015, 411). Mountain Chief was a frequent visitor to Washington and the Smithsonian, where he consulted with Gen. Hugh L. Scott on Native American sign languages.

Photo sessions took place both inside and outside the Smithsonian's Seneca red sandstone castle. Between them in each session sat an Edison cylinder recorder—Joan Jensen and Michelle Patterson (2015, 410) identify it as a Columbia Graphophone—its horn pointing toward the Native American informant. Three images from those sessions are still available through archives at the Smithsonian and the Library of Congress. In each, Densmore is seated behind the Edison recorder on the left of the image, Mountain Chief to the right, facing the horn. The first was taken outside the Smithsonian. In it Densmore has turned her head to observe Mountain Chief, her sight line following the angle of the recorder's horn (figure 2.1). In the second, also taken outside the Smithsonian, Mountain Chief is gesturing actively while Densmore looks down at the machine, perhaps making a mechanical adjustment (figure 2.2). Leaning against the music stand that supports the phonograph's horn sits a bow, an additional layer of technological mediation and affiliation, simultaneously bridging and separating the two sitters. The third picture, taken a month earlier, on February 9, was shot indoors, in a room within the museum building (figure 2.3). In this version of the image, Densmore was again preoccupied with the mechanical technology, while Mountain Chief appears to look off into the distance above the line of the horn, perhaps lost in thought, perhaps listening intently.

Neither the original purpose of the photographs nor the aspirations of their sitters or creators is discernible from their contents. The photography studios credited with creating the images—Harris and Ewing and the National Photo Company—were Washington-based news services, providing wire-service photographs of important people and events to out-of-town papers. By no means were they the only photographs of Densmore ever taken, nor of Mountain Chief. It certainly was not the only photograph ever taken of a morning glory–horn cylinder recorder, the profile of which stood for many years as an iconic image of U.S. technological innovation and modernization. But this particular conjunction of ethnologist, informant, and recording device has, for many years, circulated as one of the most frequently reproduced images of the ethnomusicologist at work, appearing on the covers or in the pages of books about Native American poetics, modernity, technology, the history of anthropology, field methodology, and ethnomusicology. Roshanak Kheshti (2015) interprets the images as fundamental representations of the feminization of mediated listening practices and of comparative musicology in the early twentieth century. John Cline calls it the "primal scene" (2014, 271), and he may not be far off. So frequent are the sightings and citings of these images in professional publications that it may be difficult to think about the role of sound recording in twentieth-century ethnography without thinking about them.

The original intentions of the people who organized, posed for, and captured the initial photographs are obscured by the pictures' subsequent circulation and the verbal captions that have framed that circulation. The images of Densmore and Mountain Chief may have escaped the fate described by Martha Sandweiss of photographs, over time, "[slipping] the bonds of biographical explicitness . . . to assume more metaphorical meanings in the eyes of a beholder" (2002, 215). The principal figures in these photographs have escaped anonymity, yet they have not escaped the process of becoming metonyms, to represent something larger and more retrospective than the initial moment of shutter-opening aperture might have encompassed.

The images of Mountain Chief and Densmore working with the Edison machine, like some of the western landscape photographs Sandweiss discusses, place past and future in an arresting visual juxtaposition. Unlike those landscapes, it is uncertain which aspects of the images of Mountain Chief and Densmore evoke

Figure 2.1. Mountain Chief, chief of Montana Blackfeet, in native dress with bow, arrows, and lance, listening to song being played on phonograph and interpreting it in sign language to Frances Densmore, ethnologist, March 1916. INV 00327300, National Anthropological Archives, Washington, DC.

Figure 2.2. Frances Densmore, listening to a wax cylinder phonograph with Mountain Chief, a Blackfoot Indian. LC-USZ62-6701, Library of Congress, Washington, DC.

Figure 2.3. Piegan Indian, Mountain Chief, listening to recording with ethnologist Frances Densmore, February 1916. LC-USZ62-107289, Library of Congress, Washington, DC.

which end of that polarity. Rather, they reinstate the "metaphorical dreamscape" of intercultural performance that in other instances "had receded into a more dualistic figuration" (Deloria 2011, 312). The photographs capture a moment in flux, multiply imagined emergences and imagined disappearances, an accounting of which can be performed only with hindsight. Viewing them produces an effect not of nostalgia, exactly, but of a layered sense of comings and goings, of things that were to pass and things that were yet to be.

It is easy enough to read the photographs as depicting the extraction of data in an encounter between the modern scientist and the primitive informant.[1] In 1916 the photographer Edward S. Curtis was midway through the publication of his twenty-volume *The North American Indian* (1907–30), and in 1913 the photographer Joseph K. Dixon had published *The Vanishing Race*. Dixon's title notwithstanding, however, by the middle of the war the idea that Indigenous North Americans were a "vanishing race" was already springing leaks. Both demographically (F. Fox 1919; Bynner 1923; Vestal 1928) and culturally—in sports (Swift 2008; Buford 2010), music (Curtis 1913), and art (Weigle and Babcock 1996)—Indigeneity was emerging, albeit problematically, as an important aspect of modernity.

No, whatever nineteenth-century photographs of Indians might have been, these images are doing another kind of work. Far from depicting the demise of Indigenous people in the face of progress, they reveal the contradictions and temporal fracturing of loss, preservation, continuity, and adaptation in the trauma of modernity. Any simple linear reading of the "crisis of temporality" (Zamir 2014, 5) contained within these pictures of Densmore and Mountain Chief consulting over the cylinder machine is quickly belied by the seemingly almost deliberate anachronisms of their principal subjects. If the technology sitting between Densmore and Mountain Chief appears outdated to the contemporary viewer, for example, the same might well have been said even in 1916. By about 1905 the Victor Talking Machine Company had already folded the horn downward so it sat out of sight in the cabinet below the apparatus (Millard 2005, 58). Over the next ten years all recording companies except Edison effectively abandoned the cylinder market in favor of discs—and in favor of phonographic equipment that would play only prerecorded material. Edison continued to manufacture recordable cylinders until 1929, which was appreciated by a devoted clientele of folklorists and ethnographers (Brady 1999). But the Edison Company had itself introduced a disc phonograph in 1913. So, even in 1916, the image of an Edison cylinder recorder with an external horn may have appeared out of step, or at least a bit scholastic.

Densmore dressed for the session in a fairly contemporary Edwardian outfit, "the working clothes of the 'new woman,'" as Jensen and Patterson note (2015, 410). Mountain Chief, for his part, dressed in feather headdress and fringed and beaded buckskin for the photo shoot. Perhaps he was acknowledging the session as an opportunity to place Indigenous tradition on display. But his couture also enacted an emerging and still-powerful contemporary intertribal style denoting new recognition of Indigenous identities in the twentieth century. The reading that sees Densmore's dress as modern and Mountain Chief's as ancient struggles against the understanding that hers was quickly overtaken by emerging trends in fashion after the war, whereas his remains a crucial aspect of contemporary Indigenous self-representation.

INDIGENOUS MODERNITIES

Modernity, as many have noted, is a noun with a somewhat fluid denotation, more of a project—and an "incomplete project" at that (Habermas 1981)—than a thing. While it is generally accepted that modernity purports to be a moment of separation from something prior to it, those proposed temporal points of separation have been many and varied: print capitalism, Luther's theses, the rise of probability and statistics, the emergence of single-point perspective, Leonardo's anatomical studies, the American Revolution, the French Revolution, the acceptance of the scientific method, the Industrial Revolution—the list goes on.

Whatever its point of origin or original manifestation, modernity arises in contexts of political, social, economic, and spiritual upheaval. Its emergence is based in trauma, for the European center as much as for its colonial peripheries. Indeed, Europe's peasantry was dispossessed of common land by enclosure laws and fraud laws during the period Karl Marx termed "primitive accumulation" ([1906] 2011) just as surely as Indigenous people were dispossessed of land by the tentacles of settler colonialism. Huntly Carter's 1910 description of the effects of industrialization in the former commons of Lancashire suggests the rapacious dispossession and degradation of natural and human resources at modernity's centers: "Tall shafts uplift a shroud of black smoke against its sky. Black arid wastes, spotted with horrible black, naked mounds, flow in all directions, intersected by rows and rows and rows of little flat featureless and unutterably dreary black dwellings, in which men, women and children wilt and wither and waste pledged to the hopeless drudgery of producing machine-made utensils, clothes, household goods, vehicles, and, in fact, the necessities and comforts, so-called, of civilized life" (8). This entwinement of trauma, distinction, and upheaval is captured in Stephen Toulmin's (1992) locating the roots of modernity in the Thirty Years War. It was in the wake of this violent sectarian conflict, in which subtle articles of faith could become death sentences, that René Descartes produced philosophical tools to determine what could be known for certain and what was mere sectarian opinion. Thus Toulmin linked modernity, its signature rationalist, and its emerging political organization of nation-states to the search for solutions to deep spiritual crisis and a violent maelstrom of uncertainty.

Indigeneity arises out of waters from the same stream—for whatever modernity's referent, it measures its motion against something that stands still: the rational and the irrational, the literate and the oral, the national and the tribal, the *Gesellschaft* and the *Gemeinschaft*, the organic and the mechanical. Indigenous communities were not alone in the worries about modernity's effects. In order "to preserve the memory of vanishing phases of the national life," Mary Bronson Hartt in 1912 called for living American folk museums based on the "Skansen idea" in Sweden (see also Kammen 1993, 233). Hartt enumerated some of the "bygone fashions" and "obsolescent types" that were quickly fading: "Old New England is passing away; the pioneer cabins of the Middle West are going one by one; the Western cow-boy life is dying out; and before many years the last relic of the gold-camps will pass forever beyond our reach" (920).

Binary oppositions distinguishing center and periphery dissolve all the more when we acknowledge Bruce Knauft's contention, in response to problems arising out of too-uniformizing theories of modernity, that "modernity has been plural from the start" (2000, 23).[2] We ought not, for example, subsume what we might call Indigenous modernities under the broad umbrella of "resistance," finding Indigeneity exclusively in an allegiance to sonic markers ideologically considered icons of traditional forms.[3] This reads modernity as a uniform, global phenomenon to which local communities are either compliant or resistant. Moreover, resistance, by this model, when it occurs, is relegated to the cultural and aesthetic spheres, thus uncoupling it from economic and social aspects of struggles over material and symbolic resources.

VERNACULAR MODERNITIES AND ETHNOMUSICOLOGY

If modernity has always been Indigenous, and Indigeneity has always been modern, two questions arise for us who study sonic expressions of culture. First, how might music sing to larger issues of modernity and Indigeneity? And, second, or more precisely, was there ever a time when ethnomusicologists were not studying Indigenous modernities? Taking on such questions opens the possibility that Indigenous modernities may not be simply a way of rethinking problems of modernity but a way of rethinking the problematic history of ethnomusicology in its involvements with the unitary and categorizing ideologies of modernity as well.

Robert Stevenson implied as much in discussing the Pueblo songs Densmore collected. Overthrowing her distinction between "old" and "comparatively modern" songs, Stevenson argued that the songs were all, in a sense, comparatively modern and required "careful sifting" before endorsing the idea of their Indigenous traditionality:

> Obviously European music—no less than horses and weapons—went with the Spaniards wherever they penetrated. The Franciscans who followed Juan de Oñate into New Mexico brought with them, for instance, organs, programmed instruction in plainchant and polyphony, and music books. At Hawikuh, the Zuñi pueblo used as Coronado's first headquarters, Fray Roque de Figueredo taught organ, bassoon, and cornett, as well as Gregorian chant and counterpoint, in the 1630's. Since other pueblos enjoyed similar programs of intensive instruction in European music throughout the Spanish period, any thesis that the 82 songs relayed from early missionary centers to Frances Densmore for publication in her *Music of Acoma, Isleta, Cochiti and Zuñi Pueblos* (1957) . . . embody pure tribal tradition, untainted by any European intrusions, requires careful sifting. (1973, 5)

Stevenson's reading inserts a centuries-long cacophony of economic, religious, ecological, and musical upheaval into any researcher's simple equation of "traditional songs" and "the oldest songs they remember." Regarding these images of Mountain Chief and Densmore through the refracting lens of Stevenson's early insight—not one that was generally heeded—gives some sense to the historicizing interpretive moves embedded in some current manifestations of the photographs, opening another avenue by which to overcome monolithic notions of the modern that have lent a strong ideological charge to ideas like "traditional" and "authentic."

Willard Rhodes's evolving work on Native American hymnody and Native American songs with English texts offer other traces of ethnomusicologists' emerging awareness of Indigenous modernities. Beginning during World War II Rhodes documented the revitalization of the Sun Dance, the Native American Church, Indian Shakers, Flag Songs, and a form of Round Dance song with English texts now more commonly known as "Forty-Nines." A chronology of a handful of Rhodes's essays reveals the difficult terrain he trod in both placating and challenging his own and his readers' expectations of purity. In 1940 Rhodes recorded the Boys Chorus of the Santa Fe Indian School performing what he titled "Three Modern Love Songs." A dozen years later he published an essay in which he argued that Native American song was relatively stable, affirming Curt Sachs's assertion that music was a robust, change-resistant cultural form (Rhodes 1952a). In November of that same year, Rhodes wrote an article for the Sunday Arts and Leisure section of the *New York Times*. Headlined "Songs of American Indian Still Live," it introduced readers to Rhodes's discoveries of a "new literature of modern Indian music that has developed out of the contemporary culture." But Rhodes immediately stepped in to reduce his audience's cognitive dissonance. The songs were contemporary, yes, "and yet so firmly rooted in the music of the past, that one can only regard them as the continuation of a musical tradition centuries old" (1952b). In 1954 the Library of Congress released *Music of the American Indian*, containing the modern love songs recorded in 1940 (Rhodes 1954). Finally, in 1963 Rhodes published a brief article about Forty-Nines. There he observed that the song texts were "obvious imitations of the popular songs and ballads that . . . find their way across the country through the media of phonograph records, radio and, more recently, television." Although the history of this song form was unknown, Rhodes surmised that the oldest examples "are associated with Indian theatrical shows" of the late nineteenth century (10). Rhodes's concession that these songs extended back to Wild West shows implied that ethnomusicologists had neglected a half century or more of Indigenous modernity's musical expression.[4]

THE TECHNOLOGY OF MEMORY

By 1905, then, when Densmore began her first formal fieldwork at White Earth, Minnesota, the hybrid song forms discussed by Rhodes may have already been circulating for years.[5] By 1918, certainly, her treatment of "comparatively" modern Lakȟóta songs can only be taken with a grain of salt. Rhodes's 1963 nod to popular music and its circulation on phonograph records returns us as well to the photographic images and the alinear temporalities of the sonic mediations of Indigenous sounds they frame. For there it sits between the two representatives of dying cultures: the preserver and destroyer of the oldest songs they remember. To the extent that the images are "about" the role of mediation in preserving and understanding music in human life—or to the extent this interpretation is in some sense encased in the ways the images now circulate—the photographs of Densmore and Mountain Chief represent the Edison machine not as a purveyor of disparaged Tin Pan Alley ditties but as an instrument of science.

Debates about the phonograph keyed thoughts about the fate of earlier forms of community in the face of technological modernity. When Densmore and Mountain Chief sat for these photographs, music was considered by many as a public good, fostering community cohesion and moral uplift. During the war, community singing was placed under the direction of the civilian War Camp Community Service.[6] At war's end, Dir. Orlando F. Lewis pleaded with music educators to continue their community work "as a part of your permanent, continued service to the people of this country" (1919, 121).[7] Not all music was equally blessed, however. By 1916 pianos, player pianos, and cabinet Victrolas competed strongly with one another for prominence in living rooms and parlors across the United States. Piano rolls, discs, and sheet music of the latest hits provided multiple alternative means of exposing customers to popular music for sale. The role of popular music in community health was already a thorny issue, and questions abounded about how to ensure that the new forms of mediation, which promised so much, would not become overrun by the lesser rubbish of manufactured music.[8]

Luckily, social scientists demonstrated through phonographic field recordings that communities still existed in the world in which people's moral, social, and ethical lives were bathed in community music making. If the world's peasants and primitives could enrich their everyday lives and most formal rituals with music that supported the well-being of the community, could—should—not the most modern of us do the same? Arts critic Carl Van Vechten remarked how this emerging global musical experience demonstrated the limits of the Western art tradition. "Think of the range of sounds made by the Japanese, the gipsy, the Chinese, the Spanish folk-singers," he wrote. "Why should the gamut of expression on our opera stage be so much more limited than it is in our music halls?

Why should the Hottentots be able to make so many delightful noises that we are incapable of producing?" (1918, 101).

Reclaiming the human in the face of modernity's tone-deaf cacophony required a rededication to songs that were not merely on the public's lips but emanated from the social body. Henry Krehbiel of the *New York Tribune*, Henry T. Finck of the *New York Times*, and others championed a scientific definition of folk songs. The definition, in Krehbiel's version, had three parts: first, folk songs were "not simply songs that are popular in the countries whence they emanate, but songs which are created by the people who sing them." Second, folk songs were not consciously artful but had emerged "among the peoples of the world as a spontaneous utterance." Third, they gave voice to the feelings of a community, "and they are therefore correctly described as the fruit of the creative capacity of a people instead of the product of a single creator" (1910b).

The matter was not trivial. Krehbiel wrote these words for the program notes to a concert by the renowned soprano Marcella Sembrich. In December 1910 Sembrich, recently retired from the Metropolitan Opera, performed a full afternoon of world folk musics at Carnegie Hall. Krehbiel's review the next morning called it "the most interesting experiment that any student of music within a generation can recall." But Krehbiel took more than half his review space to chide the *Evening Post* reviewer who had, the day before, complained that Sembrich omitted any songs by Stephen Foster. Sembrich, in Krehbiel's view, had properly relied on the scientific view of folk songs in creating her program. True folk songs, in the scientific sense, Krehbiel retorted, were "creations of the people, and not of a composer who happened to hit the popular taste in his creations" (1910a).

The photographs of Densmore and Mountain Chief consulting over the Edison machine display ethnology as a crucial means of accessing these valuable human expressive resources. They also display a crucial aspect of Indigenous modernity. Mountain Chief's familiarity with and command of modern technology is essential to the success of the process, an understanding acknowledged in Mary Anne Kenworthy and others' caption accompanying the photo in their book about archival practices. Unique among the captions I discuss here, theirs is the only one in which Mountain Chief is the topical focus. Their emphasis on his role may be in part because of their point that "analysis of information is as critical as its collection" (1985, 11). That analysis, of course, was part of debates about modernity, technology, and popular music that concerned Mountain Chief's community as surely as Densmore's.

It is perhaps because the carefully staged photographs depict neither field-work nor recording in any definitive way that they prompt viewers to reflect on the nature of field recording. The improvisatory nature of ethnographic fieldwork in sound has gone hand in hand with an increasing portability of mediating sound technology. My thoughts turn in this direction when I think about the bulkiness of field managing the phonographic apparatus in the photo. In the mid-1990s I went into the field with about thirty-two ounces of recording equipment. In the 1930s John Lomax tore out the back of his Ford sedan, packed five hundred pounds of recording equipment into the trunk, and celebrated how convenient the new technology was to transport (see Szwed 2011, 43). The posed and curated photographs do not depict the messy business of making a recording any more than production stills show the messy business of making a Hollywood film. More important, despite misinterpretations to the contrary, the photographs do not depict a recording session at all. What we see in the pictures is not the long and tapered recording horn, whose design was meant to capture and concentrate the acoustic signal onto the inscribing needle, but the shorter and stouter listening horn. That the images are so often interpreted as depicting an act of recording, as Michael Asch explains, rests in part on the lost knowledge of how this technology actually worked and in part on assumptions about the appropriative nature of encounters between ethnologists and Indigenous people (2007–8).

As depictions of sound mediation, these photographs are in conversation with other visual images weaving sound and music into the expressive fabric of modernity. The iconic image of Nipper attending to "his master's voice" similarly makes the aural emanations of the phonograph horn the focal point of the scene. For contemporary viewers, and perhaps also for those at the time, the photographs invite reflection on domesticity and gendered ideas about "an-tique" or "quaint" forms of technology (Kammen 1993; Keightly 1996). The images seem to capture a moment in which modernity emerges into the beacon of consciousness by revealing its romantic attachments to earlier forms of logic and expression (Clemens 2003). The images in this sense now exist in interroga-tive mode, scaffolding a reflection on the aboutness of modernity and on what the passage of time might mean. Fascinations with the "retro" and the "classic" reveal contemporary viewers, like Densmore, thinking about the oldest songs they can remember.

THE PHOTOGRAPHS IN CONTEMPORARY IMAGINARIES

These layers of (mis)recognition, nostalgia, critical distance, and reflexivity—Densmore both is and is not modern; Mountain Chief both is and is not primitive; the Edison machine both is and is not recording—inform, in part, the photographs' continuing circulation and resonance in recent decades. The modern circulation of these images appears, as with so many things in the history of ethnomusicology, to have begun with a recording issued by Folkways Records. *Healing Songs of the American Indians* featured as its cover image the photograph contained here as figure 2.2 (*Healing Songs* 1965). The collection was edited by Charles Hofmann, whose memorial volume, *Frances Densmore and American Indian Music* (1968), used the same image as his figure 6 on page 150. Just in the past twenty years, one or another of the three photos has adorned the covers of important works about audio ethnography (Makagon and Neumann 2009), the history of the culture concept (Hegeman 1999), Native American verbal art and poetics (Clements 1996), the history of ethnomusicology (Myers 1993), the history of recording technology in anthropology (Brady 1999), emergent Native American musical expression (Troutman 2009), and the expressive ideologies of modernity (Bauman and Briggs 2003). The cover illustrations for William Clements's 1996 book about Native American poetics and for Helen Myers's 1993 history of ethnomusicology use only the right-hand side of the photograph, the depiction of Mountain Chief. This cropping choice seems to invite the misinterpretation that Mountain Chief is performing rather than listening and interpreting. In its full frame, on the other hand, it certainly seems to be modernity that is at stake in selecting the image. For the books by Susan Hegeman, Richard Bauman and Charles Briggs, and Erika Brady, the depicted encounter between European American researcher and Indigenous culture bearer—mediated, crucially, by the technology of sonic capture and inscription—contributes to a reader's thoughtful consideration of culture in the wake of colonialism and collecting.

Authors do not necessarily control the images that appear on the covers of their books, however, and we ought not read any author's intention into decisions made by art directors, designers, and publicity offices. The choice of interior illustration is a different matter, however, and here the photograph has served a number of purposes. Authors have chosen one of the photographs to illustrate points—usually historical—in Densmore's biography (Hofmann 1968), oral literature theory (Niles 1999), the history of women anthropologists in the Southwest (Babcock and Parezo 1988), the history of American music (Tick 2008), the history of Indian delegations to Washington, DC (Viola 1981), an introduction to ethnomusicology (Bohlman 2002), the history of ethnomusicology (Bohlman 1991), the history of the packaging of Appalachian folk culture (Becker 1998), the history of world music recording (Hart 2003), the anthropology of media and mediation (Brady 2002), the history of the ethnographic use of audio technology (Brady 1999), a reflection on the politics of collecting Indigenous culture (Guilford 2000), the history of visual representations of Native American music (Levine 2002), an interpretation of the powwow (Browner 2002), a comprehensive encyclopedia of folklore (McCormick and White 2011), and a discussion of cultural property issues (Brown 2004). From the twenty-four publications I consulted, it appears the consensus is that the figure 2.1 image is the most evocative and visually arresting of the three.[9] This version, which presents Densmore and Mountain Chief as linked across the transparency of the recording technology, appears on six of the seven book covers in the publications I located and in twelve of the seventeen interior illustrations. The figure 2.1 photograph was used sixteen times by thirteen authors, the figure 2.2 photo was used twice, and the figure 2.3 image four times.

Potential meanings of cover photographs tend to be left to the imaginations of readers or purchasers of the books. But interior illustrations are inevitably accompanied by captions, which, as Sandweiss notes, "carr[y] the weight of descriptive labor" (2002, 185).[10] Spare as some captions accompanying these photographs may be, still they contain revealing variations. In naming the event participants, Densmore is never misidentified, an item that perhaps denotes the power relationships between the two sitters in spite of the seeming egalitarian framing of the event. Mountain Chief is generally identified as well, and accurately, but Barbara Babcock and Nancy Parezo (1988) mistakenly record his name as "Big Bear," and on the cover of the Folkways recording *Healing Songs* (1965) he was simply called "Indian singer." As Asch notes, Mountain Chief is always referenced by his English name—although omitting the given name he chose for himself, "Frank"—and never by his name in the Blackfoot language. Conversely, Densmore is never referred to by any of the Indigenous-language names by which she may have been known (Hofmann 1968, iv, 33). Caption writers sometimes identify Mountain Chief's tribal affiliation. The designation is generally accurate in noting him as Blackfoot or Piegan. Hofmann (1968) and Babcock and Parezo (1988) mistakenly refer to him as Sioux, perhaps on account of the clothes he wore for the photographs. Babcock and Parezo add a somewhat inexplicable "White Mountain reservation" to their annotation. Densmore's tribal affiliation seems unworthy of mention.

When the captions place the photograph in time they are generally accurate. Three of the captions, Hofmann's, Folkways', and Babcock and Parezo's, date the image to 1914. As all three of these are using figure 2.2, and two of the instances are related to Charles Hofmann, it is possible that Babcock and Parezo based their caption on Hofmann's original, although this still leaves us with the mystery of where they got the name "Big Bear." Both Jane Becker (1998) and John Niles (1999) date the photographs to 1906. None of the captions mistakenly report that the images were captured *later* than 1916. The misdatings always appear to shift the images further in the past and not in the opposite direction. This data skew is, I think, suggestive of the photograph's self-historicizing resonances for the viewer.

A number of captions offer descriptions of Densmore and Mountain Chief beyond their names. Both Becker (1998) and Philip Bohlman (1991) refer to her as an "ethnomusicologist," Herman Viola (1981) as an "ethnologist," and Niles (1999) as a "collector." These designations may have as much to do with how the photographs fit the frame of the authors' themes as with knowing what to call her. Mountain Chief is designated as a "leader" by both Bohlman (2002) and Mickey Hart (2003) and as a "singer" by Brady (1999, 2002) and on the Folkways record cover (*Healing Songs* 1965). Identifying Mountain Chief as a "singer" resonates with misconceptions about what the photographs depict, as well as understandings of what Densmore, as a "song catcher," did in her work for the Bureau of American Ethnology. But only two of the interior captions misidentify what is happening in the photo as a recording session. The consistency with which interior captions overtly frame the event as an instance of listening suggests to me that uncaptioned cover photographs may be easier to misinterpret as depictions of Mountain Chief making a recording. This may be especially true of uses in which only Mountain Chief's half of the photograph is displayed to the viewer.

Finally, as with the fact that her name is never mistaken, the colonial power embedded in the photographs is underscored in the syntax of the captions. All but one make Densmore the topical focus of the independent clause, despite the fact that it is Mountain Chief who is the agent performing the action. The predicate often turns on whether "playing for him" or "interpreting for her" is the activity foregrounded in a caption, but even in captions that emphasize the latter, the verbal construction still tends toward "Frances Densmore with Mountain Chief, who interprets a recording."

DYING CULTURE SYNDROMES

On the afternoon of January 4, 1917, about a year after Densmore and Mountain Chief sat for the photographs that have cast them permanently onto the history of ethnomusicology, Marcella Sembrich performed the first in a subscription series of four concerts covering the world history of song at Aeolian Hall in New York City.[11] To open her history, in keeping with her dedication to the scientific approach to song, Sembrich chose to again present a concert of world folk musics.[12]

On the foundation of her still-discussed 1910 recital, Sembrich was widely acknowledged as "probably the greatest artist of the folk-song living today" (*Miami Herald* 1917). The accolade appeared in a wire-service story that ran in multiple newspapers across the United States and Canada over a period of several months. The headline subject of the story, however, was not the soprano herself but rather the "Indian melody" that Sembrich sang in her recital and the work of Frances Densmore in collecting and disseminating these songs. The selection, performed immediately after the first intermission, was "Wanbli iyali heyele," a Lakȟóta song of the Sun Dance, originally sung for Densmore by Tasi'na-skwin (White Robe). A year later it appeared as example 22 in Densmore's classic *Teton Sioux Music* (1918), but its only published version at the moment was in Alberto Bimboni's piano arrangement. As with every other song on the program of more than a dozen languages, Sembrich avoided English translation, however poetic, and sang the song in Lakȟóta. The audience loved it so much they demanded that the singer repeat the number.

Sembrich's concert, hugely successful, was also her last. In the week following the recital, Sembrich fell ill and canceled the remaining three concerts of the series. Some months later Sembrich's husband died of complications following a simple surgical procedure. Not long after that Sembrich, now almost sixty, fell and fractured her shoulder. She never returned to the stage for another public performance.

The finality of Sembrich's final performance resonates with the sense of dissolution that seems to occupy the space of the images of Densmore and Mountain Chief. Whose culture was dying? Within months the United States would enter World War I. Nine thousand Native Americans, not yet citizens, would serve (Appleton 1919). When they returned home, Densmore would record their newest songs. After the war the critical approach of Krehbiel, Finck, and other champions of folk music as a source of human value and resource of art music would be dismissed as the "Old Guard" (W. Bailey 2008; Thompson 1937). With them would go an inherently conservative evolutionist perspective, but also a sociological approach to musical forms that would eventually be thrust on the emerging discipline of ethnomusicology.

And this, in a sense, may be why we continue to care about and to be affected by these photographs. The particular theoretical arguments that occupied Densmore neither concern nor inform the discipline anymore. The compromised politics that accompanied her dedication to collecting Native American songs have been well rehearsed, perhaps overrehearsed, to the point of obscuring her foundational role in the formation of an ethnomusicological enterprise.[13] Yet when we look at them, they continue to draw us in and seem to arrest those other concerns. Their continued circulation in the published record attests to that.

As with any photograph of musical practice, the silence of the cylinder fixed in motion by the camera's shutter plays both on viewers' imaginations and their frustrations. The sense of sonic loss bound up in these images reconstitutes, perhaps, the sense of loss that inspired the original photographs in 1916. "Nothing is lost so irrevocably as the sound of a song," Densmore wrote. "Indian music must be heard in order to be appreciated, and those who have not heard it on the reservations may study it on the recordings, the earlier ones of which were made by old Indians who sang in the native manner" (1945: 637). The primitive and peasant fountain source of organic power might succumb to the melancholy fact of modernity, but the communitarian values of their music were salvageable for the redemption of that modernity. For a true scientific understanding of music on a global scale, singing in the Native manner was indispensable. To achieve this purpose a recording device was key.

Within the silent frame of these images, ethnologist and consultant negotiate the path forward through this fracturing of past and future in the shared traumas of modernity, this crisis of sonic loss. Densmore came of age, as Van Vechten wrote of the now-obscure writer Edgar Saltus, "in the days when mutton-legged sleeves, whatnots, Rogers groups, cat-tails, peacock feathers, Japanese fans, muskmellon seed collars, and big-wheeled bicycles were in vogue" (1918, 64). Whose culture was dying? When I look at these photographs now, the only thing I think I know for sure is that both of them know the world is changing, and both are girded to do something about it. The temporal indeterminacies of the moment are captured in the images, none of which promise either redemption of, or resolution to, their contradictory tensions. The Recording Angel offers no guarantees of stability, and there is little sense of what that stability might portend.

GORDON E. SMITH

3. Reclaiming Indigeneity

Music in Mi'kmaw Funeral Practices

One of the best places where you'll see all kinds of music working
together is the church. Actually, if I think about it, a funeral is where there's
a real mixing of music. Traditional, modern, and the two going together.
It's best if you go to a funeral and see for yourself. Why not go to my funeral
if you're around? [laughs]. If you can't make it, maybe someone
will make a movie of it [still laughing].

Wilfred Prosper, pers. comm., Eskasoni, February 16, 2004

From when I was a child I learned our songs and dances and ways
of knowing from my mother and other family members, as well as elders,
who were keepers of our culture. I would say we are now more than ever
claiming our culture in our daily lives and celebrations. That video of my
mother's funeral I gave you shows what I'm talking about—not just keeping
our culture but reclaiming it through family and community voices.

Joel Denny, pers. comm., Eskasoni, August 3, 2009

During the 1980s I spent seven years on Cape Breton Island, where I taught music
at what is now Cape Breton University. My music courses often drew Mi'kmaw
students, affording me a valuable opportunity to discover other perspectives
on teaching and learning about music.[1] Building on this experience, I began researching musical traditions and practices on the Mi'kmaw reserve of Eskasoni,
a community located on the Bras d'Or Lakes twenty miles west of Sydney, Nova
Scotia, on the east coast of Canada. I worked with individual elders, notably Lee
Cremo, Sarah Denny, Rita Joe, and Wilfred Prosper. Since then, each of these

elders has passed away. Although I didn't attend their funerals, on subsequent visits to Eskasoni I learned that each funeral continues to be discussed and remembered by family and community members as a pivotal event in the person's life experience, a powerful expression of Mi'kmaw tradition, and an important venue for recovering identity. Parts of three of these funerals were recorded on videos, which were given to me through the generosity and trust of the Cremo, Denny, and Prosper families. In this chapter I discuss the funeral ritual as a site of reclaiming Indigeneity by examining the videos as ethnographic documents and drawing on excerpts from two of them.

The discussion of Mi'kmaw funeral videos is inspired by the Eskasoni experience of funeral rituals as a means of affirming identity and facilitating processes of healing. In this context tradition and modernity are not separate concepts for Eskasoni Mi'kmaq. As with related binaries (e.g., Native and non-Native; us and them), such dualisms exist on a continuum, which for many Mi'kmaq serves to reinforce their Indigenous identity (A. Robinson 2005). My research focused on receiving the videos from family members, watching the videos with them, hearing about the funerals, listening to stories, and engaging in conversations. Following Kisliuk (1998) and Nicole Beaudry (2008), among others, I engaged with my consultants in ongoing informal conversations that led to mutually beneficial social interactions and the sharing of knowledge and stories. As Margaret Kovach writes, "Stories remind us of who we are and of our belonging. Stories hold within them knowledge while simultaneously signifying relationships" (2009, 94). Beverley Diamond observes that stories in Indigenous contexts are not simply fictional accounts of the world but are often rooted in keen observation and constitute a form of Indigenous theory. Diamond argues that "'theory' in the sense of deep thinking about the issues that matter in our lives is not separate from practice, nor restricted to the academy" (2015c, 155; see also Simpson and Smith 2014). The voices in these funeral videos, and the stories surrounding them, map onto sensitivities and tensions behind processes of tradition, modernity, and change in Mi'kmaw religion and social life and can be heard alongside and within expressive frameworks that serve to heal and affirm community identity.

I begin with Eskasoni and its importance as a site for understanding historical and contemporary expressions of Mi'kmaw Indigeneity, followed by a discussion of the Mi'kmaw funeral ritual and how its music can function as an innovative process in recovering Mi'kmaw identity. I then draw on excerpts from the videos to illustrate. To frame this discussion I consider questions related to the video camera and field research and the process of reclaiming Indigeneity and articulating Indigenous modernity in a community such as Eskasoni. Considering content, meaning, and interpretation as a critical matrix, I ask, What is captured and highlighted on the videos and what is not, and what determines these choices? What does the video represent within a context of reclaiming Indigenous culture, and how does religion figure into healing and social practice? Given that videos and the Internet are part of a growing network of exchange both on and off reserves, what kinds of narratives are being promoted—traditional or modern, or both? Blended through these frameworks are questions related to the influence of modern media and technology in a community such as Eskasoni, as well as increasingly significant issues related to ownership and ethical responsibility.

In formulating these questions I consulted literature on fieldwork in ethnomusicology, anthropology, and visual technology, along with research on reclaiming Indigeneity in global and local contexts.[2] Questions of this sort also served as points for discussion with consultants throughout my research. The postmodern shift in the social sciences and humanities begun in the 1980s resulted in debates and experimentation in representational practices in ethnography. As Chris Scales has observed, "ethnomusicologists continue to grapple with the problematic implications of 'writing culture'; however, the field has far less engaged in critical debates surrounding the issue of 'recording culture'" (2012, 262). The funeral videos anchoring this study are texts that can be viewed through the lens of recording culture. They can also be viewed from reflexive angles that call into question who is actually "doing" the ethnography. The makers of these videos, and the subjects and rituals in the videos, are often adjacent in unusual roles and spaces in unexpected ways (Deloria 2004). Thus, the videos serve as living documents that preserve traditions while creating new ones, simultaneously affirming religious and spiritual beliefs and reaffirming the importance of family and social engagement throughout the community.

FUNERAL RITUALS AT ESKASONI

Eskasoni, where Wilfred Prosper and Sarah Denny lived, is the largest Mi'kmaw reserve in Atlantic Canada, with a population of approximately 3,500. The total estimated population of the Mi'kmaw Nation is 20,000.[3] The Mi'kmaq are an Algonquian people who reside in what is referred to as Mi'kma'ki, traditional territory in northeastern North America, comprising parts of Newfoundland,

Nova Scotia, Prince Edward Island, New Brunswick, the Gaspé Peninsula of Quebec, and Maine. Eskasoni became a reserve as part of the centralization program established by the Canadian federal government in the 1940s. For many Mi'kmaq the centralization and Residential School programs represented a climax of hostility toward Aboriginal peoples in the Atlantic region. Centralization resulted in the resettlement of at least half of the Mi'kmaw population on two reserves, Schubenacadie on the Nova Scotia mainland and Eskasoni in Cape Breton. Although the major goal of centralization was to facilitate the education of the Mi'kmaw people and to provide them with an economic base, the coercive tactics and empty promises used by the government to force Mi'kmaq from their homes left many Eskasoni Mi'kmaq with feelings of cultural deprivation and economic annihilation. As Marie Battiste writes, "Centralization reduced the rural Mi'kmaq to absolute poverty for the first time in their history. Free, prosperous and self-sufficient on their own farmlands and fisheries throughout the Great Depression while Gaelic-speaking coal miners nearly starved, the reserve Mi'kmaq faced starvation in the midst of postwar prosperity" (1988, 69).

The other negative legacy still pervasive in Eskasoni and throughout Mi'kma'ki is Residential Schools. Schubenacadie, on mainland Nova Scotia, was the site of the Mi'kmaq Residential School from 1930 until its closing in 1966. During that time more than a thousand Mi'kmaw children attended the Residential School. The federal government established church-run, government-funded Residential Schools for Aboriginal peoples as a means of facilitating religious conversion and assimilation. More than 130 Residential Schools operated across the country; the last school closed in 1996. Mi'kmaw teaching models emphasized observation and the experience of elders and natural surroundings. By contrast, the Schubenacadie Residential School, based on European educational concepts, weakened the social structure of Mi'kmaw communities in significant ways. It also served as an enormously detrimental force toward the loss of language and culture. In addition to a hostile living and learning environment, children at Schubenacadie were forced to participate in farm labor to support the school. Only in 2008 did the Canadian government formally apologize for the negative effect of Residential Schools. In the same year the Truth and Reconciliation Commission, organized by the parties to the Residential Schools Settlement Agreement, began to formulate a comprehensive response to the Indian Residential School legacy. Completed June 2015, the response is intended to help facilitate healing processes for Residential School survivors and their descendants.

During the 1950s the residents of Eskasoni, with other Mi'kmaw communities in Nova Scotia, began taking control of their affairs. They established a band council (Sante' Mawio'mi) in 1958, and there are now community-operated elementary and middle schools, as well as a secondary school, on the reserve (figure 3.1). Preserving the Mi'kmaw language and culture through the educational system is a priority, and young people now have the opportunity to become knowledgeable participants in the maintenance of Mi'kmaw traditions and the forging of a proud Mi'kmaw identity. In addition, the development of economic, public-works, and health-and-wellness infrastructures is now providing leadership and hope for a reserve that continues to experience the economic and social disadvantages and challenges faced by many Aboriginal communities.[4]

The Eskasoni reserve is the only Aboriginal Roman Catholic parish in Nova Scotia, the others being served by the Catholic mission system.[5] The Holy Family parish was established in Eskasoni in 1944, prior to which residents in Eskasoni, as in other Mi'kmaw communities in Atlantic Canada, had limited access to Catholic priests (figure 3.2). Angela Robinson emphasizes, "Evidence shows that the Mi'kmaw actually revised Catholicism to accommodate their beliefs and values. . . . Prior to this time [1940s] the Mi'kmaw had carried out religious services as they had for generations. Most Mi'kmaw communities had mission churches where members of the Sante' Mawio'mi [Grand Council] met with the people each Sunday to say prayers and sing hymns. They received services from a priest only on special occasions such as Christmas and Easter" (2005, 29).

Robinson also problematizes the ambiguity of the word *traditional* in the context of religion in Eskasoni, noting that many Eskasoni residents use the term *traditionalist* to refer to specific persons or groups of people within the community who follow what are considered to be authentic pre-Christian religious practices exclusive of Catholicism. For many Catholic Mi'kmaq—including Wilfred Prosper and Sarah Denny—traditionalists can hold Mi'kmaw culture and tradition while accepting Catholicism as a primary religious orientation. For many Mi'kmaq in Eskasoni, tradition, religion, and spirituality are "fluid concepts that are often intertwined and open to interpretation" (2005, 12). As these two funeral case studies demonstrate, expressions of tradition are hybrid and often linked to processes of invention, innovation, and modernity.

Funerals in these contexts are pivotal events, where elements of Roman Catholic liturgical practices and Mi'kmaw traditionalism are combined. The Mi'kmaw filmmaker Catherine Martin emphasizes the importance of funerals in

Figure 3.1. Aerial image of the western section of the Eskasoni reserve, showing the band office, 2012. Photo by Derek Denny. Used by permission of the Eskasoni Band.

Figure 3.2 Aerial image of the eastern section of Eskasoni reserve, including Holy Family Church, 2012. Photo by Derek Denny. Used by permission of the Eskasoni Band.

Mi'kmaw communities as powerful and unique sites for family and community engagement. She also commented that the priest often plays a role in determining liturgical practices at funerals, including the choice of music (hymns, Mass acclamations); the use of Mi'kmaw traditional practices (the Mi'kmaw language in readings, prayers, and hymns); and the use of drumming inside the church (pers. comm., Halifax, May 30, 2014). In Eskasoni, funeral masses typically occur in Holy Family Church at eleven o'clock in the morning, in between the wake—usually held in the deceased person's family home—and the *salite* (auction and feast), held in the church hall following the burial in the church graveyard. This four-part process (wake, Mass, burial, salite) has important religious and social implications in the Mi'kmaw life cycle. Rita Joe describes this process in a poem, and I cite her words in full as a powerful articulation of Mi'kmaw funeral customs.

POEM 15

The customs of various tribes
Are many,
The Mi'kmaw observe the rules
Of guiding traditions
[1] *When a native dies, immediate supplications for the dead are said by a member of the family of the nearest relative. Then they wait for the prepared body for a three day wake, at which native prayers and hymns are sung and food and comfort given freely.*
[2] *Then the Mass for the dead is sung by the priest and we answer prayers by the priest in Micmac. The hymns that we hear in our own tongue often move the native people to tears, for they are more beautiful to us in our own language.*
[3] *When the body is being lowered into the ground, the native choir members sing a hymn that has been handed down for centuries:*
Ma'lta elasnl Se'susil,
Saqamaw, wula I'mu'sipn,
Mu pa npisoqq wijikitiekaq,
Skatu kejitu nike',
Kisu'lk iknimutal msit ta'n tel-tamjil.
[4] *Then the Grand Chief tells the people that there will be a gathering at the community hall where food, donated by the people from the reservation, is served to the other visitors.*

Then the deceased's personal belongings and donations from the people are gathered together and an auction is held. There are instances where people will give the last they have to the auction. Then, when it is over, the bills are paid and if any money is left, it goes to the surviving family.
Habits of Old
Our elders teach;
We honour, and we tell. (Joe 1978)

Along with distinctive Mi'kmaw religious practices of honoring and telling about the deceased person through the wake, funeral, and burial, the salite is a significant and uniquely Mi'kmaw social practice that provides comfort and support for the family and community. The etymology of the word is unclear. I have been told it is of French origin, but there is no equivalent or derivative term in French. Robinson speculates that the word may be "Miklish" (Mi'kmaq and English), suggesting a "sale day" (pers. comm., October 20, 2008). She notes that the salite is widespread throughout Mi'kma'ki (Eskasoni, Membertou, Potlotek, Whycogomagh, Wagmatcook, Schubenacadie, and Elsipogtog), but does not exist in all Mi'kmaw communities. Historically, salites have undergone numerous changes since their inception in the postcontact period. In their current form an important feature is to assist the family with the cost of the burial. With the increased use of professional interment services in the 1960s on reserves, raising larger sums of money at salites became common practice. Previously, internment and attendant funerary practices were the responsibility of the community, including the making of the casket.[6]

The Eskasoni community has a long association with the T. W. Curry Funeral Home in Sydney. Leo Curry (founding director of the business) recalled the association, dating from the 1960s, between his funeral business, Eskasoni, and the Sydney reserve of Membertou. Both Curry and his son emphasized the importance of the salite as a vital social event in the funeral process, an event for which they handle the arrangements regularly. They emphasized that Mi'kmaw funerals are religious as well as social events, a feature they see as different from non-Mi'kmaw funerals (pers. comm., Sydney, Nova Scotia, October 3, 2008). These narratives situate the salite at an intersection between traditions and modern practices, reinforcing the social and religious elements of the Mi'kmaw funeral cycle as practiced in Eskasoni.

MUSIC AND MI'KMAW FUNERALS

More than fifteen years ago, Wilfred Prosper described to me the important role played by Sister Mary Gouthro in the musical life of the Holy Family parish and in the Eskasoni community. Trained through the Royal Conservatory of Music system in piano performance and theory and in music education at Alverno College in Milwaukee, Wisconsin, Gouthro spent two periods at Eskasoni as the music instructor in the elementary school and the choir leader at Holy Family Church (1972–76 and 1979–1992). She was a pivotal figure in the musical life of the community and parish, leading the choir and encouraging choir members, including Wilfred Prosper and Sarah Denny, to translate Catholic hymns into Mi'kmaq for use in the liturgy. Two other musicians echoed Prosper's comments: Elizabeth Cremo, Lee Cremo's daughter and the former church organist; and Arlene Stevens, who became choir director after Gouthro left.

Stevens provided information on music at funerals in Eskasoni, especially the choice and sources of repertory as well as details about Christian and Mi'kmaw elements. The Mi'kmaq Choir sings at funerals and masses at Holy Family Church. A mixed choir of men and women of all ages, the choir sings hymns, psalms, and responses in English and Mi'kmaq; Mi'kmaq is most frequent at funerals. Generally, the Mi'kmaw pieces are Mi'kmaw translations of the English words from well-known Catholic hymn books, such as the *Catholic Book of Worship II* (1980) and *Glory and Praise* (1984), as well as biblical texts such as *Glorious Mysteries*.[7] Yet the choir does not sing from these books; instead, local sources in English and Mi'kmaq have been compiled from them. These include a text-only songbook for Mass celebrations and another for funerals; the latter contains Mi'kmaw translations of English hymns and acclamations sung by the choir at funerals.

An important source for Mi'kmaw songbooks is the *Micmac Hymnal*, which includes a collection of sound recordings compiled by the Micmac Association of Cultural Studies in the early 1990s. The book contains more than forty hymns and prayers in Mi'kmaq, divided into sections for Christmas and Lent, Saint Anne (patron saint of the Mi'kmaq), "Niskam" (God), and funerals. The Mi'kmaw songbooks draw significantly on the *Micmac Hymnal*, which has been integral to revitalizing the Mi'kmaw language in the celebration of liturgies.[8] Wilfred Prosper and Sarah Denny each played a role in translating the English words into Mi'kmaq, as well as singing in the choir that recorded the hymns. Gouthro's musical influence at the Holy Family parish appears to rest with her encouragement of elders such as Prosper and Denny to recover Mi'kmaw hymns and prayers through translation and musical adaptation of existing Christian melodies, rather than teaching elders and choir members to read music notation. As Gouthro explained,

> When I started directing the music for Holy Family parish liturgies, I discovered that they had been singing before my time but most were the old sacred songs that I believe had been translated from the French by the missionaries. There was no notation for these songs and I had to listen over and over in order to play them by ear. . . . I tried teaching some of them to play the organ or piano in order to play at church. I didn't feel I was very successful in this area as they played by ear a lot and didn't want to take the time to learn notes. . . . I didn't have any special strategies for teaching the music. The singing was all learned aurally. . . . As for resources I had few. The people had some old prayer books that had words but no music. They had produced a hymnbook that contained some of their more popular hymns. This was mainly words, not music notation. This book was produced by Sarah Denny who was then working with the Micmac Association of Cultural Studies in Sydney, Nova Scotia. (Email corr., October 2006)

Well-known Catholic hymns that have been translated into Mi'kmaq include "The Lord Is My Shepherd," "How Great Thou Art," "Prayer of Saint Francis," and Christmas carols such as "O Holy Night," "Il est né le divin enfant," "Silent Night," and "O Come All Ye Faithful." The practice of translating English hymns, prayers, and songs into Mi'kmaq is pervasive in Eskasoni, as it is in secular contexts on the reserve.[9] Song translation establishes music as a powerful means of recovering the Mi'kmaw language, thereby helping to affirm Mi'kmaw identity. Gouthro's account confirms that this is a postcolonial practice. The history of Christian singing in Mi'kmaq is much longer, dating to early stages of the colonial encounter in the seventeenth century. Priests and other clergy regularly used translations of biblical stories into Indigenous languages to missionize Aboriginal peoples. Janice Tulk (2009a, 2009b) has demonstrated connections between singing prayers or hymns in Mi'kmaq and Gregorian chants.[10] Similarly, Anne Spinney has argued that it "seems most accurate to acknowledge Wabanaki Catholicism as a syncretic expression of both Native and European cultural systems, a combination with a unique dynamism—and tension" (2006, 58).

The old hymns to which elders such as Prosper and Denny often referred appear in *Alasotmamgeoel: Le paroissien Micmac* ("prayer book"), a source of hymns, prayers, and liturgies in the Mi'kmaw language, used in Eskasoni until the arrival in 1944 of the first parish priest, Father A. A. Ross (A. Robinson 2005, 54). Prosper believed the old hymns were actually biblical passages set to poetic meter in Mi'kmaq, a method used by priests to teach the bible to Mi'kmaw people (pers. comm., Eskasoni, February 15, 2004). Prosper and Denny both had a particular interest in and knowledge of chanting and believed that *histories* (i.e., "stories") were the foundations of religion. This informed their work as Mi'kmaw tradition bearers, as well as inspiring others to reclaim Mi'kmaw Indigeneity through music.

THE FUNERAL OF WILFRED PROSPER (1927–2005)

Wilfred Prosper died on Good Friday, March 25, 2005, and his funeral was on Easter Monday. The news reached me almost immediately through family members and others at Eskasoni. As Prosper himself predicted, someone did "make a movie" of his funeral, and I received a copy of it from his wife, Bessie, on my next visit to Eskasoni. Prosper was a traditionalist in that he was keen on seeing traditions—"the old ways," as he called them—continue among younger generations. To this end, he cultivated his knowledge of the Mi'kmaw language, the anchor, he believed, of Mi'kmaw cultural transmission. In addition to his Native identity, which Prosper expressed through music as a prayer leader and a chanter, he was a fiddler in the Scottish tradition, another identity of which he was proud. For Prosper, music could be a means of crossing boundaries, at the same time expressing profound religious meaning and creating contexts for social interaction. He was one of the few remaining elders who could read Mi'kmaw hieroglyphics, and he could play music by ear.[11] Gouthro taught Prosper to read music notation; he was one of the few who responded to this teaching initiative. His desire to learn how to read what he called the "language of music" speaks to his intellectual curiosity and his motivation to learn about music generally (figure 3.3).

Prosper's son-in-law, George Paul (Eskasoni), made the funeral video, and although the two excerpts I discuss focus on music, the full video is approximately forty minutes and shows a major portion of the funeral Mass, including the homily, readings, hymns (in Mi'kmaq and English), and fiddling. I watched the video with Bessie Prosper and various family members several times. For the family and congregation, the fiddlers who performed at Prosper's funeral were a highlight and moving tribute; twenty members attended from the Cape

Figure 3.3. Wilfred Prosper on the waterfront in Castle Bay, at the western end of Eskasoni, early 1990s. Photo by Barry Bernard. Used by permission.

Breton Fiddlers Association, of which Prosper was a member. Funeral masses at Eskasoni follow Catholic liturgical practice, but readings, prayers, and hymns are typically in Mi'kmaq. Sometimes, at the request of family members, there are traditional practices such as the burning of sweet grass, drumming and pipe ceremonies, or other distinctive features connected to the deceased. That is the case in the first video excerpt, which features the fiddlers. Note also, however, that the choir is prominent in these images, since it plays a critical role in the unfolding of the liturgy of the funeral Mass.[12]

"Video Excerpt 1" (2015) shows the music played at the offertory of the Mass.[13] There the fiddlers performed an old Gaelic song known in Cape Breton as "My Home," which is often played at funerals as a lament.[14] Note the fiddlers standing in loose formation, the keyboard accompaniment (typical of Cape Breton fiddling), and the icons at the front of the church. Also notice the statues of Christ to the right of the altar and of Saint Anne to the left of the altar directly above the tabernacle. The Mi'kmaw flag draped over the coffin is a typical practice. The combination of Mi'kmaw and Christian traditional elements, and a Gaelic lament played by an ensemble of Cape Breton fiddlers honoring a Mi'kmaw elder, illustrates hybridity in the funeral ritual and models the expression of identity in a sacred space. "Video Excerpt 2" (2015) is a solo, "Bovaglie's Plaid" (by J. Scott Skinner), played by the well-known Cape Breton fiddler Carl MacKenzie, accompanied by Fr. George MacInnis. The intricate rhythmic turns and ornamentation in this piece are noteworthy, as is the prominent piano accompaniment, a hallmark of Cape Breton Scottish fiddling. As the fiddle accompanist Doug McPhee observed, "The music is like a 'duet' between the fiddle and the piano" (pers. comm., Sydney, Nova Scotia, October 7, 2008). Prosper would have described this piece as "complicated" and would have loved it because of its ornamentation and slow, expressive style. It is a fitting musical tribute.

The music at Prosper's funeral also included the Mi'kmaw hymn, "The Lord Is My Shepherd," in his own Mi'kmaw translation, and Mass acclamations sung in English and Mi'kmaq by the Mi'kmaw parish choir, accompanied by guitars. At communion the choir sings "How Great Thou Art" in English with guitar accompaniment. The choir also sings the funeral song of farewell, "I Know That My Redeemer Liveth," as the priest blesses the casket at the conclusion of the Mass. Then the fiddlers play a full set of well-known and loved tunes as the casket is moved in a procession down the aisle out of the church. The set includes the lament by the Cape Breton fiddler Jerry Holland, "In Memory of Herbie MacLeod," a strathspey by the Cape Breton fiddler Brenda Stubbert, "Tracy's March," and the famous Scottish reel "High Road to Linton." The fiddlers mirror the progression from sorrow to joy in this set through their interpretation and facial expressions as they play.

THE FUNERAL OF SARAH DENNY (1925–2002)

Sarah Denny was a singer, chanter, and dancer. As an elder and "keeper" of Mi'kmaw culture, Denny believed strongly in the retention of the Mi'kmaw language, history, culture, stories, songs, and dance. To that end she formed the first Eskasoni drum and dance group with her children and grandchildren, known variously as the Sarah Denny Singers, the Denny Family Dance Group, or the Eskasoni Mi'kmaq Dancers. Denny held the position of cultural officer with the Mi'kmaq Association of Cultural Studies for almost three decades and, during that period, was regarded as a leader in reviving Mi'kmaw traditions. Denny was a revered elder in Eskasoni and in the wider Mi'kmaw community; the Sarah Denny Cultural Centre was built adjacent to the band office in Eskasoni and named in her honor following her death (figure 3.4).

Denny's son Joel made the video of her funeral, together with Catherine Mar-

Figure 3.4. Sarah Denny in the garden at her home in Eskasoni, early 1990s.
Photo by Joel Denny. Used by permission.

tin and a friend of the Denny family. Joel gave a copy to me. About forty minutes in length, the footage on which I focus is an aspect of the funeral that the family and community considered significant: the funeral procession from the Denny home through the main street of Eskasoni to the church, a walk of more than a mile. Significantly, the procession is accompanied by singing, dancing, and drumming. This is unusual, because current practice is to carry the casket from the house to the church in a hearse from a funeral home. Joel Denny described carrying the casket in procession as a "return to the way it was always done" or "reviving" a tradition. He saw filming the procession as a means of "building" the revival process (pers. comm., Eskasoni, August 3, 2009).

"Video Excerpt 3" (2015), from Denny's funeral video, shows the casket being carried out of the house, and the singers (her daughters and granddaughters) begin the Mi'kmaw Friendship or Round Dance song, "Ikwanuté," alternated with "I'ko." These dance songs formed part of the Mi'kmaw traditional repertory Denny revived through the Sarah Denny Singers and other artistic manifestations. "Ikwanuté," for example, inspired the Mi'kmaw filmmaker Catherine Martin's 1991 film of the same name. The elder George Paul (Metepenagiag [Red Bank], New Brunswick) emphasizes the significance of the Round Dance: "This dance is to recognize the teachings the Creator has given us since the beginning of time and the cycle of life itself. And everything moves in clockwise fashion" (qtd. in Tulk 2008, 225).

"Video Excerpt 4" (2015) shows the procession on the main road in the reserve leading to the church, accompanied by the "Mi'kmaw Honor Song" ("Kepmitelmnej"), attributed to George Paul (Metepenagiag) in the 1980s. Rita Joe explained that Paul received this song in a vision: "One evening, as a group of us were sitting in Steven Augustine's living room on the reserve, George talked of how this song came to him during a fast in Alberta. He spoke of having been deeply saddened by the fact the Micmac [sic] Nation did not have an honour song, and that the spirits responded to his grief by giving him this song for the Micmac [sic] people. According to George the song was needed, it was asked for appropriately and it was given. Nobody in the room questioned its authenticity and the community had officially accepted it as their honour song" (qtd. in Von Rosen 1998, 238). The song, described as an anthem for the Mi'kmaw Nation, has been circulated widely and frequently recorded. Stylistically, this song does not resemble Mi'kmaw social dances such as "Ikwanuté," which features a relaxed singing style and limited melodic range. Instead, it has the melodic shape and prominent drumbeat of powwow songs. It is significant that the "Honor Song" figures so prominently in Denny's funeral procession. It is sung by male singers with hand drums, who are later joined by the women we heard singing "Ikwanuté" in the opening excerpt. Later in the excerpt we see a powwow drum group to the side of the road, and they join the procession. In addition to the regalia worn by some participants, note the ribbons worn by members of the Sante' Mawio'mi (Grand Council).

"Video Excerpt 5" (2015) shows the procession on the hill leading up to the church. Music is heard in the background, and dancing creates a celebratory tone against the somber images of the graveyard and the church coming into view. Located on top of a hill overlooking the graveyard and the Bras d'Or Lakes, Holy Family Church is prominent from the eastern entrance of the reserve and stands as a beacon for religion and social engagement for the Eskasoni community (figure 3.2). The procession's upward climb to the church in this excerpt is symbolic, as it represents ascending to what is considered by many to be a special place of "spiritual affirmation and comfort" (Rita Joe, pers. comm., Eskasoni, August 20, 1992).[15]

"Video Excerpt 6" (2015) shows the casket arriving at the church and being met by the parish priest in buckskin vestments, who says a Christian prayer of welcome and blesses the casket with holy water. The casket is then carried up the steps and into the church, accompanied by "Ikwanuté," sung by Denny's family members. This arrival scene represents the end of the funeral procession to the church and parallels the start of Denny's funeral video, which shows the casket being carried out of the Denny home accompanied by the same song. "Video Excerpt 7" (2015) shows the beginning of the funeral Mass, including the opening procession in the church, with the choir (accompanied by guitars) singing "Glorious Mysteries" from the Catholic rosary in Mi'kmaq to the well-known Catholic hymn tune "Immaculate Mary." This is followed by words of welcome by the priest, with responses in Mi'kmaq. As the choir director, Arlene Stevens, pointed out, "Glorious Mysteries" is often sung as an opening hymn at funerals in Eskasoni, and the choir sings other standard hymns throughout the liturgy, such as "The Lord Is My Shepherd" in Mi'kmaq and "How Great Thou Art" in Mi'kmaq or English. Stevens noted Denny's participation in the Mi'kmaw church choir as well as her much valued leadership in recovering Mi'kmaw traditions, including hymns. For Stevens and other choir members, Denny's funeral was an opportunity for the community to honor her life and Mi'kmaw traditions, old and new (pers. comm., Eskasoni, May 2, 2014).

———

The content of the funeral videos analyzed here was determined by the individual motivations of the videographers. In the case of Sarah Denny's funeral video, her son Joel wanted to make the video. He explained, "I thought it would be worth it to have a record of this outdoor procession celebrating our [Mi'kmaw] traditions—singers, dancers, drummers, family and community members moving together with our mother on the way to the church" (pers. comm., Eskasoni, August 4, 2008). For the Denny family, the video was a powerful way of celebrating their mother's life through Mi'kmaw traditions. "Ikwanuté" and "Mi'kmaq Honor Song" have become part of a canon of the Mi'kmaw musical repertory, created in large part through processes of discovery, performance, and recording by the Denny family and others. Translating Catholic hymns and biblical texts such as "Glorious Mysteries" into Mi'kmaq is a common practice in Eskasoni, as it is in other Mi'kmaw communities and in many First Nations contexts. By contrast, the video of Wilfred Prosper's funeral came about when Wilfred's wife, Bessie, remembered there was a video camera in the car and asked her son-in-law to record the funeral. The Prosper video focuses on the Mass inside of the church rather than the outdoor procession that is shown in the Denny video. The Prosper video includes hymns, readings, and prayers in addition to the homily by the priest, which is as remarkable for its humor as it is for its uplifting messages of comfort. At the end of the Prosper video is a touching scene at the salite, where one of Prosper's grandsons is shown trying out one of his grandfather's fiddles that is up for auction. Fittingly, the instrument was ultimately "bought back" by the young boy's parents (Vivian Jeddore, pers. comm., Eskasoni, August 5, 2008).

Meanings and interpretations of Indigenous culture exist on multiple levels in these videos. In addition to Mi'kmaw traditional music, the videos reveal the importance of place, including the home, church, and, more abstractly, natural surroundings. Furthermore, the idea of progression from one place to another parallels the concept of circular movement, an important symbol in Mi'kmaw culture. Also significant are the regalia worn by many in Sarah Denny's procession, the dancing, and the presence of people of all ages (children are prominent). Mi'kmaw spirituality and the Catholic liturgy are intertwined in hybrid elements such as translated hymns, prayers, and readings in Mi'kmaq; the priest's buckskin regalia over the standard vestments; and the flag of the Mi'kmaw Nation draped over the funeral casket. Music, woven through these narratives, plays a powerful role in binding together historical and modern practices, as well as engaging people in ways that help to commemorate, to celebrate, and to ensure hope.

Videos like these, which now also circulate on the Internet, are part of a growing network of exchange both on and off reserves. In this kind of decontextualized existence, various traditional, modern, and hybrid narratives are being promoted. These funeral videos highlight the narrative of *celebration*, a word frequently used on the occasion of a funeral in the Eskasoni community and a word invoked many times when watching the videos with members of the Prosper and Denny families. Also important are interpretations of what this kind of celebration is about, depending on which family members are speaking. Whereas some might highlight the funeral celebration of Prosper's and Denny's lives and the combination Mi'kmaw traditions and Christian beliefs, others speak about the mixed messages such celebrations send to outsiders who do not know how integral such hybrid productions are in the processes of healing and reclaiming Mi'kmaw Indigeneity. Not surprisingly, these voices are layered, reflecting generational, gender, and familial positioning. Such nuances raise questions about changing perceptions of what constitutes an important figure in the Mi'kmaw community. In the past, was it a chief or an exceptionally good hunter or trapper? Is it now an elder or culture bearer, such as Wilfred Prosper or Sarah Denny, or is it a new kind of warrior, such as Donald Marshall Jr.?[16] And what about a Residential School survivor or a suicide victim? How does the honoring at a funeral ritual reflect these kinds of shifts?

The Prosper and Denny funeral videos are isolated examples of funeral videos made in Eskasoni. If there is a connection between these funeral videos from a Mi'kmaw community in Nova Scotia, Canada, and filming funerals in other global contexts, it might be the importance of social frameworks interacting with religious and spiritual observances.[17] Citing Victor Turner, Gail Valaskakis emphasizes the importance of the social dimension: "ritual and ceremonies are not just passive cultural repositories, they are active agents of cultural creation in which symbols not only transform and maintain cultural forms but also express meaning in social action" (2005, 153). The Mi'kmaw funeral ritual is a powerful site of embedded interaction between religion, spirituality, communal participation, and healing. The musical, religious, and social elements we see in these videos show the rich layerings of remaking tradition and reclaiming Indigeneity that can occur within the context of funerals in Eskasoni. Tradition and contemporary practice are conjoined and, in fact, actually may be said to engage each other in creative ways—"traditional" and "modern" and "the two going together," as Wilfred Prosper stated (pers. comm., February 16, 2004). His concept resonates with James Clifford's notion of understanding culture as a series of "hybrid productions" (1997, 154).

It is important to view these videos as partial records, a point reinforced in the following comment by Walter Denny Jr., who is now a chanter at funerals in Eskasoni: "I'm known now as a chanter in the tradition of Wilfred and Sarah, and I sing at many funerals. Those videos are great memories for the families, but the real important part is that we are recovering our culture through these celebrations—claiming back our culture. We need to remember that there are real traditional elements you don't see in the video—the wake and the grave—that's where we sing and pray to Saint Anne, our great Mi'kmaw grandmother" (pers. comm., Eskasoni, November 29, 2009). Denny also emphasizes the theme of *healing* through all parts of the funeral ritual and the importance of understanding the multiple nuances of healing in these contexts. More than simply making people feel better at a time of loss, healing includes celebrating an individual's life through religious affirmation, readings, prayers, music, and social interaction, including gathering together as a large family in an affirmation of Mi'kmaw identity (See also Denny 2012). Denny's words help to remind us that considering videos such as these as field documents and as a means of reclaiming Indigenous identities can be risky if we are not cognizant of the multiple narratives embedded in how they are interpreted. As Robin Ridington writes, "The meaning of . . . [video] clips is doubly contextualized. They make sense in relation to the larger narrative of which they are a part, and they also make sense in relation to the ongoing relationship between storyteller and listener" (2006, 48). Ridington's comment reinforces the idea that, as fieldworkers, we must be not only listeners but also storytellers, with the challenges and responsibilities that entails.

Do funeral videos such as these record culture and document a moment in time that may never be seen again? Whereas such video tell us how and what we choose to remember about people, events, and traditions, in time they may also become documents of fading historical narratives. Meanwhile, though, these videos serve to remind us that in a community such as Eskasoni, technological production is often now in the hands of the people, allowing them to control narratives, in essence becoming ethnographers. As such, Indigenous people move past being representatives of tradition to become agents of modernity.

This chapter is published here with the permission of the Mi'kmaw Ethics Watch (Cape Breton University, Sydney, Nova Scotia, Canada). I am grateful to those who assisted with the research, including members of the Prosper and Denny families, especially Bessie Prosper (Eskasoni), Kenny Prosper (Halifax), and Joel Denny (Eskasoni), as well as George Paul (Eskasoni) and Barry Bernard (Eskasoni). I also thank the many individuals who assisted and supported me in multiple ways, including Elizabeth Cremo, Walter Denny Jr., Tom Johnson, Catherine Martin, Fr. Martin McDougall, Doug McPhee, Angela Robinson, and Arlene Stevens. Finally, special thanks to Janice Tulk, who provided invaluable insights throughout the genesis of this project.

ANNA HOEFNAGELS

4. Indigenous Activism and
Women's Voices in Canada
The Music of Asani

On April 26, 2014, at the Givens Performing Arts Center in Pembroke, North Carolina, Ulali Project premiered their new song, "Idle No More," dedicated to the four women who founded the Idle No More movement.[1] The YouTube video of this performance, posted the next day, circulated throughout online forums and was received with great enthusiasm, owing to its message of solidarity: "[they] walk in the light, with [their] brothers and sisters [they] stand and fight with a drum, a song, a prayer, this change of time."[2] The song, cowritten by Pura Fé and Cary Morin, was performed by four female singers accompanying themselves with the "heartbeat" pattern (short-long) on hand drums. The singers included Jennifer Kreisberg and Pura Fé, two original members of Ulali, with Chary Lowry and Layla Rose Locklear.[3] The song alternates between vocables and English text reflecting on the Idle No More movement and the joining together of people in locales such as shopping malls, city streets, and government buildings to raise awareness of Indigenous issues and environmental concerns and to encourage the empowerment of First Peoples across Turtle Island. The song is significant because of the grassroots political climate in which it was released, characterized by activism and advocacy for Indigenous rights. It shows U.S. Indigenous female musicians responding to a Canadian-based political movement, illustrating the internationalization of Indigenous activism. The performance and release of "Idle No More" by Ulali Project—a reconstitution of the popular Indigenous women's trio that inspired the formation of other Indigenous women's ensembles throughout North America—completes a circle of relationships between music making, political activism, and women's empowerment.[4] In many ways it illustrates the intersectionality that characterizes Indigenous modernity in North America at the start of the twenty-first century and the important role that women have played in contemporary artistic and political forums.

Ulali Project's song "Idle No More" illustrates how contemporary artists are engaging with traditional instruments and musical idioms for current purposes and with modern aesthetics, an artistic form of "Indigenous modernity." Although Indigenous modernity assumes many guises and is specific to particular peoples, places, and situations, Ulali Project and many other Indigenous artists are using traditional art forms to address political issues affecting Indigenous people living in today's world, at the local, national, and international levels. These artists employ modern technologies for music production and dissemination, showing currency with broader social trends through the use of social media such as YouTube, Facebook, Twitter, and online blogs. As I illustrate in this chapter, Indigenous women have been instrumental in shaping contemporary activism, particularly in Canada, in many ways reflecting the attention to Indigenous women's issues and empowerment that marks the scholarship and activism at the turn of this century, while continuing a lineage of female leadership within Indigenous communities.

Indigenous women are instrumental in contemporary political activism, assuming leadership roles and exerting a significant impact on the shift in dynamics between Canadian politicians, the public, and Indigenous communities and individuals. Paralleling the increase in political activism for Indigenous rights in Canada is the growth in the creation of music by Indigenous women, notably of commercially available recordings of traditional and newly composed music. This chapter examines *Rattle & Drum* (2004), the debut recording by the Alberta-based, award-winning female ensemble Asani, to trace the links among Indigenous women's political activism, cultural revitalization, empowerment, and musical creativity. Through their song lyrics, these musicians invoke traditional Indigenous knowledge, the historical mistreatment of Indigenous people, the strength of Indigenous women, and their central roles in cultural continuity and vitality. In addition to discussing the album's song lyrics, I address prominent musical features, including creative vocal techniques and instrumentation used for musical effect. This analysis illustrates the variety and complexity of contemporary Indigenous women's music and the ways in which Indigenous women use music to negotiate and celebrate their heritage vis-à-vis modern politics and social issues in Canada. I demonstrate how women's musical creation, recreation, and performance fits into the general reawakening of Indigenous pride, heritage, and political activism for Indigenous rights in Canada, and I argue that that their artistic practices and creativity express a particular type of Indigenous modernity characterized by connections with the past and visions for the future.

INDIGENOUS WOMEN'S POLITICAL ACTIVISM IN CANADA

The roots of the Idle No More movement originated far from North Carolina in Saskatoon, Saskatchewan, Canada, and it followed years of political activism by Indigenous people contesting Canadian policies of assimilation and colonialism.[5] Indeed, Idle No More could be viewed as a "movement moment" (A. Barker 2015), one stop along a trajectory of Indigenous activism that accelerated with the Red Power movement of the 1960s, resistance to the White Paper in 1969 that would have seen the abolishment of the Indian Act in Canada, and in the 1990s a series of conflicts that put Indigenous land rights issues and environmental concerns at the forefront of mainstream media in Canada, including the 1990 Oka Crisis in Quebec, the 1995 Ipperwash Crisis, and the 2006 Caledonia resistance in Ontario, among others. Indigenous groups continue to protest resource development and exploitation of their traditional land and agitate to protect their rights as outlined in the Indian Act, the legislation that dictates the responsibilities and relationship between the Canadian federal government and First Nations communities and individuals. These protests culminated in the Idle No More movement, which began in November 2012. Members of this movement protested legislation (Bill C-45), which was passed by the Canadian federal government on December 14, 2012. Now known as the Jobs and Growth Act, the bill erodes Aboriginal control over the waterways on their lands and allows for the development of infrastructure on reserve communities. Authors of the "The Idle No More Manifesto" explain that the movement seeks respect for treaties that had been negotiated between the Canadian government and First Nations, respect for the rights of Indigenous people in Canada, respect for the land and its treatment, and responsible and sustainable development of environmental resources (Gordon and Founders 2014).

The early twenty-first century clearly marks a turning point in Canada for Indigenous rights and activism, with a significant increase in media attention to activist groups. Following Idle No More were antifracking demonstrations in the Elsipogtog First Nation in New Brunswick and the examination of the Indian

Residential School system through the Truth and Reconciliation Commission from 2008 to 2015. Between 2014 and 2015 national attention turned toward the disproportionate number of murdered and missing Indigenous women in Canada, resulting in the establishment of the National Inquiry into Missing and Murdered Indigenous Women and Girls in 2016. Complementing activist agendas is the increase in discourse by activists and Indigenous scholars calling for change to improve the lives of Indigenous people across the country. The increased political activism and cultural revitalization of Indigenous people has been noted by many media outlets, as well as by academics. Scholars such as Leanne Simpson (2011), Glen Coulthard (2014), and Taiaiake Alfred (2009) constitute the vanguard of scholarship on decolonization in Canada and a revisioning of settler-Native relations, influencing Indigenous and academic communities to rethink cross-cultural relations and respect for traditional Indigenous knowledge and lifeways. Marlene Brant Castellano, a Mohawk social worker, professor of Native studies, and long-term political activist, notes a marked shift in political activism and cultural renewal in Canada with an increasing presence of Indigenous women in transnational activist alliances:

> The last quarter of the twentieth century was marked by the emergence of First Nations, Inuit, and Métis peoples from virtual invisibility in Canadian cities and relative isolation on reserves . . . and rural settlements into the forefront of national affairs. Encounters that drew media attention were typically political and often confrontational as land claims and assertions of nationhood and self-determination were put forward. The voices of women were heard occasionally in political forums, but their work more often was carried out on a different stage. Their concerns centered around the family and quality of community life, hearkening back to their understanding of values and knowledge passed on by the grandmothers. With increasing frequency, they were stepping outside the private domain of family to lead initiatives in their communities and to network with women across the country who shared their concerns. (2009, 203–4)

Indigenous women are serving as the primary instigators of much recent political activism and are at the vanguard for many protests and demonstrations. Sheelah McLean, Nina Wilson, Sylvia McAdam, and Jessica Gordon initiated Idle No More during a teach-in in Saskatoon, Saskatchewan, and the hunger strike by Chief Theresa Spence of the Attawapiskat First Nation in northern Ontario catapulted this cause into the mainstream media of Canada.[6] Images associated

Figure 4.1. Drummers at Canada's federal legislature on Parliament Hill, Ottawa, Ontario, January 28, 2013. Photo by Melody McKiver. Used by permission.

with contemporary Indigenous activism taken from the Idle No More Facebook page, various online media outlets, and blogs from Idle No More supporters regularly feature women at the forefront of such demonstrations, often with drums in hand, as evident in the photo taken at the Idle No More demonstrations at Canada's federal legislative buildings at Parliament Hill in Ottawa, Ontario, during the winter of 2013 (figure 4.1).

Indigenous women are fulfilling important leadership roles in contemporary efforts to support their culture and community while agitating publicly for the reclamation of Indigenous identity, voice, and rights in Canada. Specific issues confronting First Nations women began to receive significant media and political attention during the latter half of the twentieth century. Indeed, since at least the 1960s, there has been increased awareness of the marginalization of Indigenous women in their own communities and in Canadian society generally. Organizations such as Indian Rights for Indian Women and the Native Women's Association of Canada have paid attention to Indigenous women's issues in Canada. Groups such as these agitated for improved living conditions for Indigenous women and sought significant changes to the Indian Act, making it less discriminatory against Indigenous women and allowing them to retain their rights regardless of whom they married.

From the time it was first introduced in Canada in 1876 until revisions beginning in 1951, the Indian Act was unapologetically patriarchal and assimilative. Under the Indian Act, First Nations people are categorized as "status" or "nonstatus" Indians according to whether they are registered with the federal government. Status Indians are able to access various programs and services, such as education, health care, and housing, and, according to certain provisions, they are exempt from paying taxes. Until amendments to the Indian Act in 1985, First Nations women who married non-Native men lost status and all benefits granted to status Indians. Benefits and status were also denied to their offspring, meaning that generations were denied their legal rights and identity as "status Indians" in Canada. The Indian Act revisions of 1985 addressed this discrimination against First Nations women, and the amendments to the act (known as Bill C-31) reinstated the status of about 117,000 people. In 2010–11, the Canadian federal government debated the details of and passed Bill C-3, which involved further amendments to the Indian Act, addressing gender inequalities that granted status to about 45,000 additional First Nations people whose grandmothers had lost status because they married non-Indian men (AANDC 2011; see also Hurley and Simeone 2010).

Despite concerns expressed about the financial implications of extending health-care, tax, and education benefits to more people, amendments to the Indian Act reflect the ongoing interests and organization of disenfranchised First Nations women and their children. In addition to those officially denied their cultural identity, many other Indigenous people in Canada were raised in non-Native families after being stolen from their home communities by federal children's aid workers and adopted by non-Natives in what is referred to as the "Sixties Scoop."[7] Others grew up in families that denied their Indigenous ancestry as a means to "fit in" better with the rest of Canadian society (S. Maracle 2003; Schwager 2003; Spears 2003). Indigenous identity, particularly vis-à-vis the federal legislation that determines who has status, and the rights status entails, is a truly complex issue. It can be quite divisive because of the rights accorded to "status Indians" that "non-status Indians" do not have. The issue is further complicated for Métis and Inuit peoples. Various other issues, such as land claims, environmental concerns, governance, and murdered and missing

Indigenous women in Canada, remain at the forefront of activists' minds, who continue to use their voices and musical instruments to raise awareness about these issues at demonstrations, rallies, and parades.

Historically, Indigenous women held leadership roles within their communities, and some First Nations communities were traditionally matriarchal and matrilineal. Although the Indian Act imposed patriarchy on reserve government structures, compromising these women-focused governance systems and power relationship within communities, many women remained active within their communities as leaders, but often in supportive capacities to elected male chiefs and councilors of First Nations bands. More recently, women are assuming greater public roles in social and political movements and local governance. This has been paralleled by an increase in academic literature, music recordings, writings, and other artistic expressions by Indigenous women. Their empowerment is also seen in the wide range of materials published in the latter quarter of the twentieth century by and about Indigenous women, critically countering the erosion of their narratives and the silencing of their voices.[8]

The anthology *Restoring the Balance: First Nations Women, Community, and Culture* (Valaskakis, Stout, and Guimond 2009) includes a wide range of writings that address Indigenous women's historical marginalization and the important roles they have within their communities. Kim Anderson and Bonita Lawrence (2003) write extensively about Indigenous women and their roles in today's society, challenging readers to consider identity issues and the intergenerational effects of the assimilationist policies of the Canadian government.[9] Susan Applegate Krouse and Heather A. Howard explore Indigenous women's issues in urban contexts, recognizing the important role women play in maintaining cultural continuity in cities. Many authors emphasize the role of women in generating the webs of social relations that sustain Indigenous culture and community. For example, Krouse and Howard write, "Women's activism has been crucial to building Native communities . . . not only through their direct participation in political and social movements, but also through their roles behind the scenes, as keepers of tradition, educators of children, and pioneers in city life . . . ensuring stability and continuity based in Native cultural and social practice, while also tending to the flames of resistance and asserting tribal sovereignty" (2009, x).

Indigenous women's activism is often framed in relation to their traditional roles within their communities as nurturers of their families and transmitters of cultural teachings and values. Castellano explains, "Women often describe their work as healing, in the Aboriginal sense of restoring physical, emotional, mental, and spiritual balance to the lives of individuals, families, and communities. As their work reverberates beyond their communities, they can be seen also as healing their nations, bringing a distinct approach to renewal that asserts the authority of experience and the wisdom of the heart" (2009, 203–4). Furthermore, she connects Indigenous women's political activism to their roles as nurturers of their cultures and families: "Almost without exception, the women were motivated by a desire to maintain their own and their peoples' culture, language, and identity. Most acknowledged the importance of support from their husbands and parents in taking on new challenges, balancing their responsibilities to home and children with involvement in the community. Their interests spanned a broad range of issues, with the needs of children and youth especially prominent" (208).

Drawing connections between the advocacy work of contemporary Indigenous women in Canada and their roles as nurturers of their families and communities is important in the context of contemporary political activism. Indigenous women are, in some cases, reclaiming their voices and heritage, and many are having their voices and messages heard publicly. As they continue to nurture their families and communities, many are also using their musical skills and talents to send out messages of empowerment and justice to a broader audience.

WOMEN'S MUSIC FOR SOCIAL CHANGE, MUSIC FOR WOMEN'S EMPOWERMENT

Within the private and public realms of resistance and empowerment, music has been, and remains, a critical and powerful tool for Indigenous people. From the protest music of Buffy Sainte-Marie in the 1960s, whose songs include "Universal Soldier" and "Now that the Buffalo's Gone," to more recent examples such as "E5–770, My Mother's Name" by Lucie Idlout and "Idle No More" by Ulali Project, Indigenous women have long used music to address social issues and political injustices. Female musicians continue to create commercially produced music that raises awareness of contemporary Indigenous issues and serves to empower First Peoples in Canada. Crystal McKinnon, writing about Indigenous music as a tool of resistance, states, "The strength and power of Indigenous music lies in its capacity to build community, culture and identity as Indigenous musicians communicate across, between and within their communities. Indigenous music is a critical foundation for the larger schema of Indigenous resistance and protest practices" (2010, 268–69).

Indigenous women's traditional recordings on which artists use hand drums and rattles as primary instruments surged in Canada during the mid-2000s. For example, in Alberta the Edmonton-based trio Asani released two albums of original music, *Rattle & Drum* (2004) and *Listen* (2009). In addition, the Women of Wabano from Ottawa released their debut album, *Voices*, in 2006; the Spirit Wind Singers based in Toronto released three albums, *Breathing the Wind* (2001), *Soul Talkin'* (2003), and *Awakening* (2004). In 2006 an Aboriginal women's support center in Ottawa, Minwaashin Lodge, likewise released the album *Our Songs Are Our Prayers*, made up of various traditional songs performed by women. Solo albums were also released and celebrated within the Indigenous community in Canada, including three albums by the Toronto-based musician Brenda MacIntyre (Medicine Song Woman): *Medicine Song* (2009), *Spirit Connection* (2007), and *Thunder Mountain Healing Songs* (2005). Fawn Wood, who hails from Saddle Lake, Alberta, released a solo album titled *Iskwewak* (2012), and Olivia Tailfeathers, also from Alberta, released *Ninihkssin* (2005). The noted recording artist Jani Lauzon from British Columbia released *Mixed Blessings* (2007), which is characterized by a return to more traditional sounds and instrumentation, illustrating the interest in traditional instruments and repertories among female performers in Canada at the start of the twenty-first century.

The surge in recordings by women's musical ensembles and female soloists can be attributed to various factors. Native American women's ensembles such as Ulali, active as a trio from 1987 until 2005 and reconstituted in the 2010s, and later Walela, a group founded in 1997, were highly successful in the music industry. Compilation albums of Indigenous women singers were released and positively received, such as the *Heartbeat: Voices of First Nations Women* and *Heartbeat: More Voices of First Nations Women* CDs by Smithsonian Folkways in 1995 and 1998. Similarly, the CDs *We Are Full Circle: An Aboriginal Women's Voices Concert* (2003) and *Hearts of the Nations: Aboriginal Women's Voices in the Studio* (1997) featured Indigenous women and were created through the Aboriginal Arts Program at the Banff Centre in Alberta. A nonmusical phenomenon that further contributed to increased musical output is the political activism and cultural milieu that characterized First Peoples at the start of the twenty-first century in Canada, a context that encouraged cultural expression and arts activism.

Many commercially produced CDs of traditional music by female Aboriginal artists share common features: the performers are respected musicians in their local and national communities; all use voice, traditional hand drums, and rattles as primary instruments; some songs invoke musical idioms and genres not necessarily identified as traditional Indigenous music, including jazz, hip-hop, and top-forty styles; many of the recordings were produced in a recording studio; performers make extensive use of vocables in their songs; song lyrics use humor for social and political commentary; and the lyrics often address the changing cultural landscape for First Peoples in Canada and cultural renewal. Furthermore, female Indigenous musicians are raising awareness and agitating for improved conditions for Indigenous women through their song lyrics and political statements, resonating with the Indigenous feminist movement that began in the 1980s and 1990s.[10] But, despite the similarities, significant sonic markers and repertory choices distinguish these performers, illustrating the colorful and creative music of Indigenous women. An analysis of an album by the successful Canadian trio Asani demonstrates how female musicians are engaging with contemporary issues confronting Indigenous women, using familiar musical idioms with a unique sound and aesthetic quality.

FINDING SUCCESS IN ASANI'S *RATTLE & DRUM* (2004)

Asani, which means "rock" in Cree, define themselves as a contemporary Aboriginal women's vocal trio. They are an Edmonton-based musical group that formed in 2001, composed of Debbie Houle (Cree Métis from the Elizabeth Métis Settlement), Sarah Pocklington (Cree Métis), and Sherryl Sewepagaham (Cree from the Little Red River Cree Nation) (figure 4.2). All three come from communities in Alberta and perform throughout Canada and around the world. All members studied voice at the postsecondary level, and all three sing, drum, and play rattle. Most of the songs performed by Asani are written by Pocklington or Sewepagaham.[11] Together the trio creates songs that draw from various musical influences and address both political issues and the importance of cultural traditions to Indigenous people. They have released two albums, *Rattle & Drum* in 2004 (figure 4.3), produced by Winnipeg-based Arbor Records, and *Listen* in 2009, by Meta Music. Their music is characterized by complex harmonizations of original melodies with vocables and lyrics in Woodland Cree and English, often accompanied with drums or rattles. They have gained significant accolades for their music. In 2005 they won the Canadian Aboriginal Music Award for Best Female Traditional/Cultural Roots Album, in 2010 they were presented with a Canadian Folk Music Award for Aboriginal Songwriter of the Year, and also in 2010 they received an Indian Summer Music Award for Best Spiritual Song (Asani 2013).

Asani often invokes common values associated with Indigenous cultures, such as the protection of Mother Earth, connections with nature and the environ-

Figure 4.2. *above* The members of Asani (*left to right*): Debbie Houle, Sarah Pocklington, and Sherryl Sewepagaham, n.d. Photo by Darren Greenwood Photography. Used by permission.

Figure 4.3. *right* Album cover of *Rattle & Drum*, by Asani, released 2004. Photo by Darren Greenwood Photography. Used by permission.

ment, the importance of family and community, the blessings and gifts from the Creator, and the importance of caring for future generations. In addition to these themes, however, are recurring messages about Indigenous women's historical mistreatment and marginalization, the power and strength of women, and the important roles that women have in their families and communities. They articulate these messages most notably on their debut album, *Rattle & Drum*. On this CD four of the eleven songs specifically address women, their historical mistreatment by the Canadian government, or women's strength and importance in building strong communities. "Bill C-31 Blues," "Rez Sister," and "Iskwesis" draw on blues and pop music, whereas "Rattle Dance" is a more traditional song, using vocables and rattles. All songs are characterized by Asani's dense harmonizations with drums and rattles, and in these four songs the attention to women's issues and their importance to Indigenous culture resonates with the general themes of Indigenous women's empowerment and activism.

The lyrics of "Bill C-31 Blues" address various issues that confronted Indigenous people in the twentieth century because of the assimilationist policies of the federal government as outlined in the Indian Act. The song comments on the pre-1985 laws about First Nations women's status and the conflicts that arose during the negotiation of Bill C-31, as well as the importance of Indian status to cultural continuity and vitality. The lyrics also reference the high proportion of Indigenous men who fought in Canada's military during the world wars and their mistreatment and forced enfranchisement upon their return to Canada.

BILL C-31 BLUES

I really wanna go home
Back to the roots that make me strong
I wanna be with my people
But many say I don't belong
Well I married out of love
How can that be so very wrong?

Well now . . .
Bill C-31, honey, now that's a real treat
If you wanna cause dissention, it can't be beat
Yeah divide and conquer that's the name of the game
Now I can't go home and it's a cryin' shame.

Mmmmmmmmm hmmmmm, I got the blues
Ooh I got them Bill C-31 blues.

My *Moosum* fought in the war
To keep this land true, strong, and free
So they took away his status
And said it was equality
Well, now he doesn't have a home
But you can't say that man's not Cree
'Cause how can that be?

Bill C-31, my friends, it doesn't bode well
For future generations it could be the road to hell
'Cause status begets status, yeah that is the law.

Mmmmmmm hmmmm, yeh, I got the blues
Oooh I got them Bill C-31 blues
Mmmm Hmmm, I got the blues
Oooh I got them Bill C-31
Yeh yeh ye, I got those dirty ones
Oooh. I got them Bill C-31 blues.

In the CD liner notes, the song's creator, Sarah Pocklington, explains that she drew inspiration from "the challenges faced by many Aboriginal people in Canada as a result of legislation passed by the Federal Government in 1985 — referred to as Bill C-31." She writes, "I believe humour can really be a source of strength in a tough situation, and I hope my attempt at combining it with musical stylings reminiscent of the 1950s and a dose of reality is successful in bringing to light some of the issues raised by this legislation and the Indian Act" (Asani 2004).

Musically, the song draws on doo-wop singing styles of the 1950s and 1960s, blues scales and vocalizations, and a mixture of solo and group singing, all a cappella. The overall musical form of the piece is ABAB. The piece closes with vocalizations, creative harmonies, and pitch bending, which are common to scat singing. The text of the A section draws listeners' attention to two key issues highlighted in the song: (1) the historical loss of status to which women were subjected if they married a man without First Nation's status prior to Bill C-31; and (2) First Nations men who lost their status after fighting in Canada's military. The piece opens with a solo voice asserting, "I really wanna go," with the others adding their vocal parts on the word "home." The second A section likewise starts with a solo declaration, "My *Moosum* fought" with the others joining on the word "war." The remainder of each A section is characterized by a main melody performed by one singer. A second singer performs a walking bass line typical of the blues (1,3,5,^{b}7, sung to "bum, bum, bum, bum"), providing a harmonic framework of I-I-V-I. The third singer adds "shoo, shoo be do wah" (with mediant-subdominant-mediant motion) to the last word of each line. On the fifth line of the A section, all three singers join together, harmonizing the text to emphasize it. In the first A section, the text is "Well I married out of love," and in the second A section, the text is "Well, now he doesn't have a home." These lyrics illustrate the emotional conflicts and challenges many First Nations people confronted owing to the assimilationist policies of the Canadian government. The lyrics emphasize the desire to maintain connections with culture despite imposed laws making that difficult, illustrating the tensions between cultural continuity and the Canadian government's policies and practices.

The lyrics in the contrasting B sections raise awareness of the effects of the Indian Act and Bill C-31, recognizing the fact that there was no consensus around the changes in status the bill enacted. The primary issue surrounding Bill C-31 — forced enfranchisement of First Nations women and their offspring through marriage to a non-Native or nonstatus man — reflects the assimilationist policies imposed on First Nations individuals and communities. The importance of cultural continuity between generations is highlighted in these sections, allowing listeners to contemplate the complicated nature of federal interference in Indigenous governance and the intergenerational effects of such policies. Indeed, the line "Yeah divide and conquer that's the name of the game" summarizes the underlying philosophy that influenced many federal policies. Importantly, however, the line "But you can't say that man's not Cree" reinforces the fact that culture and identity are not dictated by outsiders but by individuals and the communities to which they belong. Poetically and musically, this song illustrates the tensions between Indigeneity and colonial assimilationist policies and philosophies, and it highlights some of the key issues around Indian status and how federal legislation affected, and continues to affect, First Nations people in Canada.

Another song from *Rattle & Drum* that addresses contemporary Indigenous women is "Rez Sister," also composed by Pocklington. Through the lyrics of this song, Asani comments on the connections between urban and reserve life, celebrating the resiliency of Aboriginal women and their importance in passing knowledge between generations.

I'm a Rez Sister, that's a who I am
Even tho I'm livin' in the heart of downtown
I'm a Rez Sister, and I'm doin' alright
Never gonna give up the fight!

. . . .

Workin' hard for this lousy pay
Just to make sure that my kids are okay
I love my man with all of my heart
Tryin' hard just to do my part

'Cause I'm a Rez Sister
Gonna shout it out loud.
A Rez Sister of that I am proud
'Cause I'm a Rez Sister workin' for community
And someday we are gonna be free

Holdin' hands and a healin' hearts
My Kokum says that's how community starts
Feel it in your bones, mmm smell it in the air
And if you catch it with your feet
You can feel it there . . .

'Cause you're a Rez Sister, yeah a shootin' star
A Rez Sister and your gonna go far.
You're a Rez Sister and you're doin' alright
Never gonna give up the fight!

. . . .

'Cause I'm a . . .
Rez Sister, that's a who I am
Even tho I'm livin' in the heart of downtown
I'm a Rez Sister and I'm doin' alright
Never, never, never
Never, never, never . . .

'Cause I'm a Rez Sister!!!!!

This song refers to urban women's affiliation with reserve life and acknowledges the fight in which "Rez Sisters" are engaged to support their families and communities financially, emotionally, and culturally. The song also references teachings from the grandmothers to unite for community strength and well-being. Indeed, the values espoused by this song resonate with common themes of family through references to children, husband, Kokum (grandmother), and community and comment on the importance of female empowerment in urban environments. Listeners sense the permeability and movement between urban and reserve living and the fact that both can exist simultaneously within one person, a "Rez Sister." The liner notes indicate that the song "celebrates the contributions made by Aboriginal women who work tirelessly sometimes under the most stressful circumstances, to keep their families, communities and nations united and strong. Whether you live on a reserve, a Métis settlement or in the city it doesn't really matter—ancestral ties to family and the land run very deep. I like to think there is a little rez sister in all of us" (Asani 2004).

Musically, "Rez Sister" features a swing feel and pitch bending in the vocal parts. The singers are accompanied by congas and rattles at various points, although emphasis is placed on the text and vocal lines of the singers, and the overall musical form involves an alternating chorus-verse structure, with the chorus opening and closing the piece. The song opens with a solo voicing of the chorus lyrics, with a shaker added at the ends of phrases and to emphasize particular words or phrases. Pauses are inserted throughout the text of the first statement of the chorus, and the word "never" is repeated six times before the accelerated statement of "give up the fight." Finally, the other voices join in the repetition of the chorus text. Similar to "Bill C-31 Blues," "Rez Sister" is characterized by vocal play, including a section of scat singing, and the song features rich vocal harmonizations and effective uses of pause, delay, and silence. A strong statement of "'Cause I'm a Rez Sister!!!!!" sung by all three women closes the song with a sense of celebration and strength.

A third song on *Rattle & Drum* that focuses specifically on Indigenous women is "Iskwesis," composed by Sewepagaham. "Iskwesis" translates to "little girl," and it questions women's suffering and death and calls on the strength of women for survival and the pursuit of happiness. The CD liner notes explain that the song "follows the life of a girl growing up and questioning the choices she's made in her life" (Asani 2004) and the lyrics suggest that the song is about domestic violence and the promise of a return to happiness and laughter. This is a song of resistance, encouraging young women to choose their partners carefully, so they do not fall victim to a pattern experienced by many other Indigenous women, and calling on women to find "the strength to resist and survive."

ISKWESIS

Iskwesis, you ask me why
I don't know the answer to why women die
Iskwesis, you ask me why
The women who suffer and stifle their cries.

Should we ignore her pain and to be fought again?
Sing out! [Chant]
Grant us the strength to resist and survive.
Sing out! [Chant]
Oh, bring us the wisdom to staying alive.

Iskwesis, oh how you've grown
And found you a lover to call your own
Iskwesis, I should have known
The pattern you followed to be so alone.

Should we ignore their pain and to be fought again?

. . . .

Iskwesis, you ask me when
The fighting and hurting and sorrow will end
Iskwesis, you ask me when
The smiling and laughter will see you again.

Should we ignore the pain and to be fought again?

. . . .

Sing out! [Chant]
Grant us the strength to resist and survive.
Sing out! [Chant]
Oh, bring us the wisdom to staying alive.

"Iskwesis" has an overall verse-chorus form, with the verses sung by a solo singer in English and the chorus sung by the trio using a combination of English lyrics and harmonized vocables. As the song progresses, it shifts a step higher with the start of each new verse, creating a sense of increasing tension. The women accompany themselves on hand drums with a quick heartbeat drum pattern (short-long). Sewepagaham writes,

> When I went back to teach in my community in northern Alberta, I was invited to a traditional Tea Dance in the nearby community of Fox Lake. I was immediately intrigued by the rhythm of the hand drums played by a men's hand-drum group. I danced with the women in a connected sideways shuffle while other men danced to the beat of the drum with hands connected in front and behind like a chain link. The women and men danced in independent clockwise circles. The drum group stood on the outside of the two moving groups. The beauty and power of this drumbeat haunts me and is the basis for this song. (Asani 2004)

The drumbeat she describes is often used in social dances such as the Tea Dance, as well as Forty-Nine and Round Dance songs. The social commentary that characterizes "Iskwesis," especially in the reiteration of the lines "Grant us the strength to resist and survive" and "Oh, bring us the wisdom to staying alive," is not uncommon in other social dances. But the themes of domestic violence and the cyclical pattern of abuse are very pointed in this song, and, paired with the messages of empowerment, strength, and wisdom, this song speaks to Indigenous women's issues specifically and the need for healing and an end to cycles of violence.

The final song on *Rattle & Drum* that addresses Indigenous women is "Rattle Dance," also composed by Sewepagaham. Here the singers accompany themselves with rattles to acknowledge the fact that women in many Indigenous cultures customarily play these instruments. Whereas the song text itself consists entirely of vocables, the repetitions are characterized by full harmonies, interesting call-and-response interplay between the voices, and a quick pace. The CD liner notes indicate that the purpose of this song is "to honour the women of the past, the present and the future" (Asani 2004). This is a song of celebration, which listeners can join in singing with relative ease owing to the use of vocables and a repetitive structure.

Asani's debut album, *Rattle & Drum*, was created by three strong Indigenous women with an agenda of empowerment and celebration. The songs "Rez Sister," "Bill C-31 Blues," "Iskwesis," and "Rattle Dance" all address specific women's issues, drawing listeners' attention to the plight and determination of First Peoples in the twenty-first century, through thoughtful lyrics set to catchy melodies, creative harmonies, and strategic use of accompanying instruments. Their emphasis on celebrating women's strength and resiliency and their importance to contemporary Indigenous communities resonate with common political priorities of Indigenous people throughout Canada. As Houle states, "You have to have faith that when you put it out there that you let it go, and you have the faith that it's going to get to the people it has to get to and will move them people that need to be moved, and it isn't something you can see directly. It's something that you have to have faith that it's making a difference" (Asani 2009b).

Asani has performed for a wide variety of audiences nationally and internationally, for both Indigenous and non-Indigenous listeners, who regularly greet them with accolades. Their success is because of their creativity in songwriting and their inspirational live performances, in which they use traditional hand drums and rattles in a wide range of styles and repertories in their music, demonstrating the versatility of contemporary Indigenous artists. Indeed, Asani's approach to instrument use, vocal style, and song themes clearly position them as performers of *modern* Indigenous music informed by contemporary social and political issues. Their music continues the lineage of activist female Indigenous musicians—one that extends beyond Buffy Sainte-Marie's work in the 1960s and Ulali's inspirational writing in the 1990s—and illustrates the variety of musical styles created by Indigenous women as they fulfill their important roles both as nurturers of their culture and as activists. The celebratory nature of the music created and performed by Indigenous women allows for inclusive participation and music consumption, and the songs and sentiments expressed reflect the context in which they are created, a context characterized by women's empowerment, social and political activism, and the cultural revitalization of First Peoples throughout Canada.

As women and men continue to organize and to place Indigenous issues at the forefront of the Canadian media, through artistic creations, performances, and various artistic and social platforms, we are reminded of their engagement with contemporary technologies and the ways in which they demonstrate their own "Indigenous modernity." Narratives about women's rights, empowerment, and self-identification as Indigenous people resonate with the current advocacy for Indigenous rights and a renewed sense of cultural pride among Indigenous people throughout Canada; the innovative ways in which artists are projecting these issues position them as leaders in contemporary politics and activism in Canada.

CHRISTINA LEZA

5. Hip-Hop Is Resistance
Indigeneity on the U.S.-Mexico Border

"Hip-Hop Is Resistance" is the movement slogan for Shining Soul, a hip-hop group based in Phoenix, Arizona. Shining Soul is fronted by emcees Bronze Candidate (aka Franco Habre), a Chicano native of South Phoenix, and emcee Liaizon (aka Alex Soto), a Tohono O'odham Nation member, backed by Navajo Nation member DJ Reflekshin (aka Lawrence Martinez).[1] Shining Soul promotes hip-hop as a force for resistance, emphasizing hip-hop's origins among the disenfranchised of black urban America. Initially inspired by socially conscious recordings such as Grandmaster Flash and Melle Mel's "The Message" and Blackstar's "Respiration," Shining Soul draws from their own cultural backgrounds and sociopolitical experiences in the creation of conscious hip-hop.

Beyond emceeing, Shining Soul contributes to local activism through protest movements and the educational empowerment of youth. Their Beat Making workshops introduce youth to beat production and to hip-hop as a tool for empowerment, engaging students in discussions of social issues relevant to their home communities. In 2010 Habre and Soto bound themselves together, using PVC pipes and bicycle locks, with other protesters at U.S. Border Patrol offices. The protesters placed a banner in the lobby reading, "Stop Militarization on Indigenous Lands Now." One protest statement written on the PVC pipes was "Stop SB 1070," referring to the Arizona State Senate bill requiring law enforcement to request proof of citizenship from individuals suspected of being undocumented immigrants. The law enabled the targeting of Latinos, or those resembling Latinos, as suspected lawbreakers. Whereas supporters claimed that the law did not invite racial profiling, the bill did not define "reasonable suspicion," leaving this open for interpretation by law enforcement. SB 1070 was enacted in April 2010 with an amendment clarifying that "reasonable suspicion" should not include consideration of race or national origin (Morse 2011). Critics, however, remained unconvinced that such an amendment could provide equal protection for all citizens.

For many, legislation such as SB 1070 illustrates the deep anti-immigrant sentiment in Arizona and the need for a pro-immigrant movement to protect human rights throughout the border region. Following decades of escalating border enforcement and consistent mainstream support for a local sheriff notorious for employing constitutionally questionable anti-immigrant practices, SB 1070 seemed a culminating statement by the region's white mainstream against brown-skinned peoples on the border. Less than a month after signing SB 1070 into law, Arizona governor Janet Brewer signed HB 2281, the law banning ethnic studies in public schools. No population felt the impacts of this bill more strongly than Tucson youth, particularly those involved with the Tucson Unified School District's Mexican American studies program (Orozco 2012). Both SB 1070 and HB 2281 triggered a wave of protest. Youth of all ethnicities rallied to oppose both bills, perceived as a racist attack on their civil rights. Ironically, HB 2281, designed to eliminate classes that "advocate ethnic solidarity," created an explosion of protest solidarity among youth of color, as the law also threatened African American and Native American studies. In dismantling the district's Mexican American studies, the district also removed Native American– and African American–authored books included in its curriculum from all classrooms. For many SB 1070 and HB 2281 were two sides of a single political coin—legislation designed to further marginalize the region's peoples of color.

Local activism defending cultural rights in Arizona has been portrayed as anti-American and dangerous. Pauline Wakeham (2012) similarly observes that Western "War on Terror" rhetoric facilitates the portrayal and treatment of Indigenous activists as terrorists within their own homelands. Nevertheless, human rights activism challenging the escalation of federal border enforcement, state anti-immigrant and antibrown legislation, and racial profiling practices has intensified in southern Arizona. Shining Soul's song "Papers," from *We Got This* (2011b), expressed a "brown" perspective of border enforcement as militarized action against people of color with its chorus, "Click-clack / Where your papers at? / We're under attack / Fight back. It's war." A counterdiscourse to mainstream rhetoric, "Papers" portrays border enforcement as colonial warfare against Indigenous peoples. The song's lyrics frame border militarization as an Indigenous rights issue, a perspective further explained in the video's introductory text:

The militarization of the U.S.-Mexico border has led only to cultural and environmental destruction of the Indigenous peoples whose land is on or near the border. . . . Border militarization brings death and terror to Indigenous peoples from other parts of the continent migrating to this land. The immigration struggle is also an Indigenous struggle.

For Shining Soul the struggle for immigrant rights is about protecting Indigenous and human rights. For Soto the struggle is about defending his people's sovereignty, as the U.S.-Mexico border cuts across O'odham lands. Shining Soul's music has become a venue for voicing the struggles of those in Soto's community facing the daily realities of Border Patrol presence. In light of SB 1070, "Papers" emerged as a significant statement about the shared struggles of Latinos and Native Americans on the border, as Soto and Habre blended their distinct sociocultural voices to oppose anti-immigrant policies.

In many ways Shining Soul embodies the interethnic solidarity that has emerged in southern Arizona over border-related rights issues. Whereas "Hip-Hop Is Resistance" serves as rallying cry for the activist emcees, the overarching message of Shining Soul's music is solidarity through respect. In emphasizing this message Habre and Soto present an ideal model for social movement rooted in notions of mutual love and solidarity despite differences. The emcees recognize that this message must remain central to grassroots social movement from the margins, so often marred by factionalism, including internal conflicts over ethnic identity and cultural appropriation.

Latino and Native American youth on the U.S.-Mexico border may appear to have set aside ethnic differences to unite over joint issues. With young Native American and Chicano activists assembling together, communicating through such slogans as "Stop militarization on Indigenous lands" and "We didn't cross the border, the border crossed us," it might appear that border-activist youth are embracing a broad notion of Indigeneity, one that accommodates the Indigenous identity claims of both Native American and Latino activists. In reality ethnic-identity construction among youth on the border is much more complex, and conflicts over ethnic-identity claims threaten productive communication between the groups. Differing notions of Indigeneity remain present within the border social-justice movement and continue to disrupt united action. Such conflicts must be negotiated as border activists of different ethnicities seek support from one another in shared struggles. Soto and Habre offer a critical perspective on existing interethnic conflicts and the process of social negotiation necessary to maintain solidarity among the movement's warriors. As partners in musical production and creators of that movement's message for over a decade, Bronze Candidate and Liaizon offer special insight on this process, working together to bring their experiences of the world to their musical message.

By critically examining the collaborative work of a Latino and a Tohono O'odham hip-hop artist, this chapter explores how contemporary Indigenous individuals articulate particular Indigenous identities and ideologies through a shared musical medium. As Philip Deloria (2004) illustrates, Indigenous individuals have historically negotiated their identities and public performances in "unexpected" ways, revealing their continuous, though largely unacknowledged, contributions to modernity. This chapter highlights some ways Indigenous people reconstruct and articulate Indigeneity through a musical medium not typically recognized as "traditional" to Indigenous peoples. Yet, as Bissett Perea argues in her contribution to this collection, it is important to think beyond the "unexpected indigene" to processes of Indigenous alliance making common in the ongoing formation of identities and ideologies (see also B. Diamond 2007b).

One significant aspect of Shining Soul's collaborative work is the performance of distinct sociocultural voices through language and other style choices made by the artists in individual songs. Analyzing the strategic use of cultural style within songs, I attempt to merge a Bakhtinian framework for understanding code switching and code mixing with an alliance-studies approach in understanding style mixing in cross-cultural musical collaborations. In doing so, I explore how cultural code switching and code mixing occur at the levels of both sound and linguistic code selection. This analysis considers the symbolic imagery (visual and sonic) employed by Shining Soul to communicate both shared and separate sociocultural identities.

WHERE I'M FROM

My chapter derives from ethnographic field research in the Phoenix-Tucson area between 2006 and 2012. At the time my research focused on Indigenous activist movements in response to U.S.-Mexico border-enforcement policy. I became familiar with Shining Soul through contact with other Indigenous activists in the region, first meeting emcees Liaizon and Bronze Candidate at a fund-raising performance in May 2012. I recorded interviews with the two artists in August 2012, with follow-up interviews in June and July 2014.[2]

Initially, I was drawn to Shining Soul's work as an Indigenous youth statement on current border politics. Yet, as I learned more about the hip-hop duo's identities, I became fascinated with both the ways their collaboration symbolized a Native American–Latino interethnic communication and the ways it symbolized my own ethnic background. As an individual of Yoeme (Yaqui) and Chicano paternal descent and mixed Indigenous and Chicana maternal descent, I have always been conscious of the conflicts between Latino and Native American Indigeneity. Throughout my life I have been asked by strangers and friends alike, "Are you Indian/Native American?" In my responses I have always felt a certain ambiguity. Preferring always to see myself simply as Indigenous, inheritor of both a proud Yoeme cultural history and mestizo (mixed-blood) Indigeneity, I have never known how to comfortably articulate this personal sense of Indigeneity without providing both a complex history lesson and a personal autobiographical account. Often, aware of the expectations of "authentic" Indigeneity, I opt to identify as simply Yaqui. After all, despite the common colonial blood-quantum mentality present among both non-Indigenous and Indigenous peoples, one is either a Yaqui person or not. But to identify simply as Yaqui has always felt like a traitor's act against my Chicana roots. To somehow "defend" my Indigeneity by affiliation with a "real" Indigenous people has always felt like a subtle attack against the legitimacy of Chicana(o) Indigeneity and my own cultural ancestry.

This personal struggle to define Indigeneity frames my analysis of Shining Soul's work, as does my personal connection to Indigenous border activism. I believe that my particular connection to the themes and imagery present in Shining Soul's work illuminate my analysis in productive ways. The issues of where one is from in terms of origins and experience and where one is physically, emotionally and intellectually hold thematic importance for the artists. They serve as critical points of reflection in Shining Soul's self-identification, collaborations in and out of the group, and in their work to build a social consciousness among youth of color.

WHERE THEY'RE FROM

For many hip-hop artists, a hip-hop sound is fundamentally a street sound. James Spady identifies "the street" as the "rhythmic locus of the hip hop world" (Spady and Eure 1991, 406–7). Confirming one's origins in urban street culture may be the prerequisite for acceptance of one's rhymes by the hip-hop community (Alim 2004; Keyes 1991; Spady, Lee, and Alim 1999). Whereas black emcees may declare themselves "straight outta the muthafuckin streets," Shining Soul declares their hip-hop origins with "straight outta the desert borough." Shining Soul recognizes black urban life as the origin of hip-hop, but for this duo it is not the physical space of urban streets but the socioeconomic struggles experienced in those streets that define hip-hop culture. Hip-hop, as resistance in general, is born in response to socioeconomic and sociopolitical inequality. According to Shining Soul's philosophy, hip-hop is a culturally diverse space, but one where a true recognition of, and critical perspective on, one's social background is essential. Both Habre and Soto were brought up in socially conscious environments, and, for both, hip-hop culture emerged as the ideal space for expression and pursuit of conscious action (figure 5.1).

Born and raised in Phoenix's Southside, Franco Habre became conscious of his urban environment through his father's involvement with the Chicano movement, the Mexican American cultural and civil rights movement of the 1960s and 1970s.[3] The label *Chicano*, promoted during this period, derives from *Mexicano* (Me-shi-ka-no), the Nahuatl-language name for the Aztec and the self-identifying term still used by many contemporary Aztec (Nahua) in Mexico.[4] The adoption of the term *Chicano*, and of *Chicanismo* as an ideological perspective reflecting a Chicano mentality, marked the birth of a new generation of activist youth (Muñoz 2007, 96). Habre describes how Chicano liberation–movement *encuentros* (summits) taught his father and other Chicano youth "to be critical about their environments" and to "get involved in community and make affirmative change" (interview, Phoenix, AZ, August 19, 2012).

The Chicano activist culture of his father's youth shaped Habre's own youth. He was exposed to the movement's messages through

> patches, posters, the music—the *corridos*—this protest music back in the day.[5] It's parallel to what hip-hop is. . . . It [hip-hop] was there as a tool for me growing up, and in the city that probably was the first most tangible culture that I applied myself to. . . . It was a natural progression, seeking out music and doing production, and actually rapping. That part is about sharing, sharing my story. My father would always say, "You should speak your heart," or "Tell your story." It's what you begin to do when you start rhyming, because I came from that critical background of Chicanismo. . . . It just fell in-line with the origins of hip-hop, which is speaking about where you're coming from, what's important to you, and how you can change very dark situations that are developing and that are systematic and that other people are feeling as well (interview, August 19, 2012).

Figure 5.1. The members of Shining Soul (*left to right*): Bronze Candidate/
Franco Habre, Liaizon/Alex Soto, DJ Reflekshin/Lawrence Martinez, n.d.
Photo by Thosh Collins. Courtesy of Shining Soul.

Alex Soto's activist and traditionalist orientations were influenced by both
O'odham elders and youth activists within his O'odham community. While
Soto also grew up in Phoenix, he originates from the community of Sells in the
Tohono O'odham Nation. Much of his youth was spent visiting relatives on the
reservation during weekly trips with his grandparents. Soto joined the O'odham
Solidarity across Borders Collective, an O'odham youth organization working
with elders in Mexico and mobilizing against policies destructive to the O'odham
Him'dag (traditional lifeways). As border enforcement on his lands increased,
Soto's appreciation of hip-hop culture deepened. He states, "Just the level of
militarization in our community—checkpoints, agents everywhere, hearing our
relatives share these stories of getting harassed . . . that sounded like some LA
riot shit, with Ice Cube saying, 'Fuck the police.' That was my way of looking at
it. Same thing going on in the hood is going on in the rez" (interview, August
19, 2012).

At a 2012 poetry event in Tucson, Shining Soul shocked some audience members by exclaiming, "Fuck the Border Patrol!" at the conclusion of "Papers," a song
that also features the lyric, "Fuck the National Guard and the *frontera* (border)."

Soto admits that such exclamations are inappropriate in some contexts but believes that a rap performance is always an appropriate venue for such statements. Staying true to where one is from in hip-hop also means staying true to feelings about where one is from, particularly in regard to feelings of oppression. In their youth workshops Shining Soul stresses recognizing one's origins and the sociocultural struggles inherent to those origins. While youth come to the workshops hoping to reproduce the hip-hop sounds and materialistic themes heard on the radio, Shining Soul emphasizes the value of finding one's personal voice through rap. Soto recalls a recent workshop interaction with one young man: "'So you have a voice, right? Where are you from?' And he was like, 'Oh, I'm from down the street.' I'm like, 'No, no, where are you *from*?' His parents actually were undocumented. And I was trying to explain to him, 'Well you should be saying something about that. At the very least, be aware of who you are and where you're from'" (interview, August 19, 2012).

Issues of documentation, immigration policy, and border enforcement are critical not only to Latino experience on the U.S.-Mexico border but also to the experiences of many Native people in the region. The following section discusses some impacts of border policy on the Tohono O'odham Nation, along with related issues of Indigenous sovereignty and oppression emphasized in Shining Soul's music.

THE MILITARIZED REZ

Immigration and customs policy at the U.S.-Mexico border impacts numerous First Peoples of North America. There are twenty-six federally recognized Native nations in the U.S.-Mexico border region (Ganster and Lorey 2008, 196) and approximately eight First Peoples with historical ties to Mexico. U.S.-Mexico border enforcement particularly impacts the Tohono O'odham Nation, where the border bisects the O'odham traditional territories. The Tohono O'odham reservation is 2.8 million acres of desert in which both drug trafficking and undocumented-immigrant movement have increased because of heightened border-enforcement measures at urban ports of entry. Threats posed by illegal drug and human trafficking concern reservation residents, but so do border-enforcement strategies. Community members have voiced opposition to the environmental, cultural, and human destruction associated with border enforcement, including border-wall construction and the Department of Homeland Security's U.S. Immigration and Customs Enforcement surveillance and search practices.

Between 1995 and 2005 border-related migrant deaths more than doubled, and more than three-fourths of recorded migrant deaths occurred in the Arizona Border Patrol sectors (Rubio-Goldsmith et al. 2006). In 2002 the tribe's vice-chair stated, "We are very opposed to any kind of policy that would cause harm toward human beings. . . . [The policy] stains our land with the blood of our neighbors, and pierces the hearts of our people" (Tedford 2002). In a 2007 statement to the UN special rapporteur on migrants' rights, Tohono O'odham activist Ofelia Rivas stated that the blood on her lands could not be cleaned until border-enforcement violence came to an end. Joseph Joaquin, an O'odham elder and Tohono O'odham Nation cultural-resources specialist, states that "We were brought into this world for a purpose, to be the caretakers of this land." Because of present border enforcement, however, "ancestors' graves are unvisited; relatives go years without seeing family; and fiestas, wakes, and ceremonial offerings go unattended. Elders, hampered from crossing for a number of reasons, fail to share traditional stories and to pass on knowledge about the past, about plants and animals, and about caring for their desert home" (Arietta 2004). O'odham healers without required travel documents cannot attend ceremonies. Agents may search and confiscate medicine bundles or other traditional items, regardless of the holder's documentation. And while the tribe grants membership to Mexican community members, benefits on reservation lands may be inaccessible to enrolled members lacking required travel documents.

Border Patrol questioning and detention often disrupt O'odham deer-hunting and salt-gathering ceremonies in the desert (Norrell 2006). Tohono O'odham are often approached by Border Patrol to prove their identities as U.S. citizens. On the International Cry website, one Tohono O'odham member comments, "on my way down from Phoenix to my home in Pisin mo'o, I can count 30+ Border Patrol vehicles on the drive down. Then while I'm there visiting it feels as though we're in a Prison Camp, we can't go for drives on our own land without getting pulled over and interrogated." Another community member writes, "I could go on and on with border patrol, military stories that only the o'odham [sic] know" (Schertow 2008).

Shining Soul's "Papers" video (2011a) starts with footage of Border Patrol stopping Soto's (Liaizon's) vehicle for inspection. In response, Soto states, "You can check my vehicle all you want, but you have no right to do that. This is our land, not your land." The lyrics that follow express a Tohono O'odham perspective of border enforcement, yet "Papers" further expresses a Latino experience of oppression through Habre's (Bronze Candidate's) contributions:

Liaizon (emcee), Verse 1

Up in the city, yall know the deal
but back on my reservation, it's been the ordeal.
Red light, blue light, keep still
Checking for ID, you get the ideal.
"Who your family be, where your papers at?"
Don't it sound like, a chopped and screwed track?
Feds on my back, taking photos
Border Patrol, equals Gestapo.
They out to get ya . . .
I'm just minding my biz.
Officer tripping like our land be his.
Pop quiz . . .
How did we let it get this far?
Spy drones got me on radar.
Star Trek lights at night, minus Picard.
All up in my backyard.
Fuck the National Guard and the *frontera*.
Yo, we under attack.
Time to do it like Pi'Machu and fight back!
It's like that!

Chorus [repeated four times]

Click Clack
where ya papers at?
We under attack, fight back.
It's war!

Bronze Candidate, Verse 2

I don't know what's worse
Gringos constructing another green zone or Republican Latinos.
The persecution is threefold.
We broke, brown is the pigment, and they assume that we speakah no English.
We all heathens in the eyes of the state.

They raisin' the stakes.
Lockin' it down from "TJ" [Tijuana]
All the way to Matamoros
up to Brownsville, back to San Diego
lay low!
I said, "They out to get ya,
enforcing arbitrary lines with vigilante militias;
get the picture?"
White supremacists come in many facets,
and most of these bastards uphold the law and wear badges.
Click clackin', point-blank blastin',
they killin' in cold blood
with impunity, no judge.
Fuck that! We will not budge.
They push, we push back.
Watch these tables turn and witness the blowback!

With lyrics contributed equally by each emcee and a title referring to the border-related discrimination experienced by both Latinos and Native Americans, "Papers" expresses shared aspects of marginalization. While Liaizon's lyrics are specific to the border-reservation experience, Bronze Candidate's lyrics reference a Latino perspective, building on Liaizon's previous statements of Indigenous marginalization. The lyrics, "The persecution is threefold. / We broke, brown is the pigment, and they assume that we speakah no English. / We all heathens in the eyes of the state," highlight a "we" identity broad enough to include both Latinos and Native peoples, for whom racial marginalization has gone hand in hand with economic marginalization. In their track "No Mercy," Shining Soul further reiterates a "no borders" position. While Liaizon and Bronze Candidate contribute individual cultural perspectives, a united "we" identity is forged with the lyrics:

Our communities have been militarized. Open your eyes.
What we need is a military response, a hood renaissance with a heavy dose
    of upheaval
And it starts with one conversation.
Power concedes nothing without confrontation.

Chorus

We from that ground zero, antiheroes, sayin' that shit that you can't say,

Like smash borders, *chinga la migra* [fuck the border patrol], middle finga' to
   la linea [the line, or border].[6]

We from that desert borough. We keep it thorough, sayin' that shit that you
   can't say

like smash borders, *chinga la migra*, middle finga' to *la linea*.

Shining Soul's protest music presents a united Native-Latino voice, expressing shared brown oppression on the militarized border. Yet there is a limit to
the extent that Latino and Native experiences on the border can be conflated,
particularly regarding notions of Indigenous homeland. The following section
explores some of these tensions as well as points of resolution critical to continued unity and collaboration.

KNOWING WHO THEY ARE AND
WHERE THEY'RE AT

Shining Soul's "Get Up," from *Sonic Smash* (2013), is a statement of hope and
brown unity:

Young, gifted, and brown,[7]
I say we be doin' it now.
We be puttin' it down with that profound sound.
We infinity bound, to the top.

Bronze Candidate opens the piece, soon referencing Latin American Indigenous revolution with the lyric, "What I really want to say is ¡*Ya basta!* This is
for *La Raza*."[8] Liaizon parallels the opening lyrics with

Young, gifted, and red,
Us Indians ain't dead.
Meet a modern-day warrior with some street cred.
A tomahawk to the head? I use a mic instead.

Liaizon further references brown identity with

Brown and proud, say it loud, boogie down.
Native American, my rap's genuine.
I keep it real like Indigenous medicine
to make rap look cool again.

Ultimately, as stated in its lyrics, "Get Up" is a song about "our pain," whether as Latino or Native peoples, and it is a "get up, stand up, raw, uncut" statement about the power of brown people to transcend pain and fight against an oppressive system:

Shining Soul has the plan, goddamn.
Let it rain.
We make it bang on the system
through our pain.
Rearrange.
This is wisdom blasting through your system.

Yet Liaizon's lyrics further express that whereas all the voices of the song are "brown," only some are both brown and red. In this sense Liaizon's lyrics represent a Native American identity and experience of the world distinct from those of other brown peoples. Liaizon speaks from what he refers to as a "privileged place," as an O'odham person who knows "who I am, where I'm from" and "where my relatives are buried" (interview, August 19, 2012). Soto sees his privilege relative to that of most Latinos, whose exact knowledge of their Indigenous ancestry has been stolen from them through colonialism. During the Chicano movement, embracing mestizo Indigenous roots became critical to empowerment, as Chicanos strove for liberation from a colonial mentality. Descendants "of both conquered Indians and conquering Spaniards and Indians, Chicanos would vacillate between a self-identity as foreigners and a self-identity as natives" (Chávez 1984, 10, cited in Navarro 2005, 52). Reviving connections to precolonial Indigenous roots mentally liberated Chicanos from oppressive European colonial roots.

The ancient Aztec empire became a symbol of Indigenous nationhood that could be referred to as a point of origin (Navarro 2005; Muñoz 2007; de la Torre and Gutiérrez Zúñiga 2013). The processes of colonialism erased knowledge of Indigenous lineages for most Chicanos, so that few can trace a lineage to Aztec peoples or any specific Indigenous nation. Yet symbolic connection to the Aztec and Aztlán—the mythical Aztec homeland—has become critical to many Chicanos in identity construction. During the Chicano movement, Aztlán was popularized as the term for an imagined Chicano nation. Aztlán also inspired a spiritual movement, with ceremonial practices developing based on the ancient Aztec religion (de la Torre and Gutiérrez Zúñiga 2013).

In the U.S. Southwest, however, the Chicano concept of Aztlán has created tension between Chicanos and Native Americans. Tom Holm, Diane Pearson and Ben Chavis (2003) have proposed the "peoplehood matrix" to conceptualize Indigenous group identity. Peoplehood has four aspects: language, sacred history, ceremonial cycle, and place/territory. Although all parts are linked, place/territory embodies a people's sacred history and ceremony communicated through language (Basso 1988, 1996). For Native Americans, place/territory is evident in one's physical homeland, as are the other aspects of peoplehood within the homeland that they or their relatives inhabit. For this reason many Native Americans, particularly those with homelands that lie within the territories claimed as Aztlán, are troubled by the concept of it. Referring to a general history of early Indigenous migration and the U.S. acquisition of Mexican territories, Chicanos who identify with Aztlán include much of the U.S. Southwest in their claimed territories. Among many Chicano activists, Aztlán has become a synonym for the Southwest (Muñoz 2007, 94; Navarro 2005, 55, 317). This is a claim that many Native Americans cannot reconcile with their own origin stories or with their traditional sense of homeland as embodied space.

Soto explains, "I do take issue with the idea of Aztlán. . . . How I've been raised, you've got to recognize where you're at, in the areas you're at." Whereas he understands Aztlán as a "point of empowerment" or a "mind frame," for Soto, these claims on "physical land" are not rooted in the sacred histories of other peoples within the region. He states, "I'm not aware of that area [Aztlán] in my story. This is Tohono O'odham land, Akimel O'odham land." For Soto, then, an acknowledgment of place and one's presence in the traditional places of others is central to Indigeneity and in building respectful relationships with other peoples. From his perspective, an Indigenous person constructs identity by three main criteria: "(1) this is who I am; (2) this is where I'm from; and (3) this is the land of my ancestors." Soto believes refusal to acknowledge the ancestral land of others when identifying with one's Indigenous roots is the behavior of a "culture vulture," someone who picks and chooses convenient cultural traits for identification, even if it means claiming the cultural inheritances of others (interview, August 19, 2012).

For both Soto and Habre, identification with Aztlán can perpetuate colonialism if not done with respect for Native peoples' histories and sense of place. Habre states, "You know where you're at, where you're from, and know that our presences are not equal. . . . People get defensive and say, 'It's not land-based. It's all a mental thing,' but I think, for the most part, the narrative is, the Southwest is Aztlán. It's about reconquering a place of origin. But that's totally false. There are Indigenous peoples all across this so-called Southwest." Habre believes that being Chicano means "honoring your migration lineage," part of which requires recognizing "forced relocation" through the territories of other peoples. In the past the members of Shining Soul have introduced themselves as "Straight outta occupied *je:wed* [O'odham term for land]," declaring their presence on O'odham territories as well as the colonially occupied state of the region (interview, August 19, 2012).

Soto's and Habre's conversations about Indigeneity over a decade have shaped their shared perspective regarding Indigenous homelands. They see continued misunderstanding and conflict between Native Americans and Chicanos as they interact both with other activists and with hip-hop audiences. Soto points to Shining Soul's experiences on stage as a precipitant for conversations about Indigeneity. He recalls that "being at an event, and I'm saying what I'm saying, and he's saying what he's saying, and we just pissed off a whole part of the crowd. And we're like, well, what do we do? We haven't even rapped yet?" (interview, August 19, 2012).

Habre and Soto recognize that Indigeneity on the U.S.-Mexico border is a complex and sensitive issue for many Chicanos and Native Americans. Each may perceive the identity claims of the other as an attempt to "culture vulture" the other's Indigenous roots. For Native Americans, certain Chicano claims to Indigeneity seem to appropriate Native culture, denying the historical experiences of specific Native peoples. For Chicanos, Native American resistance to concepts such as Aztlán communicates a denial of Chicano Indigenous roots, reinforcing the loss of Indigenous lineage suffered under colonialism. Soto recalls describing the Native perspective of Chicano cultural imperialism to his grandfather and other elders who, baffled, described their experience with Chicanos "back in the day" of movement solidarity, when they lived together in the same urban communities, listened to the same popular music, followed the same popular fashions, and were inspired by many of the same leaders (interview, August 19, 2012). Not much has changed for Chicano and Native youth regarding a broadly shared popular culture and various points of shared inspiration. Yet Soto observes that the situation has somehow become more complicated in regard to ethnicity and self-identification.

A difference in generational perspective may be the result of an ethnic consciousness promoted during the civil rights movement, later strengthened in academic literature on race and ethnicity and the 1980s multicultural movement. My fieldwork with elder activists, however, indicates that some Native activists of the earlier generation also view Chicano Indigeneity claims negatively. The Chicana civil rights activist Enriqueta Vasquez observed similar tensions, noting that Native Americans she spoke with during the 1969 Alcatraz Island occupation "felt threatened" by and "had a hard time grasping" the concept of Aztlán (qtd. in Oropeza 2006, xxxix). While today's Native and Latino youth may be more sensitive to issues of ethnicity, the conflict between Latinos and Native Americans over Indigenous identity claims is long-standing.

This conflict certainly interferes with solidarity among Latino and Native activists on the border. Habre and Soto observe that certain gatekeeper organizations limit joint movement. Field research verifies that whereas many activist organizations on the border share social-justice goals, this conflict discourages certain organizations from collaborating. The situation is unfortunate, as Habre observes, since border activists are a "fragmented few" (interview, August 19, 2012). Shining Soul finds hope, however, in their musical collaboration. Habre sees Shining Soul as a manifestation of early interethnic solidarity movements. As "manifestations of solidarity," Shining Soul sees its work as "bigger than" conflicts that currently fragment their movement. Soto states, "Through hip-hop, we've been able to cut through all this drama and just be like, 'This is how we rock it. Dope hip-hop. Dope beats.' We have that support, that solidarity within the group, that understanding. This is real, and, at the end of the day, this is bigger than both of us. We can't be fighting each other. We can't be building on top of each other's backs" (interview, August 19, 2012).

CODE SWITCHING, CODE MIXING, AND ALLIANCE MAKING

Some linguists have applied a Bakhtinian approach to analyze language and dialect selection, viewing languages and dialects as codes for sociocultural voices (Bakhtin 1981, 1986; Woolard 2006). Harris Berger similarly views artists' language choices in musical works as identity statements, positioning a musician within particular sociocultural groups (2003; B. Diamond 2011b).

In cross-cultural collaborations, choices are made to incorporate the different cultures represented (B. Diamond 2011b). Through the strategic articulation of voices, Shining Soul articulates both a Tohono O'odham Indigeneity and a Chicano Indigeneity, while voicing a shared "we" identity through joint lyrics and the mixing of codes. Similarly, Ben Rampton (1995) observes code mixing or "code-crossing" practiced among British youth negotiating their identities within mixed-ethnic peer groups. This practice involves the selective use of another ethnic group's code to establish an alliance with its members. Such practice points to the importance of code choice in alliance making and, as Diamond argues, the importance of alliance making in producing identities. Code mixing and code switching are significant aspects of Shining Soul's work as they negotiate and perform a shared Indigenous hip-hop voice.

Shining Soul's sound has been described as "vintage," with a late 1980s and early 1990s feel reflecting the influence of that period's experimental hip-hop groups (e.g., the Native Tongues posse), as well as the influence of harder-edged groups like Public Enemy and NWA. With an average speed of ninety to ninety-six beats per minute, Shining Soul's music also carries the "vibe of the desert," comparable to "a typical human heart rate where the subject is in a relaxed state" (email corr., July 14, 2014). The duo's sound has also been greatly influenced by its primary beat maker, Bronze Candidate, who draws from the Latin American and African American funk sounds of his parents' youth as well as mariachi and salsa. Although Liaizon primarily contributes to sound as an emcee, his parents' influence is also evident with the sampling of late 1970s and early 1980s vintage vinyl and emcee rhythms reminiscent of that period. The cadence and flow of the duo's emcee voicing intertwined with its instrumentals establish that vintage feel of early conscious hip-hop as much as the duo's lyrics.

In a remix of "Niche," Liaizon credits his mother for the introduction of old school hip-hop and its empowered mentality, but he also pays homage to both "Mom and Pops," his grandparents, and ancestors in "Remember," which emphasizes the importance of his peoples' memory as "ancient weaponry" against genocide. Liaizon refers to his "rhyming addiction" as "cognition of tradition." In O'odham culture, song is prayer and medicine. Liaizon's chosen musical medium is his means of maintaining his culture's spirit:

My rhymes carry-carry on like my people's songs.
Indigenous protocol that's far from gone . . .
Put your body and soul towards whatever you got inside that's sacred.

Live outside the matrix.
These modern ways don't make us, they break us.
That's why I choose to remember.
What you thought was lost I keep it hot like embers.
I remember
being a young one, doing what Grandpa said.
I remember
bumpin' A Tribe Called Quest, going against the trends.
I remember
way back when the border did not exist.
I remember
seeing my relatives, city to the rez.

Whereas Liaizon is leery of "modern ways," he sees no conflict between "doing what Grandpa said," following the words of his elders, and "bumpin'" to conscious hip-hop. Recalling the words of an elder on activities not tradition-ally O'odham—"put the O'odham in it, make it O'odham" (email corr., July 14, 2014)—Liaizon views his hip-hop voice as O'odham expression. Playing on Na-tive Tongues, in "Remember" Liaizon highlights the use of his hip-hop "Native tongue" in the lines "Remembering where I'm from, hearing the gourd swung / Words sung in my language I could only hum, looped in my cerebrum." Tradi-tion as cognition is manifested in the body and soul of his rhymes. And while he acknowledges the challenge of walking in two worlds, maintaining roots on the rez while surviving the rat race and *milagahn* (Anglo) ways of urban Phoenix, Liaizon credits his regular transitions between city and rural rez as shaping him. For Liaizon, the increasingly marked border dividing his people is the greater conflict.

The convergence of hip-hop with O'odham song prayer and a rural des-ert–urban continuum are also emphasized through "Battle Phoenix," which concludes with the sounds of cicadas, a gourd rattle, traditional singing, and rain, all symbols of the O'odham rain ceremony as experienced on the desert rez during the summer monsoon season. These sounds briefly overlap with the sounds of an urban travel terminal. The transition is a smooth fade from one world into the other, the difference between environments evident only after the ceremonial calm of desert song is sensed in striking contrast to the political battlefront of urban Phoenix.

Sonic symbols of rain ceremony are set apart from the duo's joint vocals and

Bronze Candidate's distinctive beat contributions—a moment of sonic code switching where rural ceremony is distinguished from urban Indigeneity. Code switching is evident as well in the linguistic performances of the individual artists within certain tracks. In verse 1 of "No Mercy," Bronze Candidate states, "We from that home of the *sí se puede* [yes, we can]," a reference to the farmworkers movement led by César Chávez. In verse 2, Liaizon parallels this statement with the line, "We're from that home of the Man in the Maze," a reference to *I'itoi* (Elder Brother) portrayed in the O'odham maze pattern representing one's journey through life. The emcees never double each other's lines when referencing the southern Arizona home region in their own distinct cultural terms. In the jointly performed chorus, the emcees instead double the culturally neutral phrases: "We from that ground zero" and "We from that desert borough." In addition, Bronze Candidate's use of the Spanish language in "No Mercy" and other tracks is not mirrored in Liaizon's statements; Liaizon uses the Spanish language sparingly. This underscores Spanish as a marker of Chicano identity that can be freely used by Bronze Candidate but only selectively used by Liaizon to mark joint Latino-Native experiences of the border. Similarly, Bronze Candidate does not use O'odham cultural terms in his individual rhymes. This pattern is also seen in the duo's video imagery. In their "No Mercy" video, Bronze Candidate holds up a Spanish-language immigrant rights protest sticker, while Liaizon holds up a protest sticker in English. Man in the Maze iconography is also selectively used in the "Get Up" video with Liaizon's poetic and visual statements and one joint statement calling for defense of "the sacred."

Carlos Santana's "Yours Is the Light" is sampled for the primary instrumental rhythm of "Get Up." Original lyrics are rhythmically fused with the sampled lyric, "Yours is the light that will shine and shine eternally." With the featuring of Santana's sound, "Get Up" offers Bronze Candidate the sonic landscape to express a Chicano experience. With Bronze Candidate's opening references to his "personal memoir" and "La Raza," the track appears to express a dominantly Chicano voice. But once Liaizon's voice enters, the song emerges as an example of code mixing. As Liaizon's statements merge with the sampled lyric, "Yours is the light," the Santana sample transforms from a Latino love song to the duo's shared symbol of "soul shine." This cultural code mixing becomes more evident with the careful blending of O'odham iconography into the symbolism of the song's video. The jointly performed chorus of "No Mercy" is a further example of code mixing, as the duo's use of the terms *migra* and *linea* highlights the negative connotations that the terms evoke among both Native Americans and

Latinos on the border. Shared experiences related to these terms and their use in the chorus justifies Liaizon's further use of *la migra* when speaking in first person about border enforcement on O'odham lands.

Such careful negotiation of cultural code use is critical given sensitivities about cultural appropriation in Chicano–Native American interethnic communication. Shining Soul's strategic voicing in their intercultural productions is important to their ongoing alliance making, as they continue to define themselves in contrast to and solidarity with each other. The language of hip-hop, with African American dialect origins and ever-changing vernacular, also serves as a neutral language for such alliance making. Activist pop-culture references, such as the sampling of Malcolm X's voice and politically radical film quotes, also communicate an activist consciousness across ethnic lines.

PROJECTING SOUND IN A HIP-HOP SPACE

In Shining Soul's "Get Up," a final parallel statement to "Young, gifted, and brown" and "Young, gifted, and red" are the lyrics, "Young, gifted, and hip-hop / It don't stop." In Shining Soul's philosophy, hip-hop is the intercultural space where all can remain "real" to themselves and to the world around them and through which "all things are possible": "Unstoppable / Another world is possible." Their beat-making workshops focus on the hands-on production of music that was common in early hip-hop. This means that they use vinyl records, cassette tapes, and CDs for sampling and mixing sounds rather than digital technology. In doing so, the members of Shining Soul teach students to be patient with the production of beats and rhymes. Habre and Soto believe this process creates a better sound, but hands-on production is also part of an embodied theory of hip-hop. For Shining Soul, hip-hop should be tangible, with physicality extending to the messages it delivers. As Soto states, hip-hop production should require one to "really dig into" one's "heart and project." You may have only forty seconds to "spit your heart out," but you cannot do so unless you have reflected on where you are from and the messages that emanate from that place of origin (interview, August 19, 2012).

In "Get Up" the lyric, "So I speak from the abdominal, expand my lungs," articulates this embodied theory of hip-hop sound. "Funk from the trunk, we expand" reiterates this theory but also articulates the related concept of hip-hop as social resistance, embedded as it is in the larger chorus phrase:

This is that get up, stand up, raw, uncut
Get your hands up.
Funk from the trunk, we expand
What?
This is that disrupt, get your fists up.
Erupt from the scene with a list of demands.

For Shining Soul, hip-hop is the space where "we" can expand; where we can remain as true as possible to ourselves while respecting one another's differences in solidarity. This does not mean, however, that issues of Indigenous identity claims, including questions of cultural appropriation, can be dismissed easily. Soto and Habre continue to struggle with, and to evolve, in their understanding of these issues as they collaborate with each other, and with others, on the U.S.-Mexico border. And although hip-hop is a space where all things are possible, the obstacles to Indigenous rights on the border are recognized. In "Papers" Border Patrol questions are compared to "a chopped and screwed track," a track that slows and repeats certain thematic phrases by overlapping a delayed phrase with the same phrase at regular speed. "Papers" employs a chopped voicing of "Who your family be, where your papers at?" to represent the repetitive oppression of Indigenous peoples at the border. Concluding with media coverage of the Border Patrol headquarters protest, the song's take-home message is persistent direct action against that old colonial theme (telephone interview, June 27, 2012).

One might wonder whether interethnic discourse through a hip-hop medium can be considered a truly Indigenous articulation of culture. As Justin Richland argues, "to ignore the sociopolitical contexts in which Indigenous notions of tradition and claims to cultural difference emerge is to ignore the primary force of their meaning." For Indigenous peoples on the U.S.-Mexico border, collaboration with all those negatively impacted by border-related policies has become critical to Indigenous resistance against these impacts. Any discourse that speaks to and builds such collaboration must be examined critically as an expression of Indigenous experience. If hip-hop is the medium that some Indigenous individuals are using to express this experience, it certainly cannot be ignored or cast off as an inauthentic articulation of Indigeneity. Temporally fixing Indigeneity according to imagined notions of "authentic" Indianness in "traditional" forms severely limits the ability of Indigenous peoples to represent their voices both as modern and as articulable within modern contexts (2008, 161, 152–54). Deloria states that the agency of Indigenous peoples "has to be seen less in the terms of 'we had a voice' or 'we were there too' and more as an affirmative statement: 'We have always participated in the *production* of modern discourse—and of modernity itself'" (2004, 238). After all, as Liaizon explains in "Get Up," it is not rap that is making him a cool and modern Native American but rather his genuine Native American rap that is making rap cool again.

ELYSE CARTER VOSEN

6. Singing and Dancing Idle No More

Round Dances as Indigenous Activism

I wondered why they were drawn to the shopping mall,
and I attended several all over Canada and the United States. What I
saw and experienced has changed me forever. I saw elderly grandmothers
openly weep, and hold each other as tears streamed down their faces,
and I saw women form barricades around men who sometimes were
assaulted. I saw children holding signs and singing along with the adults.
I saw white women join the circles and dance with tears streaming down
their faces and white men stand with our men, as they were also moved to
tears by the drum. . . . The conscious realize that these institutions are part
of the game, a manufactured colonial culture that keeps people tied
to predatory consumerism. . . . We are just beginning, and have a
lot of work to do as we follow the original instructions of spirit.

Nina Wilson, The Winter We Danced

Song and dance feature prominently in the Idle No More movement, embody-
ing the fundamental principles of the movement during protests, rallies, and
teach-ins. The Round Dance, in particular, moves people, physically, emotionally, spiritually, and politically, from the "Round Dance Revolution" of Idle No
More to its enduring impact in circles of Indigenous community organizing,
decolonization, and cultural revitalization. In this chapter I focus on the work of
Anishinaabe and Cree singers, dancers, and activists from Winnipeg, Manitoba,
and Duluth, Minnesota, tracing the border-crossing arcs of the Round Dance in
its many forms: from highly visible public protest to technologically mediated
performance and from social assembly to spiritual ceremony. No matter the set-

ting, all engage in a politics of reclamation, forming a counterstory to dominant narratives of market capitalism and exploitation of land and people.

The Round Dance speaks a language that emerges directly from Indigenous experience but resonates with the dynamics of other liberation movements throughout history. Through five vignettes I identify common steps in a process of struggle: an awakening of consciousness that leads to critical reflection; envisioning and envoicing an alternative reality; and ultimately mobilizing others to make social change. These processes occur in revolutions regardless of time and place but manifest in Idle No More in uniquely Indigenous ways in that no pronounced distinction is made between spiritual and intellectual awakening, analysis, and action. Additionally, many of the revolutionary concepts explored here exist only in Indigenous languages and perceptual categories.

The Round Dance is a flexible entity, having been on the move for decades. Lac Courte Oreilles Anishinaabe linguist and singer Michael Sullivan notes that the family- or community-sponsored winter Round Dance of today did not formerly exist in Ontario, northern Minnesota, or Wisconsin but "has been making its way east and south of Saskatchewan and Alberta over the course of the past twenty years . . . an adaptation of the Cree Round Dance ceremony" (interview, Hayward WI, July 21, 2014). Anna Hoefnagels (2007a) traces its historical journey from healing dance to social dance, today encompassing both "social and ceremonial goals." Hand-drum contests, emerging from Round Dance settings, have proliferated in the past twenty years, with a scoring system that evaluates rhythm, vocals, lyrics, and synchronization (Locke 2012). The rollicking sound of the "snare beat" provides a lilting, swinging feel and a bit of swagger. It is a powerful medium for singers—especially young men—to distinguish themselves and enrich community life. Sullivan (2006) emphasizes the restorative component: "These songs are 'feel good' songs, and are intended to be humorous and to make people laugh and feel happy."

The Round Dance is uniquely suited to this historical moment of structural disruption and cultural healing because of its physical and symbolic circularity. It is multigenerational. It is conveyed solely by oral tradition and thus is highly flexible. It intersects with other artistic expression, including popular music, and moves smoothly into the realm of social media. Indigenous men and women play complementary but overlapping roles in the Round Dance, both on the ground and in the way they mobilize it for social, spiritual, and political purposes. Whether accompanied by hand-drum or hip-hop beats, broadcast from a bullhorn or podium, men's voices usually project into more highly audible and visible places, while women dance. Some women, however, are taking more public leadership roles that propel them into new social, political, and cultural spheres.

In the context of Idle No More, the Round Dance represents a purposeful intersection point with the non-Native public. It illuminates a point of tension for cultural workers who frequently situate themselves in a whole range of intermediary positions and for Indigenous activists who ask themselves how far into "the system" someone in a marginalized position should go. When does collaboration—which leaves individuals and organizations open to political and economic exploitation—become complicity? Can collaboration and decolonization be held in tension? Today's Indigenous activists and artists—who are often one and the same—have a chance to exert influence in crucial political conversations. As Bear Witness from the deejay collective A Tribe Called Red observes, "We're coming into a really exciting time where we're starting to take control of our own image, and that's starting to happen more and more, and we're taking that power. But we're still in a transitional phase" (Witness 2013).

Modern Indigenous artists thread their way in and out of a dramatic range of institutional structures. In the current landscape, where corporate interests; tribal, city, and federal governments; academic institutions; and nonprofits are all jockeying for position, the complexities of performance allow artists, as Margaret Werry argues, not only to critique but also, when necessary, "to navigate, to inhabit, and even to trick systems not of their making" (2011, xxxiii). Modern Indigeneity is generated through mobility, shape shifting, and resourcefulness: a savvy balancing act between harnessing and disrupting capitalist institutions and structures of power. Helen Gilbert notes that "artists hold the tools . . . to decolonize, to transform, to manipulate the structure" (2013, 11). Social media, which is both tied to and independent of organizations and institutions, extends artists' and organizers' ability to draw in audiences or participants. Artistic expression has a unique ability to move and persuade, especially in the sometimes volatile and often entrenched setting of settler-Indigenous social relations. Within this chapter, the face-to-face, hand-to-hand, voice-to-ear contact supplied by the in-person version of the Round Dance provides intimacy for movement building and alliance building, while its technologically mediated forms extend engagement outward.

"WE SPOKE, WE WALKED, WE DANCED":
ROUND DANCES AND THE RED WINTER

In the winter of 2012–13, Round Dances made a rapid shift. Within a period of a few weeks, they moved out of the semiprivate spaces of Indigenous communities to serve as nonviolent occupations of public space, in concert with other forms of protest against Canadian antienvironmental legislation. Beginning in major Canadian cities, they quickly crossed the border into the United States, and hundreds of "flash mob" Round Dances took place.

On Saturday, December 21, 2012, ten days after Chief Theresa Spence began her fast in protest against Bill C-45—removing protection of land and waterways against industry—and three days after the first flash mob Round Dance at Cornwall Centre in Regina, the Native people of Duluth, Minnesota, went to the mall. It was not a spectacle on the scale of the Round Dance on Ottawa's Parliament Hill, nor at the Mall of America, but it got attention. Amid last-minute Christmas shoppers, near a bright red Corvette parked on the mall concourse, eight Anishinaabe hand drummers began to sing. Snaking among perfume kiosks and jewelry stores, a modest-sized group of dancers held hands, while others used iPhones to capture the sound of the drums and the spectacle of Indigenous faces and bodies moving in this very public place. Young and old, men and women, pipe carriers, college instructors, and minimum-wage workers all circled, sidestepping with their linked hands rising and falling to the Round Dance's heartbeat rhythm. The high-pitched sounds of the singers ricocheted off the walls and cavernous ceilings. Onlookers gathered with puzzled looks on some of their faces. By the time three songs were sung, the number of singers had grown to sixteen, the dancers to a hundred, and a cluster of worried-looking mall cops gathered around the mall manager. They looked around anxiously but were no match for the wall of sound made up of soaring voices, ringing drums, and stepping feet. It was now a Native space. It was a modest protest, but it was enough to say, "We are here."

The non-Native Duluthians who wandered the mall likely wondered what prompted such a display, but the singers and dancers had no time to explain. They were busy building a new reality, a step and a beat at a time. Niigaanwewidam James Sinclair writes of a parallel experience in his poem, "Dancing in a Mall":

We spoke we walked we danced
we dreamed

and we said no more and
we remade
we remade
we remade
the paper walls.
we remade
we remade
we remade
the world . . . our births
our families
ourselves
in the hole of fluorescent light
we continue
Ha ya hey ya
we live. (2014, 149)

The voices rose—men on the melody, women an octave higher, singing in Ojibwe, vocables, and English—growing stronger, pulsing through the heating ducts. After twenty-five minutes the singing peaked, then ceased, and the crowd dispersed, but not before some Native community members exchanged polite yet charged words "in defiance of mall officials" (Krueger 2012). As the footage went up on YouTube and Facebook that night, a comment on one Duluth Ojibwe-language instructor's Twitter feed reflected the wry humor that characterizes so many of these postcolonial encounters: "Hate to be a mall cop these days, lol" (Defoe 2012).

In no place was the strategic use of media and technology more apparent than Idle No More; during the height of the movement, the hashtag melded with the name. The Round Dance achieved a highly public profile during the "Red Winter" of 2012–13 in part because its sound and movement came across so powerfully on-screen. Round Dances helped form a public face of the Idle No More movement to such an extent that it quickly became known as the Round Dance Revolution. On December 20, 2012, Ojibwe-Métis comedian and activist Ryan McMahon (2012) commented on the growing momentum: "Just look at how many #rounddance posts there are on Twitter. On Wednesday, we saw YouTube video surface of a group of native brothers and sisters from Minnesota singing the 'AIM Song' in the Canadian Consulate office in Minneapolis.[1] Incredible. The round dance revolution. It's happening. Right? . . . It's a beautiful, peaceful and inclusive action. We are being led by our drums. It's perfect. It's accessible. It's transportable." From Indigenous podcasts and YouTube music videos to mainstream news media and talk shows, the songs and dances of Idle No More provided Indigenous activists with a vehicle as powerful as the songs at the height of the American Indian Movement. In at least a dozen songs crafted to reflect and fuel the movement, Canadian Indigenous recording artists engaged with the many strands of political discourse associated with Idle No More.

"AND WE'RE BRINGIN' ALL OUR COUSINS": INDIGENOUS HIP-HOP HARNESSING THE ROUND DANCE

Among all of the popular song expression associated with the movement, Indigenous hip-hop proved particularly suited to making a dynamic political statement. Its offbeat critical consciousness served an experimental quality of resourcefulness that has always characterized Indigenous communities. Blogs and podcasts sprang up to create a rich interface with journalism and academia, all springing from the second post-American Indian Movement, college-educated generation. Indigenous hip-hop artists have multiple, increasingly visible public faces, engaging in language and cultural revitalization, university-level administration, business entrepreneurship, radio and television news, and political activism.

Indigenous hip-hop has also exerted a political impact by finding meaningful points of resonance with older cultural practices and aesthetics. Some hip-hop artists are hand-drum or big-drum singers, powwow dancers, or Midewin members, and many espouse a conception of hip-hop as part of a broader continuum of oral tradition. Cree First Nations hip-hop artist DJ Creeasian (Matthew Wood) compares Grass and Fancy Dancers to break-dancers in their prowess and intensity; a deejay to a powwow drummer, preserving the flow of dancing; and a hip-hop emcee to a powwow emcee, connecting to the crowd through storytelling. Mohawk-Cherokee hip-hop artist Lakota Jonez asserts that the appeal of rap for Indigenous communities lies in its narrative possibility. Because of its pacing and intensity, she says, "So much more can be said [than in other popular genres], so much more that can be expressed. . . . Native people, we like our stories" (Jonez and Creeasian 2011).

Whereas some women artists make hip-hop their home, Indigenous men's voices more frequently fill public spaces. During the past two decades, through hip-hop and hand drums, many young Indigenous men have found expression

Figure 6.1. Album cover of *Red Winter*, by Drezus,
released May 17, 2013. Used by permission.

as storytellers. Each musical medium makes a place for an Indigenous masculinity that is both strong and vulnerable, that allows for self-expression and also for taking care of those who come next. Many hip-hop videos associated with Idle No More gave a group of dynamic young men—both as rappers and hand-drum singers—a voice in telling the stories of the movement. A month of great creative intensity, from mid-December 2012 to mid-January 2013, bore witness to the creation of half a dozen songs released by Canadian hip-hop artists articulating the concerns of Idle No More, many employing video footage from Round Dances occurring at that same time. Two of the most significant are Winnipeg-based Saulteaux and Cree artist Drezus's song "Red Winter" (2013; see figure 6.1) and "Idle No More" (2013) by Rellik, a diverse group of urban artists from western Canada.

In "Red Winter," released on December 25, 2012, the effectiveness of the song's sound and imagery lies in its entwining of multiple generations and attention to the circle. A slow, swinging beat creates an empathetic cradle for the visceral opening lyrics: "My skin's red, I bleed red, I'm seeing red / I'm praying for my people out there who haven't seen it yet." The video's opening images feature Round Dances in every imaginable context in cities across both Canada and the United States. These sentiments of pain and awakening are complemented by the closing lyrics:

And we won't stop for nothin'
And we're bringin' all our cousins
And we're gettin' educated so the fighting ain't for nothing.
Stand up for your people, our time for power is coming.

The matter-of-fact declaration dedicates itself to the long haul and the large scale.

The video's motion fully lets loose in the chorus, which juxtaposes a muscular male Hoop Dancer in street clothes, arms outstretched, spinning in slow motion against the backdrop of an Idle No More logo, with shots of a lithe female break-dancer with her braid flying, against the lyrics, "Cause I've been quiet for too long, it's time to speak / we've gotta stand for somethin' to keep us free." The song ends with a Fancy Shawl dancer whirling defiantly in the driving sleet and wind to a chorus of hand-drum singers intoning, "We're Round Dancing around the world" (Drezus 2013). Spiraling outward, then inward, then outward again, the dancers serve as a force for political organizing and movement building.

As marches, teach-ins, and dialogues continued in the winter of 2012–13, intensity grew out in the streets, and the songs grew angrier. Métis artist Rellik's "Idle No More," released on February 17, is driving, aggressive, and sprinkled with expletives, with a percussive flow and wry delivery. "Will you fight to be Indigenous? Will you die for your identity? Will you fight for the future? Will you fight for these children?" is the call to arms recorded at a rally and used to begin the song. The questions, accompanied by uninterrupted, insistent staccato synthesizer chords, stress an awakening consciousness, set against images of young people in motion: first singing, then marching, then dancing, often in the snow. It raises incisive questions about the Canadian government's omnibus bills designed to sneak in exploitative legislation without a vote, in the name of "economic growth":

What's the future hold now?
See that's the question that we're askin'. . . . It's been too long, you've held it
    all for ransom
Since colonization and the Royal Proclamation
It was told my generation'd be the one to awaken (Rellik 2013)

Technology weaves a companion narrative through media that serves an interpretive function; artists can manipulate images through editing and sound by sampling, invoking activist voices in duet with their own. Like the iPhones that captured the footage at the mall in Duluth, the resourceful use of technology in these settings reflects an ongoing process of reworking the tools at a community's disposal in culturally compatible ways to accomplish practical ends. All represent manifestations of what Fond du Lac Anishinaabe musician Lyz Jaakola (2011) calls "Indigenuity," deftly harnessing the tools of industrial capitalism to assert communal consciousness and establish political capital. The founders of Idle No More began the movement technologically: a string of emails led to a Facebook page, blog, website, and Twitter feed, #idlenomore. In the winter of 2012–13, during the height of the frenetic holiday shopping season, the Round Dance Revolution embodied tribal connectedness and collectivity in a packaging that captured mass-media imagination and broadcast vibrant, unthreatening images of Indigenous people.

"WHAT A BRIGHT BEAUTIFUL NIGHT": THE MEDIA INTERFACE

In Canada a network of Aboriginal actors and popular musicians played a significant role in mass media, acting as cultural emissaries of Idle No More. They contributed their analysis through blogs and interviews, but they know as artists that performance itself is uniquely moving, in every sense of the word. Wabanakwut Kinew's strategic organization of a Round Dance during his January 2013 appearance on the CBC's show *George Stroumboulopoulos Tonight* displays its flexibility. Like the Round Dance itself, Kinew's life as hip-hop artist, Sun Dancer, news correspondent, university administrator, and in 2017 elected leader of the Manitoba New Democratic Party—amid controversy over misogynist tweets and past domestic assault accusations—reflects an ongoing series of savvy transformations and tactical border crossings. Appearing on *Strombo* during the height of Idle No More's visibility, he made a seemingly spontaneous decision to stand in suit and tie and invite the studio audience into a Round Dance accompanied by his voice and clapping hands:

Hey yo hey ha
Hey yo ha yo
Hey yay ya yo
Hey yo way ya. . . .
What a bright beautiful night
To show you how I love you.

Ya way ya. . . .
Look to the sky and see how the sunlight shines for you.
Ha way ya. . . .
Oh, how I miss our time together.
Can't wait 'til you get home.
Hey ya way ya ho. . . .

Charismatic and completely at home in front of the camera, Kinew was hard to resist. His radiant smile and warm voice brought the intimacy of the Round Dance into the television studio. He invited Indigenous women of the studio audience to "show our non-Native brothers and sisters" how it was done. One of the women grabbed George. The others joined Wab, spiraling their way around the set. With each push-up of the song, the mood in the room grew more joyful (figure 6.2). Chatting online later, Native and non-Native women alike swooned. Familiars burst with pride: "Wab is so bad *ss," one woman commented on YouTube, while another said, "What a hoot to hear that voice in a suit. Sweeeet." Still another added, "That felt like sweet hugs and home. Thank You!!!" In a more philosophical turn, one commentator said, "I like to think of the round dance as a representation of the sacred circle. . . . I'd like to see everyone come and claim their spot in it. All colors of the rainbow of people we have here now." Someone else matter-of-factly concluded, "And that is what it's all about, our non-indigenous brothers and sisters" ("Wab Kinew Surprises" 2013).

The Round Dance is uniquely suited for intercultural exchange. Nestled in a framework of vocables, each song's brief verse must be highly evocative to capture a glimpse of the relationship it describes. A Round Dance song performed by Northern Cree belts out love at its most painful:

I can't believe this night
I've only seen you once or twice
I'm dying inside
I need to see your eyes tonight. (Big River Cree 2011)

Meanwhile, Pipestone singer Mike Sullivan proclaims with gentle humor,

I would do anything for you
Anything you asked me to
I would run away, wait for you
I'd even lose some weight for you. (Sullivan and Day 2009)

Figure 6.2. Still shot of Wab Kinew,
from *George Stroumboulopoulos Tonight*, January 19, 2013.

After all, Round Dance songs are courting songs, with all the vulnerabilities those entail. Kinew's CBC rendition of "Bright, Beautiful Night" captured the yearning and longing, but he toned down the nasalization and wide vibrato of the usual singing style to make his words particularly clear to audience members unaccustomed to the hand-drum circuit. With the aid of his broadcasting knowledge and rap skills, he tuned his voice to translate Indigenous experience. His role as a cultural ambassador in this television context—with all of its conciliatory possibilities—hinted at the deeper challenges he faced as a highly visible public figure engaging with economics and politics at the interface between Indigenous and dominant cultures. In an interview with Joseph Brean for the *National Post* (2014), Kinew highlighted complex negotiations taking place between First Nations chiefs and the Canadian government. He saw a shift in emphasis from social and spiritual healing toward attention to economic development as the key to Indigenous sovereignty. While he recognized this as a "time of transition," his media work and high-profile presence bring to the fore the irksome question of whether sovereignty is indeed strengthened by, in his words, "participating in the global economy that's developing all around us," and whether it is possible to participate while simultaneously questioning ongoing exploitative principles that consume and damage Indigenous lands and peoples.

The problem with such economic development lies in what S. Lily Mendoza calls an accompanying acceptance of "civilizational violence." Mendoza and others express deep concern for Indigenous communities, made vulnerable by poverty, at a crisis point of searching for economic solvency, falling prey to the unavoidable allure of evolutionist principles. As Mendoza explains, pressure is continually growing toward "a now globalized culture wedded primarily to wealth accumulation, individualism, private ownership . . . and consumption as the taken-for-granted key signifiers of being human" (2013, 3). During a panel discussion that used Kinew's *8th Fire* series from CBC as a point of departure to analyze these ideological questions, Stó:lō educator Wenona Victor expressed concern with the show's assumption "that capitalism and a free-market economy is something that all Indigenous people are aspiring to achieve" ("8th Fire Panel" 2013).

"YOU DON'T GET PAID IF YOU TALK BACK": RESISTING EXPLOITATION

Idle No More is a movement started and run by women: three Native and one non-Native woman, forging their relationships through passionate emails about the violent impact of Bill C-45 on their families and making the choice to stand with the fasting Chief Theresa Spence. In the blockades, protests, and rallies they organized, these women strove to ensure a core of relationship, consciousness raising, education, and an ultimate goal of restoration. Febna Caven (2013) writes, "The nature of the fluid, nonviolent, unifying movement is one that both reflects and engages women's agency. . . . The fact that the movement's leaders speak so openly about the pain they [themselves] have experienced is one of the things that sets Idle No More apart. . . . Idle No More is a personal, global, and spiritual movement."

One of the movement's founders, Sylvia McAdam, describes her conversation with elders after the first teach-in, upholding these principles. They offered their support and underscored the necessity of using "our own laws," especially *nahtamawasewin*, the duty to defend all children—trees, plants, and animals as well as humans. They told her, "You ladies must invoke this law and let it guide your actions" (2014, 66). Cofounder Priscilla Settee saw the movement as a chance for the next generation to decide whether they would "go on the same train-wreck that we're on . . . unbridled so-called 'development' that goes at any cost" or find a new direction. Settee noted an awakening and a desire to ask questions ("Idle No More—Priscilla Settee" 2013) about what John Trudell has named "Civilization: the greatest lie that has ever been told . . . the predatory impulse that erases the memory of being a human being" (qtd. in Rae 2007).

The damage runs deep—the overburden of trees and soil scraped away, pipe-lines tearing up the earth, shafts of burning steam forced into tar sands, and the exploitation of Indigenous women. The year before Idle No More erupted, the news media on the Minnesota side of the border revealed a dirty secret: that for at least forty years, First Nations women and youth from Thunder Bay, Duluth, and surrounding Minnesota and Wisconsin reservations had been sexually traf-ficked via the ore boats on Lake Superior to Chicago and Milwaukee. During the following year the protests of Idle No More dramatically intensified the issue, bringing it more quickly to the general public. Anishinaabe researcher Christine Stark noted in a public-radio broadcast that pimps had unlimited access to these boats in the 1970s, 1980s, and 1990s. With increased security after 9/11, there has been a slight decrease in the flow of victims, but trafficking continued because of a network of connections the pimps maintained and protected within the shipping industry. When asked, "Why Native women?" Suzanne Koepplinger, executive director of the Minnesota Indian Women's Resource Center, responded, "Many pimps will view Native women as exotic, and highly marketable. . . . Coming from communities of color, coming from disenfranchised communities with high rates of poverty, intergenerational trauma is high—those are very vulner-able young people" (Koepplinger, Rubin, and Stark 2013).

The findings of a four-year study by a group of women researchers were not surprising to members of Minnesota Indigenous communities. The study con-cluded that racism was "an emotionally damaging element in the women's lives and a source of ongoing stress." The researchers found that nearly 80 percent of the 105 Native women they interviewed had been sexually abused as children, more than 90 percent had been raped, nearly 70 percent had relatives who had attended boarding schools, and 70 percent made a connection between their own prostitution and the process of colonization. The report revealed that these women carried the pain of a lifetime of physical, mental, and emotional abuse. More than 50 percent had post-traumatic stress disorder at the time of the interviews, a rate comparable to combat veterans. They had been emotionally brutalized by white johns' remarks, so painful that many of them couldn't be printed in the report. A silencing took place that one woman expressed as "You don't get paid if you talk back" (Farley et al. 2011, 3, 32).

Dakota scholar and activist Waziyatawin suggests two potential paradigms for transformation: one of countering civilizational violence with a form of what Frantz Fanon calls "absolute violence," the complete destruction of the imperialist colonizer-colonized system; and another proposed by Paulo Freire

(Waziyatawin and Yellow Bird 2012, 5). Within Freire's model, breaking down the colonizer-colonized divide is accomplished through engagement in dialogical relationships and makes room for non-Native allies. Fanon suggests that both the predatory desire of the colonizer and the desperate hunger toward success of the colonized are so strong the binary cycle cannot be broken. Many Indigenous activists oscillate out of necessity between Freire's collaborative yet still critical model and Fanon's separatist model, occasionally taking space to process anger or to get centered in one's own ways before reengaging with dominant culture projects or institutions.

"SHE'S NOT FOR SALE": WOMEN LEADERS, ROUND DANCES, AND HEALING

In Duluth Indigenous leaders are painstakingly building connections with city government and the criminal-justice system, and a number of these leaders are women. Renee Van Nett is one of them, a Round Dancer, spiritual leader, and activist. For her, like so many Indigenous community leaders, these spheres are inextricable from one another in spurring social transformation. Raised in the traditional village of Ponema on the Red Lake Reservation, Van Nett sang backup as a young woman for Eyaabay, a Drum known across the United States and Canada. Because of her spiritual capacity, she was also gifted as a young woman with the title of *ogichidaakwe*, a protector of Anishinaabe cultural ways. Her spiritual gifts protect her as she advocates for urban Indigenous people: "I know every single day I'm here because the spirits put me here. Every day, everything I do, it's coming from our people. . . . I knew I was born into abuse, but I knew I'd be able to turn it around, and I knew the Creator would be right there with me. That's what we agreed to, and I just take that agreement with me" (phone interview, November 7, 2013). Van Nett's spiritual focus has allowed her to parent five kids, chair the Citizen Review Board partnership with the Duluth police to address long-standing systemic racism in the city's criminal-justice system, and create or serve on several nonprofit boards aimed at fighting poverty and building cultural resilience.

Van Nett participated in the 2012 Round Dance at the mall in Duluth, singing behind the men. She views this form as an effective vehicle for expressing the concerns of Idle No More. The dances show "a positive way to protest with a cultural presence. Taking a stand: we won't stop being who we are. Unity, a circle. Men with drums. Women support and sing, provide the backbone structure.

The outside circle of . . . like protection. We give life, so we're stronger. . . . Men do the labor [of singing]. We support." She stresses the relationship-building function of the Round Dance inside a Native community, reaching out to other Indigenous communities and to non-Native people too. "I like how it brings people together. How we play out our traditions right down to our children. Where we teach them by example. They just seem to know it's a connection" (phone interview, November 1, 2013).

What is most impressive in the work of so many activists on both sides of the border is their stalwart insistence on relationship. They get at the heart of vulnerability in a way that still forms a protective circle, and the circles widen outward from humans to all beings. Anishinaabe elders have increasingly in-structed Indigenous women to assume their rightful places in taking care of land and water, thus ensuring physical and spiritual nourishment for everyone (Josephine Mandaamin, interview, Duluth, MN, April 3, 2013). Symbolically, the rippling of connections is well illustrated through Round Dances performed by Jingle Dress dancers. The Jingle Dress, *ziibaaska'iganagoode*, was gifted to the Anishinaabe people, carrying a story of healing sickness and caring for the earth. When a woman wears it she takes on spiritual responsibility, carefully sewing on each of the hundreds of jingle cones. The morpheme *ziib* is related to the word for "river," and the cones make a gentle sound similar to running water. In Minnesota women use Jingle Dress Round Dances to apply their deep principles to a set of borderless concerns: sulfide mining and its consequences for watersheds, wolf hunting, police brutality, and that unthinkable selling of Anishinaabe girls and women, carried over the water on boats designed to carry away the iron ore from the land.

On a cold night in January 2013, another Duluth community leader, Babette Sandman, had a dream. In it she wore her Jingle Dress and danced in an alley. She looked up and saw that she was not alone. Alongside her, other Jingle Dress dancers carried the sound. The tinkling of the metal cones swept through the alleyways of her city, into the shadowy corners on First Street, where she used to go to find her father. Her vision, relayed on social media, brought a group of Jingle Dress dancers of all ages, hand-drum singers, men, women, and children, together with non-Native allies, including the mayor, in front of city hall on Janu-ary 11. The hope expressed on that day was that "the resonation of the words, the sounds of the drum, would come down these alleys and heal our people suffering down here" ("Skip Sandman" 2013).

In her dream Babette saw the healing borne on waves of sound, reaching into

Figure 6.3. Jingle Dress dancers (*left to right*): Raven Jackson, Babette Sandman, Téa Drift, and Pat St. Germaine, at the demonstration on January 11, 2013. Photograph by Ivy Vainio. Used by permission.

the darkness. She reached out to her network of people, and they came. This Round Dance event emerged organically from her dream, with no official leaders, and with men and women performing equally important but often complementary roles. It moved in powerful symbolism through the city, marching from the government to commercial sectors of town, dancing onto the shores of the lake, and, finally, soaring onto the airwaves and social media (figure 6.3). The event was represented by Indigenous media people who asked the right questions, amplified the organizers' voices, and transmitted images of the marchers and dancers. They captured the event for the Anishinaabe community and translated it for the non-Native people of Duluth.

Every Round Dance carries circles of significance stemming not only from the human beings but also from the ceremonial items and spirits they hold. This event reverberated with the spirits of drums, Jingle Dresses, and other sacred items. After a pipe ceremony in front of city hall, fifty people marched down the main street, led by an eagle staff, followed by men with hand drums, Jingle Dress dancers, other Anishinaabe community members, and finally non-Native people, standing behind them (figure 6.4). The songs echoed off the concrete buildings, and the women danced on all four corners of the busiest intersection. Water from

Figure 6.4. Poster from the Jingle Dress demonstration on January 11, 2013. Photograph by Ivy Vainio. Used by permission.

Lake Superior was carried in a copper pail by the son of water walker Josephine Mandamin. Between 2003 and 2008 this Anishinaabe elder from Manatoulin Island walked around each of the Great Lakes, carrying their water. She did it to awaken people to the way in which human beings had, in her words, "prostituted our mother." It was important for women to protect water, she said, "because we carry water in our bodies" (interview, Duluth, MN, April 3, 2013).

As the women danced, the water followed them, underscoring the interconnection. Medicine man Skip Sandman noted in an interview that what happens to the water in Canada will impact northern Minnesota too. "The border is mythical. Water does not honor the border," another elder reflected. As Sandman explained the significance of the Jingle Dress, of its healing of the city, what he ultimately spoke of was the land itself, of the spiritual umbilical cord of the language, teachings, stories, and songs connected to it. He observed, "Duluth is new, but Indian people have been here forever. . . . Our presence has always been here. You can put up all the buildings you want, all the sidewalks," but, as he noted, the land endures ("Skip Sandman" 2013). Healing came from the spirits that sat in all four directions of the busy intersection and from the dresses of the women, dancing near the iron-ore boats at the shore of the lake.

Traditional protocols, not hierarchies, govern Indigenous community organizing. In describing the difference between working within city government and with Indigenous activists, Van Nett noted a dramatic contrast. Whereas the police department has a chief of police, and the mayor tells everyone what to do, an Indigenous system is more like a series of concentric circles: "[They're] the exact opposite of each other. For instance, [on one issue], [our Indigenous nonprofit] was the hosting program. But we aren't in charge. We just do what the community wants us to do. We take orders, so to speak. . . . It's the way of our people. We do things the way our people did them during that time of season, and the way a ceremony was held. The protocols are all the same almost" (interview, Duluth, MN, July 25, 2014). Likewise, when asked about her role in leading the Jingle Dress Round Dance event, Babette Sandman noted principles of circularity, complementarity, and the importance of spiritual forces over all: "It depends upon what your definition of leading is, because we have a whole different definition of leading. But right now what we're saying here is none of us are leaders. We're all teachers; we're all learners; we're all leading; we're all following. We're following our hearts, and right now this is such a pure moment. And we do have people who speak . . . do the media . . . yeah, us women, we're acknowledged as leaders, but not in the dominant worldview of that" ("Babette Sandman" 2013).

An important decolonizing move of Idle No More was women's public acknowledgement of their skill for pulling people together, within and across generations. Sandman reflected on the circularity of walking, in her Jingle Dress, down the same street where she used to find her father. She spoke of a time when she was nineteen, hearing of girls "going to the boats." She actually went herself once. "I knew a lot of young women that were going, so I asked if I could go with . . . they were getting all dressed up, and I was thinking of it as the Love Boat. I was horrified at what it really was. . . . It could've happened that fast. I know some were already in the trap." She emphasized spiritually anchoring the next generation of girls to end a destructive cycle: "Here's my little we'enh [namesake] here. She's ten years old now. . . . Someday she'll become a woman. And when she is, I'm gonna be there for her, when she becomes a woman, and she'll receive all those women teachings. And she'll spend a year in those teachings, and she'll know who she is. She's not for sale" ("Babette Sandman" 2013).

A powerful shift is taking place, as more and more Indigenous women move into politics and community organizing. Minnesota Anishinaabe activist Patricia Shepard (2013), in a radio report on murdered and missing Indigenous women, saw her job as grappling with issues mainstream media does not cover. To break the cycle, she believes, transformation must move in two directions: "things we need to do, internally, within our own nations, within our own people" and also addressing what she calls a "societal devaluing of Native people" at a systemic level. "We're battling on a number of fronts. We're also dealing with the impact their schools and institutions are having . . . participating in an ideology that hurts everyone." The solution entails "aligning ourselves with everyone, from all genders, all races, and crossing all those lines and involving everyone with this movement—because I think this really has to be a movement—I think Idle No More, because it addresses all of these issues on all of these levels."

"THE INTERSECTION RANG OUT WITH JINGLES": ROUND DANCING, PUBLIC POLICY, AND DECOLONIZATION

Cultural practice drives political action in Indigenous communities. Community-based and higher-profile Round Dances parallel political efforts on local and international scales. In October 2013 a momentous healing dance took place in response to the historic visit to Canada of James Anaya, the UN special rapporteur on the rights of Indigenous peoples. He made three requests to visit Canada within a year and a half, and on his third attempt reluctant government officials approved his request. At the busiest intersection in downtown Winnipeg, he was greeted by more than six hundred Jingle Dress dancers, hand-drum singers, and non-Native allies. The intersection, with no pedestrian crossing, where "vehicles reign supreme," instead "rang out with jingles, drumming, whoops, and singing on Saturday morning" (Friesen 2013). The visionary behind this event was Shannon Bear, a University of Winnipeg graduate.

Winnipeg-based Indigenous journalist and filmmaker Crystal Greene created a video, #JingleDress Healing Dance (2003), to help Bear call people together. In Greene's short film Bear carries the listener through her own journey as a dancer, bringing the healing power of the Jingle Dress to a personal level. She speaks of dreaming the dress and of its power to help a new generation of young people to heal from suicide, mental health issues, and sexual exploitation and to believe in themselves. The artistry of this short film, a study in contrast, features Shannon donning her regalia in a stark, glossy public restroom and gliding on a shiny escalator with her to-go cup of coffee up to the busy street corner, where she dances to the accompaniment of her iPod, alone. Solitary on the corner, her jingles moving like waves, she alone hears the music. She would not be alone for

Figure 6.5. Still shot of Shannon Bear from the promotional video *#JingleDress Healing Dance*, October 11, 2013. Video by Crystal Greene, CBC *Manitoba Scene*.

long. Singers with drums come. Jingle Dress dancers arrive by the dozens, then the hundreds, filling the intersection with color and sound (figure 6.5).

The event had it all: a protest that stopped traffic in a busy legislative district; a spectacle on the scale of the mall flash mobs that drew national attention but began with the vision of one young woman; a grassroots effort powered by social media and technology. In a Facebook post Bear thanked the hundreds of singers who came, reflecting that despite "the difficult circumstances under which we live, the drums cannot be silenced, the powerful voices of our men and women at the drum cannot be denied and the beauty of our people will always be reflected in the beauty of our culture and our dance." The healing dance was aimed at strengthening Anaya, a man who, as Bear put it, "packed on his shoulders a great burden of pain and emotion in hearing the trauma of our people in our current reality." She expressed her gratitude to the Jingle Dress dancers for bringing "medicine in their thoughts, their actions, and their dance" and for inspiring the children who would inspire their children and ensure "the strength of our roots in these lands" long after she and her generation are gone ("Jingle Dress Healing Dance" 2013).

In Anaya's preliminary report, following the Round Dance and the completion of his visits to Indigenous communities across Canada, he framed the crisis, highlighting the socioeconomic disparity, the "well-being gap," overcrowding, suicide rates for young people, murders of Aboriginal women, and the "lack of mutual trust and common purpose." He acknowledged the Residential School period continuing to "cast a long shadow of despair" that would need many years to heal. He encouraged extending the mandate of the Truth and Reconciliation process as long as needed and, most significant, urged building avenues of communication and trust to counter the government's "adversarial" position (Anaya 2013). That day Wab Kinew tweeted Anaya's statement that he would take the memory of the Jingle Dress healing dance "with me for the rest of my life."

The sounds of Idle No More and the movement itself became inseparable as alliances continued to build. The idlenomore.ca website resonates with the sounds of drums and the images of dancing. Discussion and action across the Canada-U.S. border continued to unfurl in 2014 around protesting mercury poisoning in Grassy Narrows; striving to abolish the Redskins mascot; seeking justice for murdered and missing Indigenous women on both sides of the border; carrying out the Fifth Annual Tar Sands Healing Walk; killing Canadian Bill C-33, which would limit Indigenous control over education; and organizing the Reject and Protect event aimed against the Keystone XL pipeline. The posting on the INM website from that time in 2014 read, "Round Dance Revolution Comes to Washington." Speaking of the international momentum she has witnessed, McAdam writes, "I am forever changed by Idle No More. This journey has not ended; it's still unfolding as I write this. . . . It is in the lands and waters that Indigenous people's history is written. Our history is still unfolding; it's led by our songs and drums" (2014, 67).

Many scholars and activists have argued that the most important legacy of Idle No More will be the movement from mobilization to full-scale decolonization. The process must necessarily impact Native and non-Native people, policy, and cultural life, but to achieve true transformation, Indigenous principles must form the core. In Minnesota an agile network of activists continues its momentum. Many local Idle No More leaders support working with non-Native allies, but with an intentional framework in place, like Anishinaabe scholar Lynn Gehl's "Ally Bill of Responsibilities" (n.d.), which begins by asking that allies be firmly grounded in their own cultural heritage and continually reflect on their own privilege and their Indigenous colleagues' experiences of oppression. Toronto activist Syed Hussan notes, "Decolonization is a dramatic reimagining of relationships with land, people, and the state. Much of this requires study. It requires conversation. It is a practice; it is an unlearning" (Walia 2014, 45).

Freire notes that the burden to educate the oppressor often falls to the oppressed. In 2013 medicine man Skip Sandman took the bold step at age sixty of running for the Duluth City Council, and in 2014 was a Minnesota Green Party candidate for the U.S. House of Representatives. Though he won 9 percent and 4 percent of the vote in these respective races, he wove his voice into every public discussion leading up to the election. A corrections officer for twenty-five years and partnered with a Western physician on the Mille Lacs reservation for twelve, Sandman is a bridge builder, "kind, but no 'yes' man," a colleague noted. Van Nett commented, "He's done his job. He's paved his way for the next one of us" (interview, Duluth, MN, July 1, 2013). Van Nett mounted a campaign for the Duluth School Board in 2015, which she lost, but in 2017 she ran for city council with the Democratic endorsement and won.

In January 2018, as Van Nett was inaugurated to the Duluth City Council, Jingle Dress dancers and drummers transformed the space in the council chambers, buoying her up with their sound and movement. Dancer Alicia Kozlowski Cyr (2018), who herself served on a committee to help craft the new Comprehensive Plan for the city, celebrated the momentous event on Instagram:

> Sometimes you've got to create the path and space to the places you want to exist. Tonight we celebrate Renee Van Nett who envisioned and carved her way here. Incredibly humbled and honored to dance beside Renee as she steps into her role as the first Anishinaabekwe to serve on the Duluth City Council. Heart bursting kind of pride here. ♥ ♥ ♥ ♥ #duluth #anishinaabe #leadership #mn #nativewomenrising #duluth #nativewomenrising #anishinaabe #mn #leadership

Thus, the medicine people, pipe carriers, singers, and dancers are the change makers. Their activism is not merely fueled *by* cultural practice; their cultural practice *is* the activism itself. As Jeff Corntassel (2012) argues, claiming the deep knowledge of day-to-day, place-based cultural practices shifts emphasis from human political authority to Indigenous spiritual principles. Waziyatawin notes that the formation of a sustainable modern Indigeneity begins with each tribal community "revaluing" traditional ways of life and using them to fuel the struggle to transform institutions, a generative cycle that works both from within and without: "[When] you start to put them into practice, you bump into these more powerful systems and institutions that are really fundamentally harmful, and as I've written, very flawed. That again, I think, leads to more action" (2012, 149).

The relationship between the Round Dance and resistance, participation in the circle and participation in public policy, continues to emerge. Idle No More and the local Indigenous movements it has seeded will remain complex and lasting because of their organic, adaptable, and inclusive nature (Bruce 2013). Not linear but circular or, perhaps more aptly, spiral in shape, this cycle of action echoes the Round Dance in all its forms, enlarging, then circling back into itself to take hold within the smaller circles of local communities. The Round Dance does not so much alter as it migrates. Something new is not created, but rather it moves. The Round Dance is the captivating flash of the hand-drum contest and the disruptive mob, a tool of diplomacy, and an instrument of community healing. It is a woman in a Jingle Dress dancing beside a protester-become-politician. It reaches out to allies and knits Indigenous communities and generations together. In all its Indigenuity, the Round Dance sets in motion a complex spiritual politics.

7. Get Tribal

Cosmopolitan Worlds and Indigenous
Consciousness in Hip-Hop

BATTLE ANNOUNCER: MC on my left, introduce yourself.

HELLNBACK: Hey, if you don't know . . . man, my name is Hellnback.
[Turning his head to glare at RedCloud] I'm about to go buy some
oranges from a Mexican. [Hellnback turns to smile coolly at camera
as audience chuckles, laughter.]

BATTLE ANNOUNCER: [Announcer's eyes narrow and small laugh as
the jab sinks in.] MC on my right, introduce yourself!

REDCLOUD: [RedCloud looks directly into camera like a happy game-
show contestant with a gentle smile.] Hi! My name is RedCloud,
from Los Angeles. And, I'm about to sell some oranges to an Asian
[big audience laughter, clapping to his return].

This emcee-battle introduction took place in a Winnipeg, Manitoba, nightclub
and travels distance with economy. Hellnback opens in regional dialect, reminding the Canadian First Nations audience they should already know who he is.
Then he throws the first verbal jab, smearing the Los Angeles–based emcee Red-
Cloud as an urban Mexican American poser by emphasizing his national origins
rather than ethnic allegiance. "You aren't Indian," Hellnback tells RedCloud
bluntly. Choosing a dizzying headshot based on the raw physical appearance of
Hellnback's mug, RedCloud responds that Hellnback is not Indian but Asian.

But what does this exchange mean? What is at stake calling a Los Angeleno
"Mexican"? How is calling a Canadian "Asian" a slam? Both emcees deny the

other's Indigeneity. On one level these slams are superficial smears that deploy cultural assumptions, even stereotypes, to de-pant opponents through verbal sparring. The terms are general, but their inflection within this emcee battle makes all the difference in understanding their humor, wit, and hip-hop brilliance.

On a deeper level both intensify their blows with truth expressed simply through humor. Hellnback is a Sampson Cree emcee from Hobbema (near Alberta, Canada) and is known for work with the First Nations hip-hop crews War Party and Team Rezofficial. Implicit in his cut is derision for entrepreneurial acumen ("freeway exit orange seller") and Aboriginal doubt about RedCloud's legality as a second-generation urban (im)migrant squatter or, more specifically, his lack of relationship to ancestral land.

RedCloud is a modern manifestation of the deeply Indigenous heritage of Mexican *mestizaje*, with roots in the mingling of Aztecan temple builders and his own Huichol or Wixarika people. Emboldened by that heritage, RedCloud dismantles Hellnback's "Indianness" by destroying his claims of land tenure. "You aren't even North American—get your @$$ back across the Bering Strait, where you came from," he humorously blasts back.

These guys know what they are doing. A sense of belonging, being down, or representing the hood or gang—or its Indigenous equivalent, the *rez* and *tribe*—is central to hip-hop identity. There is something deeply grounded or fixed about the geography of the hood and rez. And there is something embracingly reciprocal in the familial closeness of the gang or tribe. Without belonging, they don't have much.

By evoking the distant migrations of Native North American peoples and the widespread influence of Mesoamerican culture, both emcees suggest that profound geographic movements and sophisticated social accomplishments are as typical of Indigenous peoples as any timeless relation to ancestral homeland. If some presume emcee battles like this mimic global hip-hop style, they miss the weighty issue confronted in the ritualized exchange: *realness*, or perceived authenticity of identity and belonging, is among the toughest personal, political, and historical issues confronted by modern Indigenous peoples.

So why are we getting precontact with this emcee battle in a book about modernity? Modern North American Indigenous peoples fashion their futures on the continuities of their pasts, and they are increasingly empowered to party like it's 1491. Battle attendees even today have differing opinions about who won. But RedCloud, based on audience response, won that point. He simultaneously dismisses his friendly opponent Hellnback from the emcee battle and this chapter with both jaw-dropping humor and an honorable shame that undeniably provoked laughter even from its target.

Ceremonies like this end on the best occasions in pats on the back and joking acknowledgment of the best slams. This is hip-hop tradition. These emcees embody the sweep of North American experience: Mexico, the United States, and Canada. They are divided by tribal language, hometown, and nation. Despite these differences, they unite through colonial experience; political and social marginalization; and tribal, national, and global movement and aspiration. These cosmopolitan hip-hoppers are of the same "tribe." They are *Indigenous*.

NATION-STATE, TRIBE, AND
INDIGENOUS COSMOPOLITANS

This chapter continues a series of articles exploring the rhymes of three Indigenous emcees: RedCloud, Emcee One, and Quese Imc (Aplin 2012, 2013). These children of the late 1970s were raised on hip-hop and specifically address the Native experiences of North America — across Canada, the United States, and Mexico, nation-states that each define Indigenous differently. Canadian Indigenous peoples are organized into First Nations *bands* and American Indians into *tribes*, but Mexican nationhood highlights its origins in Indigenous Aztecan civilization rather than from its *indios*. Rooted in evolutionary theory, colonial powers once rationalized dispossession of Indigenous North Americans through such classifications.

Tribe has been a particularly important concept for U.S. ethnomusicological research. But the common claim that tribal people walk in two worlds too frequently creates assumptions of Indigenous versus non-Indigenous conflict — that is, that Indigenous people live perilously between tribal and colonial worlds of experience. A measure of this expectation rests in the limitations of sociological theories of modernity (e.g., Giddens 1991). A general assumption of modernity is individual and local sublimation under the broader and more abstract social and organizational needs of a nation-state. And if one were to posit an Indigenous modernity, they might note Native peoples' incorporation into modern nation-states through long-term, powerful acts of colonial violence. This is a valid starting point. But the symptoms of modernity are as a result sometimes described like an external contagion — something imposed from the outside without consent, complicity, or opposition. As a sociological term, modernity-as-concept can be as indeterminate and mysterious as the alienating bureaucracy, industry, and technology it critiques. But in what ways have citizens and tribes acted strategically within modernity? From my perspective we need to know more about Indigenous peoples' strategic positions for understanding action and strategy within historical, cultural, and musical borderlands (Brooks 2002; Hamalainen 2008).

Assumed conflict between oppositional cultures obscures the daily strategic actions of worldly tribal people, since, in actuality, Indigenous peoples cross many borders. Anthropological theory assumes transcontinental peopling of the Americas across the Bering Strait, whereas Mesoamerica influenced the economics, architectures, languages, and beliefs of the U.S. Southwest deep into its plains and prairies. Furthermore, U.S. tribes forged reciprocal alliances across Indigenous social boundaries, from the long-standing relationships of the Cheyenne and Arapaho to the Muscogee and Euchee, among others. Indigenous peoples built strategic relationships with Spanish, French, and English colonial powers, as well as with diasporic African-derived peoples. They traveled the Americas by foot, boat, and horseback, as well as to Europe as diplomats, military personnel, entertainers, and entrepreneurs representing the opportunity of North American vision. Urban Indians in Los Angeles, Minneapolis, Dallas, and other cities are commonplace. And the term *Indigenous* is now used globally to describe diverse peoples with common precolonial land tenure and a determination to defy national subordination by perpetuating ethnic heritage, often through shared cultural acts like music, language, and religion (de la Cadena and Starn 2007; Niezen 2003). This connectedness breathtakingly contradicts mid-twentieth-century cinematic depictions of nameless whooping Indians violently chasing wagon trains across the western United States.

Though many still imagine Indians as "primitive," Quese, RedCloud, and Emcee One show Indigenous peoples and nations more accurately as cosmopolitan.[1] This chapter describes how these emcees' samples and rhymes take us from primitive Indian stereotypes to a richer Indigenous perspective. They travel musically from the rural tribe to the urban center of Los Angeles, where they ally with worldly neighbors through common alienation from ancestral homeland, social marginalization, and colonization by others. They travel from Mexico to the United States to Canada and beyond in global Indigenous unity through rhyme. Their hip-hop communicates to multiple audiences through musical and textual signposts of allegiance, both geographic (the rez) and social (the tribe). The examples presented here speak through three different communication markers. *Hard* markers refer to sounds, symbols, and rhymes that communicate an affiliation to tribe or rez, evident even to the uninitiated. *Soft* markers communicate through indirect nods to audience members who are in the know, without disturbing noncommunity comprehension of broader musical and textual action. *Neutral* markers communicate broad symbols that speak differently to two or more audience constituencies. Communications to audience segments are ambiguous for the uninitiated but are nonetheless intentional. The tribe remains fundamental to the emcees' North American Indigenous consciousness because it unites diverse peoples through common colonial experiences. RedCloud, Quese, and Emcee One demonstrate that their cosmopolitanism—their sociomusical mastery of cross-border movement and artistic synthesis—has always been the best way to get tribal.

COLONIAL EXPERIENCE: FROM SAMPLING SAVAGES TO REPRESENTING THE TRIBE

The Lakȟóta scholar Philip Deloria wrote of his torment as his preadolescent son blasted "Shake Ya Tailfeather" from his room (2004, 224). A hip-hop track written by Nelly (featuring P-Diddy and Murphy Lee), "Shake Ya Tailfeather" (2003) was composed for the Bad Boyz II soundtrack, a movie about two Miami cops. Nelly localized the track by using the Florida State University Seminole's "Tomahawk Chop" as the melodic backdrop for its chorus. Contrary to the honor FSU and the Seminole tribe claim the "Tomahawk Chop" pays Indigenous peoples, for Deloria it is a musical caricature. It begins with a pulsing four-beat rhythm accenting beats one and three (DUM-dum-dum-dum), followed by a descending gapped-scale melody, complete with Scottish snap accents emphasizing the off-beat (two sixteenth notes followed by an eighth; see figure 7.1). Nelly, Diddy, and Lee's version is inverted, with the sung pentatonic melody, lacking the snap ornaments typical of the tune, and is followed by a straight hip-hop beat (figure 7.2). The descending gapped melodic material and simplistic rhythms of "Tomahawk Chop" are key Indian gestures for Western musical imaginations.

Non-Indigenous musicians have depicted Indigenous peoples as primitive in musical sound for centuries (cf. Browner 1995; Levine 2002; Pisani 2005). And the continued prominence of stereotyped imagery—whether through musical convention or the use of Indian mascots for sports teams—rankles Indigenous intelligentsia. Quese Imc (Seminole-Pawnee) shows this in the song "I Am My Ancestors" (2006): "And it pisses me off when I get on stage of an emcee battle /

Figure 7.1. Musical excerpt from the Florida State University "War Chant" fight song, by Tommy Wright, 1950. Transcribed by T. Christopher Aplin.

Figure 7.2. Musical excerpt from "Shake Ya Tailfeather," by Nelly, 2003. Transcribed by T. Christopher Aplin.

When I'm winning with punchlines and the guys just babble. . . . Dancing around like a cartoon Indian while the crowd is hooraying." Quese's frustrations led to humorous hip-hop violence in rhyme. He titled "I Pulled a 187 on a Mascot" (2008) for the California penal-code statute adopted globally as hip-hop slang for murder. The song begins with a campy hard marker: the drums. Quese toys with convention by performing his rhythmic introduction on the tom-toms and snare drum of a trap set but flavors its Scottish snap rhythm with a loose groove. He then turns mascot savagery on itself over a funk beat and stereotyped accompaniment of "Tomahawk Chop" on *Bluelight* (figure 7.3):

[I pulled] a 187 on a mascot.
Man, I ain't no mascot.
[I pulled] a 187 on a mascot.
I took my tomahawk
did a tomahawk chop
on the forehead of that mascot.

Through rhythmic groove, vocal inflection, and rhyme, Quese's violence is more comic than savage.

By contrast, RedCloud's "Native Threats," from *1491 Nation Presents: MC Red-Cloud* (2011), owns stereotype with ironic cool. It begins with a quick scratch by guest DJ Young Native, followed by a repeated tonic note that establishes the pedantic tom-tom of a midcentury John Ford movie score. An "Indian" theme

Figure 7.3. Musical excerpt from "I Pulled a 187 on a Mascot," by Quese Imc, 2008. Transcribed by T. Christopher Aplin.

enters in low-brass (figure 7.4), featuring a simple four-beat rhythm and a repetitive pentatonic melody with a triplet–eighth-note Scottish snap ornament. The comedian Dave Chappelle's sampled routine about his first encounter with an Indian in a New Mexico Wal-Mart rises over this absurdist accompaniment, before DJ Young Native drags the turntable, giving the Indian-themed horns a downward glissando, a screeching interruption of reality. The beat kicks in as RedCloud layers in a "1491" station-identification tag followed by luluing, a musical decolonization that repurposes stereotyped sound as Indian country. RedCloud starts to rap, using his throat voice and a limited melodic range rather than his more usual nasal voice, "stoically" intoning the many tribal peoples he has known.

Quese, RedCloud, and Emcee One mock stereotypes that gloss Indigenous peoples without regard for their distinctiveness. Musical coding in "Tomahawk Chop"—pedantic drums, Scottish snaps, a descending gapped-scale melody, and cultural othering through the use of low brass instruments—overlays European

Figure 7.4. Musical excerpt from "Native Threats," by RedCloud, 2011.
Transcribed by T. Christopher Aplin.

musical conventions within the context of the Americas. Musical conventions in turn associate distinct Indigenous peoples with immoral "savage" mascots and reinforce outdated theories about musical and cultural primitivism. Through juxtaposition of sound and image, these emcees dismantle impoverished musical imaginations that portray tribal peoples simplistically.

The Tribe in Music and Rhyme

Emcee One, Quese, and RedCloud use several tools to counter tribal expectation. They exert distinctiveness through their selection of musical samples.

Quese's "Medzeez" (2008), for example, connects his rhyme to earlier popular music by sampling Redbone's seminal Indigenous pride rock song, "We Were All Wounded at Wounded Knee" (1973). Redbone's chorus reminds audiences about the historical significance of both the 1890 massacre of Lakȟóta peoples at Wounded Knee, South Dakota, as well as the 1973 American Indian Movement's seizure of the same site against the Federal Bureau of Investigation and U.S. Marshals Service. Quese then links these historical struggles to contemporary youth activism and future Indigenous prosperity through musical and lyrical content. While Redbone's original track connects to the stereotyped Indian sound through the rhythm of the trap-kit toms, Quese reorients symbolic meaning for contemporary audiences by layering in a straight hip-hop beat and an original vocable-driven melody. Interweaving more than a century of Indigenous history, music, and rhyme, Quese uses "Wounded Knee" (the massacre, the activism, and the song) as a *hard* marker of modern American Indianness that communicates specifically to Indigenous audiences.

These artists sample Indigenous traditional musics too. Whereas RedCloud layers powwow sound and image into the skits that unite *1491 Nation*, Quese uses Indigenous music as the foundation for rhyme, as in "The Youth Conference" (2008) and "Medzeez" (2008). Lyrics sometimes describe the social nature of the powwow or its related Forty-Nine songs. Quese, in particular, threads references to his Pawnee and Muscogee-Seminole spirituality throughout his rhymes, as in "Bounce" (2008), "Greencorn" (2008), "Morningstar" (2008), and "Houston Tiger Speaks" (2006). These emcees offer a corrective to primitivist musical depictions by providing brief windows into specific, community-based Indigenous musics.

They also use metaphors that might surprise pop-cultural expectations but reaffirm ties to Indigenous audience subgroups. RedCloud uses Christian soft markers on "Guns and Roses" from his album, *Hawthorne's Most Wanted* (2007). Here he blends gangster rap violence, West Coast holy hip-hop, and a subtle revelation of Indigenous identity in linking the blessings of his rap to a metaphor of Indigenous spirituality, the drum: "I'm blessed with my raps / My pen and pad are my drum / Faith, like Abraham holding a sword to his son." Emcee One similarly describes his mother's battle against death in strongly Christian terms, but connects it to the drum ("Like drums at a powwow / Somehow it's all circular") as he suggests in "Mom's Song (Keep on Flying)" (2007) that her struggle generated new life. The *soft* articulation of the drum appears as a metaphorical flourish amid Christian imagery, except to listeners aware of RedCloud and

Emcee One's heritage. Through these metaphors the artists Indigenize Christianity by linking religion to self-identity while also speaking subtly to distinct Indigenous, Christian, and global hip-hop audience constituencies.

Evoking Elders

RedCloud and Quese liberate the tribe from musical primitivism through a technique connecting to widespread Indigenous values. They layer albums with spoken oral histories and skits depicting elders as revered bearers of community history and wisdom. Quese relies on spoken narratives by elders as a form of ethnographic sample or an expression of community oral tradition, in "Orrolope Muccvsepen" (2006) and "I Am My Ancestors" (2006). Although not without redemptive hope (as in "That Good Medicine" [2006]), Quese's quotations of elders address bitter aspects of colonization, missionization, boarding schools, reservation confinement, treaty abrogation, land dispossession, family and community dysfunction, and language loss. RedCloud, by contrast, uses elders' voices as playful comedic glue within skits on his album *1491 Nation*. Written collaboratively with and performed by Crow MC Supaman, the album from RedCloud uses fictional host Larry Chokes-the-Chicken to go rural by narrating it as equal parts rez radio deejay and powwow emcee. Similarly, Larry introduces a word from his sponsor in "Frybread Special," where "Grandma"—entrepreneurial, down with hip-hop, cosmopolitan in her diverse approaches to making fry bread—sweetly peddles her fare. Larry's easy-paced, elder male patter and Grandma's old-fashioned hospitality humorously communicate the respected status of elders within Indigenous communities.

Family Origins

RedCloud, Quese, and Emcee One use autobiography to reveal their personalities, family histories, and heritage. RedCloud's "Boulevard Knights" (2007), for example, makes peace with his relationship to his father. He references his urban origins and youth on "Upside Down" (2011):

Let me take you on a trip to 1978
Where some Southside Indians were fenna get laid.
In a span of ten months a young Native was made
And he never knew his Dad, even his Mom was like "late."

His lyrics express a sense of distance from family unity but try to place emotions of alienation within a positive framework for progress.

Quese provides a detailed history of his great-great-grandmother, Martha Lena Choko, in "Greencorn" (2008). His narrative is accompanied by a Muscogee Stomp Dance song, which begins with the relaxed, walking-pace rhythm of women shell shakers.[2] Male call-and-response vocals gain momentum as Quese speaks of the Seminole wars and removal.[3] As he describes Martha's devastating walk with the Seminole on the Trail of Tears to Oklahoma, the rhythm of the shell shakers becomes constant, evocative of a freight train. The vocal and percussive rhythms intensify as Quese's voice rises to describe his great-great-grandmother as an empowered elder. Although the removal should have foreshadowed doom for the Seminole people, Quese's sound portrait argues the opposite: the shell-shaker rhythm and vocals converge in sync, gaining power. Male vocalists begin singing jubilantly as Quese describes his grandma with humor and reverence. Layering family history with Woodlands song, Quese intertwines collective intergenerational memory into an unexpectedly triumphant whole.

Emcee One's spoken introduction on his album *Introducing for Again for the First Time: Emcee One* (2012) reveals his heritage like an announcer proclaiming a returning heavyweight boxer. Describing his movement from urban San Jose, California, to rural Pawhuska, Oklahoma, Emcee One pays homage to the tributaries that converge in his being. A cosmopolitan, he notes that "I have a problem with how the system of identifying ourselves within tribes has been set up to slowly erode us as a people . . . making us one tribe" (pers. comm. June 6, 2011). He therefore not only introduces himself, his Indigenous creds, and his urban-to-rural experience; he also stands against the tribal consolidation typical of colonization. Rather than simplify his identity as Osage owing to specific enrollment, he explains his more complex and accurate identity as Osage-Potawatomi-Delaware–Puerto Rican.

Indigenous Language

Indigenous emcees often reference or use Native languages within their recordings. Quese infuses his music with community languages to represent self and culture. He is aware that language skills are a keystone of Indigenous identity and has indicated that he was able to acquire his linguistic knowledge only through the study of his tribes' songs (interview, Pasadena, CA, June 17, 2011), a common entry point for language acquisition.[4] Quese typically uses Indigenous language in his recordings to flavor conclusions and encourage audiences. His most painful and fully developed exposition on language appears in the form of an ethnographic oral history introducing "Street Indian" (2004), where he engages an unnamed gentleman on the street in conversation about being Indian. The unnamed man equates language endangerment with the fragility of Indigenous communities, as indicated by the audible breaking of his voice. "I learned my language," he says, "a lot of people don't. And sometimes it's hard, because I don't have nobody to talk to." The song ends as the man bids farewell in the Muscogee language. To counter linguistic erosion and display his own efforts at perpetuation, Quese sprinkles his songs with blessings such as *Aho* (an intertribal term that alternately means "thanks," "I agree," or "amen"); *herre mahe* and *momen herkv* (Muscogee for "I feel good" and "peace"); and *tataciks'tahu* and *iriwe turahe* (Pawnee for "thank you" and "right here, it is good") in songs including "I Pulled a 187 on a Mascot" (2008) and "California" (2008). He uses a wider range of spoken community languages as a form of ethnographic snippets in songs like "Orroloope Muccvsepen" (2006), "Houston Tiger Speaks" (2006), "I Am My Ancestors" (2006), "Morningstar" (2008), "The Bird Song" (2011), and "State of Mind" (2011).

URBAN INDIANS: SOCIOPOLITICAL MARGINS AND BORDERS

Western music depends almost single-mindedly on iconic rhythmic and melodic gestures of Indianness. But these emcees mock assumptions while also expanding audience expectations: rather than pounding war drums, we discover shaken ceremonial shells; in contrasting tribal languages we find agreement, goodness, and talk of peace; and we find quirky elders that feed family spirits with tribal memory. In contrast to Indian acts of war, violence, and stoicism implied by Western musical depictions, our emcees portray their allegiance to rural homes of tribe, ceremony, and family.

Paradoxically, these emcees' family histories also betray the worldliness of their origins: all three of the emcees in this study have both Indigenous and Latino heritage. Many assume that hip-hop itself is a fundamentally African American musical expression. Its foundation on the four elements (emcees [rappers], deejays [turntablists], B-Boys [break-dancers], and graffiti), social consciousness, sampling, and popular culture references may be traced to hip-hop's origins in urban boroughs of New York City during the 1970s and 1980s. Yet the genre originated through a conflation of sources; rather than a strictly urban African American expression, Puertorriqueño communities also significantly influenced its development. While many simplify hip-hop origins by glossing complexity, shared histories and values between social communities contribute to the worldly character of both people and music. Bridging the Other and its West, the tribal and pantribal, the rural margins and urban centers, these emcees too navigate multiple geographic and social worlds through hip-hop.

Rural to Urban

Home to Reba McIntire, Garth Brooks, and Toby Keith, country music is omnipresent in Oklahoma life and identity. Quese and Emcee One rightly reflect Oklahoma's embrace of the country, a value-laden space of geographic and musical meaning. One example is Quese's "Them Country Roads" (on *The Betty Lena Project*, 2006), which builds on the harmonic foundation of John Denver's "Take Me Home, Country Roads" (1971). Quese refashions its refrain to pay homage to Indigenous peoples living along America's rural routes:

Yo, the old dirt roads
The country woods
And the back towns
It's all good because, yo, I'm down.
I'm Native American.

Quese also draws on country sampling on "Loosecannons" (using a version of the gospel standard "I Saw the Light") and on "Superbrightstar" (using Bobby Goldsboro's *Honey* [1968]). Emcee One defines his poetic style by country influences. Hip-hop forced One to emphasize the realness of personal experience through autobiography. Country music, by contrast, "was based in storytelling." By overlaying first-person hip-hop realness, country-music storytelling, and commitment to Indigenous social uplift, One crafts a music "intent on trying to tell stories that share a positive moral along the way" (pers. corr., June 6, 2011).

On one hand, country music's evocation of *rural* places and values to consumers and performers is a point of pride. As a place, country is earthy and real for Quese, and he engages with land in songs such as "Them Country Roads" and "Southern Plains" (2006). More specifically, he turns the rural backwaters or boondocks into a positive in his songs "Oklahoma" (2006) and "Superbrightstar"

(2006; "Yo, here I am / Creeping out the boondocks / Through your boombox"), where he describes himself as a diamond in the rough quietly creeping from rural margins to overtake urban centers. On the other hand, country-music "hick-hop" sampling by Quese also represents the Oklahoma soundscape surrounding him and its social limitations. They remind hip-hop heads that horizons of understanding are not fixed or unchanging; rather, they are a launching point for experiences within broader worlds, as in these lines from "Life So Great," on *Hand Drums for Whiskey Bottles* (2011):

> In a small town in the Midwest
> Growing up with no door
> Of opportunity, one stoplight, one store
> Was deemed an outcast cause I didn't praise the Lord.
> In the Bible Belt slain in the spirit, I hit the floor
> But I hit a glass ceiling with the feeling that there was more
> beyond the borders to shores.

Though bittersweet in sentiment, Quese and One are connected to the boondocks of Oklahoma's southern plains.

Madness, Hegemony, and Love in Los Angeles

On *Hand Drums for Whiskey Bottles* (2011) low-income and boondock limitations gave rise to dreams of travel for Quese and One, growing from rural margins to "Make It Big" in the urban center. For Quese, as for One, this meant moving to Los Angeles as young adults. Los Angeles has been RedCloud's home from birth. Despite differences in perspective because of personal experience and senses of "home," Quese expresses a value important to all three emcees in his "Life So Great," a love of margins and disregard for borders ("This goes out to you in that city, on that rez, in that little town just outside of nowhere . . . to anyone living just beyond the borders of somewhere"). Of significance in understanding their work is how each develops his sense of marginality in rhyme and music, particularly as it relates to his understanding of the urban center.

Though Emcee One enjoyed the attention of record executives and the adventure of living in Los Angeles, he describes his experiences like a missionary confronted by urban madness in "Gotta Make Moves," on *Somebody's Gotta Tell 'Em* (2007):

There's this man on the corner with nobody to talk to.
I'll hop to this mic to help this man try to walk through.
Dues is paid, I've stayed on couches, pounded pavement, sleeping in stranger's houses.
Been out in crazy places—that was a trip.
Off of Western and the Sunset strip.
I seen the Hollywood sign, but I don't think it saw me.
There were prostitutes and crazy dudes that could rob me.
I'd be safer anywhere, but that's where God had me.
And I'd gladly do it again if it's at the price of a Grammy.

Emcee One depicts himself missionizing within an indifferent bedlam of vice and inconstancy. He dutifully performs godly service ("pounding the pavement") even if it precludes that preeminent worldly pleasure of Los Angeles industry: a Grammy.

Quese reads the city as a site of colonization (figure 7.5). He develops the corrosive effects of urbanity across his Los Angeles–period albums, *Bluelight* (2008) and *Hand Drums for Whiskey Bottles* (2011), in terms of gentrification, for example, in the latter album's "Fame":

Man, it's kind of crazy
When you notice how many people are shady.
Climbing a ladder, building a fence
Pushing us out like gentrification, raising the rents.

Here Quese Imc (2011) links gentrification to the building of borders ("a fence"). But who builds these borders? Who are the agents of gentrification? Rather than large corporate interests, Quese (along with the *Los Angeles Times* and area Occupy LA activists and residents) points to unwitting foot soldiers of neocolonial expansion: hipsters (see *Los Angeles Times* [2012]). The hipster is a socially constructed phenotype describing predominantly male, white, middle-class twenty-somethings endowed with the luxury of urban relocation to New York or Los Angeles to be an artist. They embody millennial "apathy, refusal to engage [in] politics, participation in gentrification, [and] mindless consumerism paraded as uniqueness" (Tortorici 2011).

Quese develops his theme of hipster-initiated gentrification in detail in his Woody Guthriesque "California," on *Bluelight* (2008):

Figure 7.5. Quese Imc, n.d. Photo by Brian Frejo. Used by permission.

Echo Park, gentrification after dark . . .
Hipsters belligerent on Sunset
Walking pets, talking nonsense about artsy-fartsy art that has no content.
Once they arrived the rent went up, go figure.
Couldn't afford the rent, had to move east of the [LA] river.
It's like manifest destiny, history manifested
Manifest hipster repeating the oppression . . .
As they are raising cats and dogs, we are raising kids.
Start a business, make moves, fuck [hipster] scenes.
ICE raids, check points, this is their American dream.
Filipino, South and Central America, Chinese
Echo Park, hold it down
Nahui ohlin.[5]

Echo Park is one of many Angelino neighborhoods affected by gentrification. Quese portrays hipsters in songs including "Fame" (2011), "Whiskey Bottles" (2011), and "California" (2008) as a vacuously aggressive alien force within established communities, unaware of the colonial displacement they reenact and the families they affect. The hipster-as-colonizer is representative of a broader, unjust U.S. immigration system against which diverse immigrant Angelino neighbors should fight. Through development of the hipster, gentrification, and immigration themes, Quese joins others connected to the Occupy LA protests. These themes also connect him to his East LA community and extended family, whose roots trace to Guanajuato, Mexico. In Los Angeles Quese's rhyme freshly engaged his Latino heritage since he was not, as he says, "raised in the community" (pers. comm., August 19, 2013). This exploration is evident in several songs dating from his West Coast residency.

RedCloud's "405," from *Hawthorne's Most Wanted* (2007), touches on the corruption, poverty, and incarceration of LA gangs. His ode to one of Los Angeles's most traveled freeways is affectionate, however, with the "405" linking Hawthorne to other near and far southern California "hoods" in rhyme. RedCloud describes his city in a gritty sepia-toned film noir mumble, like a wise-talking, all-seeing LA gumshoe: "Corruption—yeah, utter it low / Keep it underground and low like it's lottery dough." His rhyme references cinematic imagery and action in visually descriptive songs like "405" and "100 Cholos," forcing reconsideration of the Hollywood Indian. And since California represents a global hip-hop center, "405" speaks in a mainstream tradition that mixes Angelino cultural indices and urban corruption with optimistic affection. He creates in the process a song with the ability to translate nationally, such as Tupac's "California Love" (1995), rather than speaking to audience segments based on narrow geographic, religious, or ethnic affiliations.

The multicultural diversity of Los Angeles sets RedCloud apart from rural expectations, but his "South Central Farm" (2007) ruralizes the urban and explores a range of Latino experience within Los Angeles. The song begins with a skit in colonial Spanish ("Tio RedCloud, puedes contarnos una historia, por favor?"), in which RedCloud reads to a group of children. He then raps the story of South Central Farm, a community garden. This site opened just after the 1992 Compton riots following the Rodney King verdict and closed just before the release of *Hawthorne's Most Wanted*. The South Central Farm rose from the ashes of the riots as a utopian response initiated not by Latinos but rather by Indigenous Mexica (the term preferred by RedCloud), those decolonized descendants of the Aztecs who still claim the Americas as Indigenous land:

With leadership Mexica in a rugged neighborhood
'Til they turned the soil over and they saw that it was good.
Families deep, real deep they came together
Tethered fences together, soiling sessions together.

Eagle and Condor feather, the smoggiest weather
Xicano ties don't sever, the tougher the better.

RedCloud Indigenizes Los Angeles, linking its Mexica to the land in a gesture meaningful within pan–American Indigenous experience. The "Eagle and Condor" establishes solidarity between Central American Indigenous peoples (the "Condor") with the European-derived modernity of urban Los Angeles (the United States, or the "Eagle") to seek reconciliation through a return to the earth. His language broadens, directing attention from Mexica Los Angeles toward U.S. Indigenous consciousness ("350 families tasting some sovereignty on private property / Although they're stricken with poverty"). This incorporation is reaffirmed as his language expands again, uniting the "Eagle and Condor" across spiritual, national, and Indigenous borders: "On a rainy day they got a letter from the owner / But not from *the Creator* / From a lawyer and a bulldozer [emphasis added]" (RedCloud 2007).

RedCloud's engagement with the pluralism of Los Angeles extends beyond Mexica Indigeneity too. This is most apparent on his LA-focused album, *Hawthorne's Most Wanted*, in which he lays his allegiance bare from the opening track, "Welcome All." His street values reflect southern California's vaunted cultural diversity in the way he transcends boundaries:

I'm an originator, so read my lips
I roll with Eses, Asians, Crips.
Armenians, Indians, come back dissin'
I'll immortalize my beef unto a compact disc.

Regardless of the Latino/Mexica "Eses" and African American "Crips," gangsters that made LA hip-hop famous, RedCloud declares himself a local son by spelling out the range of immigrant communities—often marginalized refugees of warfare and genocide, including Koreans, Armenians, and Cambodians—he hangs with in Los Angeles.

INDIGENOUS MOVEMENT: TRIBAL, NATIONAL, AND GLOBAL TRAVEL AND IMAGINATION

Metaphorical and physical hip-hop travel enables Indigenous emcees to reach pan-American and global audiences. Emcee One expresses this connection most generally on "Fresh" (*A Collection of Demos*, 2004), as he notes that people too often place borders on themselves: "I find it's all in your mind / (That's where you're battling). . . . You need a horse for saddling / A boat for paddling / Hip-hop is a vehicle for a different kind of traveling." Their lyrics describe a range of geographic and cultural movements, such as in One's "Mom's Song (Keep on Flying)" (2007), in which he describes receiving news of his mother's passing: "Living in DC, but out in LA when the call came"; or in Quese's "I Am My Ancestors" (2006): "From New York to LA / In the middle—Indian country / Oklahoma to the four directions / This is my story."

For Quese, these travels link to the historical displacement and sorrow of his Indigenous ancestors, as in "The Bird Song" (2011): "We have traveled many miles / On the Trail of Tears of blood / But, we're laughing now. . . . We are the movement, the culture / We can't be beat. Whether from warfare, exile, or adventure, movement through travel colors their view of their world.

Each emcee travels North America extensively, particularly within the continental United States and Canada. This creates the sense that they have seen it all, a sentiment Emcee One (2012) expresses poetically in "Regals and Olds," through urban-to-rural movement, biblical evocation, and decadent hip-hop metaphor: "I'm from the West Coast / Some call it the killer Cali / Traded in my earthquakes for tornado alley [Oklahoma] / Been to the mountaintop / And through the valleys / Working in the clubs and them car-show rallies."

Quese and Emcee One have also toured western Europe. Yet it is in the ambitious imagination of RedCloud's collaboration with Crystle Lightning, in a duo called LightningCloud, that global travel and imagination find voice in songs such as "Zoom" and "Gravitron": "Put it on my landing strip / That I'm equipped to handle this / Rock a show in Edmonton and fly back to Los Angeles / Lay over in London with an artist and a vandalist" (RedCloud 2012).

Borderland Tensions

The lyrics these three emcees write make clear that friction is common at the frontier of musical, social, and geographic travel. In "Whiskey Bottles" (2011), Quese historicizes borderland conflicts ("Trading stolen land with the land-mine, the borderline / They sent us on the reservations"), using the "borderline" to represent a marginal purgatory, a place of exile. In this sense frontier conflict is social. It is also synonymous with questionable treaty practices and the subsequent marginalization of Indigenous peoples within U.S. history and consciousness. Although the U.S. national narrative valorizes flexible borders and migratory openness, Quese expresses skepticism through his gentrification, hipster, and colonization themes. Confrontation marks his spoken introduction to "California" (2008). But his most forceful critique of immigration policy appears in "Red Zeppelin" (2011). Imagining modern technology as empowerment for Indigenous peoples, "Red Zeppelin" describes the breadth of his travel and cross-border American experience and allows him to condemn U.S. immigration policy as dishonest ("Since when did immigration become so racist? / Isn't that how they started this nation?").

Emcee One, Quese, and RedCloud connect through music to marginalized immigrants and outcasts in the friction of the border zone. Quese develops this theme in "Hero" (2008) a song dedicated "to the outcasts, the weirdos, the ones not in the popular crowd." Cast in neutral imagery of the unpopular kid at school, the protagonist emerges within the lyrics and contemplates a school shooting. Quese hints at redemptive love as his protagonist halts his schoolyard violence when a love-interest hero, in Japanime style, beats down unnamed bullies and jocks and departs happily with her protagonist. Quese dedicates "The Youth Conference" (2008) to "anyone that has ever been left out." "I Am My Ancestors" (2006) links this spirited underdogism more specifically to Indigenous peoples' alienation from American land, political power, and historical memory, by calling them "the invisible people" (a literary play on Ralph Ellison's *The Invisible Man*) and the "minority of the minorities." His diminutive phrases describe the subaltern position of Indigenous peoples in terms of national consciousness and politics.

Global Consciousness

The hip-hop travel of these emcees imagines a border-crossing consciousness in a world without boundaries: that is, recognition of borders within rhyme defines them as obstacles to be transcended. If music transcends boundary, it is for these emcees a result of commonalities shared by the diverse residents of this planet. Quese's dance-grooved, electronic "Radiation" (2011) argues as much:

Music and dance give you the chance
We breaking through borders
We taking no orders
Recording resistance
We witness, we listen
Our culture, traditions.

If "Radiation" breaks down borders, however, its message is marked softly toward Indigenous audiences with its emphasis on "our culture" and "tradition." Quese's "Rebel Music" (2008), by contrast, expands its worldliness through its reggae-influenced groove and poetic hook:

We are building from place to place
We are building from nation to nation
We are building communication
We are building liberation.

These emcees communicate international consciousness, a world without borders, through poetic messaging to multiple audience constituencies. Emcee One, Quese, and RedCloud all demonstrate their interest in being inclusive through musical accessibility. Emcee One, for example, has commented on the difficulty of shaping narratives for multiple public audiences as he writes a motivational book tentatively titled "Youth Are Not the Future" ("Like Dr. Phil meets Tony Robbins, for the rez" [pers. comm., March 8, 2013]). Though his music is aimed at Indigenous audiences, Quese has also commented on his desire to provide a window into Indigenous communities and histories for wider audiences.

As much a product of the diversity of his urban home as his multifaceted and open character, RedCloud also draws in wider audiences through nuanced messaging. Whether emphasizing a point regarding Christianity or Indigeneity, RedCloud's poetic voice consistently speaks in soft (rather than proselytizing or militant) terms across his recordings. This trait is most evident in his recent release with the actor, vocalist, and DJ Crystle Lightning (Hobbema–Enoch Cree) on their self-titled group debut, *LightningCloud* (2012). Listeners might interpret "Light Up the World" (2012), for example, as a statement on masculine-feminine relationships, since the hook is delivered by his romantic performance partner, Crystle:

I've had this burning; I've had this feeling
You can catch me overheating
Everybody needs to see him
So together now we can be in
We'll light up the world; we'll light up the world.

In these terms Lightning delivers potentially suggestive praise over sustained keys and a straight dance beat before RedCloud seconds her desire to bring light to darkness. The verses are couched in general terms of light-versus-dark antipathy or male-female complementarity, so the listener might not notice amid its optimism and humorous human want ("for this jar of peanut butter, though there's very little left") the sprinkling of Christian-tinted language as the song progresses ("divine," "Hallelujah," "preach the news," "blessed," "tribulations"). Not until the listener combines softly marked cues and reorganizes the chorus—"Everybody needs to see Him"—does an electrohouse, hip-hop track emerge as a song of praise. As appropriate for cutting a rug as spinning at the neighborhood gym, "Light Up the World" widens LightningCloud's audience with broad language that communicates to spiritual and nonspiritual audiences in different ways.

RedCloud's (2012) neutral messaging is also evident in "Casino Money" (2012). His performance partner, Crystle Lightning, speaks to key materialist themes in hip-hop: "Baby I'm filthy, filthy rich / Got casino money, oil money, all the money / That a daddy's girl ever needs." Its poetry and pulsing dance beat might evoke for global audiences materialistic hip-hop "bling," Scorcesesque violence, and Daddy's-girl rock attitude. Yet it is this very combination that elicits enthusiastic response from Native audiences, since it simultaneously suggests increased Indigenous wealth and autonomy through casino gaming and oil leasing (which significantly affect Lightning's home community near Edmonton, Alberta). Both artists value the song's ability to communicate to contrasting audience segments. As RedCloud noted, "We wrote ['Casino Money'] with the idea that it could be taken in an Indian way, or in a Vegas way . . . but when the Natives jump on it, that's even cooler" (interview, Studio City, CA, March 9, 2013). RedCloud uses neutral markers as signposts of allegiance, but he invites audiences to fill prominent symbols with personal meaning. Neutral articulation allows him to touch lightly and continue beyond musical, cultural, or ethnic boundaries by drawing attention to shared points uniting different audience constituencies: the toughness or danceability of a beat, a faith in some higher power for those struggling, or visually evocative cinematic images well known to North American audiences (figures 7.6 and 7.7).

A fusion of two booming styles—hip-hop and electrohouse—RedCloud's collaborative album, *LightningCloud*, is his global album. Crystle Lightning relies on her acting skills to introduce the track "Get Tribal" with a detached, British-inflected spoken dialogue. "Zombie Love" uses a tango-influenced harmonic backdrop for RedCloud's rhyme and features an internationally minded introduction by Crystle Lightning, singing in French. "Hang It Up, Daddy," points in many directions at once, beginning with the use of France Gall's chorus from

Figure 7.6. LightningCloud (*left to right*): RedCloud and Crystle Lightning, with DJ Hydroe. Photo shoot for winning Power 106 Best of the Best MC Battle, n.d. Photo by Joshua Tousey (JT Pro Imaging). Used by permission.

Figure 7.7. RedCloud and Crystle Lightning at Mexika New Year's Eve, Boyle Heights, Los Angeles, 2014. Photo by Gonzalo Rios Photography. Used by permission.

the 1964 *ye-ye* hit, "Laisse Tombe les Filles."[6] With campy horror screams and cringe-inducing lyrics of female-on-male violence, it also links to April March's cover of Gall's hit featured in Quentin Tarantino's ode to slasher violence in *Death Proof* (2007).

Nowhere is LightningCloud's global consciousness more apparent than in the dance track "Zoom." The chorus delivered by RedCloud is inclusive, urging audiences to put their hands up, bob their heads, and get down. Lightning's verses, however, take the listener on a prophetic tour of the world that LightningCloud desires to conquer, from the Space, Pacha, and Amnesia electronic festivals on the Mediterranean island of Ibiza to the clubs of England; house festivals of Germany, Japan, and Singapore; and U.S. performance venues (Coachella, South by Southwest, the Vans Warped Tour). "Zoom," sings Lightning in an ascending and descending glissando in the second verse, evoking an aircraft engine's liftoff and landing. An aspirational "dreaming aloud" (interview, Studio City, CA, March 9, 2013) about the places they would like to perform, "Zoom" has proven prophetic for LightningCloud. They performed at South by Southwest after RedCloud defeated large numbers of southern California's emcees to represent West Coast rap for America's number one hip-hop station, Power 106. LightningCloud also received studio time with renowned beat maker Timbaland after defeating the East Coast representative in an emcee battle at South by Southwest. The result is their release "Sake Bombs" (2013). The Aboriginal People's Choice Music Award led them twice to Winnipeg, Canada, where they won Best Rap/Hip Hop Album in 2012 and Best New Artist in 2013.

Tribal Roll Call and International Indigeneity

These emcees' lyrics importantly broadcast an Indigenous pride spanning from the rural to the urban, the local to the global. Emcees make shout-outs for people and places to stir the consciousness of audiences. But Indigenous compasses emphasize unexpected tribal priorities, as in the popular blues-rock style of Quese's "Whiskey Bottles" (2011): "Where ya from, yo?—Oklahoma / Where ya from, yo?—California / Where ya from, yo?—North Dakota. . . . Where ya from, yo?—the reservation!" In "Mouse" he conjures an Indigenous movement united through land stewardship and moving from the abstract ("from battling mics") to the concrete ("to battling for rights") to oppose environmental degradation across geographies and communities. Quese's "I Resist" (2011) embodies this technique in its most jubilant form, as he eradicates Indigenous marginalization and invisibility in the United States:

> We're young, warriors
> Paths we roam
> This ain't Hollywood
> Yo, this is our home. . . .
> We made it this far 'cause our grandmas survived.
> Indigenous pride as we ball up our fist
> Five hundred years—'cause we say, "I exist."

Hopi reggae star Casper Lomayesva lifts audiences higher in "I Resist," chanting the warriors of the past into the boundaryless future:

> Warriors, Warriors
> Come cross the border.
> Always looking forward
> Watch your back
> Never falter. (Quese Imc 2011)

He then departs on a brief tribal roll call in which he names and describes aspects of the tribes and Indigenous people he has known and performed for. By calling out tribal names and locations of the Southwest and beyond, Quese and Casper gesture toward tribal inclusivity while calling attention to the distinctiveness of Indigenous peoples and places.

Quese's "Bounce" (2008) suggests a broader pan-American cosmopolitanism through use of a Quechan harp loop and poetic content that defines Indigenous identity positively, despite alienation within national law and global economy. It links Indigenous experience in the Americas through shared oppression under police power and economic inequality, yet rises above, as Quese urges the listener to bounce to the rhythm, to "live carefree and don't care." He defines Indigeneity in terms of relationship to culture and tradition and takes for granted an international Indigenous value placed on community reciprocity rather than engagement in a global marketplace.

RedCloud's "Native Threats" (2011) takes Indigeneity around the world. Providing a tribal roll call, he first tours the United States from the Plains to the Southwest, the urban East Coast to the tribes of the Southeast, uniting them through common musical, food, and gaming activities:

East Coast Indians with fry bread, cheese steak
Cherokee, Choctaw, Chippewa, Chickasaw, Cree, and Creek peep
They deep, just look at ya'll
Florida Indians, those Seminoles strong
[Trade me your per capita], I'll write you a song.

His eye wanders north of the fortieth parallel to Canada ("Moosonee, Moose Factory, there's Moose River, Fort Albany / Teachers and students in Kashechewan want to remember me / [I] got 'em yelling 'orale' in mother-freaking Thunder Bay").[7] He meanders south from California to take pride in Mexico's tribes and civilizations ("Mexico is the Mecca for every Native, and here it is / Every single Indian should visit the pyramids"), and he swims beyond North American shores ("Pacific Island, Maori, Hawaii, Havaii, Aussies and Kiwi Fam"). RedCloud connects Indigenous peoples across rural and urban, North American and global boundaries, highlighting their geographic breadth, commonality, and distinctiveness.

The realness or accuracy of Indigenous identity has been skewed by primitive expectation. If Indigenous peoples are of the tribe, that is because it reminds them of their links to ancestral home and social reciprocity. For these emcees and Indigenous peoples, the tribe is a diminutive but affectionate term, conveying the closeness of their home communities, even within wider Indigenous and national incorporation. Being a member of the tribe is flexible, but one must show memory, commitment, and reciprocity to gain entrance. When tribes cross rural and urban as well as national and international borders, they transcend to the global. They also take us beyond expectation, allowing a cosmopolitan understanding of their character.

I once told RedCloud about my amusement attempting to interpret who he was through the layers of his recordings: Los Angelino, Latino, Indigenous reservation player, Christian, gangster, visual and musical artist, wise-guy comedian. To him, these categories were not exclusive—they were just him. Instead, he emphasized a desire to make a "good hip-hop album" (interview, Studio City, CA, July 22, 2011) that reached the broadest possible audience without constraint by any one aspect of his identity—geographic, religious, ethnic, or otherwise. RedCloud's unbounded ambition opens his music to larger audiences and allows him to represent himself in his multiplicity. This is important, because it is not simply two worlds through which the Indigenous peoples of North America stride.

Cosmopolitanism, in its philosophical sense, means simply "of the world." Cosmopolitans can be thought of in terms of possessing not only a philosophy or worldview but also a capability gained through life experience and travel. This attitude on a community level represents a sociocultural condition that values ethnic pluralism and cultural hybridity. Cosmopolitans can be read with both positive and negative meanings: as one unexpectedly open to the world and sophisticated in articulating its (often inverted) wisdom or, alternately, as one of ambiguous origin, superficial allegiance, perhaps even dangerous rootlessness. Scholars sometimes interpret Quese's invisible people, or urban RedCloud, within a sociological frame not unlike colonial modernity, as representing a people of fragmented, irreconcilable identity tossed by wicked cultural winds casting about them. But, frequently, they are instead underground underdogs, surviving champions, and cunning cosmopolitans—not a people trapped and uncertain between opposing worlds but a daring people of the world capably crossing and synthesizing across borders. This distinction helps us think through individual and tribal strategies within broader systems. It also connects our pastiche-synthesized present to the past—despite obfuscation by primitive assumption—in a way that renders modernity less unexpected and more Indigenous.

Here the tribe links to its modern equivalent, Indigenous, which better evokes the worldliness tribes lived throughout history as they built culture through geographic movement and social accomplishment. Indigenous peoples get tribal by crossing borders to speak with contrasting audiences through hard, soft, and neutral forms of communication, creating bonds with those sharing alienation from home, social marginalization, and colonization. Native emcees and performance crews perform throughout Indian Country. Hip-hop today, then, is as evocative of Indigenous unity and consciousness across the Americas as it is of earlier exchanges shared among the cosmopolitan bands, tribes, and civilizations long before 1492.

JOHN-CARLOS PEREA

8. Native "Noise" and the Politics of Powwow Musicking in a University Soundscape

Singing and drumming are embodied practices that create access to deep narratives of Native American history, aesthetics, and lived experience. The powwow drum, in particular, becomes a fluid space through which Native people can form a personal identity, emphasizing the diverse ways in which it is possible to be Indigenous. As a Mescalero Apache, German, Irish, and Chicano man who was raised in San Francisco, I learned powwow singing and drumming in the early 1990s during my undergraduate years at San Francisco State University (SFSU). In 2010 I myself began to teach powwow singing and drumming at SFSU after I joined the American Indian studies faculty in the College of Ethnic Studies. I quickly learned that listeners unfamiliar with Native singing and drumming may experience powwow music as "noise," a response shaped by religious, social, and political concepts that are deeply rooted in the North American consciousness. This led me to explore the role of performance in teaching intertribal powwow music and how to facilitate it in a university setting.[1] Drawing on sources from ethnomusicology, sound studies, and American Indian studies, this chapter analyzes the non-Native reception of powwow music as noise from an Indigenous perspective and demonstrates the ways in which sound is disciplined in a university environment. I argue that the university constitutes a sonic environment within which unexpected forms of musicking, such as powwow performance, can sound freely, beyond the bounds of the campus powwow and other identifiably Native events.[2] A discussion of Indigenous modernity, soundscapes, and musicking provides a framework for analyzing powwow musicking in a university classroom.

INDIGENOUS MODERNITY, SOUNDSCAPES, AND MUSICKING

Powwow singing and drumming in a university class highlights the complexity of Indigenous modernity by foregrounding divergent expectations about the role of Native music in contemporary life, acoustic environments, musical rehearsal, and performance on campus. My understanding of Indigenous modernity in relation to music has been informed by Philip Deloria and Beverley Diamond. Deloria explains that in the early 1900s, "according to most American narratives, Indian people, corralled on isolated and impoverished reservations, missed out on modernity—indeed, almost dropped out of history itself" (2004, 6). Rather than accepting that narrative, Deloria explores the many ways in which Native people have actively participated in constructing and performing modernity, though not from equal social, political, or economic positioning. For example, historical trends such as the formation of brass bands at Indian boarding schools reveal the underlying complexity of Indigenous modernity. While the brass bands reflect cultural loss and assimilative music education, they simultaneously illuminate the ways in which Indian students exercised their own agency in mobilizing music education as a means through which to survive (Deloria 2004, 183–223; see also Troutman 2009; O'Connell 2012). Similarly, Diamond explains that "concepts and social relationships of the past are embedded in the present" (2007b, 171). She critiques the expectation of tradition in the singular and explores the many ways in which Indigenous musicians negotiate genre and technology, language and dialect, citation and collaboration, and access and ownership to create music that articulate the sound of Indigenous modernity in various political and socioeconomic contexts (173). Indigenous modernity, therefore, is an ongoing state, not a recent condition; it has always been traditional for Native people to be contemporary in their own lives and in the many ways they produce and consume music. One of the most powerful ways to create and express Indigenous modernity as part of a university campus's soundscape is through courses on American Indian music that include a performance component.

The composer R. Murray Schafer coined the term *soundscape* in the 1960s, defining it as "any portion of the sonic environment regarded as a field for study. The term may refer to actual environments, or to abstract constructions such as musical compositions . . . particularly when considered as an environment" (1994, 274–75). Schafer further defines *acoustic ecology* as "the study of the effects of the acoustic environment or SOUNDSCAPE on the physical responses or behavioral characteristics of creatures living within it" (271). The entry for "acoustic ecology" in *The World Soundscape Project's Handbook for Acoustic Ecology* asks readers to reference the definition for "soundscape ecology." Barry Truax expanded the definition of soundscape to mean "an environment of sound . . . *with emphasis on the way it is perceived and understood by the individual, or by a society. It thus depends on the relationships between the individual and any such environment*" (1978, 127, 126; emphasis added). In other words, Truax uses the term *soundscape* "to put the emphasis on how that environment is understood by those living within it—the people who are in fact creating it" (2001, 11). Following Schafer and Truax, I understand the university campus as a socially constructed sonic environment in which the teaching and reception of powwow singing and drumming contributes to the larger soundscape ecology. The university soundscape functions as the environment in which the social and sonic interactions for powwow singing and drumming take place, both inside and outside of my classroom. Understanding the soundscape ecology of the university sheds light on the hierarchical relationships among sounds and sound makers on campus and encourages reflection on how these relationships might change in a productive and sustainable fashion.

The musicologist Christopher Small introduced the term *musicking*, explaining that "*to music is to take part, in any capacity, in a musical performance, whether by performing, by listening, by rehearsing or practicing, by providing material for performance (what is called composing), or by dancing*" (1998, 9). Small's definition is essential to my music class, since it reinforces the fact that everyone contributes to the collective production of a musical moment, whether they are performing, listening, or engaged in other actions. Whereas my class emphasizes powwow singing and drumming, listening also plays an important role in generating both positive and negative reactions from people inside and outside of the classroom. The concept of musicking therefore provides a framework for understanding performing and listening as complex and interrelated acts that cannot be separated. In my use of the term *musicking*, I hope to subvert expectations by using an unexpected word to describe the musical process that takes place in my classes. The term *unexpected* describes powwow musicking on campus because the sound and presence of the drum in a university setting confronts expectations of Native assimilation and disappearance that continue to manifest in our media and academic landscapes. I was trained as a powwow singer, and I teach my students the rudiments of this style, but I find that the words *singing* and *drumming* often obstruct the more complex student experience in which physical, mental, and cultural competencies become interwoven. The multilayered quality of Small's term, *musicking*, allows me to refer to the simultaneity of positive and negative reactions with physical, mental, and cultural domains in ways that challenge preconceptions of what it means to sing and drum.

PAST(S): POWWOW MUSICKING AND NATIVE WORLDVIEWS

I joined the American Indian studies faculty at SFSU in 2010 and since that time my teaching responsibilities have included AIS 320, American Indian Music, which examines the music and dance of intertribal powwows. The class offers students the opportunity to learn about Northern Plains powwow singing and drumming through participation at a powwow drum under my direction as instructor and lead singer. Every semester students learn to perform between five and ten powwow songs, and, if circumstances allow, they present those songs in public. For example, students from my 2014 class performed an Honor Song at the graduation ceremony held by the Student Kouncil of Intertribal Nations, SFSU's Native student organization.

I learned to apply the powwow drum as a teaching tool in this fashion from Dr. Bernard Hoehner, a respected Lakȟóta elder, singer, powwow emcee, and Northern Traditional dancer. He taught American Indian studies at SFSU for more than twenty years, until his passing in October 1995. Born and raised on the Standing Rock Reservation in South Dakota, his Húŋkpapȟa and Sihásapa lineage includes his grandfather, Chief John Grass, a leader in his nation's struggle for land rights. Hoehner served in the U.S. Marine Corps during World War II, and in 1970 he joined the American Indian studies faculty at SFSU, where he taught courses in music, language, earth science, and religion. His many accomplishments at SFSU included founding the Blue Horse Singers, a Northern Plains style drum group made up of SFSU faculty and students as well as local community members, and producing *Hymns in Lakota*, a recording of hymns sung in the Lakȟóta language (Hoehner n.d.). I was fortunate to take American Indian Music with Hoehner as an undergraduate in the early 1990s and to sing with him as a member of the Blue Horse Singers. Reflecting on my experiences as his student, I can recall multiple instances in which faculty and administrators confronted him for "making too much noise" when he used the drum to teach. On one occasion in particular, I remember an administrator interrupting

Hoehner in front of students as he sat at the drum. I could not hear what the administrator said, but I clearly remember Hoehner standing up and exclaiming, "This isn't noise. Do not call my music noise."

Hoehner's teaching pedagogy may be located within the larger history of other American Indian music ensembles at U.S. universities. These include, but are not limited to, the E-Yah-Pah-Ha chanters led by Louis Ballard (Quapaw, Cherokee) at the Institute of American Indian Arts in the late 1960s (Flahive 2012, 66; Institute of American Indian Arts 1972, 20–21); the American Indian Ensemble at the University of California, Los Angeles in the 1970s taught by Charlotte Heth (Cherokee); and the residencies conducted by William Horncloud (Lakȟóta) at Wesleyan University in the 1970s and by Helma Swan (Makah) at Colorado College in the 1970s and 1980s. In addition, Hoehner's use of the drum as a teaching tool resonates with the fish-camp science odyssey curriculum developed by the Yupiaq scientist and educator Oscar Angayuqaq Kawagley. The fish-camp curriculum provides a means through which to seek praxis in the teaching of subjects ranging from science to music to philosophy (2006, 107). Kawagley explains, "Students can first learn their language, learn about themselves, learn values of their society, and then begin to branch out to the rest of the world. They may later make a choice as to what they want to do and where to live. Given such a foundation, they can fearlessly enter any world of their choice, secure in their identity and abilities and with dignity as human beings" (87). The fish camp and the powwow drum both become fluid spaces through which Native students can form a personal identity while also learning how to navigate different sociocultural contexts. The diverse ways in which it is possible to be Indian are emphasized, as opposed to the expectation of singularity and stasis.

Student and faculty responses to my class have been mostly positive, but there have been moments of tension between myself and other members of the campus community who find my class disruptive. In the course of teaching powwow singing and drumming, I have been interrupted regularly by instructors from neighboring classrooms who ask me to "stop making so much noise." On one occasion, while I was giving a guest lecture on powwow music, someone stormed into the classroom and demanded that I stop singing or he would have me arrested by the campus police for creating a disturbance. Sometimes when my class meets outdoors, we have been surrounded—at a distance—by university police officers either because of a noise complaint or an unspoken concern that this "noise" could be a precursor to a campus protest. My students become aware very quickly of what constitutes acceptable music and what constitutes noise in a university setting. To ground my students in Native concepts of powwow music, I explain the sounds of the drum and singers using the concept of the four circles of the powwow as taught to me by Hoehner. Different articulations of the four-circles model exist in tribal worldviews and in the ethnomusicological literature (cf. Browner 2002; Young Bear and Theisz 1994). Given my training in Lakȟóta powwow practices through Hoehner, the following discussion privileges Lakȟóta oral and written sources.

The Lakȟóta word for drum is čháŋčheǧa, which translates as "wooden bucket." The drum occupies the first circle of the powwow because its voice gathers the people who make up the other three circles: singers, dancers, and other community members. The voice of the drum is commonly referred to as a heartbeat, because, according to the Lakȟóta elder Severt Young Bear, it represents the heartbeat of uŋčí, or grandmother earth, "the sound vibrating in the earth" (Young Bear and Theisz 1994, 47). The drum is placed at the center of the dance area out of respect for the symbolism embedded in its construction (J.-C. Perea 2014, 25–28). Wooden drum frames and animal-hide drumheads are not simply decorative; they also symbolize the relationship between human beings and the environment of which they are a part. Young Bear explains that the sound of the powwow drum signifies both social and sacred relationships: "If there was going to be a *tokala* warrior society dance, they'd hit [the drum] in a certain way. If it was another type of event, they'd hit it in a certain other way. . . . The sound of the drum would add a loud sound that accompanied your voice to give it strength and power, or for the Great Spirit to hear your songs beyond your own limits" (Young Bear and Theisz 1994, 47). The voice of the drum, then, is not simply the sound of an inanimate object; it is the sound of the relationship between human beings and the world around them. The act of striking the drum also implies a responsibility in that one may be asking for strength or undertaking sacred communication by drumming and singing. This fluid relationship between the social and sacred sound of the powwow drum carries over into the second and third circles of the powwow and the sounds made by men and women singers.

Hoehner referred to a male singer as ȟʼokȟá wičháša, or "a man who knows how to rattle his voice." The term rattling refers here to the use of vibrato as part of Northern Plains singing technique. The ethnomusicologist William K. Powers provides other useful information on the sound of powwow singing from an Oglála Lakȟóta perspective. He writes that "the proper way to sing the introduction is *pan* 'to whine, cry'; the second should be sung *akiša*, a general term relating to both human and animal cries of a piercing nature. . . . *Yupesto* is used to indicate excellent attack in the introduction of [the] second. It means 'to sharpen,' as one would sharpen a pencil or stick" (1986, 56). These terms speak to both the rattling quality of Northern Plains singing and its characteristic high pitch. Hoehner often explained that the high pitch of the Northern Plains style was meant to communicate in the same way as the urgent cry of a newborn baby (J.-C. Perea 2014, 27; see also Hatton 1990). That sonic analogy relates to the third circle, the women singers who stand behind the drum. Hoehner referred to the female singers as *wičháglatA*, which he translated as "songbirds." Powers translates *wičháglatA* as "responders," since the women singing from behind the drum "trail slightly behind the men's [singing] at the end of each song" (1986, 58). The gendered dynamics present in these explanations and in the four-circles model continue to be the subject of scholarly and community debate (cf. Hoefnagels 2012), and such concerns are crucial to understanding recent changes in powwow musical practice, such as the founding of all-women powwow drums. Hoehner maintained that the third circle of the powwow separated women from men singers as an acknowledgment of the power and responsibility of motherhood. In this interpretation the sound of powwow drumming and singing references familial relationships and also signals the creation of new kin groups over time. The interpretation does not detract from research on gender and power in powwow singing; rather, it nuances the complexity of powwow musicking in diverse social contexts. The fourth circle of dancers and community members dance and move according to their own responsibilities throughout powwow space, and those movements are related back to the drum as it sounds throughout different events in the powwow agenda.

Whereas Hoehner's model of the four circles is useful in the classroom to address the physical, spatial, and gendered relationships present in powwows, similar models have been articulated by Severt Young Bear and Tara Browner. Young Bear expands the idea of the four circles to delve more deeply into Lakȟóta identity formation (Young Bear and Theisz 1994, 176–77). He begins by discussing his experience of the use of space at the Sun Dance, where the first circle comprises "two thin circles . . . *wawiyokpia* (spreading of humor), where the sacred clowns do their antics to take the edge off feelings with their humor" and "*otakuye* (relatives) ring, where honorable relatives take part with their kids." The second circle is "*wawaynaka* (looking at something clean) . . . witnessing and observing what is being done in the center, but [it] is often passive and lets the center do those things." The third circle is "the courting circle . . . *wiyapaya* (by choice you bump into each other)." Young Bear's fourth circle is a space in which people have "lost their ways or they don't want to be identified with what's being done out there. They don't understand what's going on in the center two circles, so they stay back in the dark. This is the circle of the *omuniyata* (lost or disconnected)." This formulation may be useful in terms of developing an Indigenized map of the university soundscape that could locate culturally relevant relationships in spaces such as classrooms and other public meeting areas where powwow musicking occurs.

Browner juxtaposes two diagrams of powwow space, one given to her by George Martin (Ojibwe) that contains seven circles and one she calls a typical perception of powwow space among non-Indians (2002, 98). The diagrams by Hoehner and Martin are similar, except that the latter adds three additional circles to include elders, audience members, and spirit beings. It is interesting to note how Martin distinguishes elders from other audience members in his formulation and, as Browner notes, also includes spirit beings as social participants in the powwow.

PRESENT(S): POWWOW MUSICKING AND "NOISE"

Understanding the roles and meanings of singing and drumming within the contexts of powwows and classrooms marks both activities as musical and articulates tribal worldviews relating to ecological and familial relationships on social and sacred levels. How, then, have these sounds come to be heard as noise within the university soundscape? Schafer provides four possible definitions of noise: unwanted sound, unmusical sound, any loud sound, or a disturbance in any signaling system. He notes that the most satisfactory of these definitions is unwanted sound but recognizes the subjective quality of such a distinction (1994, 273). Truax also recognizes the subjectivity inherent in defining noise, adding that "although the subjective definition may be adequate in some situations, it should be realized on the larger scale it reflects, supports, and encourages desensitization of the majority at the expense of reactions and feelings of the minority" (2001, 95). At SFSU I have experienced the subjectivity of these definitions and therefore find them useful to frame a discussion of selected reactions to my class as noise.

Since I began teaching the course, American Indian Music has been housed in a number of different campus locations, so the question of space has influenced the reception of my class. At first I taught the class in Burk Hall, occupied primarily by the Graduate College of Education. In this location some faculty found the incursion of powwow musicking noisy in that the sounds were unwanted and loud in the context of their own classroom environments. I respected faculty complaints at the time because the classrooms in Burk Hall lack sound mitigation, and the building is not zoned for sound in the same way as is the Creative Arts building, which houses the School of Music at SFSU. Brandon LaBelle considers the issue of zoning and appropriate use according to "the logic of place, and what appears *out of place*. . . . Noise by definition is that sound which occurs *where* it should not. It finds its way in, to disrupt the particular setting" (2010, 47). Yet LaBelle also finds positive outcomes in the process of disruption, however, and argues that "noise might act as a form of deviation that . . . can fully aid in the *emergence* of a community" (84). Therefore, it is also important to consider the productive moments that emerged from these interactions in the early history of the class.

Noise complaints in Burk Hall did generate a sense of community. Because of campus space constraints at the time it was not possible to house the class in Creative Arts, so I reached out to the other faculty housed around me to try to form alliances from our shared experience. In some cases I was able to speak to the instructors with whom I shared space in Burk Hall to inform them about the particulars of my class. I made it a point to invite those faculty and their students into my classes so that they could see and learn about what was taking place. Some faculty told me that when the sounds of our musicking became audible in their rooms, former students in my class identified themselves and explained what was happening, even translating the songs being sung to explain their significance. This helped to contextualize the sounds being heard and so changed their reception from intrusive noise to music, which could be understood and incorporated into the acoustic ecology of the university soundscape. An unexpected community emerged as students began to enroll in American Indian Music after having taken a nearby class that submitted a noise complaint. In other words the early experience of receiving noise complaints had both positive and negative effects that continue to characterize the class to this day.

In 2011, after receiving a noise complaint from a colleague in Burk Hall, I asked to move American Indian Music to the Creative Arts building. It took a few weeks to get the change approved, and, given the fact that I no longer wished to sing in a room where I had received complaints, my class sang outdoors in front of the ethnic studies and psychology building. University police officers then began to observe the class from a distance. On one occasion a police officer actually approached one of my students while we were singing to ask what was happening. The student explained that we were a scheduled class and were singing outside because we were in the process of moving to a new classroom. The officer thanked the student and left the scene. I was unaware of the interaction at the time because I was leading the class in a song, but the student recounted what had happened as soon as I finished the song. In discussing the interaction the students suggested that since ethnic studies and psychology are located directly across from Burk Hall, the sound of the drumming and singing may have bounced back and forth between the two buildings, increasing the reverberation and volume. Jean-François Augoyard and Henry Torgue note that the psychological and physiological experience of reverberation embodies a number of factors, including "the presence of something or someone beside oneself," "the feeling of 'collectivity' and the sharing of social communication," and "the propensity toward a narcissistic attitude as a sound mirror in situations of individual sound productions" (2005, 115). Whereas the class tends to experience these factors in a positive fashion owing to the cultural knowledge the students acquire throughout the semester, any of these factors may have caused the singing to be perceived as unwanted or loud sounds that may have motivated a noise complaint.

Our physical location in front of the ethnic studies and psychology building may also have suggested the start of a protest action, given the long history of my department and the College of Ethnic Studies on campus. The college emerged as the result of student demands articulated during the Third World Liberation Front Strike of 1968 (cf. Whitson 1999; J. E. Perea 1985). Luis S. Kemnitzer notes that, after the strike, Richard Oakes (Mohawk), Al Miller (Seminole), and several other Native students were admitted to sfsu and went on to play central roles in the occupation of Alcatraz Island in 1969 (1997, 115). In relation to music studies, Sherrie Tucker further explains that "it is crucial to recall the five-month Third World Strike at San Francisco State University in 1968 that mobilized, and was part of, a larger movement in which students, faculty, and staff risked degrees, jobs, and careers because it was *that important* to infuse the academy with hitherto marginalized perspectives, theories, experiences, histories, and insights. The invigorating shake-up that awoke the critical potential, interdisciplinary possibilities, and social relevance of the university in the 1960s and 1970s transformed American studies and facilitated much American music scholarship of those years" (Garrett et al. 2011, 704). These histories recirculate on a constant basis throughout the campus through classes, yearly anniversary events, and conferences. Additionally they recirculate in student-led creations of exhibits such as *We Are Still Here*, which provides a permanent acknowledgment of the 1969 occupation of Alcatraz for visitors to the island, which is now a National Historic Landmark (San Francisco

State University 2013). Therefore, our location in physical and, for some listeners, historical proximity to these events may have been a cause for concern.

When considered in relation to the long history of student activism at SFSU, the presence of police during our outdoor singing sessions assumes important implications with regard to both the disciplining of noise and the disciplining of student bodies. Schafer clarifies his fourth definition of noise, "a disturbance of any signaling system," as referring to "electronics and engineering . . . static on a telephone or snow on a television screen" (1994, 273). If, however, one understands the university environment as its own signaling system, then why would powwow musicking function as a disturbance that necessitates police intervention? In his analysis of Jeremy Bentham's Panopticon, a circular prison in which inmates could be observed at all times and from all directions, Michel Foucault writes that "the Panopticon . . . must be understood as a generalizable model of functioning; a way of defining power relations in terms of the everyday life of men. . . . It is the diagram of a mechanism of power reduced to its ideal form" (1995, 205). The university environment similarly represents its own generalizable model of functioning based on the definition of power relationships among students, faculty, staff, and administrators. Those power relationships are in part dependent on the disciplining of unwanted, unmusical, and loud sounds and the bodies that make those sounds, since they represent static in the signaling system of education.

Whereas Foucault emphasizes the visual throughout his analysis, he qualifies the sonic aspect of the Panopticon as surveillance in silence: "in these conditions, its strength is that it never intervenes, it is exercised spontaneously and *without noise*, it constitutes a mechanism whose effects follow from one another" (1995, 206). LaBelle's research on the Auburn State Prison in New York also addresses the relationship between silence and noise: "The silent system is a disciplinary silence designed to bear down on the body as the final mark of the law and to force the criminal into a state of deep solitude while quite often leading to insanity" (2010, 71). Applying this to my class, the recognition of the function of silence as a mode of discipline raises several questions with regard to the disciplining of sound in a university context. Does powwow musicking represent a disturbance in the signaling system of the university because it interrupts the transmission of knowledge? Or does powwow musicking represent an interruption in an educational system that has normalized Native American disappearance as a consequence of genocide and forced assimilation, making the contemporary performance of that music a radical act on campus?

Like the social encounters in Burk Hall, the outdoor class experiences generated both positive and negative outcomes. The noise complaints we received while
singing outside caused concern for myself, my students, and my department,
but they also provided another form of publicity that exposed a larger cross-
section of the campus community to powwow singing and drumming. From the
students' perspective, singing outside was difficult for a number of reasons. We
held discussions around the drum in an attempt to alleviate frustrations, and,
whereas there was support for my decision to move outside, many students felt
that their rights were being violated because they were paying for a class that
lacked a classroom. Students were also concerned about the police presence
but tended to take it as a point of pride because it made them feel connected to
campus histories of activism. In general, students bonded through the experience and went on to advocate for the class in their own circuits across campus.

Since 2011 American Indian Music has been housed in the Creative Arts
building. I hoped that this move would prove friendlier and that perhaps the
class could work in tandem with courses in jazz and world music to mediate the
university soundscape.[3] But this move has not been without its problems. When
the class first landed in Creative Arts, we were assigned to a multipurpose "green
room" in a heavily trafficked hallway directly across from the recital hall, which
is used for rehearsals and performances by string, wind, and jazz ensembles.
By the end of our first semester in Creative Arts, campus administrators told
me that the class would have to move again because of noise complaints. We
relocated to another room in Creative Arts away from the recital hall and in a
lower traffic area. To my knowledge there have been no noise complaints yet.
Ironically, the migration of my American Indian Music class around the SFSU
campus recalls the forced removals and relocations of many Native peoples since
the colonization of North America.

Classroom location and volume have no doubt influenced the reception of
powwow musicking as noise at SFSU, but I do not believe that the issues I have
faced, or Hoehner before me, are solely a matter of finding the appropriate venue.
Under these circumstances it is also important to reflect on other factors that
may influence the reception of powwow musicking on campus. The historian
Richard Cullen Rath addresses the question of religious and social influences
on the reception of Native voices, explaining that early European colonists used
the soundscape of the "howling wilderness" as a means through which to define
space and place. He writes, "Puritan chroniclers used the howling or roaring
wilderness to hold down the outer reaches of their landscapes. In Deuteronomy

[32:10], the Hebrew God is said to have plucked Jacob out of such a 'waste howling wilderness' to found Israel, so the Puritan errand to the wilderness was a symbolic return to the place where God had chosen his people. . . . What howled most often in colonists' perceptions of their wilderness were not wind or wolves, but Indians. Colonists did not have to imagine the voices of those they fashioned their wilderness demons" (2003, 147). The concept of the howling wilderness had a lasting effect on the way non-Natives perceive and conceive of American Indian music.

Religious narratives also had an impact on Euro-American perceptions of, and federal policy toward, Native music and dance. Scholars cite the example of the Bureau of Indian Affairs commissioner Charles Burke, who wrote in 1921 that Indian dancing "under the most primitive and pagan conditions, is apt to be harmful, and when found so among Indians we should control it by educational measures as far as possible, but if necessary, by punitive measures when its degrading tendencies persist" (cf. Browner 2002, 29; Troutman 2009, 67–68). Burke's circulars restricting Native dance and music remained influential until 1934, when John Collier Sr. became head of the Bureau of Indian Affairs. John Troutman illustrates the ways in which attitudes of this kind came to influence the educational philosophy of early Indian boarding schools, which were intended to force assimilation and cultural loss, but he also highlights moments of resistance and survivance emanating from Native nations in response to these policies. Diamond discusses similar situations in Canada's Indian Residential Schools (2015a). Many students in my American Indian Music class are surprised to learn that federal restrictions on Native music and dance were relaxed only in 1934 and that the historical trauma from those restrictions continues to resonate in the twenty-first century.

Religious, social, and political restrictions on Native music and dance were motivated to a great degree by fear. Fear as an affective factor in the reception of sound has been addressed in several sources. Karin Bijsterveld writes that "the historiography and anthropology of sound make clear that noise and silence refer to deeply rooted cultural hierarchies" (2008, 40). She cites the work of the historian Peter Bailey (1996), which outlines "three types of socially defined noise: noise as merriment, such as laughter; noise as embarrassment, such as a fart; and noise as terror" (qtd. in Bijsterveld 2008, 32). Here again cultural context plays a significant role in conditioning the reception of powwow musicking. At the beginning of every semester I conduct an exercise in which I ask my students to listen to a recording of Northern Plains powwow music and to write down their impressions of the music. Many of those first impressions involve descriptors that, over time, have included yelling, shouting, screaming, and shrieking. My students therefore emphasize terror and embarrassment in defining the "affective tone" (Goodman 2012, xiv) of Northern Plains powwow singing. Over the course of the semester we work together toward a shared sonic space in which students come to acknowledge that they do not have to love powwow music, but they do have a responsibility to understand the songs as articulations of lived experience and meaningful cultural expression and not simply as noise.

I find it useful to show the students that terror in relation to American Indian music may be discerned very early in the ethnomusicological literature. For example, Alice Fletcher wrote in her 1893 study of Omaha Indian music that "I think I may safely say that I heard little or nothing of Indian music the first three or four times that I attended dances or festivals, beyond a screaming downward movement that was gashed and torn by the vehemently beaten drum." Of course, she follows this description with an account of her journey toward a better understanding of the context and musicality of what she was actually hearing: "I therefore began to *listen below this noise*, much as one must listen to the phonograph, ignoring the sound of the machinery before the registered tones of the voice are caught" ([1893] 1994, 7; emphasis added). Fletcher recognized the need to listen below the noise of her own fear to achieve a better understanding of what she was hearing, and this process of learning to listen below the noise remains very relevant to my students.

FUTURE(S): SOUNDING THE DRUM AT SFSU

To find a safe space for powwow music within the university soundscape, it is necessary to address the legacies of terror and embarrassment as articulated through religious, social, and political restrictions that have shaped the reception of powwow music among non-Natives. An important aspect of the continuing research on the intersections between Indigeneity and noise involves examining how anamnesis affects the reception of powwow musicking among the SFSU campus community. Jean-François Augoyard and Henry Torgue define anamnesis as "an effect of reminiscence in which a past situation or atmosphere is brought back to the listener's consciousness provoked by a particular signal or sonic context." They note that "the more distant and *unexpected* the reference the more the emotion may overwhelm the listener. The effect is not based on the sound or on its meaning. It is rather the listener who gives it anamnesic value" (2005, 21; emphasis added). When students discuss their first reactions to powwow music in my class, many focus on the high pitch and bright timbre of Northern Plains singing, which triggers their associations with warfare and violence. Augoyard and Torgue explain that "sound colour has such an influence on emotional response that anything linked to *timbre*... may be likely to induce anamnesis" (23; emphasis added). The questions of timbre and whether powwow musicking represents an interruption in an educational system that normalizes American Indian disappearance have significant implications for the future of Native music in the university soundscape. Attention to the phenomenon of anamnesis may provide data as to the positive and negative reactions listeners associate with their experience of music. In the case of powwow musicking, such data might suggest avenues through which to generate dialogue between the lived experiences listeners bring to their reception of powwow musicking and Native ways of knowing and understanding the voice of the drum and the singers. This resonates with current research on weaponizing sound (cf. Volcler 2013) and may facilitate interdisciplinary studies relevant to a wide range of interested communities.

From my perspective it is important to continue to sound the drum at SFSU, regardless of noise complaints. In response to Andra McCartney's call to "approach complexity in thinking about sound environments" (2013), I also want to account for the partiality of my own experience by considering silence in the design of future classes. Nomi Dave has written about violence and protest in Guinea, noting that "young musicians in Conkary use silence, quietness, and inarticulation as tactics of playful evasion to balance their aspirations and needs. Silence thus represents not just the denial or lack of voice, but a particular strategy of communication and being in an authoritarian state" (2014, 2). Whereas the political contexts are obviously different, the mobilization of silence raises important questions relevant to the long-term sustainability of the class. In years past I have alternated singing during the spring semester with a fall survey class that lacks the performance component. Students in the fall survey ask where the drum is and why they do not get to sing. This leads to powerful discussions on the nature of powwow musicking in the university environment and its reception as noise, which furthers many of the points raised in this chapter.

There are no simple answers to the questions I've raised. To paraphrase the Comanche museum curator Paul Chaat Smith (2009, 36), I prefer to continue to pose questions, since the process of questioning facilitates discussion and continued journey. In the context of teaching powwow music in a university setting, I find it important to continue to engage in research and dialogue because it illuminates the many nuances through which the social activity of music is received by and transmitted among my students. While it is tempting to assume that volume and location are the primary factors influencing the reception of my class, socialization, together with religious and political concepts of noise, also play a role in the way my students relate to powwow music and other components of course content. For many of my Native students, the experience of sitting at the drum—whether or not they continue to sing at the drum after the class ends—is an important means through which they negotiate their own urban Indigeneity as complex yet empowering (Sissons 2005). This parallels my own experience of studying powwow music with Dr. Hoehner, which gave me a sense of personal identity, because in the process of learning about his Lakȟóta musical culture, I also began to learn about my own Mescalero Apache musical culture. These complex sounds demand continued interdisciplinary attention and discussion based on culturally informed definitions of Native music that interrogates the concept of noise. In this way I hope to ensure that powwow drumming and singing remain present and accessible in a classroom environment for future generations of SFSU students.

This chapter originated as a conference presentation at the northern California chapter meeting of the Society for Ethnomusicology (University of San Francisco, March 2, 2013). I am grateful to the volume editors, Vicki Levine and Dylan Robinson, as well as to the other contributors to this volume, for their constructive feedback during our 2013 writing retreat in Indianapolis. I would also like to thank Dirk Alphin, Joanne Barker, C. D. Ka'ala Carmack, Robert Collins, Andrew Jolivétte, Phil Klasky, Eddie Madril, Kenneth Monteiro, Richard Moves Camp, Melissa Nelson, Barbara Perea, Jessica Bissett Perea, Jacob Perea, Amy Sueyoshi, and Kathy Wallace for their support of, and contributions to, my American Indian Music class and this chapter. None of this would be possible without the support and trust of students past and present who have taken AIS 320 while attending SFSU.

BYRON DUECK

9. Powwow and Indigenous Modernities
Traditional Music, Public Education, and Child Welfare

Public education and child-welfare services are widely regarded as structures that enlightened societies have established to ensure equal opportunity and well-being, yet these institutions have been responsible for some of the most disruptive consequences of colonialism among Indigenous people in Canada. Drawing on ethnographic fieldwork and interviews conducted in the province of Manitoba, mostly in 2013, this chapter explores how Indigenous people are addressing these colonial legacies; how powwow and traditional cultural practices are being incorporated into schooling and child-welfare provision; and what various parties understand tradition to achieve in these new contexts. Above all, it considers how Indigenous actors articulate Indigenous modernities around the very institutions the settler state once deployed to separate them from their culture.

A POWWOW CLUB IN WINNIPEG

Winnipeg, the Manitoban city where I have conducted fieldwork on and off since 2002, has one of the largest urban Indigenous populations anywhere in North America (see NUIFC 2008; U.S. Census Bureau 2012; Statistics Canada 2017) and is home to large numbers of both Métis and First Nations people. The majority of the latter are Northern Algonquians—Ojibwe, Cree, and Oji-Cree—but there are also Dakota and Dene and others whose traditional territories lie still farther away.[1] Not surprisingly, the city is home to a wide range of Indigenous musical practices, one of which is powwow.

My connection to the powwow scene in Winnipeg owes much to Ray and Rhonda Stevenson, who have been teaching Native children to sing and dance for more than two decades. In 2002, when we met, they ran weekly powwow clubs for Ma Mawi Wi Chi Itata, a child- and family-service organization serving an urban Indigenous population. Around that time they estimated that half of the children who came to the clubs were in the province's foster-care system. The clubs had been a great success, and, despite having daytime jobs, Ray and Rhonda ran meetings on several work nights each week.

I attended a few of these at a community center in Winnipeg's West Broadway neighborhood. They began with smudging and prayer followed by singing, with the remainder of the session devoted to practicing common dance styles: Jingle Dress and Fancy Shawl for the girls, Grass Dances for the boys.[2] The clubs were also a point of entry to other aspects of contemporary Indigenous tradition: in addition to smudging, children learned ceremonial songs and protocols related to dancing and drums. They were also offered opportunities, outside the clubs themselves, to participate in sweat lodges and receive their Indian names (sometimes called spirit names) and colors. Rhonda's remarks in a 2003 interview reflect these broader connections:

> [Ma Mawi Wi Chi Itata] offered . . . a separate component . . . linked to the powwow club, where they do sweat lodges and stuff, so a lot of [the children] learn that. . . . They've gone through sweat lodge ceremonies, where they get their names and stuff, so they do go into a bit more depth with that. . . . In the powwow club . . . we . . . explain everything that we do, even with the medicines and stuff . . . we use. There's other stuff around dancing, though, and females, that has to be said, whether it's for the parents, the foster parents, or the kids themselves. (Interview, Winnipeg, August 25, 2003)

When I visited Winnipeg in 2013, Ma Mawi (as it is often called) still ran powwow clubs three nights a week and in much the same format. As was the case a decade earlier, some of the attendees were children in foster care, although they now made up a much smaller proportion of the whole, and the gatherings were attended by larger numbers of non-Indigenous children. Ray and Rhonda had moved on and led another club that met in the student center of a downtown university campus. At one of these meetings, Ray announced that in a few days he would be emceeing a powwow at a school in the eastern part of the city. He invited attendees to come and participate; the powwow was to get underway at four in the afternoon with a pipe ceremony, followed by a meeting of participants and the grand entry. Those who took part in their powwow outfits would receive an honorarium.[3]

The powwow was a traditional event like others I have witnessed, albeit much compressed in terms of time. I arrived after the pipe ceremony but in time for the feast of stew, bannock, and wild saskatoon pie. The gathering was held in the school's gymnasium, with the emcee's table and many of the drums set up along one wall and the bleachers opposite serving as seating. There were perhaps seventy dancers and eight drum groups, as well as a large, but not capacity, audience. When the feast had finished and the dancers had gathered with the arena director, Ray announced the grand entry over the PA system. He explained that Aboriginal people believe the dance circle on earth coincides with another in heaven and that when people dance down here, our grandmothers and grandfathers dance up there. He asked the drum group to sing one verse, telling participants in the grand entry to wait until this was finished to start, so the grandmothers and grandfathers could dance first. The grand entry then began. Veterans and elders, carrying flags and eagle staffs, moved into the gymnasium, followed by dignitaries and the dancers in regalia. They processed clockwise until everyone was in, the vanguard halting in front of the emcee's table and the host drum. As the assembled participants stood, an elder prayed in Anishinaabemowin (Ojibwe), explaining something of what he had said afterward in English. There followed a Flag Song, an Honor Song, and introductions of special guests.

The dancing then got under way; eight intertribals, dances in which anyone could participate, were followed by an Honor Song acknowledging the organizing committee and a demonstration of Hoop Dancing, in which dancers used hoops to create figures, including flowers and thunderbirds. After this was a series of dances categorized by age, gender, and genre. This began with dances for tiny tots, juniors, and teens, in which boys and girls performed side by side. Then came dances for older participants in several core styles: women's Fancy Shawl, Jingle Dress, and Traditional Dances and men's Grass and Traditional Dances. The event concluded with the exit of flags. The drum groups in attendance—each comprising several men seated around a large circular drum—accompanied the dancing with songs in the asymmetrical form that has spread alongside the powwow throughout North America (see Powers 1990; Goertzen 2001; Browner 2002, 2009a; Hoefnagels 2002; Whidden 2007; Levine and Nettl 2011). They performed in the northern style, in a high range and with tense voices. As it was a traditional powwow, performers did not compete for cash prizes (see Scales

2007); nevertheless, those who had come in dance outfits received small gifts of money, as Ray had promised.

The powwow had been made possible in part by Aboriginal Academic Achievement (AAA) funding from the Manitoban government, I soon learned. As the website of the school division that hosted the event explained, the grant allowed the division to provide "authentic and successful Aboriginal cultural programming" to students and staff by integrating Indigenous perspectives in curriculum and offering a range of cultural activities, including powwows like the one I had seen, as well as presentations on drumming, dancing, the medicine wheel, the Seven Sacred Teachings, and plant medicines (RETSD 2014). The site also explained that AAA aimed to "enhance Aboriginal academic achievement." As discussed at greater length later, the Manitoban government emphasizes this last goal, rather than cultural programming, in its own descriptions of AAA funding. For example, a 2013 publication explains that it assists school divisions with programs "that target academic success for Aboriginal students" (MDEAL 2013).[4]

POWWOW, SCHOOLING, AND CHILD-WELFARE PROVISION

The incorporation of powwow and other traditional or neotraditional practices in public education and child welfare marks a dramatic historical reversal. During the colonial era, schools and child-welfare agencies separated Indigenous children from their communities and traditional ways of life; today the same institutions attempt to reconnect them to their culture. This section outlines aspects of this history, including Residential Schools, the "Sixties and Seventies Scoop," and the subsequent transfer of responsibility for education and child welfare to Indigenous communities and governments.

During the most intensive period of Canadian colonialism, the state openly attempted to assimilate Indigenous children by means of education. Between the 1880s and the 1970s, tens of thousands of students were sent to Residential Schools, where they lived, studied, and worked for months or years at a time, often hundreds of miles from their families and communities.[5] Residential Schools interrupted the transmission of Native languages, knowledge, and values, seeking to replace these with Euro-Canadian ones, although the quality of education and care was often very poor. Vulnerable and far from home, many students were subject to physical and sexual abuse.

As the era of Residential Schools was ending, another arm of the welfare state was beginning to separate Indigenous children from their families. From the 1960s, when provincial governments began to provide child-welfare services to Native communities, until the early 1980s—a period sometimes called "the Sixties and Seventies Scoop"—disproportionately large numbers of Indigenous children were taken from their homes and placed with foster parents or adoptive families, many non-Indigenous. Patrick Johnston writes that, while in some cases, the children were genuinely at risk, in many others, welfare workers seem to have believed they would be better off with non-Native families (1983, 23). Yvonne Pompana goes further, arguing that an ostensible concern for "the best interests of the child" justified the imposition of "mainstream values on Aboriginal families" (2009, 16). Even as the federal government was phasing out assimilation-oriented Residential Schools, then, provincial institutions were taking inordinate numbers of Indigenous children away from their families and placing them in non-Indigenous homes. Consciously or not, child-welfare interventions perpetuated the same kinds of cultural interruptions.[6]

Advocacy by Indigenous communities brought about changes. In 1972 the National Indian Brotherhood presented a position paper calling for "Indian Control of Indian Education" (NIB [1972] 2014). The federal government drew on this paper in establishing a new educational policy and began to transfer administrative responsibility for primary and secondary schooling to Indigenous communities during the 1970s and 1980s (Canada 2011, 8). It also phased out Residential Schools.[7] Most First Nations in Manitoba now run their own schools (see MFNERC 2013), and it is increasingly common for Indigenous-language instruction and immersion, as well as traditional knowledge, to be incorporated in curricula.[8] Notwithstanding the transfer of control over First Nations education, large numbers of Indigenous students still attend schools run by provincial governments; the powwow described earlier was hosted by one of these.[9] Here, too, there has been an attempt to consult Native groups regarding education. In Manitoba an Aboriginal Education Directorate, advised by councils representing the province's Indigenous populations, helps to develop educational initiatives and policy (AED 2014a). And since the 1990s the province has sought to incorporate Indigenous perspectives in educational curricula (MDEAL 2014a).

There has also been a transfer of control to Indigenous groups in the area of child welfare. In Manitoba this process began in 1981, when the province assigned oversight of child welfare in eight First Nations communities to an agency run by the Dakota Ojibway Tribal Council (Pompana 2009, 119). Another major step came in 2003, when Manitoba began to transfer responsibility for Indigenous child welfare to three authorities (one Métis and two First Nations) that today serve Indigenous people across the province (Pompana 2009, 236–50; FNNMCFS 2013). It is unclear how much autonomy these authorities have, since they are accountable to the province and operate under the oversight of the Department of Families. Nevertheless, Indigenous input into child-welfare provision is much more direct than a few decades ago.

Reflecting the greater input Indigenous people have in schooling and child welfare, powwow instruction for young people has become increasingly common in both areas. There was little powwow-related activity in Winnipeg schools when I began fieldwork in 2002, but by 2013 seven of the seventy-seven schools in the Winnipeg School Division (the largest of the city's six school divisions) advertised a powwow club, an annual powwow, or an affiliated drum group on their websites (WSD 2013). The most active of the schools offered a weekly powwow club, a Hoop Dancing club, and drum groups for boys and girls, among other programs. There has been a similar effort to incorporate traditional practices in child-welfare provision. In the early 2000s Dakota Ojibway Child and Family Services hired cultural workers and established a cultural camp for foster families where children could participate in activities such as drumming, singing, playing the moccasin game, and sweat lodge ceremonies (Pompana 2009, 279–80). At around the same time, Ma Mawi Wi Chi Itata, the human-service organization introduced earlier, began to offer powwow clubs and cultural instruction to children in care. State education and child welfare have thus undergone a striking shift: the same institutions responsible for interrupting the transmission of Indigenous languages and practices seem today committed to reconnecting Native children to tradition.

INDIGENOUS CHARACTERIZATIONS
OF CONTEMPORARY POWWOW INSTRUCTION

The Indigenous people I talked to often spoke about tradition using the words "the culture," by which they meant a way of life that was spiritually centered, morally right, and in touch with the Creator and "our grandmothers and grand-fathers" (spirit relations both human and more than human). As noted earlier, powwow clubs presented a range of opportunities to become familiar with the culture, and activities at these clubs were widely understood to be linked to larger realms of sacred practice. Most of the Indigenous people with whom I spoke regarded the surge of interest in the culture positively, and in this section

I outline a number of things they believed it to accomplish. First and foremost, they understood it to ameliorate the damage caused by colonialism, Residential Schooling, and the child-welfare scoop. Wayne Ruby, a powwow singer and leader at a Winnipeg powwow club, explained, "When we practiced our culture [in Residential Schools], we got hit. . . . And basically after that . . . CFS [Child and Family Services] came along. And the kids were taken away from the parents. And they weren't placed within other Aboriginal communities; they were placed within . . . basically, white man's home. . . . That's why the culture was slowly vanishing. . . . And, basically, that's why [we have] powwow club: because the culture's vanishing and it needs to come back." Patricia Olson, a teacher of traditional singing and dancing at a public school with a large Indigenous student population, said of a powwow to be held at the school: "We want everybody to have a piece of what they've lost" (interviews, Winnipeg, October 4, 2013). And Rhonda Stevenson, explaining how young people find themselves through powwow clubs, said,

> [We] still work with kids that are . . . in the [child-welfare] system. . . . It's just the history with the sixties scoop way back when. . . . We just have a genera-tion of people that didn't raise their kids. . . . [The] young people now are still . . . learning who they are. . . . If you're from a family that's always been doing [powwow], and you've . . . grown up in it . . . then you've learnt that from day one: all the skills and the dancing, the singing, the beliefs, the traditions. But a lot of the kids that are in care, they've had that disconnection. So . . . when we're doing this stuff with the kids [we're trying to make] that reconnection. (Interview, Winnipeg, September 26, 2013)

Rhonda's remarks refer not only to the cultural disruptions caused by the child-welfare scoop but to ongoing disconnections as well. Indigenous groups now have more say in the running of the child-welfare system, which takes greater care than in the past to place Indigenous children with Native families, but the number of Indigenous children in care remains staggeringly dispropor-tionate. In 2006 only 15.7 percent of Manitoban children were Indigenous, yet 85 percent of the children in care were Indigenous (Kozlowski et al. 2012). Powwow clubs do not simply address the historical legacy of child-welfare provision, then, but also its contemporary consequences.

Some interviewees characterized powwow as a way for children to develop pride in their heritage, something important in an environment where prejudice remains widespread. Ray Stevenson told me,

A big part of [powwow clubs] is finding your identity as a Native person and being proud of that identity. . . . [For] a long time, people used to hide that they were Native. . . . And I'm talking, like, forties, fifties, and sixties, even sometimes the seventies. If you were an Indian you were considered a savage or a dirty Indian on Main Street.[10] Today, that's not the same, but . . . there are some people that still look at Native people as that way. . . . But having that sense of identity . . . and being proud of, "Hey! This is who I am, this is what *we* do as Native people"—that makes them proud to be able just to participate in singing a song, just to participate [in] dancing. (Interview, September 26, 2013)

Interviewees also understood powwow and the culture to help young people avoid unhealthy and dangerous lifestyles. Ray told me that he had grown up in an environment where alcohol and drug abuse were widespread; he had been a heavy drinker by the age of twelve, and as a child had begun selling alcohol and cigarettes illegally on the reserve. The culture was his way out of that life, and he saw it offering a similar path to others:

I knew what it was like growing up. . . . I knew all of the ups and downs, especially when it came to drugs and alcohol, because that's the environment that we grew up [in]. And we got to see the effects in our lives and the damage that it did to our lives and our parents and our grandparents . . . and other extended family members. People die because of it all the time. So, when I made that choice [to follow a traditional path], I figured if I knew it and . . . how it got me away from that, why wouldn't I teach that to other people? (Interview, September 26, 2013)

People additionally understood engagement with powwow and the culture to be tied to a good life more generally. When I asked the Stevensons why it was important for young people to learn the traditions they taught, Rhonda replied, "[It's] just the beginning of understanding who you are. And it's important for them to make their way in this world: for young people to understand who they are. . . . There's a lot of aspects of it. There's the traditional part; there's the physical part of [it]. . . . [The] singing and dancing is important, because there's teachings involved with that, too, if it's done right. It's not a performance; it's not just a show. It's a way of life that's mixed in with it." Ray added, "I've been brought up in the church—going to church, forced to go to church—and I found something when I became an adult that made me feel good. It lifted my spirit, a spirit that I didn't even know I had up until the drum came into my life, and the ceremonies, and the songs that are sung in those ceremonies. That's something that [awoke] my spirit that I have within me. And that's what helped me stay away from the old lifestyle that I had" (interview, September 26, 2013).

These statements convey ideas I encountered in many contexts: that drum song, dancing, and the culture are bound up with a way of life that is both fulfilling and morally upright and that they address the whole person. They recall on the one hand *bimaadizawin* or *mino-pimatisiwin*, the traditional Northern Algonquian concept of the good life: "life in the fullest sense; life in the sense of health, longevity, and well-being, not only for one's self, but one's family" (Hallowell 1955, 294).[11] They also evoke a holistic concept of selfhood—comprising physical, mental, spiritual, and emotional aspects—that circulates in a wide range of Indigenous communications, including discussions at powwow clubs as well as literatures associated with counseling and education. The idea of the holistic self is widely disseminated, for instance, through versions of the medicine wheel in which the physical, mental, spiritual, and emotional aspects of the self are mapped onto the four cardinal directions. Both ideas (of the good life and of holistic selfhood) are evident in the following excerpt from a publication on smudging in schools by Manitoba's Aboriginal Education Directorate: "Many First Nations share the concept of 'mino-pimatisiwin,' which means 'good life' in both Cree and Ojibwe. Implicit in this is the understanding that all of life is a ceremony; that the sacred and the secular are parts of the whole; that people are whole beings (body, mind, spirit, emotion); and that 'mino-pimatisiwin' is achieved by taking care of all aspects of one's self" (AED 2014b).

To sum up, engagement with powwow and the culture are widely understood as a way to address the consequences of Residential Schooling and the child-welfare scoop, an alternative to unhealthy lifestyles, and a source of pride. They are additionally associated with a traditional concept of the good life and a notion of whole selfhood.

THE INTEGRATION OF POWWOW
INTO STATE INSTITUTIONS

The return to traditions interrupted by colonialism is no simple thing. Powwow, for example, is a relatively recent genre whose origins can be found in part in Wild West shows (Powers 1990, 161; Browner 2002, 29–30; Ellis 2003, 79–101; Ellis, Lassiter, and Dunham 2005, 13–14); its early history is thus intertwined with a form of performance closely associated with colonial ideology. The songs and dances that make up the core powwow repertories are elaborations of traditions associated with specific Indigenous groups, but they are also migrating genres that have been adopted by communities that did not originally practice them. In these respects and others, powwow is a complex, cosmopolitan manifestation of Indigenous modernity. Other factors complicate the return to tradition further: not all Indigenous people embrace all aspects of what is taught in powwow clubs; not everyone agrees that schools are a proper venue for introducing children to the culture; and a great deal of Indigenous education and child-welfare provision is still overseen by the state, whose priorities do not always coincide with those of Indigenous communities. It is to these three issues I now turn.[12]

Issue 1: A Range of Indigenous Beliefs and Practices

The return to the culture is complicated in the first place by a heterogeneous Indigenous context. There are a wide range of Indigenous groups in Manitoba, some (such as the Dakota or the Ojibwe) having closer connections to the musical and choreographic genres of the powwow. Just as significant is that Christianity is widely practiced in many Indigenous communities (see Whidden 2007; Dueck 2013) and that not all Indigenous Christians understand powwow to be a good thing. In 2003 I spoke with a singer who was both a regular performer at a gospel coffeehouse in Winnipeg's North End and a fluent speaker of Ojibwe from a First Nation in the Manitoban Interlake area. I set down what I recalled of the conversation in my field notes as follows:

> The singer told me that she had just come back from visiting a relative on a reserve near Calgary. While she was there, she attended a Christian tent meeting and also, for the first time in her life, a powwow. . . . She had been terrified. She had never seen a powwow before and found it loud and frightening. Sitting with her daughter-in-law and unaware that she was being watched, she began to pray. She asked her daughter-in-law why the people were dancing, and she replied that it was a competition and that they were dancing to win money. The singer told me she did not think dancing like that would get you into heaven, nor did she think there would be drums there like the ones they had at the powwow. She explained that they had never had powwows where she grew up—they had witchcraft, but not powwows. (Field notes, reproduced here with minor changes, Winnipeg, July 22, 2003)

As this suggests, some First Nations people have serious concerns about powwow and the culture. They are not necessarily alienated from their own heritage, as is sometimes asserted by those who would dismiss their objections; some, like the woman with whom I spoke, are fluent in Native languages and familiar with the traditions of their home communities.

Educators were familiar with such objections. One told me that she had heard some Christians describe powwow as "dancing with the devil," and I heard reports of drum song being called "the devil's music." A number of teachers discussed how they responded to such concerns. One told me that when people objected to what was taught at the powwow club he helped run, he reminded them that the activities were voluntary and that they could always leave. Another had sought to establish common ground with a couple who expressed concerns about powwow club activities, inviting them to observe what went on at the club she ran. After a visit they felt comfortable letting their child participate, a decision that suggests that differing perspectives about powwow and the culture do not necessarily lead to impasses.

Issue 2: Ensuring Respect for Human and More-Than-Human Relations

It is not only Christians who voice concerns about the teaching of powwow and the culture but some traditional people as well. One educator told me that, although she informed her students about the sweat lodge and the Sun Dance, she did not introduce them to such activities herself. She believed that it was parents who were responsible for imparting a spiritual education to their children, and they who should be involved when their children were initiated into ceremonial life. She expressed apprehension about the cavalier way in which spiritual things were sometimes treated in her community, describing her sadness on seeing old powwow outfits offered secondhand and her fear that drums, too, might be sold like everyday items. For these reasons she did not make powwow outfits or build drums with her students. She was also concerned about a fellow educator who was getting involved in traditional practices for which he was perhaps not yet ready and she seemed to be suggesting that teachers should be careful not to put themselves, or their students, in situations where ignorant engagement with spirit beings could have negative repercussions.

Her remarks underscored the spiritual aspects of the traditional practices being incorporated in schooling and child-welfare provision. Ceremonies bring together human and spiritual participants ("our grandmothers and grandfathers") and, in these contexts, a drum is more than a musical instrument, being also a way of communicating with those spiritual participants (see Dylan Robinson's chapter, in this volume). In fact, the drums used at powwows and in ceremonies are often understood to have spirits of their own, and this helps to explain why the educator felt distressed at the thought of one being sold.[13] Northern Algonquian people have traditionally been careful to show respect to spirit relations, and one problem with introducing students to the culture is that it is not certain they will do the same.

This said, educators and traditional people held a range of opinions on the appropriateness of teaching the culture in powwow clubs. One seemed to suggest that it is important to put children into contact with the culture, even if not all of them are receptive to it, and that it is necessary to accept that one cannot control outcomes. Another told me that there will always be people who respond ignorantly to the culture when it is explained to them but that this should not keep one from teaching. During interviews in 2003 and 2013, Ray and Rhonda explained that it was generally young people who came to the club over a longer period who engaged more fully with the culture, growing into it over the years.

Issue 3: Expedient Culture?

A final factor complicating contemporary powwow instruction is that it is often delivered through provincial educational institutions and child-welfare provision and that, in these contexts, Indigenous priorities may be subordinated to those of the state. Just how this can happen is evident in government literature on Indigenous educational initiatives, including the province of Manitoba's publications on AAA funding. At the beginning of the 2011 school year, for example, the province required school divisions to put together plans identifying how their programs would produce "measurable . . . academic achievement outcomes . . . including grade levels" for Indigenous students (MDEAL 2013). School divisions were also directed to submit reports showing how well they had met the outcomes identified in their previous year's plans. More recently, beginning in the 2014–15 school year, the province declared that school divisions funded by AAA grants would be expected to spend more than half of their funding on initiatives to improve the literacy and numeracy of Indigenous students. They would also be required to show whether these initiatives had been successful (2014b).

The emphasis on literacy and numeracy should be understood in the context of broader provincial and national policies. The goals of Manitoba's 2004 "Aboriginal Education Action Plan" included increased high school graduation rates, access to and completion of postsecondary education, and entry into and participation in the labor market. Similar goals appeared in the province's 2008 action plan (MDEAL 2004, 2008). At the national level, meanwhile, one of the areas of activity agreed in a 2008 meeting of provincial and territorial ministers of education was the elimination of the gap "in academic achievement and graduation rates between Aboriginal and non-Aboriginal students" (CMEC 2008).

Government literature emerging from processes that prioritize consultation with Indigenous people tends to place more emphasis on how schooling can support the sharing of Indigenous knowledge and perspectives. The guiding principles of Manitoba's 2008 action plan—produced in consultation with Indigenous groups—include support for "sharing of Indigenous knowledge" (MDEAL 2008, 2). The plan also proposes "[working] with Aboriginal organizations, schools and school divisions to incorporate strategic initiatives or activities that will infuse Aboriginal perspectives into the curriculum and professional learning." All the same, the text subordinates this objective to a broader goal of "student engagement and high school completion" (3). Even when Indigenous people have been consulted, then, questions remain about how their recommendations will be implemented and what kind of priority they will be given.

What are the goals of incorporating Indigenous perspectives and traditions in public education? Are the goals higher achievement in literacy and numeracy, higher graduation rates, and more thorough integration into the workforce; or are they a turn or return to the culture, the cultivation of alliances with human and more-than-human relations, the pursuit of *bimaadizawin*? These aims are not necessarily exclusive, but what happens when the state understands the teaching of Indigenous tradition as the means of achieving its own priorities? As George Yúdice argues, societies are deploying "culture" in increasingly expedient or instrumental ways—for example, in the service of projects that aim to foster civil society or improve the physical health of citizens.[14] At stake in the case of powwow in schools is whether culture should be understood primarily as a resource to be mobilized toward other ends (2003, 9–13) or as a good in itself.

The Efficacy of the Culture

If Indigenous traditions are being used in the service of government objectives, this does not seem to be occurring in any straightforward way. This is in part because these practices maintain an independence from schooling and child-welfare provision. Powwow is not contained by its new educational contexts (on containment, see Hermes 2005, 44; Richardson 2011; B. Diamond 2016) but rather maintains connections to broader spheres of traditional practice. Fittingly, the language in which practitioners described traditional activities tended to be encompassing rather than encompassed. When I asked Patricia Olson about the relationship between school clubs and community ceremonies, she told me, "The school day . . . may start at eight-thirty, nine o'clock, and end at four thirty. . . . [The] community . . . always has something going on. . . . Like I said, it, it surrounds us. . . . There could be a ceremony going on; there could be a feast; there could be just a thank you or a welcoming dinner going on, or a powwow" (interview, October 4, 2013). In her explanation tradition and its practitioners are surrounding rather than surrounded.[15]

Another indication that culture is not instrumentalized in any straightforward way is that activities such as powwow clubs prioritize goals distinct from those emphasized in government action plans. As is evident in the foregoing accounts, when interviewees told me what powwow clubs were for, they did not mention graduation rates, enrollment in postsecondary education, or participation in labor markets but rather how powwow clubs connect Native people to their traditions, give them pride, keep them from unhealthy ways of living, and enrich their lives. Many of these statements resonated with the concept of *bimaadizawin*, life in the fullest sense. Even the sole interviewee to mention graduation rates (an employee of a Winnipeg school division) made it clear that engagement with the culture impacted much more than this:

> How did the powwow come about [at the school we have been discussing]? School divisions in Manitoba have access to funding called the Aboriginal Academic Achievement Grant. Its main objective is to reverse . . . the rates of public school dropout . . . among our Aboriginal young people, which creates all sorts of individual and social problems and challenges on the future by having young people that have no goal and no education and no sense of purpose just floating loose in this society. So with this funding, our schools aim to teach about Aboriginal traditions—history, the peoples—in an authentic way and in a meaningful way. And the best way that we find that can be done . . . is having our people come in and tell our stories in our way, as opposed to just relying on books. And there's nothing wrong with books, but it's much more meaningful when a young child can look at an Aboriginal role model

who's speaking to them and they start getting that sense of pride in who they are. So the powwow is a bigger extension of that philosophy of wanting our young people to find out who they are and be proud of it, because the powwow is such a resplendent, exciting gathering that showcases who we are [at] our best, who we are coming from a spiritual way. (Interview with anonymized participant, Winnipeg, October 1, 2013)

Phrases such as "social problems" and "floating loose in this society" may suggest concern about low graduation rates and participation in the labor market, but just as apparent is a concern for the quality of life of those who seemingly live without purpose, grounding, or pride.

To criticize expedient uses of culture is not to take issue with the idea that the turn to tradition can effect consequences but rather to interrogate how institutions seek to make instrumental applications of it in pursuit of social and economic ends. The foregoing accounts reveal contemporary education and child welfare as sites where a wide range of understandings of the efficacy of music, dance, ceremony, and tradition are deployed. Among them are ideas about the *expediency of culture*—for instance, the notion that incorporating Indigenous perspectives and traditions in schooling may lead to measurable outcomes in graduation rates. But there are also ideas about the *efficacy of the culture*, including the idea that singing, dancing, and ceremony contribute to a full life. These goals are not necessarily exclusive; at issue is which ones get prioritized and who gets to do the prioritizing.

———

Western Canadian public schooling and child-welfare services have undergone a profound shift since the late twentieth century. At one time these institutions alienated Indigenous children from their communities, languages, and cultures; today they are seen as sites where children can be connected or reconnected to tradition. Bringing children into contact with their heritage in this way is complicated by a number of factors. One is that Native people have a range of opinions on the place of the culture in schooling: some Christians have deep reservations regarding anything connected to traditional ceremonial practices, while some traditional people worry that school may not be the right context for introducing young people to the culture. Another factor is the apparent expectation on the part of the state that cultural practice should be enlisted in the pursuit of measurable educational, social, and economic outcomes. In Manitoba, then, Indigenous musical modernities involve negotiations over what kinds of work music and dance are expected to do in institutional contexts and what kinds of work should have priority—whether the efficacy of the culture lies above all in its ability to contribute to measurable policy outcomes or in its role in the pursuit of good life more broadly conceived.

To what degree is this chapter a narrative of the triumph of what the Foucauldian tradition calls disciplinary institutions (schools, child-welfare agencies, prisons), in which even groups that have undergone immense suffering in them regard them as indispensably expedient (Gordon 2000, xiv–xv)? Readers would be right to perceive some ambivalence in my account. But my primary aim has been to consider how Indigenous modernities are elaborated around, through, and sometimes despite these institutions—how Indigenous people use education and child-welfare provision to share songs, dances, and other traditions; how they express a range of contrasting positions concerning the place of the culture in schools; how they make use of government initiatives to ensure the presence of Indigenous perspectives and persons; and how they insistently make room for the culture.

Thanks to Lisa Aymont Hunter, Wayne Ruby, Ray and Rhonda Stevenson, and Geraldine Whitford, as well as others who requested anonymity but agreed to contribute to this project. It would not have been possible without your patience and help.

JESSICA BISSETT PEREA

10. Inuit Sound Worlding and Audioreelism in *Flying Wild Alaska*

More than sixty documentary-style, unscripted, or nonfiction programs about Alaska have aired on national television since 2005; the most successful of these feature extreme or dangerous professions and lifestyles unique to living in the "Last Frontier" of the United States. Although many Alaskans and media critics alike dismiss these programs as inauthentic, their popularity speaks directly to the endurance of a frontier ethos that continues to reinforce harmful and socially engineered stereotypes, including the "rogue pioneer" or the "happy-go-lucky Eskimo," which justify destructive enterprises such as resource extractivism and racial inequality. Given the role mainstream print and audiovisual media play in social, political, and economic struggles across Alaska, it is crucial to consider the ways in which reality television shows do or do not engage the lifeways and lived experiences of both Alaska Native and native Alaskan peoples.[1]

This chapter begins by introducing concepts of sound worlding and audioreelism to pose critical questions about how music and sound effect understandings of "the real" in Alaska-based reality television shows, especially for its target audience: viewers from the "Lower 48" and their enduring fascination with Alaska's distinctive landscapes, lifeways, and natural resources. I then offer a brief history of dominant tropes portrayed in the majority of Alaska-based reality shows, "realities" rooted in settler-colonial narratives of extractivism and the dispossession and disappearance of Native peoples. Next, I turn to a more in-depth discussion of Discovery Channel's *Flying Wild Alaska* (FWA), which for three seasons followed the Tweto family and their successful airline business based in the northwest Alaskan village of Unalakleet. Regarding sound design, FWA is unique for its balance of licensed third-party Arctic Indigenous music—the overwhelming majority of which features Inuit-language rock, rap, and R&B songs—with original music, ten scores of which were later released on *Flying Wild Alaska: The Soundtrack* (2012). I conclude by comparing FWA's Inuit-language–centered approach to sound worlding with nine other top-rated shows to emphasize its radical audioreelism, especially in relation to the settler-colonial narratives that dominate what one might call a reality television industrial complex.[2]

SOUND WORLDING AND AUDIOREELISM

The documentary *Reel Injun* (2010), by Neil Diamond, Catherine Bainbridge, and Jeremiah Hayes, is arguably one of the most poignant studies of shifting stereo-types of Native American people over a century of North American cinema. The film focuses almost solely on mythic (mis)representations of American Indians of the continental United States, which makes sense, given Hollywood's domi-nance in twentieth-century cinema. Yet the film's conclusion locates the future of Indigenous cinema in one of the most unexpected places: Canada's farthest northern territory of Nunavut. Diamond, Bainbridge, and Hayes offer a brief discussion of Igloolik-based Inuit filmmaker and director Zacharias Kunuk's work, especially the award-winning film *Atanarjuat: The Fast Runner* (2001), which scholars credit with forging new paths for the next generation of Inuit and Indigenous filmmakers (Huhndorf 2003; Raheja 2007, 2010; Bissett Perea 2017).

Given this present collection of chapters on music and modernity among Native North Americans, it perhaps goes without saying that oral and written languages are but one of many ways Indigenous peoples assert their presence and worldviews in spite of settler-colonial policies and nation-state formations that sought to eradicate them. To more fully comprehend the ways in which Indigenous people *sound and perform* their lived realities, I want to listen criti-cally to the ways in which FWA's Inuit language-centered sound design can be heard as advancing an "Indigenous way of 'worlding' without 'stateness'" (Picq 2018, 26), a process I call *sound worlding*. To be sure, Indigenous worlding could be understood in relation to Martin Heidegger's understanding of worlding, a term he activated as a verb to emphasize the generative process of world making, world becoming, or world "bringing-near" ([1927] 2008). Yet Indigenous ways of bringing into being have been practiced since time immemorial. Moreover, circumpolar Inuit music always already expresses an epistemology of (re)gen-eration and transtemporality (the critical importance of incorporating the past into the present to ensure futurity) (Anawak 1989, 45; Fienup-Riordan 1990;

Kawagley 1995) and a multiplicity akin to Ana María Ochoa Gautier's concept of "acoustic multinaturalism," which postulates variation as nature rather than a variety of natures (2016, 139). Whereas settler-colonial sound worlding silences and disappears the ways in which colonized people are brought into existence and thus framed by colonial epistemologies, Indigenous sound worlding is a critical embodied practice that unsettles audible formations of colonial logics and representations. I am particularly interested in how Inuit sound worlding offers dynamic narratives of Inuit traditions of transnationalism and cosmopolitanism, traditions that question the very usefulness of modernity as a framing concept.

Despite the popularity of reality television since the turn of the millennium, little to no scholarly attention has yet been paid to (mis)representations or presence of Native American and Indigenous people in the genre. Yet the sheer number and "cacophony" of colonial representations (Byrd 2011, 53) in Alaska-based reality shows hold very real implications for social, economic, and political realities facing Alaska Native people. As Michelle Raheja observes, "The 'reelism' of film resides in its ability to function as a placeholder: as a representational practice it does not mirror reality but can enact important cultural work as an art form with ties to the world of everyday practices and the imaginative sphere of the possible" (2010, xiii). Based on prominent themes portrayed in Alaska-based reality shows, it is clear that the majority of cultural work being done reifies the state's position as an extraction colony, a predicament one might find counterproductive for the decolonial tactics of "visual sovereignty" (Raheja 2007, 1161). To push one step further, however, Indigenous media studies should consider analyses of the audio *and* visual components of popular culture and media phenomenon—which one might call an attention to "audioreelism"—to emphasize a more complete or holistic approach to mediascapes advancing Native American and Indigenous narratives of sovereignty and self-determination. An audiovisual expansion of Raheja's work necessitates critical conversations between the fields of music and sound studies and Native American and Indigenous studies, a partnership that contributes to the continued development of Indigenizing the former and sounding the latter.[3]

A CACOPHONY OF IRRECONCILABLE REALITIES: SETTLER SOCIETY VERSUS ALASKA NATIVE

Since a majority of Alaska-based reality shows champion settler and arrivant narratives of extractivism that are mapped into and over top of Indigenous narratives of self-determination, it is necessary to outline from whence this colonial cacophony comes and how it continues to operate on the ground in the present day. By 1890, not long after the United States purchased Alaska from Russia, the "free lands" promised as part of western expansion in the continental United States had closed, positioning Alaska as the last frontier. Frederick Jackson Turner declared the American frontier closed at the 1893 Chicago World's Columbian Exposition, which had a wide-reaching impact on the U.S. mainstream. His romanticized frontier thesis led to characterizations of non-Native Alaskan settlers as a hardy stock of people who were born again by testing their pioneer spirit in a harsh and inhospitable land. Stephen Haycox notes the resilience of this narrative, pointing out that Alaska served as the nation's "last frontier throughout the twentieth century, as a land where men and women might yet prove themselves capable and worthy . . . relying on only themselves for success or failure" (2002, vii). Yet despite the persistence of Turneresque romanticism of Alaska and its independent and hardy pioneers, Haycox argues that Alaska's immigrant population remained deeply dependent on the health of the politics and economics of the continental United States:

> The American period of Alaska's history is best understood in a colonial con-
> text. . . . Political and economic colonialism has characterized America's rela-
> tionship with the region. *Dependence is a central element in Alaska's colonialism.*
> Alaska's economy has been dependent on investors from outside the territory
> because the capital to develop regional resources has not resided in Alaska. But
> the only resources in the region are natural resources: hard rock minerals, fish,
> timber, and forest products, and petroleum and natural gas. Only investment
> in exploitation of those resources has provided jobs in Alaska, and the non-
> native, immigrant population has come to Alaska for jobs, not for subsistence.
> (2002, 164; emphasis added)

Haycox (2002) posits that the overwhelming majority of Alaskan residents have functioned almost solely in the service of the state's status as an extraction colony from 1867 to the present day. The dependence on outside investors—such as the mid-nineteenth-century Hudson Bay Trading Company or the present-day British Petroleum—has in fact solidified Alaska's position as one of the more lucrative extraction colonies in the United States. After Haycox's call to under-stand Alaska in a colonial context, its designation as a colony in the present day is an ironic reversal that potentially denominates the non-Native population as an economically domestic dependent nation. This notably *dependent* reality is also evident in Alaska's immigrant population's overall refusal to pursue radically alternative lifestyles, having instead sought to replicate the lifestyles from the southern places they left behind.

Whereas land was a primary catalyst for struggles between Native Americans and the Lower 48 settler society, Alaska's seemingly abundant bounty of natural resources—including whales, furs, gold, coal, and oil—held a much greater appeal than land. The gradual development of Alaska's four interlinked highways provides tangible markers of the early twentieth-century resource extraction by fur traders, gold prospectors, and miners. Although the reality television industry certainly reinforces the colonial expectation of Alaska's continuance as a resource-extraction colony in the early twenty-first century, very few nonfiction programs are based on or near the road system; the vast majority are filmed in remote villages, homesteads, or offshore (in the case of numerous fishing shows). For the past decade major cable networks, primarily the Discovery Channel and the History Channel, have revived a mainstream fascination with the last U.S. frontier. Critics and fans alike say the abundance of Alaska series is rooted in the success of Discovery's Bering Sea crab-fishing series *Deadliest Catch*, which has become a flagship for the cable network. Since the debut of *Deadliest Catch* in 2005, more than sixty nonfiction television projects based in Alaska have aired nationally, enumerated in table 10.1.[4]

One explanation for the recent explosion of interest in proposing and filming nonfiction projects in Alaska can be attributed to 2008 legislation that established the Alaska Film Production Tax Credit Program, which subsidized film and television projects with a 30 percent tax credit to any company that spends more than $100,000 in Alaska. At first, Alaskans supported the program because, in theory, it encouraged film-industry professionals to hire Alaskans and to film in Alaska, instead of the prevalence of staged Alaskan scenes in the Pacific Northwestern states, Canada (primarily British Columbia), or New Zealand. But tax credit breaks to these major films did little to boost the Alaskan economy: "for every dollar earned by an Alaskan worker under the subsidy program [in 2013], out-of-state workers earned five" (Hopkins 2014). This problem is exacerbated when one considers the comparatively fast timelines and light personnel and equipment requirements of nonfiction television projects, which make up more than half of the thirty-eight productions that qualify for the 2013 tax incentive. Kyle Hopkins (2011) asserts that "no other state . . . has more cable shows per capita." By my count there were only twelve nonfiction television programs that had aired as of February 2011. By 2014 the figure nearly quadrupled to forty-one. Ultimately, the

TABLE 10.1 Nonfiction television programs filmed in Alaska (working list as of March 2018)

TITLE	NETWORK	AIR DATE	NUMBER OF SEASONS	NUMBER OF EPISODES	THEMES
Deadliest Catch*	DC	04/2005–present	14	217	Extractivism
Out of the Wild: The Alaska Experiment	DC	04/2008–06/2009	2	18	Lifestyle
Tougher in Alaska	HC	05/2008–08/2008	1	13	Lifestyle
Iditarod: Toughest Race on Earth	DC	10/2008–11/2008	1	6	Lifestyle
Ice Road Truckers	HC	05/2009–09/2012	4	61	Extractivism, Transportation
Alaska State Troopers*	NG	10/2009–06/2014	6	71	Dangerous Work
R5 Sons	GC	07/2010–09/2010	2	26	Lifestyle
Sarah Palin's Alaska	LC	11/2010–01/2011	1	9	Lifestyle
Gold Rush: Alaska	DC	12/2010–present	8	114	Extractivism
Ax Men	HC	12/2010–03/2016	9	153	Extractivism
Flying Wild Alaska*	DC	01/2011–07/2012	3	31	Transportation
Alaska Wing Men	NG	01/2011–03/2012	2	13	Transportation
Mounted in Alaska	HC	04/2011–06/2011	1	15	Lifestyle
Big Hair Alaska	LC	09/2011	1	2	Lifestyle
Coast Guard Alaska	WC	11/2011–04/2015	4	41	Dangerous Work
Alaska: The Last Frontier	DC	12/2011–present	7	101	Lifestyle
Hook, Line and Sisters	LC	12/2011–01/2012	1	7	Lifestyle
Bering Sea Gold	DC	01/2012–10/2016	9	80	Extractivism
Mountain Men	HC	05/2012–09/2013	2	24	Lifestyle
Goldfathers	NG	05/2012–06/2012	1	5	Extractivism
Bristol Palin: Life's a Trip	L	06/2012–07/2012	1	14	Lifestyle
Yukon Men*	DC	08/2012–present	5	48	Lifestyle
Bering Sea Gold: Under the Ice	DC	08/2012–10/2014	3	18	Extractivism
Buying Alaska	DA	10/2012–03/2015	3	32	Lifestyle
Building Alaska	DIY	11/2012–01/2018	8	65	Lifestyle
Married to the Army: Alaska	OWN	11/2012–12/2012	1	8	Lifestyle
Wild West Alaska	AP	01/2013–02/2016	4	38	Lifestyle
Alaska Fish Wars	NG	02/2013–02/2014	2	8	Extractivism
Life below Zero*	NG	04/2013–present	9	93	Lifestyle
Great Bear Stakeout	DC	04/2013	1	3	Wildlife
Ultimate Survival Alaska	NG	05/2013–03/2015	3	37	Lifestyle

TABLE 10.1 *continued*

TITLE	NETWORK	AIR DATE	NUMBER OF SEASONS	NUMBER OF EPISODES	THEMES
Alaska Steel Men	DC	08/2013–09/2013	1	3	Lifestyle
Living Alaska	HGT	08/2013–01/2017	5	54	Lifestyle
Alaskan Women Looking for Love	LC	10/2013–11/2013	1	6	Lifestyle
Alaska Gold Diggers	AP	10/2013–11/2013	1	6	Extractivism
Red Alaska	NG	11/2013	1	1	Lifestyle
Railroad Alaska	DA	11/2013–01/2016	3	25	Transportation
Alaska Off-Road Warriors	HC	11/2014–01/2015	1	8	Lifestyle
Alaska Moose Men	AP	02/2014	1	1	Lifestyle
Alaskan Bush People	DC	05/2014–present	7	70	Lifestyle
The Hunt*	HC	06/2014–07/2014	1	8	Lifestyle
Escaping Alaska*	LC	07/2014–08/2014	1	6	Lifestyle
Alaska Monsters	DA	09/2014–11/2015	2	14	Lifestyle
Slednecks	MTV	10/2014–12/2014	1	19	Lifestyle
Edge of Alaska	DC	10/2014–11/2017	3	32	Lifestyle
Alaska: Battle on the Bay	AP	12/2014–02/2015	1	8	Extractivism
The Last Alaskans	AP	05/2015–05/2017	3	26	Lifestyle
Dead End Express	NG	05/2015–06/2015	1	8	Transportation
Yukon River Run	NG	06/2015–09/2015	1	8	Lifestyle
Missing in Alaska	HC	07/2015	1	13	Lifestyle
Great Wild North	HC	10/2015–12/2015	1	8	Extractivism, Lifestyle
Power and Ice	HC	08/2015–10/2017	1	7	Dangerous Work
Alaska Haunting	DA	09/2015–10/2015	1	6	Lifestyle
Dr. Dee: Alaska Vet	AP	11/2015–10/2016	2	18	Lifestyle
Alaska Proof	AP	01/2016–02/2016	1	10	Lifestyle
Big Fix Alaska	NG	02/2016	1	2	Lifestyle
Alaska Aircrash Investigations	SmC	03/2016–04/2016	1	6	Dangerous Work
Alaska Mega Machines	SC	04/2016–06/2016	1	6	Lifestyle
Guiding Alaska	TC	07/2016–08/2016	1	7	Lifestyle
Alaska Homicide	DC	06/2017	1	1	Dangerous Work
True Alaska*	TC	11/2017	1	1	Lifestyle
Gold Rush: White Water	DC	01/2018–present	1	8	Extractivism

* = Show features one or more main characters who identify as Alaska Native

Network key: AP = Animal Planet; DC = Discovery Channel; DA = Destination America; DIY = Do It Yourself Network; GC = General Communication; HC = History Channel; HGT = Home and Garden Television; L = Lifetime; MTV = Music Television Network; NG = National Geographic; LC = Learning Channel; OWN = Oprah Winfrey Network; WC = Weather Channel; TC = Travel Channel; SC = Science Channel; SmC = Smithsonian Channel.

state subsidy program itself became an unsustainable form of resource extraction, so the Alaska legislature voted to end it in June 2015 (Forgey 2015).

Thematically, the overwhelming majority of the shows present selective versions of life in Alaska that recall a paradox Haycox (2002) outlined in his critique of rogue Alaskan residents as dependent on the infrastructure of continental U.S. politics and economics. Moreover, each of these reality shows is in some way complicit in the ongoing resource extractivism that has plagued Alaska from its Russian Period (1741–1867) and into its U.S. Period (1867–present). The mainstream popularity of shows such as *Deadliest Catch, Alaska State Troopers, Ice Road Truckers,* and *Ax Men* are considered part of a recent television-programming trend that features real men in danger, by following the day-to-day activities of occupations with high fatality rates, such as crab fishing, law enforcement, ice-road truck driving, and logging, respectively. At issue is a continuation of late nineteenth-century settler and arrivant narratives that center resource extractivism as vital to the survival of the United States and as Alaska's raison d'être, both of which are achieved at the expense of Indigenous practices of cultural and environmental sustainability and stewardship.

Conversely, FWA makes visible and audible the tensions and successes of Inuit audioreelism in Alaska specifically and the circumpolar Arctic more broadly by coupling the modernity and realism of flight technology with a soundtrack predominated by Inuit language rock, rap, and R&B music. FWA was cocreated by Tommy Baynard and Ariel Tweto, who is the youngest daughter of the show's primary family. FWA aired for three seasons between 2011 and 2012, highlighting the lives and adventures of Alaskan bush pilots and the rural Native and non-Native people and communities who depend on them. Baynard, a television-industry professional, encountered the Tweto family prior to the start of FWA. He first met Ferno Tweto, Ariel's mother, when his crew arrived in Unalakleet in the spring of 2008 to work on the six-part nonfiction series *Iditarod: Toughest Race on Earth* (Discovery Channel). Unalakleet is one of the stops along the Iditarod trail, just under ninety miles to the race's finish in Nome. Baynard met Ariel Tweto again later that fall when she competed on the ABC obstacle-course game show *Wipeout,* where Baynard was working on the set as a safety coordinator. During this second encounter, they began brainstorming ideas for a show about bush pilots and pitched the show for more than a year before Discovery expressed interest and asked them to shoot a "sizzle reel," or collection of clips that illustrate the major ideas behind the show. Discovery then provided Baynard and Ariel with the resources to film ten episodes for season 1.

I asked Tweto about the primary goals for show, and she emphasized a desire to move away from the negative interpersonal drama that characterizes the majority of reality television:

I just wanted it to be an honest show. . . . I went to school for TV film production and communication, so I understand that sometimes you need drama. . . . Our lives are not exciting every day, but we wanted to capture an honest show . . . and I'm not going to be arguing with my mom and dad or my sisters. . . . So I wanted to make it clear to them that it was going to be pretty lighthearted and capture our way of life up in bush Alaska. So our only requirement was that we wanted it to be as real as possible." (Interview, Anchorage, AK, August 23, 2012)

Whereas most reality shows derive their drama from clashing personalities and unstable egos, FWA is populated by laid-back pilots, mechanics, and other employees involved in the day-to-day operations of Era Alaska. The dramatic aspects of bush pilots' lives are primarily environmental in that they encounter drama in the form of high winds, inclement weather, and bird strikes (when a plane accidentally strikes a bird). Other moments of interest are created by the unusual cargo transported by the bush pilots. For example, episodes from the first season feature a range of cargo, from wedding cakes to explosive harpoon heads for whaling. Season 2 documents the delivery of one village's first-ATM machine, complete with a cash delivery to stock it. FWA proved to be a huge success and was one of the highest-rated premiers of any show in Discovery Channel history, which led the network to green-light production on seasons 2 and 3.

Discussing the production crew's approach to sound worlding, Tweto explained that she and Baynard "wanted to keep the music pretty local and traditional, but we also wanted it to be modern because we live in a modern world" (interview, August 23, 2012). Discovery Channel executives supported their desire for unique soundscapes and soundtracks, support that is unusual for reality television and resulted in a number of firsts for the genre. Compared to FWA's nonfiction program counterparts, the show's producers took a notably language-centered approach to sound worlding while also balancing between licensed third-party music and original music.

LICENSED THIRD-PARTY MUSIC:
MODERN, DIFFERENT, AND REAL

A predominantly circumpolar Arctic soundscape on mainstream cable television is unprecedented, and its significance cannot be overstated. According to most of the people interviewed for this chapter, FWA executive producer D. J. Nurre is credited with playing a key role in shaping the show's distinctive sound, what one might call an audioreelist approach. Nurre's inspiration was first sparked by the rap song "Angajoqqaat" by the three-man Kalaaleq (Greenlandic Inuit) crew named Prussic, what he described as the "link that inspired it all." From here, Nurre and music supervisor Matt Kierscht scoured local Alaskan radio stations, the Internet, and independent record labels in search of contemporary Inuit music (email corr., September 2, 2012). Their efforts to locate unique and local music yielded a dramatically different approach to reality television sound design compared to other shows, those that came both before and after. Nurre explained, "We wanted a show that had a sound that was appropriate to the area we were shooting in. . . . You have the seal drums; you have the throat singing, but there's not necessarily an overwhelmingly melodic instrument other than the vocals . . . like an Alaskan instrument that just cuts through and the moment you hear it . . . it's the equivalent of a sitar or a didgeridoo, where you're like, 'oh, that means this region of the world.' . . . *So that's when we arrived at the lyrics, and that's where your ear immediately goes, 'Okay, this is different; this is something unique'*" (interview, Anchorage, AK, October 19, 2012; emphasis added).

The overwhelming majority of the licensed third-party music featured in FWA comes from Indigenous musicians from the circumpolar Arctic region. I created table 10.2 from the cue sheets for all three seasons of FWA, provided by the show's music supervisor, Matt Kierscht (email corr., November 9, 2012), to visualize the number of cue appearances delineated by nation-state. Approximately two-thirds of the music comes from Russia (34 percent) and Greenland (32.5 percent) and the remaining third from the United States (23 percent from Alaska and 10 percent from the Lower 48) and Iceland (0.5 percent). These numbers raise two issues. First, there are no cues from Canada—a rather gaping hole that cuts out more than one third of Inuit-language speakers.[5] Second, the range of Indigenous languages from Russia, the United States, and Greenland is quite broad and by no means limited to the local Yup'ik or Iñupiaq languages heard at the cultural crossroads that is Unalakleet.[6] In the end, the producer's desire to find and feature local music (from Alaskan Inuit) resulted in a considerably more "glocal" playlist (from circumpolar Arctic Indigenous). Broadly speaking, the third-party songs licensed for FWA foreground musical mixtures of Inuit-language lyrics and Arctic Indigenous vocal styles atop Anglo- and Afro-identified styles and genres (namely rock, rap, and R&B). On the subject of genre, most of the artists licensed for FWA resist easy categorization; as Beverley Diamond points out, the technological, economic, and sociopolitical developments of the 1990s contributed to a surge of Native American popular music that often defies typical conventional genre categorizations, complicating both their physical location (as in record stores) and discursive location (popular, traditional, world, folk) (2005, 118). So for the purpose of the analysis that follows, the genres listed in table 10.2 align with larger designations validated by the music industrial complex (e.g., Grammy-award categories), while my discussions adhere to the particularities of each musician's or band's artistic vision as it was explained to me. It is intentional to let the differences stand, as they draw attention to predicaments of what it means to be an Indigenous musician operating within and against systems of settler colonialism in general and the problematics of what I call "sound quantum" ideology more specifically (Bissett Perea 2012, 9).

The two Alaska-based Inuit bands featured throughout FWA's three seasons— Frozen Whitefish and Pamyua—offer remixed genres that they have redefined as "Yupik Rock" (Frozen Whitefish) and "Tribal Funk" or "Inuit World Music" (Pamyua). Frozen Whitefish is a Bethel-based Yup'ik rock band fronted by musician and producer Mike McIntyre, who licensed two of the band's original Yugtun-language songs, "Maani Alaskami" and "Kenkamken," which were later released on McIntyre's EP *Wiinga Ellpet'llu* (2012). The recording of "Maani Alaskami" is an up-tempo rock song featuring an acoustic guitar, an electric guitar, bass, and drums, all played by McIntyre, who explains, "I had band members, but they don't always have my drive to record. So I end up doing everything myself" (email corr., March 15, 2018). "Kenkamken" features a laid-back feel, major tonality progressions, and McIntyre singing while accompanying himself on acoustic guitar.

Pamyua is the award-winning Anchorage-based band formed by self-described Afro-Inuit brothers Phillip Kill'aq Blanchett and Stephen Qacung Blanchett (Yup'ik and African American); Ossie Aasanaaq Kairaiuak (Yup'ik) from Anchorage, Alaska; and Kalaaleq (Greenlandic Inuit) musician Karina Moeller.[7] With 19 percent of the total cues for season 1 (and similar numbers for the two subsequent seasons), Pamyua is by far the most prominent band featured

TABLE 10.2 Third-party music featured in season 1 of *Flying Wild Alaska*, 2011

LOCATION	LANGUAGE(S)	PERFORMER(S)	GENRE	NUMBER OF CUES	PERCENTAGE OF CUES
Russia	Tunguisic (Évenk, Nanaj, Oroč, Udēgē, Ulč) Chukotko-Kamchatkan (Koryak Uralic (Nenec, Sel'kup)	Various unidentified Siberian singers	World	48	34.0
Greenland	Kalaallisut (West Greenlandic)	Peand-eL	Rap	15	32.5
		Kimmernaq	Rock	1	
		Nanook	Rock	10	
		Prussic	Rap	9	
		Tuu Motz	Rap	11	
United States					
Alaska	Yugtun (Central Yup'ik)	Pamyua	R&B / World	27	23.0
		Frozen Whitefish	Rock	5	
Lower 48	N/A (Vocables)	NicholasE	Rock	6	10.0
		Jana Mashonee	R&B	8	
Iceland	Icelandic	Jónsi	Rock / Pop	1	0.5

on the show. Kalaaleq rapper Peand-eL is the show's second most prominent musician, yet he is a distant second, with approximately 11 percent of total cues (although his voice opens each episode in the main title song "Frozen Sky"). Nurre observed, "This is a unique opportunity for Pamyua to represent the Native sound of Alaska for many folks like myself down in the lower 48 who have never heard music from that region before." Phillip Blanchett responded on Pamyua's behalf by saying, "We're honored to represent bush Alaska in this series. . . . This show highlights the enduring spirit of Alaska's rural culture and its people" (*Alaska Dispatch News* 2011).

At the time FWA began filming and production, Pamyua licensed their entire catalog to the show, which then included thirty-four songs across three albums: two studio recordings titled *Mengluni* (The beginning; 1998) and *Apallut* (Verses; 2001) and one live recording titled *Caught in the Act* (2003). It so happens that the three songs with the most cues from season 1 provide a glimpse of the band's stylistic transformations developed over nearly two decades together. "Reindeer Herding Song" (from *Mengluni*) had the most cues (nine total) and showcases Pamyua's signature arrangements of traditional Yup'ik-language (Yugtun) songs performed in four-part vocal harmonizations with R&B or gospel-inflected stylings, which critics dubbed "Inuit Soul" and "Yup'ik Doo-Wop" (Dunham 1998; Pardes 1999).[8] From *Apallut* a traditional Yup'ik teasing song, "*Cauyaqa Nauwa?*" (Where's my drum?), had the second most cues (eight total) and because it was also recorded on their debut album it offers one of the clearest articulations of Pamyua's stylistic shift toward what they called "Tribal Funk" and "Inuit World" music. Stephen explains their transformations as moves to reach out and relate: "We went after it. We found those musicians. We wanted to be tribal. We wanted to stay tribal. We wanted to express Indigeneity" (interview, Anchorage, April 27, 2009). Phillip adds, "The didgeridoo itself is very vocal. It's a very earthy sound and very rhythmic, and it really blends well with the style of music that we do, especially with our world music songs or world grooves" (qtd. in Korry and Juneau 2005).

Whereas *Mengluni* features arrangements of either a cappella or piano and *cauyaq* (Yup'ik frame drum)–accompanied singing, *Apallut's* instrumentation builds out to include a four-piece rhythm section, African djembes, Australian didgeridoos, and Latin percussion (congas and timbale). Of the three songs with the most cues, "*Cauyaqa Nauwa?*" is the only word song, as opposed to the partially vocable "Reindeer Herding Song" or primarily vocable "*Inngerneq*" (from *Caught in the Act*), the song with the third most cues (three total). Pamyua's live album features remixes of core repertory (including new arrangements of "Reindeer Herding Song" and *"Cauyaqa Nauwa?"*) alongside songs that the band had not yet recorded, such as *"Inngerneq,"* a traditional Greenlandic chant, accompanied by djembe and congas with an outro section that sounds the quartet's expansion of vocal stylings to include more distinctive vocal timbres such as Inuit vocal games and overtone singing comparable to the deeper styles of Tuvan Kargyraa and Tibetan dzo-ke.[9]

The diegesis (filmic or televisual narrative world) of FWA is significantly shaped by its use of licensed third-party music in both diegetic (originating within the narrative world) and nondiegetic (originating outside of the narrative world) ways. For example, the first scene of the first episode (following the main title theme song) introduces audiences to Sam Towarak Sr. (aka Sam the DJ), one of FWA's favorite recurring personalities and one of the primary means through which licensed music is brought into the diegesis. Sam's voice opens the first episode: "You're listening to KNSA here in Unalakleet. . . . I had a request to play a song by a local group called Pamyua." The camera follows Sam's hands as he punches the buttons to cue Pamyua's "Reindeer Herding Song." The song begins but then shifts to a state of nondiegesis, serving as the score for a filmic sequence of a bush plane accelerating along a runway and taking off into flight, followed by long aerial shots of Unalakleet and its surrounding area. Pamyua also offers some of the few diegetic performances on the show, most notably on the sixth episode of the third season, titled "Radio Silence." During the final third of the episode, Ariel calls Phillip and asks if Pamyua would consider coming to Unalakleet to lead a drum-making and dancing workshop with area youth and perform for the local community, a concert she named "UNKfest 2012."[10]

Behind the scenes Pamyua took advantage of the invitation to appear on the show and initiated a Kickstarter fund-raising campaign to bring a professional film crew (Electric Igloo Creative) to Unalakleet to shoot their first music video. The song they chose to bring to life in audiovisual form is Ossie's original song "Bubble Gum," a teasing song commemorating a student chewing gum during dance class, which they released on their fourth album *Side A / Side B* (2012).[11] The song serves as the underscore for the drum-making workshop, for which Pamyua used nylon airplane fabric as the drum membrane, a common substitution for animal gut or hide that is easier to obtain and maintain while also producing a similar sound. On-screen Pamyua's UNKfest set opens with "Bubble Gum," with Pamyua singing into microphones stuck into the snow pack, surrounded by dozens of students dancing and playing along with their newly made *cauyaqs,* while audience members groove along from their makeshift auditorium seating made of wood pallets and crates atop the packed snow.

ORIGINAL MUSIC: "LOVE LETTERS TO ALASKA"

On July 5, 2012, the Discovery Music Source announced, "for the first time ever Discovery's Global Music Services Team releases a full soundtrack to iTunes [from] Discovery Channel's *Flying Wild Alaska*," a soundtrack that began with the acquisition of "six original songs co-written by series composer Doug Bossi and produced with local artists . . . [and] rounded out with four additional tracks from the show's score, all reflecting the *distinct Inuit sound* that sets the mood of the show" ("Flying Wild Alaska Soundtrack" 2012; emphasis added). As one of the few (if not only) such soundtrack albums ever released in conjunction with any reality television show, the significance of FWA's approach to sound design is reinforced further by the fact that the show's original music earned composers Doug Bossi, Tony Elfers, and Mat Morse the BMI (Broadcast Music, Inc.) Cable Music Award in 2011 and 2012. BMI awards honor "composers of the past year's top-grossing films, top-rated prime-time network television series and highest-ranking cable network programs" ("Rolfe Kent Receives" 2012).[12] Bossi notes that these awards and the show's top ratings were among some of the factors that prompted Discovery Channel to release the soundtrack.

Table 10.3 lists the tracks and artists featured on *Flying Wild Alaska: The Soundtrack*, alongside my notation of Inuit languages performed, given Nurre's earlier statement of their central role in creating a score with a "distinct Inuit sound." I asked Bossi to explain the origins of the soundtrack project, and he related that the show's original compositions were initially meant to serve as complementary aural scores for the big and epic visual montages created by Nurre's filming crew — what he called sonic love letters to Alaska (interview, San Francisco, March 13, 2018).[13] Regarding the creation of the album, Bossi described a dynamic transnational process or flow made possible by the widespread accessibility of modern studio technologies. Directed by Bossi, each track represents collaborations between two U.S.-based music-production companies — Sonix-sphere (Chicago) and iSpy Music (Los Angeles) — and Inuit musicians Phillip and Stephen Blanchett (Yup'ik and African American) and Ossie Kairaiuak (Yup'ik) from Anchorage, Alaska; and Kalaaleq musicians Karina Moeller, Peter Lyberth (aka Peand-eL) and Ajaaja Gabrielsen from Nuuk, Greenland. Bossi, Elfers, Pamyua, and Lyberth all recorded and revised their contributions from their home studios, distances that span over 3,400 miles and traverse multiple nation-states (as the crow flies).

Since the FWA narrative emphasizes the dangerous work of piloting bush planes, and not interpersonal drama, FWA sound designers approached an idea of audioreelism that balanced their desire to articulate a local and distinct Inuit sound with a need to invoke drama or tension musically, which is common throughout the reality television genre. Tension, of the sitting on the edge of the seat variety, is a constant feature across the entire soundtrack, which its composers achieved using a number of techniques, including the forward momentum of driving syncopated patterns and rhythmic grooves; an unresolved feeling produced by a majority of minor-leaning suspended chords and vamping i—VI and i—III harmonic progressions; timbral interest and variation realized by layering Inuit and Native American drums atop resonant acoustic string instruments atop buzzing synthesized distortion effects; an edginess created by Inuit-language lyrics, given the vast majority of viewers would be unfamiliar with Yugtun or Kalaallisut; and added realism through actual and simulated sounds that reflect on-screen action, including prop engines, bird strikes, and aircraft alarms.[14] This dynamic range of "electronic to orchestral to tribal to Native" tension-inducing sonic factors heard across each soundtrack score unsettles conventional musical representations of "The North" by European and U.S. modernist composers who privilege static or arrhythmic tempos, predominantly minor harmonies (if chords are heard or implied at all), sparse instrumentation and timbres, and a near absence of the human voice (Doug Bossi, qtd. in Marchant 2011). It is worth emphasizing this last point, that literal absences of Inuit voices can be heard as a colonial tactic to unpeople the Arctic, thus reinforcing an assumed availability for extractivist agendas.[15]

Individually, the tracks can be roughly grouped into three categories according to the featured language (or lack thereof), which include: three Yugtun-language songs; four Kalaallisut-language songs; and three Bossi-defined "Modern Alaska Drama Underscore" (MADU) tracks, which incorporate Inuit frame drums and Native American hand drums and are primarily instrumental or involve only sung vocables (email corr., March 18, 2018). The first of three MADU tracks, "Humpback Song," samples string instruments imitating whale songs and a woman's voice (composer Sarah Schachner) singing a vocable melody atop one of the few primarily major-leaning harmonic progressions. "Danger Ahead" and "Working Man" are the lone MADU tracks to omit the human voice and foreshadow the minor progressions and driving feel of the main title track, "Frozen

TABLE 10.3 *Flying Wild Alaska: The Soundtrack,* 2012

TRACK	TITLE	ARTISTS	LANGUAGE	GENRE
1	"Ayaa"	Pamyua	Yugtun	Inuit world
2	"Anori"	Peand-eL, featuring Ajaaja Gabrielsen	Kalaallisut	Rap
3	"Humpback Song"	Doug Bossi and Sarah Schachner	n/a (vocables)	MADU
4	"Our World"	Pamyua	Yugtun	Inuit world
5	"Dead Air"	Peand-eL	Kalaallisut	Rap
6	"Danger Ahead"	Doug Bossi and Evan Wise	n/a (instrumental)	MADU
7	"Avannaarsua"	Peand-eL, featuring Ajaaja Gabrielsen	Kalaallisut	Rap
8	"Tundra Chant"	Pamyua	Yugtun	Inuit world
9	"Working Man"	Doug Bossi and Tony Elfers	n/a (instrumental)	MADU
10	"Frozen Sky"	Doug Bossi and Tony Elfers, featuring Peand-eL	Kalaallisut	Rap

Sky." The three Yugtun-language songs are performed by Pamyua, including "Ayaa" (track 1), "Our World" (track 4), and "Tundra Chant" (track 8). While the majority of soundtrack titles are given in English, there are two Kalaallisut-language exceptions: "Anori" (track 2; translates to "Breeze") and "Avannaarsua" (track 7; translates to "The Great North"). Among the four Kalaallisut-language songs, these two are further distinguished through the use of sung choruses by Kalaaleq singer Ajaaja Gabrielsen, whose original lyrics, written by Peand-eL, describe the daring pilots and the beauty of flying, both literally and metaphorically.[16] "Dead Air" (track 5) and "Frozen Sky" (track 10) feature instrumental compositions with Peand-eL's original lyrics. The instrumental compositions for tracks 2, 5, and 7 were recorded by Bossi, which he then sent to Peand-eL to record his raps and Ajaaja's choruses. Because the majority of FWA producers and audiences are unfamiliar with Inuit languages, Bossi explained how the Yugtun and Kalaallisut lyrics had to be vetted by a third-party translator—the Discovery Channel could not risk profanities in any language slipping into their PG-rated primetime show (interview, March 13, 2018).

FWA was the first nonfiction series to feature an opening theme song with "lyric up" vocals in an Indigenous language. Nurre explained that prior to FWA, "you'd have been laughed out of the building" for the mere suggestion (interview, Anchorage, AK, October 19, 2012). According to Bossi, "Frozen Sky" features Elfer's music with Peand-eL's lyrics and was the song most labored over, as music and production crews considered more than thirty different versions before choosing the final cut (interview, March 13, 2018). The up-tempo rock groove is built from the bottom up, with the rhythm section outlining an eight-bar minor vamp, following a i—VI—II—v progression. Synthesized distortion sustains the tonic of each chord, while an electric bass and drums rhythmically emphasize the second and fourth beats (hitting an eighth note on the downbeat followed by two sixteenth notes that drive to the second beat, and the third beat is composed of four sixteenth notes driving to four [one and-a / TWO / three-e-and-a / FOUR]). This driving rhythm is reinforced by the strumming of an acoustic guitar and dramatic cymbal rolls and crashes that land on the chord changes. An orchestral string section provides a syncopated melodic counterpoint to the rock progression underneath. On the soundtrack version Peand-eL's rap enters in the fifth and final phrase, with added rhythmic emphasis on two and four reinforced with hand claps, and ultimately becomes part of the forward-moving rhythmic soundscape.[17] Peand-eL states that "I will never, ever rap in English or Danish because I honor my own language. . . . I was born with it, and it's more fitting for me to rap in Greenlandic. It's more emotional" (qtd. in Meigs 2011). Peand-eL's original lyrics (table 10.4), which he titles "Timmivunga" (I am flying), narrates from the perspective of an Alaska bush pilot, which is quite a departure from the majority of his work, which confronts darker issues such as alcoholism, sexually transmitted diseases, and loneliness.[18] Taken together, the music and lyrics produce a "wall of sound" effect in that there is literally no silence or space, which creates another level of tension, since the audience has little time to breathe in silence.

TABLE 10.4 Lyrics for "Timmivunga" (I am flying),
aka "Frozen Sky," by Peand-eL

Timmivunga qilaap nunaallu akornani	I am flying between sky and land
Qaqqarsuit inornangit	The mountains are reachable
Isigisassat nunaat	Always new land to see
Misigisassat nutaat	Always new adventure to see
Inuit tamarmik utaqqisaat	Everyone is waiting for me
Inuit tamarmik ataqqisaat	Everyone respects me
Anorersuaq perlussuaq aqqusaarlugit	Storm or the bad weather can't stop me
Pingaarutillit tuaviunniarlugit	Gotta hurry to deliver
Avannaarsuanut nunaqarfinnguamut	To the north to the small city

WHY INUIT-LED SOUND WORLDING
AND AUDIOREELISM MATTERS

Recent work on the topic of Indigenous modernity (cf. Bigenho 2002, 2011; B. Diamond 2007a; Diamond, Szego, and Sparling 2012; Hoefnagels and Diamond 2012) raises questions about the direct and concrete implications sonic stereotypes and expectations hold for Indigenous individuals and communities. I want to conclude by discussing the irreconcilable sound worlds of the colonial-versus-Inuit narratives, especially in relation to understandings and inequities among genders and races. I start from my assertion that compared to other top-rated reality shows, *Flying Wild Alaska* offers a radically different approach to sound worlding based in an audioreelism that foregrounds Inuit cultures as unapologetically modern. Table 10.5 compares *FWA* to nine other top-rated shows that either aired more than five seasons *or* aired more than sixty episodes each (these nine are also highlighted in table 10.1) and focuses on one comparable data point: each show's main title song.[19]

Table 10.5 illustrates two shifts in terms of genres represented over a nearly fifteen-year period. The first shift warrants an examination of gender. For shows that debuted between 2005 to 2010, network producers gravitated toward licensing third-party hard rock anthems to serve as theme songs—such as Bon Jovi's "Wanted Dead or Alive" (1986) on *Deadliest Catch*; Aerosmith's "Livin' on the Edge" (1993) on *Ice Road Truckers*; and Jimi Hendrix's "All Along the Watchtower" (1968) on *Ax Men*. The anthems accompany the extractivist narratives of crab

TABLE 10.5 Comparison of main title songs from top-rated, Alaska-based reality television shows

SHOW (release date on iTunes)	MAIN TITLE, ARTIST(S)	GENRE	ORIGIN	LANGUAGE	THEMES
Deadliest Catch	"Wanted Dead or Alive," Bon Jovi	Hard rock	Licensed third party	English	Extractivism, Dangerous Work
Ice Road Truckers	"Livin' on the Edge," Aerosmith	Hard rock	Licensed third party	English	Extractivism, Dangerous Work
Alaska State Troopers	"Main Title," Bleeding Fingers Music	Drama underscore	Original composition	n/a (instrumental)	Extractivism, Dangerous Work
Gold Rush: Alaska	"Intro Song," Didier Rachou	Drama underscore	Original composition	n/a (instrumental)	Extractivism
Ax Men (season 1 only)	"All Along the Watchtower," Jimi Hendrix	Hard rock	Licensed third party	English	Extractivism, Dangerous Work
Flying Wild Alaska	"Frozen Sky" Doug Bossi, Tony Elfers, and Peand-eL	Rap	Original composition	Kalaallisut	Lifestyle, Dangerous Work
Alaska: The Last Frontier	"Alaska: The Last Frontier," Atz Kilcher and Jewel	Contemporary folk	Original composition	English	Lifestyle
Life below Zero	"Naught" FineTune Music	Ambient underscore	Original composition	n/a (instrumental)	Lifestyle
Bering Sea Gold	"Gold in These Hills," Brandon Michael Kinder	Contemporary folk	Original composition	English	Extractivism
Alaskan Bush People	"The Main Bush," Bleeding Fingers Music	Contemporary folk	Original composition	n/a (instrumental)	Lifestyle

fishermen, big-rig drivers (in service of the North Slope oil industry), and logging operations, respectively. Music scholars have demonstrated a homology between hard rock musics and a particular mainstream American hypermasculine ethos (Ramirez 2012; Waksman 2001; Walser 1993), and when hard rock is deployed in relation to extractivism in Alaska, it only further accentuates these three shows' real (read: masculine) men-in-danger premise. These anthems amplify the presence of a small number of settler, primarily male workers while effectively silencing a large number of Alaska Native men and women who occupy the rural areas targeted for resource extraction, such as the Alaska Peninsula communities of Saint Paul and Dutch Harbor (*Deadliest Catch*), the southeast Alaska-Canadian border communities near Klukwan and Skagway (*Ax Men*), or the sub-Arctic and Arctic communities along the Dalton Highway and near Fairbanks, Deadhorse, and Prudhoe Bay (*Ice Road Truckers*).[20]

Mark Trahant, a member of the Shoshone-Bannock Tribe and the 2013–15 Atwood Chair of Journalism at the University of Alaska, Anchorage, noted that whereas Alaska may have led the way in terms of incorporating Native voices in mainstream media three decades ago, Native people's participation has waned significantly in recent years (qtd. in McCoy 2014). The relative absence of Alaska Native voices in the media has significant repercussions in terms of who represents our cultures and lifeways in the past, present, and future, especially in relation to the endurance of positioning Alaska as the last U.S. frontier and resource colony. The very fact that Ariel successfully advocated for and cocreated FWA despite a profound lack of women or Native presence in film and television production is significant and a testament to her vision and perseverance. At various points during the show's three seasons, Ariel tells viewers that she wants to make a positive difference in the world, especially for Native youth facing a serious suicide epidemic. In fact, Ariel explains in the "UNKfest" episode that she invited Pamyua to Unalakleet to do something nice and share the importance of drumming, singing, and dancing with local kids.

After FWA ended Tweto founded a nonprofit dedicated to suicide prevention and launched a second reality television show called *True Alaska*, which aired its pilot episode in November 2017 on the Travel Channel.[21] Describing her new show, Tweto reiterates a similar vision to that of FWA: "I want to make a show about Alaska for Alaskans, and show people that we are more than what you usually see on TV. Yes, we hunt and fish and we live in stunning and difficult terrains. But we also go to the store, live normal lives and have great families" (qtd. in Banwell 2017). Although at the time of this writing it is not clear whether

True Alaska will air an entire season, Ariel's resolve to interrupt the reality television industrial complex by insisting on real representations of Alaska Native people engages in the critical work of advancing Indigenous narratives of self-determination.

The second shift in genres outlined in table 10.5 begins with top-rated Alaska-based shows, aired from 2011 to the present day, that pivot away from hard rock and decidedly toward contemporary folk-style main title songs, two of which feature lyrics (*Alaska: The Last Frontier* and *Bering Sea Gold*) and one that is instrumental (*Alaskan Bush People*). *Life below Zero* is alone in the fact that its main title, as well as its overall sound design, could be categorized as an ambient drama underscore. Given the fact that three of these shows focus on the rural or off-grid lifestyles unique to Alaska and one on blue-collar mining culture, the use of contemporary folk music speaks to associations with the southern, white, rural, working-class United States (Filene 2008; A. Fox 2007). Whereas, on the one hand, FWA's heavy emphasis on more notably urban genres (rock, rap, and R&B musics) could be heard as liberating Inuit musicians from expected colonial notions of authentic traditional forms or genres, I would argue that this also likely speaks to an incomprehensibility or unintelligibility of Inuit drum-dance forms, styles, and grooves (as opposed to the more globally known Inuit vocal game genre) to mainstream audiences. Moreover, the few times Inuit drum-dance songs appear on-screen, the diegetic sound is silenced, and the performers are instead subsumed by a non-Inuit, nondiegetic music, which one might hear as more comprehensible owing to its vague world music or global beat characteristics.

The FWA producer's articulated desire to create a distinct Inuit sound ultimately privileged Inuit languages as the distinctive factor, a predicament related to the vexed concept of audible Indigeneity in that it refers to a subjective enterprise of how one aurally discerns music, sound, or noise as "Indigenous." Diamond explains how mainstream audiences tend to fetishize or privilege musical practices that have "'unusual' timbres, spiritual beliefs, or distinctive social practices. . . . Only indigenous music that exhibits the *expected* linkage between radical sound production and indigeneity is widely known internationally" (2007b, 173; emphasis added). In other words, Indigenous music is always already positioned as "other," and expectations of how the "other" sounds conform to pervasive historical narratives that place Indigenous peoples as having vanished long ago and far away. Colonial powers in the Americas have long aimed to silence Indigenous musical modernities by activating and maintaining agnotology (the logics of ignorance and willful deceit) regarding cultural change, insisting instead that authentic markers of audible Indigeneity are decidedly premodern or ancient. Critics note how the settler nation's inculcation of shame has become a primary mechanism of colonial invasion, alienation, and erasure of Indigenous modernities more broadly: "the policing of tradition as an essence expressive of *real* indigeneity, initially used to shame Indigenous peoples into forcibly abandoning their 'savage' practices, now serves the oppression of multiculturalism" (Amsterdam 2013, 55). In this way, Indigenous individuals and communities are continually faced with a zero-sum game of colonial silencing and shame: one chooses either to internalize or to resist marginalization.

This volume posits that it is time to think beyond what Deloria might call an "unexpected" Indigene (2004) and instead focus on the very real ways in which "it has always been traditional for us to be contemporary" (J.-C. Perea 2012b). To do so requires a radical shift in privileging Inuit- and Indigenous-led projects, especially sound worlding as discussed here. This shift would align with Comanche author Paul Chaat Smith's most recent collection of essays, *Everything You Know about Indians Is Wrong*, which invites readers to reconsider the power of popular, monolithic myths about Native American peoples by self-reflexively asking, "Who are we, and what happened to us?" As his provocative title suggests, Smith challenges Native and non-Native communities alike to pose more questions, and thus dialogue, instead of using what he views as a more standard and closed answer-centered approach: "This is who we are, and this is what happened to us" (2009, 29). As someone who was born and raised in Alaska (a native Alaskan) and who has been living in diaspora for two decades at the time of this writing, I have developed a bit of an obsession with asking questions of Alaska-based reality television. Alongside my diasporic Alaskan peers, I can count on one hand how many shows come even remotely close to representing anything I would call reality. Yet my positionality and responsibilities as a Dena'ina (Alaska Native) woman and critical Indigenous-studies scholar drive my need to amplify the direct connections between an arc of a larger reality television industrial complex and a reinvigoration of settler-colonial narratives rooted in ongoing practices of extractivism. A settler-colonial revolution has indeed been televised through the glorification of narratives that demand dispossessing Native peoples of their lands, rights, and, ultimately, presence through processes of disappearance. Following Smith, I suggest we consider Native musical modernities as invitations to ask questions about our pasts, presents, and futures, particularly those questions that open up possibilities for what could be, such as Ariel envisions, rather than what currently is. In this way, Native sound worlding contributes to critical processes of unsettling the continued maintenance of dominant settler-colonial narratives and demonstrates the ways in which we are not passive voices from the northernmost margins; rather, we have always been actively engaged in using American musical life to our own radical ends.

11. Native Classical Music

Non:wa (Now)

Today I'm modern; tomorrow I'll be modern 'til tomorrow;
yesterday I was modern for yesterday.

Sadie Buck, interview, St. John's, Newfoundland, July 16, 2011

Sadie Buck, one of the leaders in the Rotinonhsión:ni (Iroquois) traditional singing society known as the Six Nations Women's Singers, explains a prevalent understanding of modernity among Native American/First Nations peoples. The Kanienkéhaka (Mohawk) scholar Taiaiake Alfred adds that "Being *Onkwehon:we* [Indigenous] is living heritage, being part of a tradition—shared stories, beliefs, ways of thinking, ways of moving about in the world, lived experiences—that generates identities which, while ever-changing and diverse, are deeply rooted in the common ground of our heritage as original peoples" (2005, 139). In other words, tradition, modernity, and Indigeneity are dynamic processes among First Peoples. We share similar histories and challenges that unite us in common causes, and, most important, we are working toward strengthening and healing our societies for future generations. From these perspectives traditions of the past are brought into the present to be acted out in the future, continually constructing history as it unfolds in a recursive contour. Indigenous modernity is part of a process that creates and maintains Native societies that are grounded in traditional beliefs.

Processes of Indigenous modernity are embedded in Native Classical music, which is music composed by Native musicians, scored in part for Western orchestral instruments and for performance in concert settings.[1] Many Indigenous composers with whom I have worked agree that the genre of Native Classical music is defined by its relationship to a particular training and method of composition that includes performance, history, and theory of Western music. Composers use some kind of written notation in their work. Drawing on the teachings of elders from my own Kanienkéha heritage and using Indigenous language and cosmology as cultural metaphors, this chapter presents various possibilities for examining Native Classical music through Native ears and describing how the processes of Native Classical–music composition and performance reflect Indigenous values of interconnectedness, relationality, continuity, and political action.[2] I begin by examining the concept of modernity from Kanienkéha perspectives, followed by a discussion of traditional creative processes in Indigenous music as employed by Native Classical composers. I illustrate these points through the work of two Navajo composers, Raven Chacon and Juantio Becenti, as well as my own work as a composer and performer.[3] In discussing my own work, I am drawing on the Indigenous research methodology known as autoreflexivity.[4] The many compositional styles employed by Native Classical composers reveal individual personalities and artistry, while expressing certain shared Indigenous worldviews and showcasing the rich cultural diversity that exists among Native musicians.[5]

KANIENKÉHA CONCEPTS OF MODERNITY

The word *modernity* is commonly used in English to distinguish the period of antiquity from that of modernity, yet the Latin root for modern, *modō*, meaning "in a certain manner, just now" (*Free Dictionary* 2013), parallels the Rotinonhsión:ni concept expressed in the epigraph by Sadie Buck. According to Indigenous worldviews, *modern is relative* to the period in which one is living. The concept of modern is seen as dynamic, as it travels through time with us, rendering innovation and new creations as part of a time continuum that includes traditions of the past that affect the future. Similarly, the Kanienkéha concept of *non:wa* (now) refers to three modes of perception: the now of the past, the present, and the future. The word non:wa encapsulates this concept, but it may be understood more fully through three words, as explained by the Kanienkéhaka elder Jan Kahehti:io Longboat: "As Indigenous people, we don't have past, present, and future. All we have is now. *Oksa* is the first now, which means something just happened; non:wa is the second now, that means right at this moment, moving the energy of *oksa* forward. And if we don't learn *oksa* and non:wa, we won't have *onhwehn*, the third or next now" (lecture, Kanatsioharé:ke, NY, August 20, 2013).[6]

In reference to music, she explains, "The language is timeless, so for me, I don't really believe that we are offering music in a contemporary way because it's only bringing back the time to now" (interview, Kanatsioharé:ke, NY, January 12, 2012). Longboat further illustrated her perspective on modernity through a story. A visitor to her healing lodge on the Six Nations Reserve in Ontario asked how she could be "traditional" in such a nice house, getting water from her kitchen spigot. She replied that water is water and is no less precious, no less traditional, whether it comes from a spigot or she draws it from the river. "The concept of sacredness is never lessened by other means, so the fire is still sacred no matter who lights it and how they light it," she explained. "It doesn't lessen the concept of sacredness in our Indigenous knowledge base" (pers. comm., Kanatsioharé:ke, NY, August 23, 2013). Along the same lines, Tol Foster writes, "in an epistemological way, tribal peoples are not disrupted by either the notions of modernity or postmodernity." Susan Stanford argues for multiple modernities at different historical junctures, describing her curiosity about the very term *modernity* in tribal languages: "I do not believe there is any such word in Muscogee, but I suspect that if there is, it is probably 'pickup truck'" (both qtd. in Womack, Justice, and Teuton 2008, 276).

As these scholars suggest, bringing the time back or bringing it forward to now, is indicative of a worldview in which the nows of the past and future are always experienced as part of the present. With an emphasis on relationship, non:wa suggests that moving forward in the present is cyclical, as one takes from the past for the future and back again. Together these concepts point to the intersection of innovation and tradition that underlies the creation and performance of Native Classical music, and they join the existing discourse that critiques binary oppositions separating Indigenous tradition (past) from modernity and innovation (present and future). Leroy Little Bear expands on this worldview in describing our Indigenous connection to the land as the source and reason for continuity and creativity: "The Earth is where the continuous and/or repetitive process of creation occurs. It is on the Earth and from the Earth that cycles, phases, patterns—in other words, the constant motion or flux—can be observed. Creation is a continuity. If creation is to continue, then it must be renewed" (2000, 78). Little Bear cites the importance of renewal ceremonies, the retelling of stories, and the resinging of songs, but I also see newly composed works of music as part of this maintenance of creation.

Indigenous ideas about modernity reflect political and activist stances on the legacy of contact and colonization. From this perspective modernity is seen as having initiated the demise of First Peoples, including the loss of culture, land, language, family, traditions, and livelihood, from genocide, forced assimilation and relocation, and the removal of Native children from their birth families through Indian Residential Schools and adoption. Many see a return to harmony as dependent on cultural revitalization, political activism, and restoration of land rights while fighting for sovereignty to reclaim what was stolen and nearly destroyed. Alfred writes, "We are facing modernity's attempt to conquer our souls. . . . The challenge is to find a way to regenerate ourselves and take back our dignity. Then, meaningful change will be possible, and it will be a new existence" (2005, 38). He advocates for a fight "*against* the state and *for* the re-emergence of Onkwehon:we existences as cultural and political entities unto themselves. Onkwehon:we are in relationships with Settlers, but are not subsumed within the state and are not drawn into its modern liberal ideology of selfish individualism and unrestrained consumption" (133). Like many Onkwehon:we (meaning Native/First Nations or Original Peoples in Kanienkéha), Alfred sees materialism, consumption, and individualism as dangerous byproducts of colonization, having replaced spirituality, collectivism, environmentalism, and community values that have long been central to Native life.

Indigenous modernity, then, involves self-conscious traditionalism, in which First Peoples interact with their history and teachings in ways that reach "beyond reflective practices to an actual political and social engagement with the world based on consensus arrived at through broad conversation among people who are part of that culture" (Alfred 2005, 140). The dynamism in the creative processes of Native Classical composers stems from the synergy between tradition and innovation. Indigenous creative artists create Indigenously. Drawing on these perspectives, how, then, might we define the modernities of Indigenous compositional process?

INDIGENOUS CREATIVE PROCESSES
AND NATIVE CLASSICAL MUSIC

The comparative musicologist Frances Densmore was among the earliest non-Native scholars to address Indigenous creative processes.[7] Densmore wrote that Native American makers of traditional songs either received them in dreams *or* composed them on the basis of a core idea (1927, 393). Indeed, dreams are an important site for the creative process in many Native American cultures. For example, Navajo elders explain that "when we dream, that is the spirit inside of us speaking, and when we hear sounds in our ears, or feel a pricking in our throats, or a twitching of our nerves, or a popping in our noses; that is *Niltche B'yazh* (the Wind Spirit) [speaking to us]" (Lincoln [1935] 2003, 215). Elyse Carter Vosen adds, "Dreams are deeply important. They are cosmological theory put into practice, pulled along/through the fluid continuum from material to spiritual" (2013a). Dreams and music occupy similar psychological realms, "with potential for tapping preverbal, primary process thinking," which may generate a symbolic "language of the unconscious" (Sand and Levin 1992, 163). Both music and dreams may connect one to the subconscious in a kind of twinship that allows the self to be shared with others, sometimes by recreating the dream through music in the conscious world (181–84).[8]

Like traditional Indigenous musicians, Native Classical composers often find inspiration in dreams. For example, when I asked Chacon about his creative process, he replied that "much content comes from dreams. . . . I would say that thirty percent of my work or ideas (including much text) comes from dreams" (email corr., May 3, 2013). I myself wrote the trio *Konti:rio* (Wild Animals) immediately following a dream in which I could recall both the sounds of the music and the visual picture of the score. It contains some of the most interesting counterpoint I have ever written, and although I had to work out some of it mathematically after the fact, I notated most of the piece exactly as it appeared in my dream. It remains one of my favorite "compositions," since I feel no personal ownership or criticism of it, having been the transmitter rather than the composer. When I perform or hear the work, I experience a feeling of completion and centeredness. Although both Chacon and I have received musical ideas from dreams, each of us then works out the details of a piece through a compositional process. We use our dreams to express our realities through music. By recounting the dreams through music, we share our interpretation or creative telling of the dreams with others, reexperiencing the dream in a way that can create twinship, a feeling of sameness and connection.

Traditional processes of Indigenous musical creativity may also involve borrowing melodies, musical instruments, or specific components of style from other Native as well as non-Native peoples (cf. Levine 1998, 2002). Leroy Little Bear explains, "No one has a pure worldview that is 100 percent Indigenous or Eurocentric; rather, everyone has an integrated mind, a fluxing and ambidextrous consciousness, a precolonized consciousness that flows into a colonized consciousness and back again" (2000, 85). Like makers of traditional Indigenous songs, Native Classical composers employ musical borrowing. When we borrow from the Native and non-Native musical traditions to which we belong, however, I prefer to use the terms *direct* or *indirect referencing*, since this implies that these traditions also belong to us. As Native composers, we are cautioned to be respectful in how we incorporate traditional songs and to be aware of concepts of cultural propriety. Some Native Classical composers avoid direct referencing and may purposefully disengage from their communities of origin, whereas others return to their musical roots, employing both direct and indirect cultural references in their work. Nonetheless, the sounds and concepts from our communities of origin remain embedded in our music. Chacon, Becenti, and I do not usually use direct referencing in our music, but we often explain our work in terms of Native thought and employ Native concepts as part of our sonic choices, values, and compositional processes.

Chacon references Navajo concepts of time, place, and stories indirectly, without quoting specific melodic material. About the degree to which his heritage plays into his work, Chacon explains, "There is a culmination of musical experiences I've had, whether it's Navajo music, popular music, rock music, or whatever, that influenced me all up to a point. And then from there, I think I found sounds that I wanted to work with and then developed instruments and techniques and systems to make those happen. As far as consciously trying to quote Navajo music or anything like that, I don't do that. It's more just like using the tools like vocables or maybe some kind of scale that might be found in Navajo music" (workshop, Montgomery College, MD, November 2, 2013). Becenti's understanding of traditional Navajo concepts of form, balance, and cadence are prominent in his work. Describing the emphasis on structure and form in his *Cello Suite* (2009), Becenti explains, "The grounding Navajo cadence is usually in groups of four, mimicking the Navajo [concept of ritual directionality:] what's above me, below me, behind me, and all around me. The cadence is always in fours, even the stanzas are always in fours—the groupings, sets of fours, and it's very repetitive. But the whole purpose of that in my opinion is to dispel tension or evil, and I use it here to release tension . . . in the music. [I use it] not as a device for superficial reasons; it has a purpose" (interview, Rockville, MD, November 5, 2013). I have similarly referenced linguistic and cultural markers in my own compositions that avoid direct citation of individual songs or music. In my string quartet *Hohonkweta'ka:ionse* (Ancestors), for example, I based the melodic material on a twelve-tone row subdivided into two five-note rows and one two-note motif, exploiting and enjoying the stereotypes about Native pentatonicism. I ask the musicians to test their own boundaries by reciting words in Kanienkéha, thus evoking another sonic memory that emphasizes important vibrational qualities inherent in the speaking of my original language. These musical borrowings from our own cultures may not be direct, but they permeate our musical sensibilities.

Most Native Classical composers with whom I have spoken use Western staff notation as part of their compositional process, although many have also composed experimental works that are not fully notated but feature some degree of improvisation or use notational methods created specifically for that particular piece. These works occupy various points along a continuum of contemporary musical expression. On this continuum Becenti's fully notated chamber music appears on one end, Chacon's avant-garde work that may include sonic directions rather than standard musical notation falls on the opposite end, and my work, which combines graphic and staff notations with improvisation, falls somewhere in the middle (figure 11.1). Other Native composers, such as Jerod Impichchaachaaha' Tate and George Quincy, might be placed closer to the classical side, given their use of Western symphonic notation; R. Carlos Nakai and Ron Warren may be placed slightly right of center, given their incorporation of improvisation and jazz harmonies; Brent Michael Davids and Barbara Croall might be more central, given their varied repertory of symphonic, graphic, and notation for unusual instrumentation; Sadie Buck's collaborative operatic writing may be more toward avant-garde. Most Native Classical composers alternate between the use of rational composition plans for form and motivic material with more intuitive and inspirational phases, relying instead on improvisational techniques (cf. Bahle 1938). What differentiates our work from that of non-Indigenous composers are our sources of inspiration and certain working processes. The Anishinaabe composer Barbara Croall, for example, describes her own process as tending toward what Julius Bahle (1938) would call an "inspirational type" of composition:

> Even though I've had some degree of Western training, which I respect and have found enriching, I come from a very strongly intuitive way of thinking and creating. I don't think methodically about what I'm doing, I realize after the piece is done. For Aboriginal people, when you create something, it first comes from the heart, from your feelings and emotions. I'm not saying that artists from other cultures don't think that way, but many already have theoretical systems that create a see-sawing tension between intuition and theory. Songs that I learned and sang were not written down, it was all oral tradition. . . . It's all through listening. Writing things down came later. (Croall 2010)

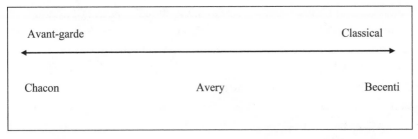

Figure 11.1. Three Native Classical composers on a continuum of style, 2014.
Figure by Dawn Avery.

Finally, underlying Indigenous artistry are layered understandings of relationship and accountability to future generations in accordance with community
needs. All the Native Classical composers with whom I have researched have
been involved in cultural revitalization projects, such as the Composer Apprentice National Outreach Endeavor and the Native American Composer Apprenticeship Program (also known as the Native Composer's Project). Similarly,
the Banff Centre for the Arts in Canada has organized programs in Aboriginal
arts since the mid-1990s. The Aboriginal Women's Music Program, directed by
Sadie Buck, was one of the first of these programs and is regarded by many as
one of the most effective means of empowering Native women creative artists.
These educational endeavors follow Native protocols and encourage Indigenous
expression through the creation of classical music. The Mohican composer Brent
Michael Davids explains, "It's teaching Western music though, not Native, in
order to expand the palette of techniques by which Native students can express
their own Nativeness (using Western-European techniques and written music)"
(email corr., September 21, 2013). Native American composition programs help
to "create a culturally rich music controlled primarily by Indian people rather
than by white composers" and to solidify "a recognizable *cohort* of Indian people
engaged in a congruent activity; the making and remaking of a spectrum of
expectations" (Deloria 2004, 210, 229). Rather than assimilating ourselves into
musical modernism, we are exploring and choosing educational, compositional,
and performance practices and refusing the Western racial imaginary of what
Indigenous music should sound like. Although Native Classical composers and
performers have existed since the 1800s, Native Classical music includes representations of Indians that are, as Philip Deloria writes, still somewhat unexpected.
I have applied the four stages of Indigenous self-determination outlined by

Linda Tuhiwai Smith (2012) to Native compositional processes and programs by superimposing them on the Rotinonhsión:ni calendar with four cardinal directions. The Rotinonhsión:ni calendar is overlaid with concepts taken from the Anishinaabe medicine wheel (figure 11.2).[9] This model suggests that the past is always present in the future and is embedded in modernity. As Pamela Karantonis and Dylan Robinson have written, rather than being understood as an "incongruous pairing of cultural traditions," Native Classical music is "used to express and reassess cultural traditions" (2011, 1). They explore Indigenous modalities specifically in the context of opera, where diverse Indigenous voices express traditions through classical music while focusing on "the potential that hybrid styles and juxtapositions may have as a decolonizing strategy" (7).

THREE NATIVE CLASSICAL COMPOSERS

Indigenous music makers are creative in the now of the past, and contemporary creative expression in various classical genres allows for a reemergence of traditional ideas and sonic landscapes in current contexts. This concept may be illustrated in greater detail through a discussion of specific works by Juantio Becenti, Raven Chacon, and myself. Becenti worked with Chacon as part of the Native American Composer Apprenticeship Program. Chacon is part of the American Indian interdisciplinary arts collective, Postcommodity, with which he has developed multimedia installations exhibited internationally, and he also performs experimental noise music as a soloist. Both Chacon and Becenti have lived and worked near the Navajo reservation in the Four Corners area of the southwestern United States. I am a composer, cellist, and vocalist, and my compositions, which I think of as a form of sensory engagement, are characterized by the inclusion of Indigenous musical instruments, themes, and languages. I often experiment with crossing the boundaries of audience and genre. Selected works of each composer are discussed in turn.

Juantio Becenti

Becenti's compositions, many of which are fully written in Western staff notation, fall farthest to the right on the continuum shown in figure 11.1. But he often looks back on his work after completion to explain what is Navajo about it. For example, he uses Navajo concepts to explain his breaks from Western form and the importance of culture-based concepts of structure in his *Cello Suite*, remarking,

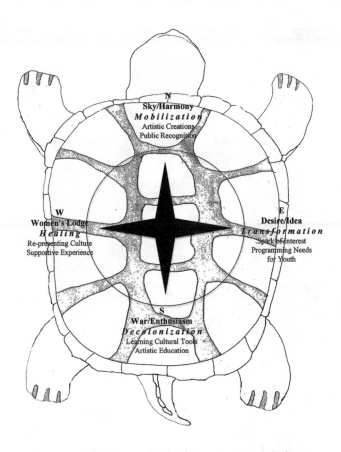

Figure 11.2. Indigenous goals of self-determination applied to
compositional processes and based on traditional symbology, 2014.
Diagram by Dawn Avery.

In Navajo we realize a concept . . . called a spirit line—basically it's just geo-
metric patterns in Navajo weaving; it's very linear, but there's a spirit line that's
broken in one space, so that thoughts can move freely in between. It's purposely
left unfinished, that one line, so it can allow thoughts to move. It's imperfect, I
guess. For example, the *pizz* [marking] at the end of "Recitative No. 2" breaks
with the form of the whole piece because it's structured to mirror one another.
The first sounding of what it would be mirroring is played with the bow, so
technically it would also need to be played with the bow, but in the spirit of
[the spirit line concept], I don't need to be that strict about it. That's just a way
of looking at it. (Interview, Rockville, MD, November 8, 2012)

Rainbow color system	Juantio Becenti

1. Falling and rising halftones   **Pink**
The falling and rising halftones are used traditionally throughout pantonal and extended tonal music and are used here to both release and increase tension.

2. Inverted halftone   **Green**
The interval is a staple of pantonal music and is generally used alongside falling and rising halftones.

3. Tritone   **Yellow**
This interval is also a staple of pantonal music and, alongside the inverted halftone and falling and rising halftones, comprises the vast majority of intervals used in pantonal music.

4. Major and minor seventh chords   **Blue**
These chords are staples of tonal music (often considered to be harmonious rather than dissonant) and are used as a grounding element.

5. Perfect fifth   **Purple**
The perfect fifth is the backbone of tonal music and is used here to complement all the mentioned intervals.

6. Major and minor thirds   **Orange**
This interval, at times quite sensual, is an integral part of tonal music construction and is used here to increase the sense of movement.

7. Navajo cadence   **Red**
In traditional Navajo music there is often a cadence of groupings in four, and the concept is applied here to balance the music.

Figure 11.3. Intervallic structures in the "Rainbow Color System," 2009.
Figure by Juantio Becenti.

His subtle "cultural accents" are part of the germinal phase of his compositional process, during which "subconscious themes, melodies, or ideas break through to consciousness and are seized by the conscious mind" (Max Graf, cited in Bennett 1976, 4).[10] He uses Navajo ideas that are unrecognizable to the listener, but some of these ideas become apparent to the musicians during coaching sessions prior to performance. Other sources of creative inspiration for Native Classical composers include deeply rooted cultural metaphors that can be expressed sonically. For example, Becenti states that he uses "musical markers" to create aural imagery, explaining that "how you remember things can be visual; imagery allows people to think better and imagine—music works that way as imagery, and it allows your mind to wander" (interview, November 8, 2012). Becenti provides rehearsal notes that employ specific cultural references to coach the performer in the interpretation of the work. As an Indigenous performer, I may embody these concepts through the physical performance of his works, but I also activate my trans-Indigenous understanding of his concepts. For example, in the *Cello Suite*, Becenti uses various metaphors to instruct the performers, such as "the faster movement is comical and exaggerated, like some of the Navajo characters"; play like "how a chant would start"; or "play cello like strong drums." His cross-cultural competency is demonstrated by "employing things you'd associate with traditional diatonic music and aspects of dissonant music, such as tri-tones [and] sevenths" (Skype interview, November 1, 2012).

Becenti's concept of musical time is flexible, but he notates intervals precisely and expects pitch accuracy. In discussing one of his works, he describes his "Rainbow Color System" to show how specific intervallic structures determined the form (figure 11.3). Becenti applies a Navajo concept of balance in his use of dissonance and consonance, and he covered this approach to creating musical tension and release during a rehearsal coaching. "These dissonant intervals are sensual and sometimes even violent," he explained. "They create tension and then there's an octave—the cake. That's the release. Let them have cake" (Skype interview, October 20, 2009). He instructed me to push and pull the time in any way that maintained the integrity of suspense and release and to hold tied notes according to the length of time needed to settle into the interval.

In his work for solo violin, titled *Squash Blossom* (2015), Becenti again uses Navajo visual concepts for inspiration. The form of the work is based on the squash blossom–necklace design whose focal point is a central ornament decorated on both sides with a set of five or six beads. Employing dynamics, specific registral timbres, ornamentation, and effects, he wrote six short ornamental passages leading to a larger center and went back through the five-six passages to create a circular imagery. Hinting at the necklace design, the bulb or central material to which he refers as the weight of the piece consists of compositional development of the ornamental, lighter passages. He noted that historically the squash blossom necklace does not have real cultural significance, other than the bulb in the center was used on top of a horse's headpiece, representing wealth and prosperity, and that it appears on both men and women in old photos, making it unisex. The design and history inspires him in his writing, but, according to him, there is no real story behind it. "It's more ornamental—just a beautiful thing to look at which inspired me as a visual concept to write something" (phone interview, August 20, 2015).

In describing what musical composition means to him, Becenti wrote, "I've dedicated myself to music more than anything I ever have in my life because it is deeply satisfying. I recall the first time I heard my music performed for me by other people; I quite literally had an out-of-body experience. A wave of absolute euphoria swept over me and I found myself looking down at myself and everyone else in the room. No experience before or since has approached the joy I felt in that moment" (email corr., May 2, 2013). Becenti achieves a state of euphoria when the performers are able to realize his work according to his vision of how the piece should sound.

Raven Chacon

Chacon's compositions fall farthest to the left on the continuum in figure 11.1. Chacon refers to a kind of cross-cultural competency in which globalization has affected his compositional process. As a member of Postcommodity, Chacon's work is characterized by Indigenous political initiatives that express cultural self-determination. In 2010 Chacon and Postcommodity created a mixed-media installation sound sculpture titled *P'oe iwe naví ûnp'oe dînmuu* (My blood is in the water). This work was commissioned as an Indigenous response to the four-hundredth anniversary of the founding of Santa Fe. The group's website explains that the work memorializes the deer (figure 11.4)

> as a spiritual mediator of the landscape and pays tribute to the traditional pro-
> cesses through which Indigenous people put food on the table—which is an act
> of decolonization against the dominant culture's process of commoditization,
> demand/supply and convenience. The work functions as a semiotic vehicle of
> continuity, connecting past and present through uninterrupted processes of
> Indigenous culture and community attached to this landscape. With blood
> dripping from the hanging deer carcass onto the amplified Pueblo drum, the
> piece becomes an ephemeral time-keeping instrument relaying the history and
> intonation of this land. (Chacon n.d.)

Experiencing this piece had an emotional and timbral impact on me. Pitch was not a dominant factor in the creation of this work, but the deep powwow drum, with a low note between C and D, created a low rumble that caused a profound

Figure 11.4. *P'oe iwe naví* ûnp'oe *dînmuu* (My blood is in the water), 2010.
Photo by Julian McRoberts/Postcommodity. Used by permission.

physical sensation owing to its vibration, resonance, and repetition. The intensity of the sound of the amplified drum was as powerful as the visual and political effect of the sculpture. There was a sense of time stretching because the drops of blood landed on the drum indeterminately, creating silence between the drum sounds. Yet that silence was filled with people talking in the background and the wind rustling the bushes in the performance area. Furthermore, the sights and sounds of the performance space, and the sculpture itself, changed as an integral part of the performance. For me the work created a visceral connection to the layered concepts of Indigenous time, history, and space, exemplifying the concept of non:wa, in which an innovative performance dynamically engages past and present.

Chacon's creative process varies according to the inspiration or motivation for a particular piece:

> It changes every time. A lot of times, more than not, it'll start off with a title or an idea, not necessarily a story or a narrative. Almost never is it a story. The title generally has nothing to do with the piece, ever, but that's the first motivation to start and finish a piece. Other than that, it might be a process or system that sets the entire piece into motion. Other times it's a group of people I'm collaborating with. There are all different kinds of processes, whether it's a recording project or a written, notated composition, or just an improvised performance situation. (Interview, Rockville, MD, November 10, 2012)

In collaborative works, Chacon further remarked that each member of the group contributes individual values and creative practices.

Chacon spoke more specifically about his creative process in a work titled *Táágo Dez'á* (Three points), which I premiered in 2007. In this case the title provided the conceptual inspiration for the piece but also determined the form and compositional approach. He stated that certain "conceptual symbols or ideas . . . get relayed through the piece in different ways. For example, the cello piece, for you, was a triangle, so the number three was a big motivation and determined the form of the piece. . . . The number three also came up with each point representing the composer, the performer, and the audience. Three was a consideration for everything that was done in the piece. If ever there was a wall I came upon, three would be the answer for that" (interview, November 10, 2012). Although the number three held no cultural significance for Chacon, he used it to explore three methods of notation: standard staff notation, images for improvisation, and oral transmission (in which I was asked to listen to a prerecorded CD). The use of these methods constitutes both a musical experiment and a political statement on the roles of Western notation and pictorial, oral, and aural modes of transmission.

Chacon explained his notation and expectations for the performance of *Táágo Dez'á* as follows: "There's different designs in here like arrows, and what some of you may call Swastika, but that's not what it is. A symbol used in Hopi and Navajo migration, this symbol means a lot of different things to different tribes, but [it] was unfortunately stolen for different reasons. But just because it means migration in some Indigenous tribes, Dawn's able to interpret it however she wants—maybe some kind of circular movement or whatever she wants to use for that symbol" (performance workshop, Montgomery College, MD, November 10, 2012).[11] In the second movement of *Táágo Dez'á*, Chacon suggested that I should "imagine being scared, looking for your grandfather, like in a desert, at night." For a passage involving triple-stopped pizzicati, he suggested that I play so that it sounds like "distorted powwow drums." At the end of the same movement, he suggested that I fade the sound like "the sound of a breeze" (rehearsal notes, Montgomery College, MD, November 2, 2008).

In another sound installation piece, *Singing toward the Wind Now/Singing toward the Sun Now* (2012) Chacon drew inspiration from the environment of Canyon de Chelly and the electrical towers along the side of the road, reminding him of Navajo deities and mythology. His piece consists of four sound sculptures that are about eight feet tall; some have sound generators, solar panels, and wind harps, which create sound (figure 11.5). Chacon explained,

That's a piece I've been thinking about since I was a child. There were these giant monsters walking through the desert. That had always been a story in my head. Those were symbols, or signs, that a bigger being was watching over you, for better or worse. I call them monsters, but I wanted them to be symbols of the Navajo Reservation rather than encroachments. It was my decision to make them a council where they would speak together, as if they were disguised as these monsters. You could stand by them and listen to them, learn from them. That was a mythology I've thought about for a long time. They're designed obviously after electrical towers; for me, I think the electrical towers also look like Navajo deities called *yé'i*.[12] They take on these designs that I believe were maybe foreseen sometime in the past and have come to actualization in the present. The shapes are very geometrical. One looks like a stalk of corn, one looks like a lightning bolt, and two look sort of like figures. It's possible that

11.5. *Singing toward the Wind Now/Singing toward the Sun Now*, sound installation by Raven Chacon, 2012. Photo by Julien McRoberts and Eileen Braziel. Used by permission.

someone had seen those in the past and had drawn them. Part of the mythology is that these shapes were influenced by Navajo mythology. (Interview, November 10, 2012)

Thus, Chacon's work does not include overt musical borrowing, nor is it simply imbued with a Navajo cultural "flavor." Rather, it derives from Chacon's current life experience and inventive experimentation with sound, while connecting to Navajo mythology in a complex way. It allows the past to blend with the future, as different environmental conditions generate continual changes in the sound. He explained, "The sound changes when the sun shines, when it's cloudy, and when birds fly through [the structures]" (performance workshop, November 10, 2012).

Chacon told me that he does not consciously compose or improvise Indigenously, but, because he is a Native person, his background and heritage emerge naturally in his work. His Indigenous focus depends on the parameters of a specific project. His concepts regarding time as flexible and pitch as secondary contrast with the usual expectations in contemporary classical music, which stress specific rhythms and pitch accuracy.[13] Furthermore, he explained that he "is not interested in conveying or relaying any personal emotions, nor emotions in general" (email corr., May 2, 2013). Interestingly, his work often stimulates highly charged emotional responses among the audience, ranging from exhilaration to rage. In the piece *Yellowface* (2005) Chacon inserted microphones into a yellow balloon, which he pushed against his face while singing a Navajo chant, manipulating the sounds using electronic effects. During a 2009 performance of this work, some audience members appeared to be upset and covered their ears, whereas others sat wide-eyed on the edges of their seats, cheering after the performance.

Dawn Avery

My work falls somewhere between Becenti and Chacon on the continuum in figure 11.1, and my compositional style is often considered ironic. For example, in *Decolonization* (2006/2018) for cello and voice, I juxtaposed a Rotinonhsión:ni Women's Stomp Dance song, a genre banned at one time by both the United States and Canada, against the U.S. national anthem, which I played in imitation of the distorted sounds produced in Jimi Hendrix's interpretation (figure 11.6). I wrote this piece following a talk by the Kanienkéhaka elder, Tom Porter, at the Kanatsioharé:ke Mohawk community, in which he asked, "How do you

11.6. Musical excerpt from *De-colonization*, 2006. By Dawn Avery.

decolonize the colonized?" His lecture combined storytelling, humor, compassion, myth, history, and current solutions. In my piece I too borrow melodic elements from various musical genres, including a Yuman healing song, an Iroquois women's dance, a Cherokee peace chant, early American blues, the National Anthem, and Gregorian chant. Thus, *Decolonization* asks many questions (Avery 2007). In creating the piece, I alternated between the inspiration of borrowed musical material, using storytelling to create a through-composed form, and specific rational manipulations of contemporary compositional and performance techniques.

Many of my works include audience participation, musicians embedded within the audience, and multimedia such as film projection, narration, and dance. They must be adapted to each performance venue, whether it is a concert stage or an outdoor arena. Adapting a work to a specific venue requires the use of performance cues, fermati, and vamps. For example, *Fringe* (2008) invites the audience to participate in a communal and cultural experience as we cross boundaries of social, political, and psychological expectations in classical-music performance. A singing and dancing audience is asked to encircle the performers, blurring audience-performer boundaries. I employ direct musical borrowing by teaching the audience to sing part of another Rotinonhsión:ni Stomp Dance, which is accompanied by Native and non-Native instrumentation. The piece uses both Western staff notation and improvisation. In an interview by Rebecca Draisey-Collishaw, I stated,

I wanted people to have a performative experience of what it means to be in, on, or witnessing the fringe. To me that may mean something very different than for somebody who isn't Native. . . . The Women's Stomp Dance is a song that is used publicly in which Native and non-Native [people] may participate. It's about Native pride. . . . So to have people singing and dancing that song on the periphery or the margins of the theatre puts them physically on a fringe. . . . There is a lot of beauty and power in the fringe, especially if we hold onto our traditions. . . . That's part of its political implication. The fact that the audience and chamber musicians are in the middle with everyone else walking around them is that you can't really forget that we're there. We have held the space for centuries and you will always hear us. (Draisey-Collishaw 2010, 4)

Sounds, language, and movement from my tradition are incorporated and shared with contemporary classical instrumentation and notation, in cross-cultural competency for the future.

When a student asked what composing is like for me, I replied, "Time stops when I compose. I forget eating, appointments, getting the mail. It becomes all-encompassing. I'm so inside the process that all else fades away. . . . Sometimes, I'd go so out of body and into a dream or trance state that when I lived in New York City, I couldn't even cross the street safely after writing. . . . It's like a deep meditation" (lecture transcription, Memorial University, NF, February 2010).

———

The work of these three Native Classical composers illustrates some of the ways in which contemporary performances and compositions "embody memories of place and personal experience, recontextualizing and resituating the past to be useful in the present and future" (B. Diamond 2011c, 130). For all three compos-ers, form is usually determined by something external: pitch for Becenti, history and sound for Chacon, and cultural melody and memory for me. Becenti's style is strongly note-driven, whereas Chacon is more interested in sonic landscapes; both composers perceive time as flexible and as determined by the performer and the performance. By contrast, most of my works are conducted or are set in a specific meter, but flexibility lies in the performer's interpretation, audience participation, and improvisation, which are determined in part by the perfor-mance space. Each of these compositional processes refuses the direct quotation of traditional music and what we might consider a hegemony or normativity of Indigenous sound worlds. Instead, the processes undertaken by each composer grapple with the question of how to render Indigenous thought in musical form. In doing so, the works described in this chapter demonstrate how Native Classical music interacts with and simultaneously embodies the past, present, and future.

Culture permeates all that we do as Indigenous people, and all societies have been affected by the consciousness of original peoples. That consciousness is embedded within the land on which we live and is reflected in the values, governance, language, place names, and intergenerational memories of all humans. Until all peoples acknowledge the rights and sovereignty of Indigenous peoples, human societies may not grow to their fullest potential. The process of decolonization or reenculturation is therefore a constructive and healing force for Natives and non-Natives alike. Native Classical composers embody this decolonizing force by presenting Indigenous worldviews and new artistic creations in performances directed at diverse audiences. As Anna Hoefnagels and Beverley Diamond explain, "decolonization is arguably needed more among populations who were historically the privileged, the colonizers. Here . . . new concepts of embodiment might be the most transformative. It is audiences whom the indigenous creators of . . . recent works are inviting into a new relationship" (2012, 56). The past is always present in the future and is embedded as part of modernity. By going back and bringing tradition forward, we are strengthened in the "modern" world. Native Classical compositions serve as a means through which we represent ourselves as Indians, to some unexpectedly, and they are part of a gift that drives us as creative beings who are also Native.

In 2007 I founded the North American Indian Cello Project (NAICP), in which I perform, record, commission, and lecture about Native Classical music. Several of the works discussed in this chapter originated through that project, and my own embodied relationships to these works is central to my musical practice. For their inspiration, I thank Howard Bass, Georgia Wettlin-Larsen, and Brent Michael Davids, who developed the first Native Classical–music program at the National Museum of the American Indian in November 2006. That program gave me the opportunity to perform with talented Native American Classical musicians who shared my interests and outlook on the role of Native Americans in contemporary classical music. The NAICP has enabled me to commission, perform, and record a small number of classical works for cello written by Native North American composers. I want to thank these composers for their collaboration and friendship. The NAICP was funded by a grant from the First Nations Composers Initiative project, which was supported by the Ford Foundation's Indigenous Knowledge, Expressive Culture grant program of the American Composers Forum.

DYLAN ROBINSON

12. Speaking to Water, Singing to Stone

Peter Morin, Rebecca Belmore, and the Ontologies of Indigenous Modernity

The phrase "Indigenous modernity" has sometimes been used to address the postcontact impact of settler-colonial culture on Indigenous peoples. It lays out one of many non-Western histories of modernity that, according to Dilip Parameshwar Gaonkar, "have arrived not suddenly but slowly . . . awakened by contact, transported through commerce; administered by empires; bearing colonial inscriptions; propelled by nationalism; and now steered by global media, migration and capital. And [they] continue to 'emerge and arrive,' as always in opportunistic fragments accompanied by utopian rhetorics, but no longer from the West alone" (1999, 1). Historians of both Western and subaltern forms of modernity, note Gaonkar, have often situated the concept along positive and negative axes, or what he calls "the irresistible but somewhat misleading narrative about the two types of modernities, the good and the bad." The narrative of "bad" modernity is a narrative of societal modernization characterized by "the emergence and institutionalization of market-driven industrial economies, bureaucratically administered states, modes of popular government, rules of law, mass media, and increased mobility, literacy, and urbanization" (2). Implicit in this societal modernization are colonial ideologies that sought to remake subaltern subjects literate (in English), productive (for the state), and law-abiding (of Western law). While historians of Indigenous and settler-colonial history continue to deconstruct the narrative of "bad modernity" that positions Indigenous peoples as helpless victims (Raibmon 2005; Thrush 2016, among others), much work remains in documenting Indigenous perspectives on the histories and impacts of colonial modernity, to trace the particularity of these histories across different Indigenous communities across Canada and the United States, and to understand the agency, refusal, and response of Indigenous subjects in such histories.

In contrast with "bad modernity," Gaonkar characterizes the scholarship of "good modernity" as that which affirms cultural innovation. Here there are "no aesthetic limits that could not be transgressed, no moral norms that could not be subverted. One must explore and experience everything . . . that would spur imagination, quicken sensibilities and deepen feelings" (1999, 2–3). With the rise of Indigenous rap, noise music, opera, and throat boxing, we witness one aspect of what has been called—in this collection and elsewhere—the musics of Indigenous modernity that bring Indigenous story, worldview, and song presented within new contemporary musical forms. Responding to Gaonkar's call to reconsider such binary narratives of modernity, this chapter critiques the usage of the phrase "Indigenous modernity" in ethnomusicological research as a consistently affirmative marker for contemporary Indigenous musical genres and questions how the rise of the term "Indigenous modernity" has predominantly tended toward Gaonkar's category of "good modernity."

The phrase "Indigenous modernity" is often used to periodize or aesthetically categorize contemporary Indigenous practices. The phrase is seldom, if ever, used to examine the ontological or epistemological aspects of Indigenous musical practices. Here we see in operation the same binary principle identified by Kofi Agawu (2003) in scholarship on African music: a separation between music's function and its aesthetic aspects. Agawu critiques ethnomusicology about African music as reinforcing traditional music's primary significance as ritual or function (such as in talking-drum practices, for example) instead of its aesthetic. In response to this binary, Agawu proposes that traditional African music should be analyzed using formalist and structural models of analysis, a position that has since been expanded through the work of Michael Tenzer (2006) and challenged by Gabriel Solis (2012).

One could similarly note how analyses of traditional Indigenous music (here using Solis's expansive and forward-thinking conception of analysis that focuses on interdisciplinary approaches rather than applying Western forms) have been a rare occurrence in ethnomusicological research of the twenty-first century. Solis's proposal for expanded conceptions of ethnomusicological analysis is important in another sense as a prompt to those who study Indigenous music to reformulate the practice of analysis itself. More particularly, Solis's work incites us to question how Indigenous-centered models of formal and structural analysis might be developed (cf. Avery, in this volume). How might specific principles drawn from Indigenous worldviews develop into what I call "sensory-formalist" models of music analysis (D. Robinson n.d.) and in doing so deconstruct the binaries of form/context and function/aesthetic that continue to underpin scholarship on Indigenous music? Questions pertaining to the development of new forms of Indigenous analysis hold great potential for the future of Indigenous studies and Indigenous sound studies.[1] In particular, given that Indigenous song has the ontological status of "work" or "doing," it is important to question how formal, structural, and aesthetic analysis proceeds along similar lines of inquiry. Beginning from an examination of how scholarship has to date neglected the ontological significance of contemporary Indigenous music and performance, this chapter contributes to a redefinition of Indigenous sound studies through analysis of the work that Indigenous contemporary sound art does.

A number of contributors to this collection theorize the complexity of Indigenous modernities beyond the conflation, "Indigenous contemporary music equals Indigenous modernity." Several authors also question whether the term should be employed at all and instead insist on establishing alternative ways to describe how innovation and change take place from the standpoint of Indigenous languages and epistemologies. Despite such reevaluation, writing about Indigenous music and modernity continues to employ the phrase "Indigenous modernity" as a synonym for "contemporary Indigenous music." One explanation for this use of the phrase to simply describe contemporary Indigenous music might be located in the history of the discipline of ethnomusicology itself. That is, "Indigenous modernity" as a phrase used to describe contemporary Indigenous music arises out of an effort to counter the binary specters of "authenticity" and "tradition" that haunt the Western discourse of ethnomusicological modernity. Using "Indigenous modernity" to describe contemporary Indigenous music effects a certain degree of legitimization that belies a history (and persistent haunting) of the disciplinary denigration of the popular and contemporary. In considering the academic credibility and affective impact (to an academic readership) that the phrase "Indigenous modernities" boldly announces, we must understand its connotations of a temporality that counters "bad modernity": "Step right up, folks, and see the amazing Indigenous modernities!" Like the circus call that proclaims a promise, the trick behind this illusion is the exceptionality and spectacle of the act that overcomes the negative perception of the aberrance. If Indigenous modernities is the miracle elixir, an "Indian Sagwa," then what are we hoping it might cure?

My critical orientation to this phrase is not mutually exclusive of scholarship that seeks to affirm the vitality and diversity of contemporary Indigenous music, and the critical perspective I offer here is not one that intends to criticize others' acknowledgments of contemporary Indigenous musical practices' significance and social efficacy. My critique instead asks how we might consider some of the blind spots and spectacle of the phrase that may not follow through on its promise. Yet I am not content to leave behind the potential of this term either, what it "imagines otherwise" (Chuh 2003; Justice 2014, 298). Rather than conceptualizing Indigenous modernity as an aesthetic or genre difference, I argue that in examining Indigenous musical modernities, we must go well beyond merely describing the contemporary aesthetics of Indigenous cultural practices and question when and how ontologies of Indigenous song continue to be articulated, renegotiated, and transformed in contemporary artistic media. To study Indigenous ontologies of expressive practice is to study how those practices and their components (oration, regalia, dance, song, ceremony, storytelling) serve functional purposes other than the equivalent Western forms of artistic expression. Specifically, this chapter's examination of Indigenous ontologies of music and oration focuses on the ways in which Indigenous songs and speech "do" things beyond their aesthetic function (for contemplation) or communicative function (for conveying information). Understanding ontologies of Indigenous cultural practice requires that we attend to the ways in which such practices achieve, enact, or bring something into being. To illustrate this, I consider how sound art by the Tahltan Nation artist Peter Morin and the Anishinaabe artist Rebecca Belmore have functional efficacy, given their situation in public, non-Indigenous presentation contexts.

SITE SINGING TO THE FOUNDATIONS OF EMPIRE

If asked to imagine the iconic landmarks of London, one might think first of Big Ben, Buckingham Palace, or London Bridge. To visit these sites is to encounter crowds of tourists snapping selfies, preserving the memory of the visit through photos. Much less frequently, however, do we encounter tourists in active conversation with these sites, for example, speaking to Big Ben, telling a joke to the Houses of Parliament, or singing to Buckingham Palace. Selfies are ubiquitous, but the "singie" has yet to materialize as a phenomenon. Singing to objects, sites, and architectures, though they may not have taken hold among tourist publics, are exactly the kind of public interactions employed by the Tahltan Nation artist Peter Morin in his 2013 series, *Cultural Graffiti*.

Whereas Morin's interventions might seem less out of place when considered alongside other musical performance occurring at tourist sites, such as busking or summer festivals, there is an important distinction between these forms of performance and Morin's work. Unlike the intention of busking to entertain a live audience, Morin's performances are—like the act of graffiti itself—created under a certain level of concealment. Although they are located in highly public tourist areas, Morin's acts of cultural graffiti are importantly "hidden in plain sight" or, perhaps, "doubly voiced in open earshot." The Western ontological understanding of song and the phenomenological framework of listening here act as screens that afford a certain level of privacy between Morin and his intended interlocutors. Though they are certainly present in great numbers at the sites of Morin's cultural graffiti interventions, the hundreds of selfie-taking tourists are not the primary public to which Morin sings. Instead, in the midst of this crowd, Morin's public is one more intimate, consisting of ancestors, both British and Indigenous, as well as other-than-human relations.

The cultural graffiti interventions that Morin vocalized across the city of London in June 2013 resulted from an invitation to take part in an artistic residency extended by the Indigeneity in the Contemporary World project at Royal Holloway, University of London. The "counter-monumental" (Young 1993) work that emerged from this residency questioned the assumption that public art must be for the broadest range of viewers (i.e., the general public). Yet these works were not the first of Morin's work to engage ancestral and other-than-human publics, nor were they the first to imbricate Western and Indigenous forms of public engagement. Morin's cultural graffiti work developed as part of a long-term exploration of the intersections between contemporary performance art and ceremony in Tahltan and Pacific Northwest First Nations traditions.

Before working with Morin on his *Cultural Graffiti* performance interventions in London, I had previously worked with him on a project called *The Aesthetics of Reconciliation*, on the role of the arts in Canada's Truth and Reconciliation Commission (TRC) on the Indian Residential Schools. As part of this project, Morin attended several of the TRC national events with a group of Indigenous and non-Indigenous scholars. After attending several of these events, Morin created a work in response and an essay that described his experience of the

TRC and the work he created. Writing about his participation in the TRC national events, Morin conveyed his disjointed experience through the poetics of a list:

Residential School survivors making public testimonies. Residential School Survivors making private testimonies. Residential School survivors sitting in a circle to make testimony with other survivors. town hall meetings. public forums for "our Canadians" to speak to the difficult histories of residential school. didactic panels that share a carefully determined language about this difficult history. linear histories. stand at one end and read your way backwards or forwards. panels to help you to get a better picture.

―――

The survivors who give public testimony are projected on large screens for viewers at the back of the room. The event is carefully choreographed, with imagined attendance numbers. Our emotions are also carefully choreographed. Volunteers walk through the aisles with tissue and kind words. Don't interrupt the live stream broadcast of the testimony.

―――

The difficult task is finding actions to activate this space where Indigenous knowledge meets settler ways of being. they are bodies of knowledge that mingle and impact each other. And often their meeting requires yet another meeting. (Morin 2016, 60, 70, 71; lowercased words are in Morin's original quotations throughout)

Key for Morin in attending the TRC events was a decided lack of ways to share his thoughts and experiences outside of the sanctioned spaces of the TRC and its predetermined forums of testimony taking. As Morin notes, different spaces for testimony included private, community-supported, and public forums, town-hall gatherings to address a largely settler public, church areas to speak with members of the churches, and even a talent show open to anyone willing (and confident enough) to take the stage. Yet, despite these various spaces, there were few culturally specific forums for sharing experiences and for spending time exclusively with the larger Indigenous community. The space that perhaps came the closest to a culturally specific forum was the talent show. Yet even this took place within a Western performer-audience dialectic on stages where survivors and intergenerational survivors shared their work in the venues' cavernous atmospheres. Although there were numerous performances by Indigenous musicians, singers, and artists, throughout the TRC's spaces not limited to the talent show, there were few instances of space dedicated for nation-specific forms of community gathering.

Similarly, as expressed by Morin, the format of the expressions of reconciliation sessions largely precluded other forms of contribution, for instance, singing to the Bentwood box, as he had hoped he might do upon attending the TRC for the first time at the Victoria Regional Event. These formats, as Morin notes, fit Indigenous experience into a series of "gathering spaces, spaces that divide up intention and accessibility. This division also effectively splits up time. Scheduled events are taking place throughout these separate locations simultaneously. This results in a disjointed experience, a broken connection with the events of the day(s)." Rather than engendering complementary relationships among its constituent parts, the TRC's segmentation of truth and time-tabling of reconciliation prescribed a decidedly non-Indigenous epistemological framework that to a large degree disallowed Indigenous practices of visiting and culturally specific formats and protocols for engagement. In such an environment, notes Morin, "My truth and reconciliation is not invited. It feels like my truth and reconciliation is not invited to the party" (2016, 70).

Motivated by this fact, for the final meeting of the Aesthetics of Reconciliation project at the Montreal TRC event in April 2013, Morin was commissioned to create a new work that would reflect on the TRC events he had attended over three years.[2] His response to the range of testimony he witnessed at the TRC was a two-part, two-evening long work titled *this is what happens when we perform the memory of the land*. The first evening of this work was a multiact performance involving videos contributed by numerous Indigenous and ally artists, as well as new regalia, dances, and oration in a contemporary potlatch, where the components of the ceremony were replaced by a range of artistic contributions from honored contributors. Drawing on the form of potlatch, our research team assembled in the performance area as honored witnesses (figure 12.1).[3] Describing the role of witnesses within potlatch ceremony, Morin notes that "witnesses are selected to act as the memory of the event. they watch, record, document, and perform the order of events. these witnesses become living memories of the potlatch. . . . we were holding something like a potlatch. we were invited to become living memories of the events" (Morin 2016, 76).[4]

12.1. *this is what happens when we perform the memory of the land*, August 2013. Photo by Dylan Robinson. Used by permission.

On the second evening the work unfolded in the form of a dance. This dance, however, was not a dance performance for an audience but a dance where everyone present was invited to participate for a specific aim. Its explicit intention was to give strength to the TRC commissioners as they continued to hear hundreds of stories from Residential School survivors about the various forms of abuse they endured while attending Residential School. In creating this two-part, two-evening performance, Morin describes his objective of continuing tradition by hosting a contemporary (art) potlatch involving settler-ally participants and Indigenous artists from across Canada who contributed video oratories, new regalia, and new dances to tell this part of the shared history of Residential Schools and to contribute to a stronger future:

> a new ceremony. a new dance to address a current historical trauma. much like a dance to remember small pox. or a mask that remembers death. thinking about the commissioners of the Truth and Reconciliation Commission. thinking about the work that is required of them. thinking about how to keep them strong. I offer this work. this dance. this remembrance. to them. to their work. to keep them strong. because we need them. we need them to finish strong. we need them to look at these stories and tell us their opinion. we need this

because it helps us to see the next steps. I honour them and their work. and I ask ahdighi denetia to keep them safe. (Morin 2016, 89)

This work, like other pieces in Morin's extensive artistic output, emphasized creating new traditions that bring together popular culture and contemporary artistic practices with Tahltan-specific ceremony, song, and regalia. During the second evening Morin used a dance remix by Calvin Harris featuring Florence and the Machine singing "Sweet Nothing." With its repeated chorus, "You're giving me such sweet nothing," Morin noted that it was "*a perfect song to sing to colonization. a perfect song to dance to*" (Morin 2016, 88).

As is the case for many First Nations peoples of the Pacific Northwest, the work that we do in our longhouses and big houses has important functions and is in most cases not carried out primarily through an epistemology of performance (and spectating) that is *for* an audience's aesthetic contemplation. The function of song—what Gary Tomlinson (2009) in reference to the Aztec *cantares* has called "songwork"—operates in numerous ways that include reaffirming rights and privileges of families and individuals, documenting important changes including marriages and the transfer of rights and privileges, healing, documenting history and rights to territory, and conveying knowledge about the lands of which Indigenous people are caretakers. These functions are what many Northwest coast First Nations communities call the "business" of longhouse gathering. In Morin's ceremony, during the second evening of *this is what happens when we perform the memory of the land*, we danced to acknowledge the magnitude of the work that the TRC commissioners had undertaken in listening to thousands of survivors but also to help give them strength and support them in finishing their work over the remaining two years, when the commission concluded in the summer of 2015 and the findings were reported (TRC 2015a). Our work, as dancers, here served a function other than as an aesthetic object of spectatorship. Our work that evening was for the commissioners.

ANCESTRAL AND OTHER-THAN-HUMAN PUBLICS

Like Morin's *this is what happens when we perform the memory of the land*, the work that resulted from Morin's London residency in 2013 was not, in the first instance, a performance directed to a physically present audience. Although tourists and members of the British public were present in large numbers at the sites where Morin sang, his intended public was one of ancestors and other-than-human relations. For example, in visiting Buckingham Palace, Morin spoke directly to British ancestors who effected colonization. Morin describes speaking and singing to these ancestors:

buckingham palace. thousands of people. set up the blanket. put on your armour. sing the song. the song that is a tahltan river rushing inside of me. the drum speaks. it says "this drum supports indigenous voice." the drum beats are bullets. does anyone know this? (only me). sing the song. fall down and sing the song into the land. drum and sing around the monument. overheard conversations: 1. i think he thinks he's an indian, 2. shhh. this is an indigenous performance.

walk up to the gate. wearing the amour. use your voice to write on the gate. the words "we are still here. we remain. we are still vibrant. you did not fucking win anything. today. you lose everything." (Morin, email corr., July 19, 2013)

In creating *Cultural Graffiti*, Morin visited two different kinds of sites over the course of several weeks in June. The first set of sites were British landmarks, many of them the support structures of colonial power and monarchy. These monuments, as Morin states, "cement colonial history, and are foundational to that history. . . . They reinforce it" (Peter Morin and Dylan Robinson, interview, Royal Holloway, University of London, May 23, 2013). The landmarks Morin tagged with song included the Houses of Parliament and Big Ben, the Magna Carta monument, the Tower of London, Buckingham Palace, the Canada Gate at Buckingham Palace, the memorial to Princess Diana in Hyde Park, and a statue of Queen Victoria at Royal Holloway, University of London (figures 12.2 and 12.3).

As is apparent in these images, Morin sang to the foundations of former empire quite literally by singing to the physical foundations of the statues and structures. In an interview with Morin following these interventions, he describes his relationships to these works, including the statue of Queen Victoria:

A lot of Indigenous communities believe that the artwork is alive; that the creation or production of artwork is imbibing it with a spiritual existence. So in some respects there is a little bit of Victoria's spirit in that statue. And so coming into contact with it, engaging it from that knowledge production framework, it becomes quite serious . . . and a little bit overwhelming. And so these interactions have been about singing Tahltan Nation songs — cultural knowledge — singing those songs into the stones; understanding that the stones are alive, they are the ancestor peoples. And so part of the work is

12.2. Peter Morin singing to the pavement at Buckingham Palace, August 2013. Photo by Dylan Robinson. Used by permission.

12.3. Peter Morin walking away after speaking and singing into the Canada Gate of Buckingham Palace, August 2013. Photo by Dylan Robinson. Used by permission.

singing directly and saying directly to the spirit of Victoria for example "we are alive, we remain, we are vibrant, you did not win." And leaving these acts as . . . I'm trying to frame them as cultural graffiti. But the act is going inside of the monument, inside of the stone . . . trying to enact direct challenge to the colonial power. (Morin and Robinson, interview)

Using his voice to tag these sites of colonial power, Morin asserted cultural resilience by singing what is commonly referred to as the "Tahltan national anthem" composed by Beal Carlick. In doing so, Morin also participated within the habitual sonic framework of public culture at these sites where the British national anthem is commonly heard. Some interventions also concluded with Morin declaring, "We are still here," to those British ancestors who took part in the colonization of Indigenous lands and waterways now known as Canada. In contrast with his visits to British landmarks, Morin visited a second set of sites in which he used a different strategy of song intervention. These visits focused on lesser-known Indigenous monuments and sites of Indigenous presence in London and included Pocahontas's gravesite in Gravesend and Kwakwaka'wakw carver Mungo Martin's totem pole at Great Windsor Park.

In a subsequent visit to London in October 2013 Morin staged a related intervention (related to this set of performances but taking place in a subsequent visit to London in October 2013) inside and outside of St. Olave's Church, where the first captured infant from the Americas was buried. In 1577 Martin Frobisher took captive an Inuit man, woman, and infant from Baffin Island. Whereas the man and woman died shortly after arriving in Bristol, the infant was taken to London, where Queen Elizabeth I was keen to claim him as a royal subject. In considering this history, Morin saw connections with the much longer history of First Nations children being taken from their families to Indian Residential Schools. After much conversation and attempted negotiation between Morin, myself, and an increasingly anxious Anglican minister at St. Olave's, Morin asked the minister, "What *would* you allow us to do in the church in order to honor this child?" The minister responded, "You are welcome to have a ceremony in your head."

Rather than considering this defeat, Morin responded to the minister's steadfast refusal of all "pagan" as well as all artistic proposals to honor the child by creating a silent ceremony. For this intervention Morin gathered together a small group of people to honor the captured infant, beginning with a procession toward St. Olave's Church. Morin led the way, silently drumming, allowing each beat of his drum stick to stop just before it hit the drum. Yet as we walked, these visual beats carried just as much resonance, if not more, than if they were aurally present, perhaps because of their sonic censorship. Morin asked us to follow behind him and take turns singing or speaking messages for the infant into a jar of devil's club tea. This act, although again nearly silencing our songs and messages, had an even more palpable resonance individually as our voices filled the jar. Before we individually entered the church, Morin asked that we each bring some of the devil's club tea into the church, take a moment to remember this child or "have a silent ceremony in our head," and then leave the tea somewhere in the church. To conclude the performance Morin took the remaining tea and washed the exterior wall of the church with it. The entirety of this action took place in silence, yet the sensory resonance was palpable.

Morin's written response on Facebook, postperformance, shared our work with members of the Tahltan community and Indigenous arts communities and was reshared widely by other networks of the small group who participated. Morin described the work we undertook that day as part of what I consider a "Facebook oratory":

> today. singing. singing to this baby. remembering this inuit baby. remembering and respecting all of our stolen babies. sitting in silence in the church. holding the medicine of our land. an important collaborator. seeing the baby. holding the baby. reminding the baby we have not forgotten. we do not forget. we love you. we are holding you. crying. laughing. dancing. heart singing. heart drum beats. holding medicine. we are working together. thank you to all of our collaborators. here in london. and there on the land. thank you medicine. you are a powerful force. and then. washing the church with our medicine tea. the words. even a buried heart is still a beating heart. thank you all for helping to remember this still a beating heart. (Morin, Facebook post, October 31, 2013)

This Facebook oratory offered a different way for the larger Indigenous community to witness the interventions that we enacted. In response to his intervention at St. Olave's one woman noted "every time I hold my daughter when she cries . . . I think of all the ancestor moms who got that chance taken from them. . . . So your post and the event hit home" (Facebook comment, October 31, 2013).

In each of these interventions, Morin enacts a form of Indigenous nation-to-nation contact with ancestors, while his Facebook oratories communicate this work across larger Indigenous communities in which Morin is a part. Whereas the phrase "nation-to-nation" has become commonplace as a way to assert the necessity for sovereign forms of dialogue between the government of Canada and First Nations, Métis, and Inuit peoples across the country, it is equally important to remember our longer history of nation-to-nation relationships, negotiations, and solidarities between Indigenous peoples. Building on contemporary protocols of acknowledgment, Morin's interventions constituted forms of visiting. In our visits he extended a similar Indigenous ethics of care we have for ceremonial objects, drums, and other-than-human relations toward the sites of Indigenous presence in London. Yet this ethics of care was not for the site itself, nor was it for the public who happened to be physically present. Rather, Morin's interlocutors in these visit-interventions were our ancestors. Although he repeated the same phrases—"we are still here" and "we have not forgotten"—as he did at colonial monuments, the meaning of these phrases differed. Instead of declaring survivance, when visiting Indigenous ancestors Morin intended the phrases to provide comfort. We were visiting with kin, reassuring our ancestors that "we are still here. We have not forgotten you. You are not alone, though you may be far from home." Morin described our visit to Pocahontas's gravesite at Gravesend, for example, as a visit to "our aunty." In these instances of visiting with Indigenous ancestors, we approached the site through a nation-to-nation politics of care and solidarity of responsibility that did not differentiate between visiting kin at home in our communities and visiting abroad.

AYUMEE AAWACH OOMAMA MOWAN ON TORONTO ISLAND: NOT SPEAKING TO OUR MOTHER

As a precursor to Morin's work, Rebecca Belmore's *Ayumee aawach Oomama mowan: Speaking to Their Mother* (1991) demonstrates another instance of speaking to place and form of care. Created by Belmore during a residency at the Banff Centre for the Arts, the central object in the work is a large ten-by-twelve-foot wooden megaphone that contains a working megaphone inside it. Over its long history of use, *Speaking to Their Mother* has traveled to a diverse range of locations and allowed participants to speak to Indigenous lands, to the Canadian Parliament buildings, and to Group of Seven landscape paintings at the Art Gallery of Ontario from 2003 through 2005. Far from being an object confined to gallery display, "the megaphone," as it is often called, is what activates community (figure 12.4). As Belmore notes, "it doesn't belong to me, it belongs to the people, it belongs to the earth. It came from the earth, it was made of materials

12.4. *Ayumee aawach Oomama mowan: Speaking to Their Mother*, the megaphone pointing toward the city of Toronto and the CN Tower, August 2014. Photo by Dylan Robinson. Used by permission.

from the earth . . . so I feel it's not mine, it belongs to people, and it belongs to the human voice to speak out to mother earth to talk about her and talk to her" (Beaucage 1992).

In 1992 Belmore brought the work to the Protectors of Mother Earth Wiggins Bay Blockade in Northern Saskatchewan for three days, where people spoke to the land in Cree and, more specifically, to a recent clear-cut that had occurred there. As Belmore describes, although her original idea for the work was to direct it toward the Canadian government and aim it toward Parliament Hill, it eventually transformed into a tool for affirming the voices of Indigenous communities: "Instead of aiming it at the government, and taking it and aiming it at that building or at those people, I wanted to instead take it out to the people, to native people, and turn it towards the land so the people could speak to our mother, to the earth, and feel very positive about speaking out and not be afraid to speak out" (Beaucage 1992).

In August 2014 *Singing to Their Mother* was situated at Gibraltar Point on Toronto Island. Many Torontonians consider the island, only a twenty-minute ferry ride from downtown Toronto, to be their refuge from the city. The island is also home to an amusement park, nude beaches, a tourist area, and Billy Bishop Airport, to which many Toronto Island residents fiercely but by and large unsuccessfully opposed plans for expansion. Toronto Island has also been a site for cruising in the queer community. For Belmore's purposes, Gibraltar Point, an area somewhat sheltered from the airport and amusement park, offered a clear vista of the city of Toronto and Lake Ontario, to which she spoke with the following oration:

> Boozhoo, Ahnee, Tansi.
> Boozhoo.
> Boozhoo, Ahnee, Tansi.
> Hello, good people of greater Toronto.
> How are you?
> Toronto, I'm talking to you.
> Hello.
> Hello, good people of greater Toronto.
> How many people are you?
> How many people are you?
> How much water do you have?
> How much land do you own?

How much water do you have?
How much land do you need?
How much water do you need?
How much land do you want!?

In addition to Belmore's oration, a small number of others spoke that day, including myself, the Anishinaabe curator Wanda Nanibush, the Mohawk curator Ryan Rice, and settler-musicologist Patrick Nickleson, among several others (figure 12.5). With our voices aimed at Lake Ontario as well as Toronto's iconic skyline, we voiced our concern about water pollution; about our relationships to the rivers, lakes, and oceans in our home territories; and about drinking water from our territories and becoming ill. I spoke about the theft of 265 million liters of water taken from S'olh Temexw (Stó:lō territory) by Nestlé to turn into bottled water. Yet despite these important messages, what struck me most significantly was the lack of voices speaking. When Belmore first toured the work in 1992, she noted that "people readily embraced the idea of speaking directly to the earth through this strange object that had come to them" (Belmore and Nanibush 2014). In a conversation at the Toronto Island gathering, Belmore noted also that in many of these community contexts, speakers often followed one after the other, immediately picking up where the last speaker had left off (pers. comm., Gibralter Point, Toronto Island, August 9, 2014). Yet this sense of oratorical fluidity was far from the case that day in August on Toronto Island.

There were resounding silences between speakers, despite the fact that many had gathered to watch, from young art students to tourists trying to figure out what was taking place. Despite the large number of bodies, the few voices who chose to rise to the occasion of speaking was notable. In contrast to Belmore's desire for the megaphone to engender the feeling of "not being afraid to speak out" (Beaucage 1992), I wondered whether this particular group on Toronto Island—as more spectators than active orators—felt afraid to speak or perhaps even apathetic. Describing her own first experience of speaking to the earth, Belmore notes, "I first spoke through it, when I spoke through it in Banff, and it echoed off the mountains and all over the place and it was my voice, I could hear my voice way over there separated from my body and bouncing off and echoing off mother earth, the land, I felt that 'wow'! I felt really humble. I felt so small . . . and I *felt* my place as a human being as part of the land and part of her but also I felt really strong at the same time. . . . It made me feel really good, it made me feel . . . like I belong here" (Beaucage 1992).

12.5. Dylan Robinson speaking into the megaphone for *Ayumee aawach Oomama mowan: Speaking to Their Mother*, August 2014. Photo by Patrick Nickleson. Used by permission.

That day on Toronto Island our voices seemed to neither resound nor reverberate. Rather than hearing an echo from the city of Toronto itself, our voices seemed to be swallowed up by the sound of the tourist water taxis and ferry and by the flights arriving and departing from Billy Bishop Airport. According to the Cree-Métis singer and artist Cheryl L'Hirondelle, her participation in a previous *Speaking to Their Mother* gathering at the Banff Centre engendered a sense of feeling the strength of community belonging (pers. comm., February 19, 2015). The impact of such a feeling must not be understated in light of the intergenerational legacies of Indian Residential Schools and resultant shame and lack of belonging many Indigenous peoples feel within their communities. Compared to Belmore's experience of feeling her place as part of the land, the silence of speakers on Toronto Island points toward the lack of community constituted by itinerant tourists and art students alike but perhaps also illuminates their *disconnection* from place in addition to the foreignness of speaking to place as a relation. Importantly, in contrast to Belmore's experience of belonging, perhaps it also made some of those who spoke feel that we did not belong there. As part of the *xwelmexw* diaspora—that is, as a person of Stó:lō descent who is a guest in the territory of the Wendat, Anishinaabe, Haudenosaunee, and the New Credit

Mississauga—speaking to a land that is not my own, *Ayumee aawach Oomama mowan* provides recognition of the fact that I have a responsibility to take part not just in learning about the lands on which I am a guest but speaking with those communities when I am asked to stand with them in opposing the ongoing resource extraction and destruction of their lands and waterways.

SONG, ORATORY, AND INDIGENOUS MODERNITY

In an interview with Wanda Nanibush, Belmore explained, "My strategy was simple, bring a conceptual artwork in the form of a functional tool to the people and ask them to speak directly to the issue, to the land itself, as we have always done" (Belmore and Nanibush 2014). The phrase "as we have always done" is particularly apposite for considering the ways by which Belmore's and Morin's actions are part of a continuum of tradition. In each of their interventions, song and oration are not merely aesthetic; they operate within a performative tradition that Western theory would call "speech acts." In the case of Morin and Belmore, we might more accurately name these "song acts" and "oratory acts." As song acts and oratory acts, they continue the work that our songs and oratory do in ceremonial contexts—they communicate with our ancestors, honor our families, and affirm sovereign rights. While our nations struggle in Western courts of law to assert our traditional, ancestral, and inalienable rights to land and water across the country, artists like Morin and Belmore are asserting such rights in a nation-to-nation context as we always have: through Indigenous protocols of song and oration.

Indigenous hip-hop, rap, opera, throat boxing, country, and noise music assert the vibrancy of our cultures on a continuum with Indigenous tradition rather than a break from it. These contemporary genres carry our cultural knowledge into the present, as does throat singing or Cree hunting songs. As scholars who study contemporary Indigenous musical genres, we are more able to recognize this continuum of cultural practice rather than categorize new genres as subsidiary to older expressions of Indigenous cultural practice. Yet we must also recognize the ways in which contemporary Indigenous performance is on a continuum not only with older aesthetics of cultural practice but with the epistemologies of doing that these traditions enact. What would it mean to understand the function of contemporary Indigenous song not simply as aesthetic, but as doing something or bringing something into being through its performance or utterance? Recognizing this fact is to reframe our ontological understanding of song and speech. When does Musqueam hip-hop, for example, not merely narrate our connection to land but act as an expression of sovereignty for the lands we have always cared for? When does Mohawk Classical music not only aestheticize history but serve as primary historical documentation, as precisely and rigorously as we consider our written research? When does Stó:lō rap not merely describe (re)conciliation but enact treaty? Importantly, these are not merely the questions I pose for the purposes of this chapter but also the questions First Peoples must now address within our own communities as we continue to innovate practices of what I call sensate sovereignty. While legal processes that seek to uphold Indigenous sovereign rights are appeals for political recognition in the eyes of the state, argued for on the terms of the state, such processes in many ways run counter to those cultural practices of sensate sovereignty, which is constituted by forms of doing in Indigenous cultural traditions—the materiality of wampum belt exchange and the singing of land rights (*Delgamuukw versus the Queen*).

Éy kws hákw'eletset te s'í:wes te siyolexwálh—it's good to remember the teachings of our elders' past. Remembering here is not a form of nostalgia but rather an action of making our traditions present across a range of contemporary forms. By doing so, we also continue the structural logics of our traditions and their power to do things in the world. Morin's and Belmore's sound art enacts healing for those not physically present, vocalizes sovereignty, and provides necessary forums for Indigenous peoples to aurally affirm kinship with other-than-human relations.

BEVERLEY DIAMOND

13. Purposefully Reflecting on Tradition and Modernity

The binary of modernity and tradition is underpinned by assumptions that are particularly problematic in relation to Indigenous expressive culture.[1] The two terms are sometimes discussed in Indigenous contexts, as I illustrate initially by describing one event in a Sámi community in Norway. Extending out from this description are references to scholars who write about the colonialist construction of the terms. In particular, I discuss the "thingness" problem in relation to tradition. The dynamism and adaptability of Indigenous expressive practices, as I have encountered them, disrupt the static concept of "things" and imply an action-oriented definition. The purposeful action orientation of Indigenous tradition, in turn, leads me to think further about the social aims of ethnomusicologists' practices. Building on Ana María Ochoa Gautier's (2014) compelling analysis of the ways sound—and listening to Indigeneity in particular—is implicated in the settler definition of modernity, I focus on practices of listening. I reflect on the colonial readings of aurality that Ochoa Gautier observes and listening strategies of Indigenous interlocutors in hopes of extending conversations in our discipline about how we might contribute to more ethical and decolonized research.

A COMMUNITY CONVERSATION ABOUT INDIGENOUS MODERNITY

The first time I recall hearing the phrase "Indigenous modernity" in an Indigenous community was about fifteen years ago, in a seminar offered in a Sámi *lavvu* (conical tent) prior to a Riddu Riđđu festival in Kåfjord, Norway—one of the major celebrations of global Indigenous expressive culture in the world. Seated in this most traditional of dwellings, we first listened to the anthropologist Arild Hovland speaking on "Modern Indigenous People."[2] At the time I thought the "modern Indigenous" juxtaposition offered a fresh perspective on a binary that had so often conceptualized modernity as characterized by rupture, newness, flux, and mobility in opposition to the rootedness and supposed unchanging authenticity of the Indigenous. Most attendees seemed to embrace the modern Indigenous designation as an obvious descriptor of their lives, but there was discussion among this mostly Sámi audience about the terms of reference.

Some Sámi questioned the priorities of *keeping* tradition or *using* it—both entirely compatible with being modern Indigenous people but suggesting different strategies in their struggle for resource rights, for example.[3] Some saw these divergent perspectives as differently embodied and place related. Language and traditional culture are vibrant and strong in the community of Kautokeino, but what about Sámi in New York, asked one individual. The comment was implicitly a challenge to the fixity of place that is so often ascribed to Indigenous people (Burton 2012, 492). "Sámi in New York" implied that geographies of circulation must be considered (J. Robinson 2013, 662). There was debate about hybridity and plurality (adopting, borrowing, or inventing new technologies, social practices, or expressive forms), which some saw as a defining feature of the modern, but others described as a negative feeling (perhaps sensing a loss of older cultural knowledge or maybe worrying about authenticity). The anthropologist Elizabeth Povinelli locates such negative feeling in what she describes as the "cunning of recognition" (2002) in relation to Aboriginal Australia in an analysis widely applicable in other Indigenous contexts: "To be truly Aboriginal, Aboriginal persons must not just occupy a place in a semiotically determined social space; they must also identify with, desire to communicate (convey in words, practices, and feelings), and, to some satisfactory degree, lament the loss of the ancient customs that defined their difference" (1999, 28). Further, she notes that because nobody inhabits these invented social spaces, "a present-tense indigenousness in which failure is not a qualifying condition is discursively and materially impossible" (29). Expectations of cultural continuity have long worked against the creation of histories of change within Indigenous society.[4] At the same time, settler cultures—particularly in the twentieth century—have often appropriated Indigenous expressive culture to give new life to modernist art, literature, and music.[5]

The cultural and political were explicitly linked at the Kåfjord gathering. The conversation gravitated toward events since the Alta River crisis of 1979–80, when Sámi communities as well as reindeer habitats and migration routes were about to be flooded by a new Norwegian dam, when Sámi activists camped out in Oslo explaining their concerns to passersby and seeking support for their land and human rights. The protests did not prevent the dam construction but did generate considerable public support and led to a renaissance of cultural production and political change (Hilder 2015; B. Diamond 2007). At the Riddu Riđđu gathering twenty-five years later, Sámi reflected on how this important historical juncture demonstrated another instance of false logic that Povinelli has also articulated: settlers often assume they possess land, whereas Aboriginal people are sometimes thought only to "need access for hunting and fishing and ceremony" (2002, 26). In the case of the Alta River, both access and living space were constrained by the building of the dam.

One Sámi political leader noted that people who have a literature in their own language (including written creations but also audio recordings, theater, dance, and other public performance) cannot be made invisible.[6] Indigenous media in decolonization initiatives, then, were known to be critical. At this point Sapmi Indigenous theater was thriving and Sámi-run publishing and recording companies were (and still are) actively creating (missing) histories of cultural and social change.[7]

A day or two later at the opening of the festival, another problem of modernity was referenced when the emcee noted that all introductions and announcements from the main stage would be made in Sámi, Norwegian, Tuvan (Tuvan musicians were special guests at this particular festival), and the "world's most widely spoken language—broken English." In this lighthearted manner, the necessity for English (a third, fourth, or fifth language for many Sámi but clearly a facility they had acquired in a cosmopolitan world) stood in for the connected histories of imperialism and colonialism about which many have written. I was reminded of Jodi Byrd's invocation of Said's contrapuntal reading, a reference to a musical practice that was certainly Euro-centered and governed: "As a musical form, counterpoint emphasizes dependent lines that exist relationally with rules to resolve harmoniously; and though counterpoint can entail secondary lines independent of the first, original line, counterpoint always relies on tension with the original melody to determine its existence and options" (2011, 93).

English is the "tonality" that governs many forms and contexts of communication. But, equally, I thought of Sámi comparative-literature scholar Harald Gaski's discussions of *joik* texts, which cannot be fully understood without deep local knowledge of individuals, places, and Sámi cultural practices. Gaski sees such knowledge as a mode of resistance to colonization, "where a subtle use of double meaning in the *joik* poetry made it possible to communicate on two levels at the same time, so that one type of message was conveyed to a Sami audience and quite a different one to outsiders" (2000, 196). Were the translations from the festival stage into Norwegian, Tuvan, and "broken English" more like tonal counterpoint or double meanings of *joik* texts, I wondered?

PROBLEMATIZING MODERNITY IN ETHNOMUSICOLOGY AND INDIGENOUS STUDIES

Scholarly attention to artistic Indigenous creation in what some might regard as modern genres or hybrid ones has a long history in North America. Prior to the late twentieth century, however, the impact of colonialism was often referenced generally and vaguely in ethnomusicological work. Politically aware interpretive strategies began to appear with the flourishing of postcolonialism, a particularly egregious term given the inequities that persist in Indigenous communities. By the 1990s scholars in all fields were aware of alternative modernities. In an influential, special-topics volume of *Public Culture* devoted to this theme, Dilip Parameshwar Gaonkar urges us to "revise the distinction between societal modernization and cultural modernity." He defines the former to include "the growth of scientific consciousness, the development of a secular outlook, the doctrine of progress, the primacy of instrumental rationality, the fact-value split, individualistic understandings of the self, contractualist understandings of society and so on." He deems societal modernization acceptable, whereas he sees cultural modernization (centered on avant-garde artistic creation) as destructive with its "pretensions, complacencies, and hypocrisies" (1999, 2). I cringe at both definitions. Whose science, whose belief systems, and whose progress? Why privilege individual over community rights? More useful, however, is Gaonkar's proposal to redefine modernity as an attitude rather than an epoch: to see modernities (plural) as multiple site-based questionings of the present (13–16), believing that "one can provincialize Western modernity only by thinking through and thinking against its self-understandings which are frequently cast in universalist idioms" (14).[8] From an Indigenous-studies vantage, however, the broad term *Western* instead of *settler* is problematic since the Indigenous Americas are part of the Western sphere geographically, historically, and culturally. Bruno Latour (1993) had similarly argued that modernity was invented to distinguish the West—with *its* particular brand of post-Enlightenment rationality, science, and law—from the rest to instantiate hierarchies that relegated Indigenous cultures to premodern status. Ochoa Gautier, however, describes how the colonial interactions of settler and Indigenous people were mutually constituting in the creation of modernity in the Americas. The aural was implicated in distinctions between human (clear pitched and inscribable) and nonhuman sounds, in the "lettered city" (2014, 145) and in the identification of certain genres of non-Indigenous song with the nationalist project in colonial Colombia. "Orality," Ochoa Gautier writes, "was not what, in the late nineteenth century, named the multiplicity and singularity of divergent vocalities but rather what disciplined the production and perception of the human voice" (167).

In the twenty-first century both settler and Indigenous intellectual leaders often embrace the language of traditional knowledge, traditional Indigenous knowledge, and traditional ecological knowledge. But the modern-traditional binary is troubled by different configurations of temporality. Both elders and scholars in various disciplines have discussed the recursivity and circularity of Indigenous constructs of history (Nabokov 2002; B. Diamond 2013). Haudeno-saunee composer and ethnomusicologist Dawn Avery (2012) has described the Mohawk concept of *non:wa*, a "now" that encompasses both past and present. The awareness of coexisting times, however, is not exclusively an Indigenous ontology. British urban geographer Jennifer Robinson, for instance, writes about the cotemporality of pasts, presents, and futures in cities. She advocates shift-ing focus from the *new* to a *now* that includes "the conditions of possibilities of emergence, and . . . the range of interconnections that produce [a city]—his-torically and geographically" (2013, 663). Similarly, the literary theorist Mieke Bal (2004) explores how different historical moments may be recast by means of socially differentiated artistic genres that retain traces of the past. She recalls childhood memories of the racist, black-face tradition of Zwarte Piet (Black Peter) in the Netherlands, while studying portraits that draw on upper-class modes of presentation for the Zwarte Piet actors. She demonstrates how dia-logue about race and class can emerge in the temporal and social disjunctures of these representations. Whereas literature or urban geography seem a long way from ethnomusicology or Indigenous studies, such temporal reorientations are fruitfully congruent. Although the teleology that defined modernity is disrupted by rethinking temporality, the term *tradition*, which has been widely embraced in Indigenous studies, often retains connotations of the past. I propose some reasons for this in the next section.

THE THINGNESS PROBLEM OF TRADITION

Modernity has been theorized more than tradition, but the latter has often taken a harder beating. In an anthology addressing the intellectual trajectory of the term, Mark Phillips and Gordon Schochet (2004) point to the dominance of authenticity issues and the influence of Eric Hobsbawm and Terence O. Ranger's (1983) invented tradition concept in the humanities and social sciences. They describe tradition as a "residual" term that "for scholarly purposes at least we need no longer (or perhaps *can* no longer) speak of . . . except in tones of irony" (2004, 4). Arguments for the continuing relevance of tradition have sometimes been harshly dismissed as socially damaging; Arjun Appadurai (1996), for instance, critiques the black box of *primordialism*, a term he equates with recent antimodernism movements (many challenging the governance of the nation-state and asserting various fundamentalisms, often in violent ways) that claim rights rooted in a place and body of knowledge by which one lives.

A problem with regarding tradition either as invented or authentic, or as antimodern, however, lies in the assumption of its "thingness," its inevitable casting as a noun in English rather than a verb. There is no "traditionize" to parallel "modernize." I'm not suggesting there should be. Rather, I draw attention to what seems obvious in Indigenous contexts: that enactments of tradition are active, purposeful interactions among humans, other beings, and environments. Action-oriented ways of being that many people label *traditional* actually imply a dismantling of the problematic modern/traditional binary altogether.[9] Indeed, Indigenous values underpinning customs, rituals, lifeways, stories, creative expression, or beliefs aim to manage relationships, social change, divergent perspectives, and conflict. In other words, the *why* of Indigenous tradition, rather than the *what*, is arguably more relevant to a global future than the why of modernity.

A purpose approach to Indigenous tradition easily accommodates a dynamic range of practices—some innovative or adaptive, others drawing on given repertories and lifeways. In some cases, of course, traditional Indigenous processes require precise specialized knowledge that is replicated exactly, with care, by those charged with responsibility for that knowledge.[10] As we consider how to bring peace to a currently unstable world, it is essential to recognize that the difficult moments of confronting change, foreignness, anger, and violence may require the repetition of a repertory of familiar and meaningful ways of acting, not simply free improvisation. This is true of all societies where formalities as simple as a handshake might be needed to mediate relationships. In other cases, new forms of expression and action may be equally appropriate and readily adopted. Perhaps because of the destructive uprootings of colonial encounters, Indigenous nations have developed multiple forms of mediating change to a larger extent than settler societies.

Whereas the many purposes of Indigenous social practices, including ceremony, vary across the hundreds of sovereign Indigenous nations, a number of common needs and issues are addressed (albeit differently) by traditional activity. Among these are the following:

1. Needing regular personal and group renewal. These may be tied to the cycles of renewal of the earth, as in the case of the agricultural ceremonies, or to cleansing of mind and body, as in the sweat lodge ceremonies of Native Americans.

2. Following respectful ways of meeting and separating. Protocols for acknowledging and asking permission to visit the territory of another group or specific ways to begin and end gatherings ensure future relationships. Parting from life on earth always demands special attention in every Indigenous (and settler) culture.

3. Giving thanks for the gifts of the earth. This is a broad category that exists in virtually every ecologically attuned society, often enacted through song and dance that animates life.

4. Healing. Common to Indigenous wellness beliefs is the view that the physical, psychological, spiritual, and social are interlinked and that song plays a central role. Classic studies in our field such as Frank Mitchell's autobiography (1978), edited by Charlotte Frisbie and David McAllester, have long taught us about some specific ceremonial practices such as the Navajo Blessingway. Recent work has explored intergenerational healing issues associated with colonial trauma, including the abusive systems of Indian Residential Schools, which operated in many countries (cf. Greenwood, Leeuw, and Lindsay 2015; Robinson and Martin 2016).

5. Rebalancing individual and group lives when they have experienced social change. Specific repertoires for this purpose may be well established, as in the case of the Navajo Enemy Way (McAllester [1954] 1973), performed when an individual has been away and seeks reintegration into the community. Or they may be less formal, as in the case of Innu sojourns in "the country" or Aboriginal Australian walkabouts, which enable a renewing of relationships with land.

6. Formally legitimizing new roles and responsibilities. Protocols involving feasting, speech making, gift giving, and performance constitute law and may be elaborately presented, as in the case of the potlatch of Northwest Coast First Nations in Canada. Ceremonies for naming or marking life cycle changes play a similar role (Frisbie 1967).
7. Defining acceptable ways to voice criticism or resolve conflict. Certain genres such as Inuit drum dances or, in Scandinavia, Sámi *joiks* may be used to point out socially unacceptable actions or personal traits. More elaborate forms of conflict resolution exist, especially in a number of African nations, where customary mechanisms that parallel and complement the laws of nation-states are constituted (Qashu 2016; Nannyonga-Tamusuza 2005). Traditional practices may be employed to reintegrate offenders or rebuild the capacity for empathy (Gow 2008, 250–56).

I am not suggesting, of course, that settler cultures should appropriate Indigenous ways in yet one more violation of the sovereignty and integrity of Indigenous culture, but rather that the active purposes of tradition, rather than its thingness, should underpin conversations. What might an action orientation to ethnomusicologists' work look like? With that question in mind, I turn to moments in our history, focusing on the purposefulness of listening within ethnomusicological research. My aim is to further conversations on *hearing* Indigeneity as a response to Ochoa Gautier's vivid demonstration that colonial listening in Colombia was a significant means of inscribing the concept of modernity.

PURPOSEFULLY HEARING INDIGENEITY
AND INDIGENOUS APPROACHES TO LISTENING

I reflect on selected examples (among many) of the explicit or implicit intentionality of listening evident in the work of ethnomusicologists, often engaging my own work reflexively in text boxes. In some cases our attitudes and aims retain hints of colonial hierarchies described earlier. In others they reflect shifts in the orientation of the senses as relationships are redefined. Implicit in my reflection is a need to think about who listens in what way, what can be heard, and what should or should not be heard. This discussion complements and builds on Victoria Lindsay Levine's excellent consideration of inscription practices in her introduction to *Writing American Indian Music* (2002). Notation itself represented the lettered classes and inscribed the colonial hierarchy that Ochoa Gautier describes. Whereas many ethnomusicologists invent ways to convey nuance by inscribing what we hear (Béla Bartók was a diligent model), few would deny that Western notation was both an inadequate visualization and a colonial imposition, a symbolically violent act (like stereotypes and other reductive representations) that contrasts starkly with forms of notation within Indigenous tradition such as visual or tactile aids to memory, including the order of songs in ceremony, or pictographs that map rich cross-references among places, living beings, spirits, and forms of human expression.

Victoria Lindsay Levine selected for *Writing American Indian Music: Historic Transcriptions, Notations, and Arrangements* (2002) a transcription of mine that raises other ethical issues. For an early study I made comparative transcriptions of variants of the same song—lining them up vertically so the differences were easy to see. This obvious gesture toward the classificatory projects of science were still encouraged during my graduate-student days, however objectifying and decontextualizing they seem to me now. Of course, when explored together with singers' narratives, variants *can* point to meaningful stories about why certain songs may be performed differently in different circumstances or about the malleability of Indigenous tradition in response to different sociopolitical sites and situations (cf. Cruikshank 1998). I did record some of the stories about specific songs, but without the sociopolitical nuance about specific performances that I would discover years later in Julie Cruikshank's work.

LISTENING TO LEARN THE MUSIC OR DANCE

Settlers often posit the right to learn as universal, yet in Indigenous contexts one often encounters a different emphasis. Individuals are encouraged to learn certain repertories or skills when (or if) they are deemed able to fulfill the responsibilities of that knowledge, responsibilities that may relate to clan, family, or social position but that may also be determined by a particular skill set. In some instances Indigenous culture bearers have entrusted scholars (insiders and outsiders) with song knowledge, although more often as recorders and preservers of knowledge in a time when it is under threat (Coleman and Coombe 2009). There are times, however, when everyone is invited to participate in some way if they can fulfill the responsibility of animating life and giving thanks for the gifts of Creation.

During a course on Haudenosaunee arts taught at my university by a Seneca-Cayuga instructor, students learned to sing Ęhsgá:nye songs (Women's Shuffle Dance songs) used for socials in the community. Students had to learn not only the songs and drumming patterns but also the dance steps and ways of providing appropriate food for a community event that they were expected to host at the end of the course—as the final exam. In other words, "listening to learn the music and dance" related to their responsibility to animate a successful event for Haudenosaunee and their friends in nearby communities, thereby contributing to the vibrant energy of life. There have occasionally been other instances where I was privileged to be able to listen to learn other music. One was a powwow drum within the federal prison for women in Kingston, Ontario, which I visited regularly from 1986 to 1988 to see two Indigenous friends who were incarcerated far from their children and other family for minor offences. I joined an Aboriginal Circle that was offering support to inmates. While female powwow drums are now more common (see Hoefnagels 2012), it was rare in that decade for women to sit around the big drum, but the constrained circumstances of a federal prison led the elders and circle leaders to teach powwow drumming and singing to all the "sisters," both Indigenous and settler. The drum hosted an annual powwow for the larger community in Kingston. It was inevitably a powerful and emotional event—an act of generosity by inmates, who created handmade gifts as well as the gift of song for all who played a role and even for authorities who were not kind to them on a daily basis. I am grateful for this opportunity to sing some powwow music even as I deplore the justice system that remains inequitable for certain populations.

LISTENING FOR COMPLEXITY TO COUNTER SIMPLISTIC STEREOTYPES

Whereas close attention to nuance is undoubtedly the mark of all good research, I suggest that listening for complexity has had a different ethical motivation—to demonstrate the falsity of racist stereotypes—in the work of ethnomusicologists who have worked with Indigenous singers and drummers or with archival materials from Indigenous communities.

In the 1980s I undertook an organology project because so many early evolutionist studies and even late twentieth-century textbooks offered dismissive representations of Inuit and First Nations music as just drums and rattles. The project was congruent with the desire of some Indigenous advisers to learn more about artifacts that were "imprisoned" in museums and archives. The wide range of technologies, artistry, and sonic nuance evident in the more than seven hundred artifacts in twenty-five museum collections that my research team studied purposefully belied such simplifications, visually and sonically. Such objects, of course, also drew attention to the loss of the embodied individual or shared experiences of using these sound producers. Some instruments were gifts of the natural world requiring no modifications (gourds or seed pods that produced the sounds of creation when the seeds dried). Others were complex assemblages of meaningful material elements with qualities, colors, or sounds needed for medicinal or other purposes; many were beautifully crafted artistic productions. The hidden-from-view materials inside shakers were particularly diverse—some fine-grained and delicate, some loud and piercing, some sound reducing, even one silent (a shaker, we were told by an elder adviser, intended for spirits). These unique creations connect the materiality of sound to environments and lives and taught me about the artificiality of a nature-culture divide.

There is evidence that other scholars were similarly motivated to listen for complexity. At a symposium in 1963, David McAllester modestly asserted that "I need more musical sophistication than I have" to study Navajo music well, noting the many genres that Navajo have created, alongside their sand paintings, silver work, and rug weaving, and arguing that "a tribal music may well be as complex as a classical music" (qtd. in B. Diamond 2015b). We consider attention to detail as a mark of good scholarship, but it belies a voracious desire to possess the knowledge of another.[11] While I can't assess the purposefulness of other scholars, I suspect that there are many instances where looking and listening for complexity was motivated by the clear need to counter oversimplified stereotypes and homogenized accounts of Indigenous sonic culture that were, and still are, prevalent in textbooks, media, and social experiences. These worthy intentions may nonetheless reflect assumptions about entitlement unless Indigenous collaborators anticipate social as well as academic benefit.

LISTENING FOR BORROWED STYLES
TO UNDERSTAND RELATIONS

Given that listening is inherently relational, it is not surprising that sharing and borrowing (as well as more coercive practices including stealing songs or foisting one's music on others) are widespread across cultures. Such repertories are neither hybrid nor outside the lived experience of people who use them. This is certainly true of Indigenous people who often gifted songs to neighbors or shared them in other ways and who learned the music of colonizers. For example, Christian hymns are the most widespread of adopted repertories that reflect changing assumptions about settler-Indigenous relationships.

More than any other genre of Western music, the Indigenous adoption of hymns has been documented since the late nineteenth century. Early collectors, including Frances Densmore (1938, 1941), Gertrude Kurath (1957, 1959), and Willard Rhodes (1952a, 1960) were students of Native American hymnody, interpreting the practice as acculturation (with its implications of inauthenticity and loss). But Densmore traced hymn influences on certain genres of traditional music, and she and David McAllester (1952) studied the syncretic Native American Church. Rhodes acknowledged the role of boarding schools, and Kurath used the language of syncretism to replace the acculturation paradigm, recognizing Indigenous agency and foreshadowing recent work by Ann Morrison Spinney (2006), Chad Hamill (2012), and Kimberly Jenkins Marshall (2016) on the adaptations and power dynamics of Indigenous and Christian leaders. Studies of Indigenous hymnody burgeoned in the late 1970s and 1980s, with more attention to usage in traditional Indigenous contexts (cf. Grant 1980; Keillor 1987; B. Diamond 1992). In the early twenty-first century, collaborative approaches have enabled more nuanced views of the ways hymns are meaningful for individuals (cf. Lassiter and Ellis 2002). The narrative of borrowed genres shifted slowly from the colonialist paradigm of inauthenticity and acculturation to syncretism, sociopolitical agency, and personal accounts of the emotional and social meaning of specific repertories.

But why hymnody? What does it say about music scholars that they focused extensively on this tool of conversion and assimilation? Why were other genres such as country music, fiddle, and band ignored by most academics prior to the 1980s and 1990s (cf. Whidden 1984; Preston 1985; Mishler 1993)? Why were individual processes of mapping meaning across generations and landscapes ignored until recently (cf. Vander 1988; Lassiter and Ellis 2002; Samuels 2004; Levine 2014b, 2015)? One might surmise that studies of rap and reggae (Vosen 2013b; Aplin 2012; Marsh 2012), as well as Indigenous opera, classical music, experimental performance, and jazz (Karantonis and Robinson 2011; Avery 2012; J.-C. Perea 2012a; D. Robinson 2012), began to appear after 2000 because they emerged recently, but opera, classical music, and jazz, of course, have deep historical roots. Did we fail to recognize Indigenous work in elite and virtuosic idioms, or did we think populist genres were more capable of articulating a politics of Indigeneity? Also relevant is how genres originating in African American culture trouble the mapping of modernity and tradition onto settler and Indigenous peoples.

LISTENING TO REDEFINE HOW HYBRID STYLES EMBODY AND COMMENT ON RELATIONS

Listening to relationality is arguably inherent when sonic styles are juxtaposed, and this has become a pressing issue in an era of industry-defined world music and digital technologies that facilitate easy production and dissemination of sonic hybrids. Most ethnomusicologists are less interested in "expert" interpretations of sonic texts than in the potential of music's polysemy. But listening to sonic mixture is often shaped by broad institutional forces, which effected huge erasures of the differences in the auralities of hundreds of First Nations, Inuit, and Métis in the public imaginary and invented stereotypic markers of Indigenous sound in North America, as Tara Browner (1997), Philip Deloria (2004), and Michael Pisani (2005), among others, have demonstrated.[12] One might legitimately ask whether it is possible to listen to Indigenous-style references without invoking the stereotypes that continue in world music and movie production. Dylan Robinson (2016a) has problematized this issue, noting even further erasures in songs with a "we are the world" message that effectively denies the specificity of colonial victimization.

Ethnomusicological studies of Indigenous music production, however, vary significantly in approaches to interpreting the juxtaposition of diverse styles. Jessica Bissett Perea (2012) reminds us of the mixed heritages that many Indigenous musicians embody. What might be heard as hybridity is unified in their own lives. Both Bissett Perea and Avery (2012) explore concepts in Indigenous languages that naturalize mixtures. But attention to the processes of production and the hierarchies reinscribed in both text and performance trouble settler and Indigenous hybrids. Both Richard Jones-Bamman (2006) and Dylan Robinson (2012) write cogently about power in cross-cultural musical collaborations, observing instances where the control of such things as tempo and balance was determined by the non-Indigenous conductor or where the enclosure of Indigenous elements in a dominant mainstream idiom replicated colonialist power dynamics. Indigenous musicians who master several styles have reflected on their personal experience of collaborating interculturally, often emphasizing common philosophies more than similar musical languages (R. Wallace 2012; Avery 2012).

On the other hand, I have suggested (B. Diamond 2007, 2011b, 2016) that listening closely to subtle cultural differences in style—to the slippages that make something not quite what one expects—might be a decolonizing strategy that resists the aforementioned elisions and stereotypes promoted under the "world music" industry label. In a genre such as opera, for instance, an Indigenous composer who juxtaposes languages, vocal timbres, and instrumental styles can render colonial relationships audible and visible (B. Diamond 2011b, 31–56). Like the cultural geographer Jennifer Robinson (2013), who looks at intersecting histories in the lives of contemporary urbanites, ethnomusicologists who explore the circulation of sonic styles can sharpen awareness of intersecting and uneven histories. I agree with the Australian theater director Rachel Swain (2014), who regards the "copresence of multiple stories" (in theater) as a way of talking back to colonial perceptions. Consider Dawn Avery's performance of a Bach unaccompanied cello suite with interspersed segments of a Mohawk song. At the very least, listeners must wrestle with the question of what these two styles have to say to each other and perhaps with their own preconceptions about stylistic coherence or even pastiche. Only with more conversation about actual divergences among culturally diverse listeners and interpreters of contemporary Indigenous music will we understand capacities and limitations of the sonically hybrid in mediating intercultural differences.

LISTENING FOR POWER, PAYING CLOSE ATTENTION, AND LISTENING TO SURVIVE

Recently, literature on music and violence has altered approaches to listening for power. Suzanne Cusick (2006) was a pioneer, addressing sound as torture, demonstrating that sound that might be pleasurable for some can be extremely painful for others. Listening for power moved in profoundly new directions in work by Martin Daughtry where, as he recounts vividly, listening for sounds of specific weapons in war zones is a matter of life and death and also relates to trauma. He recounts the "fine-grained experiences of individuals" and observes, "to say that we are always free to choose how to interpret these sounds, however, is to ignore the structural impediments that a state of profound vulnerability creates" (2015, 47). Daughtry suggests that sound "coerces bodies into involuntary vibration and co-opts them into participation, through resonance" (165). Sound, then, is potentially always violent in that it enters the body and has both physical and psychological ramifications. But the same quality that creates this potential also creates the potential for attuning positively. Such observations suggest approaches to listening in war zones or listening to orient oneself in everyday life arguably resemble ways in which Indigenous hunters and others pay attention to sonic environments.

In the context of isolated communities, I have often been astonished at the acuity with which Indigenous people hear their environment. Children distinguish the different engine noises of each neighbor's snowmobile. A hunter knows the distance away and direction a goose is flying, through knowledge of its call and atmospheric conditions. Aboriginal languages often reflect this acuity. Inuktitut, for instance, is structurally more "relational" than English, with subject and verb both indicated in the verb tenses (e.g., *tusaavaa* means "he hears something or someone"). My Inuktitut dictionary (Schneider 1985) adds further nuance: s/he *knows* because s/he hears. That basic verb can be easily modified in this polysynthetic language to indicate subtleties such as hearing only once, hearing repeated sound, or listening but not obeying. One can indicate "weather that makes hearing difficult and hunting easy," "hunting in good hearing weather," or "weather that makes hearing easy and hunting difficult." Although I am a relative beginner and ongoing learner of this language, it is clear that the many inflections relate listening to survival.

Practices of listening that Indigenous hunters employ are key to finding food or navigating space, clearly relating to survival in some circumstances. But, unlike soldiers under fire, elders engage in a sort of sonic attuning that integrates humans with the animate world they share.

LISTENING FOR MIMESIS, STRIVING TO ATTUNE

Michael Taussig (1993), among others, has written that seeing and listening to imitate something or someone is a common, often politically charged, response to the world external to one's self. Mimesis, as he defines it, is a way of miming the world into being with high stakes.[13]

I've tried to learn mimetic Indigenous genres, including Inuit vocal games or Sámi *joik*. But my skill in listening for mimesis is childlike, searching simply for recognizable resemblance. I hear the sound of the goose in a vocal game but rarely recognize the personalities or spatial nuances. In Sámi *joik* I miss the fleeting rhythm that signals the quality of movement (of a bird or animal or human) that *joik* composers are so good at, and I need help to understand the double meanings of texts that characterize people critically but lovingly or that map social and ecological relationships.

With reference to the Quechua-speaking Runa of Ecuador, the linguistic anthropologist Janis B. Nuckolls describes such vocal simulation as "sonic alignment." "Runa model natural processes with sound by imitating the resonant, rhythmic properties of experiential phenomena: ongoingness in time, distribution in space, instantaneousness, disruption, rearrangement, and completion. I want to claim, further, that in the act of constructing natural processes with ideophonic sound, Runa are at the same time foregrounding their shared animacy with such processes" (2004, 66). Paul Carter similarly observes that "echoic mimicry is communication in the absence of anything to say" but is significant because it expresses "the desire or necessity to communicate" (2004, 46).

When anthropologists have written about the way place may reflect systems of social relationships (Armitage 2011), evoke memories of people and the songs they loved (Samuels 2004), or summon stories that instruct newcomers about the teachings of the land, a similar sort of alignment seems to be at play. Anthony Seeger ([1987] 2004, 65–78) describes such a process when he writes about the Suyá (or Kĩsêdjê) in Brazil, where the sonic recreates a spatial map of relationships. Given the widespread practices of mimetic vocalization to which these culturally diverse references point, listening for mimesis—though arguably not yet a very common practice among ethnomusicologists—might be a way of respecting sonic alignment and a means to explore ontologies that emphasizes emplacement and resonance among human and other-than-human environments.

———

In her thought-provoking article "Prelude: An Accountability, Written in the Year 2108," the anthropologist Carolyn Nordstrom asks challenging questions related to purposefulness: "Did scholars at the dawn of the twenty-first century recognize that their work not only illuminated the past and shaped the present but also produced the future? Did they see in their analyses the harbingers of new kinds of wars, unprecedented forms of violence, undeveloped potentialities? . . . What intellectual and moral bearings animate the heartbeat of their epistemologies as they ripple across and interact to configure, in however large or small a way, our emergent tomorrows!" (2008, 1–2).

The aural regimes of coloniality were still evident in the mid-twentieth century, when ethnomusicology emerged as a named discipline, and I recognize them in my own work.[14] Close attention to our own intentions when we listen to Indigeneity not only enables us to see ourselves in relation to the colonial aurality that Ochoa Gautier identifies but might also assist in determining what types of purposeful listening could best contribute to an emergent tomorrow in which diverse and sovereign cultural communities could exist without one subsuming another or addressing differences violently.

It is apparent that the purposefulness that I refer to in relation to Indigenous tradition differs in scale from what I identify as some examples of the purposefulness of listening in ethnomusicology. A next step may be to identify the larger social purposes of different kinds of listening. I have signaled a few that might relate to anticolonialism and decolonization. From a utopian perspective, one might argue that such actions, if successful, could contribute to better balance, sustainable social and environmental ecologies, and less violence. But the disjunctures (like stylistic and generic sonic differences) may simply open space for dialogue about purposefulness, the content of which I would not presume to predict. Our different strategies must all take heed of a potential problem that Ochoa Gautier (among others) identified: that some practices undertaken "in the name of decolonizing" actually "recolonize" (2014, 17). To mitigate recolonization, I suggest that our scholarship continue to focus on the way that regimes of sound are mutually constitutive but use horizontal rather than hierarchical thinking and consider the many pasts that circulate and inform the present. This will be an evolving process in the work of anyone involved in Indigenous arts who is committed to recognize colonial processes that continue to shape contemporary societies but willing to accept responsibility for helping to animate a future.

TREVOR REED

14. Pu' Itaaqatsit aw Tuuqayta
(Listening to Our Modern Lives)

How do we locate Indigenous modernities? Is modernity a condition imposed through colonization that seeps into sounds Indigenous peoples create? Is it a kind of social and intellectual mobility that empowers us to speak to broader audiences through new technologies and expanded social networks? The contributors to this volume have heard *modernity* in diverse ways. Looking toward the future, I wish to explore the stakes of methodology in music research with Indigenous "moderns." Bruno Latour (1993) describes modernity as a two-part process.[1] First, it involves the strategic hybridization, translation, and interconnection of seemingly autonomous domains such as science, religion, or art into new functional combinations. Second, it involves the processes of "purification"—the means whereby these new functional combinations take on independent identities, leaving behind any remnant of the former social lives of their component parts. Once purified, the new thing that emerges is given its place in the civilized world, one partitioned by Enlightenment-era divisions of nature and culture (Latour 1993, 11). Examples of musical hybridizations and purifications abound in modernity: the domains of music and politics, mobilized together for some social end, become purified as cultural policy; sound-recording technologies employed to conceptualize and express "the environment" result in the purified art form we know as soundscape; certain categories of sound administered as medical remedies becomes music therapy.

This collection suggests that Indigenous musicians may or may not be participants in modernity's work of hybridization and purification. Rather, a significant number are involved in revealing modernity's purifications, making bare the social lives behind the components of various musical or political forms. This is probably owing to the fact that in our Indigenous worlds hybrids are constantly being generated, often against our will. Lands we conceptualize as ours are merged with oil- and gas-extraction methods, political power, and capital investment and then purified into discrete domains like economic development, pollution, and government corruption. Traditional medicines, business practices, and patent law generate valuable new drugs along with novel opportunity costs; traditional knowledge, ceremonial practices, and academic ambitions become anthropological data and carefully guarded cultural resources.

Cloaked from view, hybrids can become purified or segmented into manageable, categorizable "things" and their socially motivated aspects erased through what Ana María Ochoa Gautier has called the "epistemological work of invisibilization" (2006, 810). As long as the twin processes of hybridization and purification coexist but do not reveal each other, modernity perpetuates itself, and we believe we are in a state of stable progress (Latour 1993, 11). But, as Latour reminds us, inevitably new forms of disruption—including musical ones—manage to reconnect the erased links connecting processes of hybridization and purification, making modernity precarious if not impossible to sustain. Searching for these disjunctures may be a key entry point for understanding Indigenous modernities.

Doing anthropology of "moderns" and the purified hybrids they create is complicated because modernity is particularly opaque, despite claims to self-awareness, self-analysis, critique, and rationality (Latour 2013, 18). So much of what we see as Indigenous musical modernity may come across as resistance to settler-colonialism, yet how can we be certain we truly understand all that is happening in modern Indigenous sonic spaces? Latour argues that in modern contexts we need to bridge "the abyss that separates what the Moderns say from what they do" and to look at the "plurality of ontologies" that are swept under the rug through modernity's logics—logics that purport to be rooted in universal human values. This opens the possibility that, as anthropologists of Indigenous music, we have to engage with "entities that no longer ha[ve] a place in theory," to accurately map the sound worlds of Indigenous modernity (21).

CULTURAL PROPERTY: A MODERN EXAMPLE

Latour's deconstruction of modernity serves as a useful starting point because it asks us to look for meaning in the social powers that produce modern hybrids as well as the forces and motivations that purify them of their sometimes messy or hegemonic social relations. As the contributors to this collection argue, modernity's projects and processes do not necessarily fall along a convenient Indigenous/settler binary. Indeed, the Indigenous musicians discussed here are often doing the hybridizing, purifying, and determining which domains are modern and which are not. The logics of modernity have a direct bearing on my own research and community activism involving the repatriation of ritual song recordings to the Hopi people. Repatriation of Indigenous ceremonial culture takes as its baseline the proposition that Indigenous ceremonial performances are originally owned by those who create and perform them and, if the creators or performers are no longer living, their lineal descendants or those who carry on the ceremonial practices. Indigenous peoples, therefore, have the right to control how recordings of their ceremonial culture circulate. If a recording was made illegitimately or is circulating outside of the original owners' control, it should be returned to the rightful owners and restitution made for any harm done (cf. United Nations 2007; Seeger 1996).

At the outset of my work on Hopitutskwa (Hopi lands), I considered Hopi songs to be "cultural property" — the bundle of rights belonging to an Indigenous group by virtue of the fact that its members jointly held the culture manifest in the artifact or archival medium. I assumed all I needed to do as a researcher-activist was to discover how those rights should be distributed and then redistribute those rights to the object in legally sound ways. Over several years of meetings with Hopi community members across the reservation, I documented and began trying to make sense of Hopi people's opinions on how and to whom the recordings and their associated rights should be returned, believing that some sort of underlying traditional cultural property principle would emerge to solve a very modern problem. My efforts to locate "the sovereign will of the autochthonous Hopi sociopolitical organization" (Richland 2011, 223) did not provide the panacea I sought. I discovered that thinking of Hopi ceremonial songs in terms of property rights actually did very little to explain what should be done to repatriate the songs in any meaningful way.

Indigenous ceremonial song recordings are inevitably hybrids, products of Indigenous modernity generated from multiple, ontologically diverse networks. From their place on archival shelves, they are purified from nearly all their social relations for the sake of keeping them organized, contained, and accessible to researchers. Yet, despite their scholarly value, recordings like these hold comparatively little value outside of their uses within Indigenous networks. On one hand, they are intellectual and physical property—the exclusive fruits of Lockean labor lingering as an intellectual asset within an academic cosmology.

On the other hand, they are Indigenous ceremonial performances—the fruits of Hopi ritual labor. They are latent voices existing within a living Hopi cosmology. When they are purified as cultural and intellectual property, an Indigenous community may be empowered by reclaiming and taking ownership of songs like these as cultural resources (Yúdice 2003). But, as James Leach has warned, treating ritual songs as property may enact a modern conceptual colonialism over Indigenous groups, requiring them to rely on Enlightenment divisions of nature and culture to assert their rights, while ignoring the diverse stakes of the other actors vital to Indigenous ritual culture (2007, 99).

Some Hopis with whom I collaborated insisted that the Hopi Tribe should control access to all ritual recordings containing Hopi esoteric knowledge because they have been declared to be the "cultural property of the Hopi people" (Hopi Tribe 1994; see also Brown 2004). But to say that Hopi ritual songs do their work within the Hopi community *as* property is to adopt wholesale the hybridizing and purifying processes at play in modernity. Hybridizing Hopi ritual songs with the conceptual container of property may allow songs to be transferred back to Hopis within the U.S. legal domain, but an additional layer of analysis is needed to allow those actors necessary to a ritual song's vitality to speak to its optimal circulation on the ground. Hopi songs originate through joint partnership with humans, other-than-humans, and environmental phenomena and become owned by all those who invest their time and energy in hearing and internalizing them. Even beyond generating artistic satisfaction or entertainment value, the performance of ritual songs accomplishes work on the environment and produces transformative effects in individuals who perform and listen to them. While many Hopis with whom I collaborated supported the use of cultural property as a framework for decolonizing the voices of their ancestors, many also resisted the potential effects of transforming Hopi ritual into tribal or individual property.

In sum, without an ontologically oriented approach to understanding Indigenous musical contexts, we may lose a richer understanding of Indigenous people's interactions with modernity's processes and logics. If we fail to ontologically situate our research in modern Indigenous contexts, we may actually be enabling colonization by taking for granted the purified hybrids we encounter therein.

A MODERN METHODOLOGY

This collection deals with important contemporary Indigenous contexts in which the fusion of social forces and sonic forms is clearly evident. Some contributors unpack how musical fusions are playing out in activist Indigeneity; some focus on the recontextualization of these forms; and some consider the emplacement of traditionalized musical forms in contemporary multicultural or neoliberal spheres of governance. These chapters raise the overarching question: Is a unified goal emerging for research in the area of Indigenous musical modernities? If so, is it to interrogate the hybridizing and purifying processes happening across Indigenous sonic spaces? Is it to celebrate Indigenous creativity and activism despite modernity's forces? Or can it be both, and more?

Even with the breadth of musical activity among Indigenous peoples today, these chapters reveal a deep resonance between modernity and Indigenous activism's expression through hip-hop and powwow. But what is it about hip-hop or powwow and Indigenous social activism, including cultural revitalization, protest, and community programs, that makes us as scholars hear and see *modernity*? These chapters frame hip-hop and powwow as performative social vehicles with the ability to penetrate and then work inside and across cultures, sometimes specifically to accomplish larger social goals. Contributors take note of Indigenous artists' biographies, establish their connections to Indigenous and non-Indigenous communities, and often reveal postcolonial anger, all of which are brought into productive relationships with certain beats, timbres, performance styles, or linguistic characteristics that have acquired near iconic significance in other cultural contexts. The analyses rightly examine the political and economic inequalities in which the artists operate and their desires to remediate cultural harm caused by settler-colonialism, to reclaim or expand a particular social role or position, and to create dialogue or initiate resistance, all through exploration of the meanings generated at the confluences of music, genre, culture, or political movements.

If these contexts are in fact paradigmatic of Indigenous modernities, then we should be able to not only perform postcolonial analyses but also examine the domains that generated them and the conditions under which they have been purified into neatly segmented categories of political discourse and naturalized sound-objects. Since hybridizations of different Indigenous sociopolitical configurations with powwow or hip-hop sound are each so carefully analyzed here through lenses focused on their actors' decolonizing thrust, perhaps the next step is to consider the purifications that make these hybrids accessible or inaccessible to and for certain publics. I wonder if there is a conscious link between activist musicians' hybridizing work and the kinds of new epistemologies or ontologies of sound that seem to be emerging as they circulate: worlds that articulate who "we" are and who "they" are; that claim rights, assuming those rights have always been there; and that persistently grapple with who is a sellout and who is real. This approach to studying Indigenous musical modernities would make persistent use of audience ethnography—understanding how and what sonic messages and strategies actually link performer to audience and whether or not the ideologies or desires the artists convey are actually being realized or linked back to their hybrid forms within the Indigenous communities we are imagining. This is critical because simply hybridizing Indigenous or Indigenized sounds with modern social or political institutions does not always produce the decolonizing results we should be able to expect. What for some might be an empowering expression of collective Indigenous presence in a systemically colonized space may unfortunately be for others just another manifestation of a purified genre living up to its stereotypes. Audience ethnography can tell us about the networks in which modern Indigenous musical hybrids circulate and the entities that enable or disable them, disrupting, through diverse social vantage points, any modernizing thrust to purify Indigenous musical experience and relocate it along a predetermined nature/culture binary (Latour 1993, 11).

The empowered tone of these chapters is both intellectually and politically satisfying. It shows that Indigenous moderns are assessing and capitalizing on North American insecurities, fears, and weaknesses. They assert an Indigenous creative agency in the world and in doing so work toward a decolonization of music, anthropology, the academy, and the world in which we live. Yet there are important opportunities going forward to explore the effects these kinds of hybridization and purification are having on Indigenous *peoples* themselves.

If hybridizations and purifications are key aspects of Indigenous musical modernities, have we sufficiently explored what effects these processes are having on Indigenous communities and their cosmologies? From the point of view of an Indigenous community, is it the same thing to generate music from within local networks of exchange as it is to appropriate it from elsewhere or even to appropriate foreign concepts about music from another tribe, social group, or species? (cf. Viveiros de Castro 1992; Stolze Lima 1999). Are Indigenous musicians and their audiences hearing and being moved differently by sounds with diverse genealogies? Even for Indigenous musicians living in urban environments, I can't help but wonder how their children, elders, ancestors, or deities are hearing and thinking about their choices of musical hybrids and how these choices impact their relationships and environments.

I am in no way advocating for a racialized or essentialized notion of Indigeneity that *limits* the experiential, intellectual, or political possibilities of Indigenous actors to the constraints of imagined social groups or social stereotypes. Rather, I am suggesting that we need not confine ourselves to the partitioned, purportedly rational domains modernity has left for us. This volume is a springboard for further engagement in an expansive exploration of Indigenous musical modernities that takes into account diverse ontologies in its analysis. That these authors and the artists they study have opened up a decolonized intellectual space for this kind of dialogue is cause for celebration. *Kwa'kwhay!s*

NOTES

1. Music, Modernity, and Indigeneity

1. Protocols of welcoming and situating oneself relationally are values shared widely among the Indigenous peoples of North America.

2. Here I am paraphrasing the Tahltan artist Peter Morin (2016, 75). For additional information on how Indigenous gestures of welcome enact sovereignty and establish authority in Native spaces, see D. Robinson (2016b).

2. The Oldest Songs They Remember

1. In employing such loaded terms as *primitive* and *modern*, I invoke the lengthy, productive critique and reevaluation of their emergence as foundational and canonical for the social sciences and humanities in contexts of settler colonialism. See Clifford (1988), S. Diamond ([1974] 2018), Kuper (1988), Patterson (2010), A. Simpson (2014), Taylor (2016), and Torgovnick (1990).

2. Diamond, Szego, and Sparling (2012, 2) concur, seeing in the term "Indigenous Modernities" a call to "emphasize the fragmentation, deterritorialization, and struggles for reclamation that are parts of indigenous experience" of modernity.

3. For a discussion of the problem with reading recognizable iconicity and indexicality, see Samuels (2004).

4. Rhodes's latent critique of researchers of Densmore's generation stops short of explicitness, in part because he approached these creative processes through the zero-sum game of acculturation theory.

5. "Hybrid" is the term Rhodes preferred, using it decades before the term gained firmer theoretical footing and wider circulation.

6. A celebratory songbook based on the organization's emphasis on community music making was titled *A Singing Nation Welcomes a Singing Army* (1918).

7. The plea for community-based music was also met by the National Bureau for the

Advancement of Music and its widely successful campaign promoting Christmas caroling throughout the United States (Anonymous 1924).

8. For a discussion in greater depth, see Bristow (1996), especially 79–90.

9. My conclusion here differs from that presented by Kheshti (2015), who argues that the image reproduced here as figure 2.3 has become the most famous.

10. Writing of photographs that purported to document the "Vanishing Indian" and the inevitability of "Progress" and "Development," Sandweiss notes, "If the photographs themselves were the centerpiece of the story, they were nonetheless incapable of conveying the burden of narrative themselves. Only with words could the mute pictures speak" (2002, 272).

11. With less than half the capacity of Carnegie Hall, which she surely could have filled, Aeolian Hall allowed Sembrich's fans to hear her in a setting "that should establish the desirable intimacy between singer and audience in a kind of art whose essence is intimacy" (*New York Times* 1917).

12. Subsequent afternoon shows were titled "The Art-Song," "The German Classics," and "The Song Composers of Today."

13. Often recounted is the incident with Red Cap, in which Densmore agreed to record the Ute leader's message of complaint to the commissioner of Indian Affairs, but played it without a translator present (cf. Troutman 2009, 165; Brady 1999, 93; Scales 2012, 1).

3. Reclaiming Indigeneity

1. *Mi'kmaq* is used as the plural form and refers to the Mi'kmaw people and the Mi'kmaw language. *Mi'kmaw* is the singular and is also used for adjectival and adverbial forms.

2. For literature on fieldwork, see Feld (1976), Von Rosen (1990), Barz and Cooley (2008), Cooley, Meizel, and Syed (2008), Wissler (2009), and Deger (2006). For reclaiming Indigeneity, see Battiste (2000), Vizenor (2008), and Levine (2014b).

3. This is a contested figure when one considers patterns of identifying status and nonstatus Aboriginal people, as well as those who have lost, and are in the process of reclaiming, their identity as Mi'kmaq.

4. For descriptions of the economic, educational, cultural, and social infrastructures now in place in Eskasoni, see the Eskasoni Mi'kmaw Nation website (n.d.). Recent examples in the area of tourism include the Mi'kmaw trail on Goat Island at the eastern end of the Eskasoni reserve, opened in 2012 by Eskasoni Cultural Journeys.

5. The history of the Mi'kmaq and Roman Catholicism dates to the early seventeenth century, when Chief Membertou and members of his family were baptized by Catholic clergy who accompanied explorers from France. See Prins (1996) and A. Robinson (2005).

6. Changing funerary practices also occur in other Aboriginal contexts. See Frisbie (1978) and Griffen (1980). I thank Charlotte Frisbie for this information.

7. The choir at Holy Family Church has copies of the text version of *The Catholic Book of Worship II* (1980), the official hymnal of the Roman Catholic Church in Canada, as well as copies of the second edition of *Glory and Praise* (1984), a popular post-Vatican II hymnal from the U.S. Catholic Church.

8. Saint Anne, mother of Mary and grandmother of Jesus, became the patron saint of Mi'kmaq in the seventeenth century. A. Robinson (2005) explains that Saint Anne's relationship to Jesus (*ki'ju*, or grandmother) resonates with Mi'kmaw culture because of the importance attached to the *ki'ju* as the progenitor of the family and, by extension, as the protector and giver of life. Mi'kmaw people regard Saint Anne as a source of healing and spiritual inspiration, and she is celebrated on July 26 in the annual pilgrimage to the Mi'kmaw mission at Potlotek on Cape Breton Island.

9. Kalolin Johnson of Eskasoni has become well known on YouTube singing Mi'kmaw translations of popular songs such as "The Climb" by Miley Cyrus and "You Are My Sunshine." She became a young sensation through YouTube when she performed her Mi'kmaw version of "O Canada" at the closing ceremonies of the Jeux du Canada Games in Halifax, Nova Scotia in 2011.

10. Tulk (2009b) provides parallel sound recordings and describes her discovery of a Mi'kmaw version of the Catholic *Liber usualis* and the importance of Gregorian chants in the practice of Catholic liturgies among the Mi'kmaw.

11. Historically, the Mi'kmaw wrote in hieroglyphs scratched into tree bark or animal hides; some of these writings have been preserved as petroglyphs. Following contact, the history of written Mi'kmaq is linked to the work of missionaries in Mi'kmaw communities. See Battiste (1984).

12. The seven video excerpts illustrate the narratives in this chapter. Rather than definitive statements, the excerpts should be viewed as partial documents that initiate discussion about Indigenous identity and modernity.

13. View the seven video excerpts on YouTube; see "Video Excerpt 1" (2015) to "Video Excerpt 7" (2015). The excerpts can also be accessed by searching this chapter's title on YouTube. A compact disc with the excerpts is located at the Beaton Institute (Mi'kmaw Holdings) at Cape Breton University, Nova Scotia, Canada.

14. The text of "Mo Dhachaidh" ("My Home") appears in many nineteenth- and twentieth-century Gaelic songbooks, including Moffat (1907) and Whyte (1883). The song probably originated as a piping tune, as suggested by the modal turn at the final cadence. In the twenty-first century it is most often heard in instrumental versions. See Creighton's ([1956] 2004) recording of the song as performed by the late Cape Breton singer Malcolm Angus MacLeod. I thank Stephanie Conn for this information.

15. Alstrup (2003) contains a moving narrative of the climb to the top of the mountain where the church is located. Each Good Friday, the Stations of the Cross are observed at set stopping points along the pilgrimage climb to the cross at the top of the mountain, an event that links religious ritual to the natural surroundings for the Mi'kmaq.

16. Donald Marshall Jr., a Mi'kmaq from the Membertou reserve, was wrongly convicted of murder in 1971 and spent eleven years in prison before the life sentence was overturned. Marshall's name is synonymous with the fight for justice for the wrongly convicted, and he is a hero in the battle against racism toward Aboriginal people in Canada. His funeral in 2009 was recorded by the Canadian Broadcasting Corporation and by the Mi'kmaw filmmaker Catherine Martin.

17. Global examples include Hodges (2009), Johnson (2011), Toner (2007), and Wissler (2009), among others.

4. Indigenous Activism and Women's Voices in Canada

1. *The Winter We Danced: Voices from the Past, the Future, and the Idle No More Movement* (Kino-nda-Niimi Collective 2014) is an anthology of writings, art installations, and reflections on the Idle No More movement and contemporary issues confronting First Peoples in Canada in the early twenty-first century.

2. The earliest publication of this song on YouTube was by an audience member called "clockle" on YouTube (Ulali Project 2014). The official video release of this song on YouTube was published by Tapwe Production Projects on June 18, 2014.

3. For an overview of the origins, development, and music of Ulali, see Cain (2003).

4. For a discussion of the impact of Indigenous a cappella women's ensembles, see Cain (2003).

5. See Simpson and Ladner (2010), Obamsowin (1993), Hedican (2008), and Shore (1994).

6. For a firsthand perspective on the origins of Idle No More, see McAdam (2014) and McLean (2014).

7. For a description and account of the Sixties Scoop and its impact on the people directly affected by it, see Ireland (2014).

8. Authors such as J. Green (2007), Anderson (2000), and Anderson and Lawrence (2003) are contributing significant publications addressing Indigenous women's rights and their agitation for increased respect and acknowledgment within their communities and throughout Canadian society.

9. Anderson and Lawrence (2003) offer valuable writings by Aboriginal women who recount their experiences and relationships in the early twenty-first century.

10. Interestingly, *feminism* is not a term commonly used by Indigenous women to label female leadership and activism; however, the terms *Indigenous feminism* and *tribal*

feminism have been coined in relation to the advocacy work of contemporary Indigenous women. For a discussion of these terms, see Deerchild (2003), Huhndorf and Suzack (2010), and Hoefnagels (2007b). For readings on the reclamation of women's voices (figuratively and literally as singers and spokespeople) and Indigenous women's activism, see Amadahy (2003), B. Diamond (2002), Fiske (1996), Gould and Matthews (1999), Allen ([1986] 1992), Klein and Ackerman (1995), Mihesuah (2003), Miller and Chuchryk (1996), Mithlo (2009), and Silman (1987).

11. Additional information about Asani was found in their electronic press release (Asani 2007).

5. Hip-Hop Is Resistance

1. The Tohono O'odham Nation is federally recognized, with reservation lands in southern Arizona and approximately twenty-eight thousand members. Its traditional lands extend beyond Arizona into northern Mexico, with federally recognized tribal members residing in Mexican traditional territories as well as in the United States. The Tohono O'odham were previously and are sometimes still referred to as the Papago (cf. Erickson 1994; Griffin-Pierce 2000; Luna-Firebaugh 2005; Griffith 1992).

2. DJ Reflekshin joined Shining Soul during production of the group's 2016 album *Politics Aside.*

3. The Chicano movement was marked by Mexican American youth demanding educational equality in U.S. classrooms, coinciding with broader civil rights movements for desegregation and the fair treatment of Mexican American farmworkers (cf. Navarro 2005; Muñoz 2007; Gutierrez 2011; Ontiveros 2014).

4. Xicano (Shi-ka-no) and Mexica (Me-shi-ka) are sometimes used in preference to Chicano (Gutierrez 2011; de la Torre and Gutiérrez Zúñiga 2013).

5. *Corridos* are Mexican narrative ballads, traditionally about local heroes fighting for community justice.

6. *La migra* is Spanish-language slang for "immigration police," used to refer to Border Patrol and, previously, Immigration and Naturalization Services.

7. The line "young, gifted, and brown" is a reference to Nina Simone's civil rights anthem, "Young, Gifted and Black," inspired by the 1969 off-Broadway play, *To Be Young, Gifted and Black: A Portrait of Lorraine Hansberry in Her Own Words.*

8. ¡*Ya basta!* (Enough already!) is an anticolonial slogan popularized during the 1960s and 1970s Latin American liberation movement, later popularized among Chicano activists in the seventies (Ontiveros 2014, 24–25). First coined during Mexican nation building to instill pride in a mestizo citizenship, *la raza* (the race or people) became popularized in Chicano nation building.

6. Singing and Dancing Idle No More

1. The AIM song may be heard at "A.I.M. Song/B.I.A. Song" (2018).

7. Get Tribal

1. We encourage readers to open their ears by listening to these emcees' sound recordings, available through artist websites, iTunes, Amazon, YouTube, and bandcamp.com.

2. Stomp Dances are a social and ceremonial genre performed by Creek, Seminole, and other Native Southeastern peoples. In the dance the women wear leg rattles made of terrapin shells or condensed milk cans and are known as shell shakers (R. Green 1992; Levine 2004, 2013, 2014a).

3. Quese references the Trail of Tears, or the forced relocation of many tribes west of the Mississippi River as a result of the Indian Removal Act (1830), enacted by President Andrew Jackson (A. Wallace 1993; Levine 2014b).

4. Hip-hop artist Angel Haze (2012) reinforced this point by revealing her Cherokee heritage and speaking the Tsalagi (Cherokee) language in an interview on Hot 97 FM radio.

5. *Nahui Ohlin* (Nahuatl) means "four movement" and describes both Quese's affiliation with an Indigenous-centered store in Echo Park, Los Angeles, and a nascent cultural-political movement. The term refers to Native peoples' shared ceremonial understanding of the number four.

6. *Ye-ye* is a French popular music style prominent in the early 1960s; songwriters and performers include Serge Gainsbourg, France Gall, and Francoise Hardy, among others.

7. "Orale" is a Chicano term meaning "that's right."

8. Native "Noise" and the Politics of Powwow Musicking in a University Soundscape

1. I follow Ellis and Lassiter in using the term *intertribal* as opposed to *pan-Indian* (2005, xiii). For many of my students, the experience of a powwow is integral to their ability to comprehend the fluidity of tribal and intertribal influences, since at a powwow they can see the process taking place before their eyes. I alternate between the terms *American Indian* and *Native American* in this chapter to reflect the shared language of my classroom. First Nations is used only in reference to tribes living within the geopolitical boundaries of what is now known as Canada.

2. In my use of the terms *expected* and *unexpected* in this chapter I follow Deloria, who defines expectation as "shorthand for the dense economies of meaning, representation, and act that have inflected both American culture writ large and individuals, both Indian and non-Indian (2004, 11). He explains, "Expectations and anomalies are mutually

constitutive—they make each other. To assert that a person or an event is anomalous cannot help but serve to create and to reinforce other expectations" (5). Finally, he breaks the binary relationship between expectation and anomaly by introducing the concept of unexpectedness, asking readers to "distinguish between the anomalous, which reinforces expectations, and the unexpected, which resists categorization and, thereby, questions expectation itself" (11).

3. Nettl has noted the importance of world music as a mediator in schools of music, using the example of the American Indian Dance Theater, which "combines many kinds of Indian music and dance—material from different cultural areas, from different times, and with varying degrees of fantasy and Westernization. Thus, a concert itself may be seen as a *mediating* institution among musical cultures" (1995, 90; emphasis added).

9. Powwow and Indigenous Modernities

1. Ojibwe people also refer to themselves as Anishinaabe, Saulteaux, Ojibway, Ojibwa, and Chippewa. Swampy Cree also refer to themselves as Mushkegowuk, Woodland Cree as Sakāwithiniwak, and Oji-Cree as Anishininiwag.

2. Smudging is an act of purification in which participants wash themselves with the smoke of a smoldering medicine, often sage. The people with whom I spoke used the words "prayer," "spiritual," "sacred," "teachings," "Indian names," "drum groups," and "Aboriginal," and I follow their uses here. Terminology varies widely across North America, and some of these words may be regarded as problematic in other contexts.

3. It is not unusual for traditional powwows in Manitoba to open with a pipe ceremony.

4. AAA funding is different in a number of ways from the kinds of funding made available through the 1972 Indian Education Act in the United States. The AAA grant is a provincial (rather than federal) initiative, and it targets Indigenous achievement in public schools that are usually off-reserve and in which Native students are often in the minority.

5. For a comprehensive overview of Residential Schools in Canada, see Miller (1996) and TRC (2015b). Canadian Residential Schools were similar in some ways to Indian boarding schools in the United States; however, U.S. schools were run by the federal government, whereas Canadian ones were run by various Christian denominations (Riney 1997). On Indian boarding schools in the United States, see Lomawaima and McCarty (2006).

6. The corrections system is another branch of the state that has had immensely disruptive effects on Indigenous communities; here, too, traditional cultural activities have been made available to prisoners.

7. More recently, the federal government has apologized for the abuses suffered by Residential School students, extended financial compensation to many (but not all) who were mistreated in such schools, and funded a five-year Truth and Reconciliation

Commission to examine their legacy. The findings of the commission (TRC 2015c) can be viewed on the website of the National Centre for Truth and Reconciliation.

8. Although increased community control of schooling has been cause for optimism (see Taylor, Crago, and McAlpine 2001, 46), concerns remain about how much autonomy the federal government allows Indigenous communities in educating their young people (see, e.g., Canada 2011, 8).

9. In Canada the provinces are responsible for public education, the exception being the education of status Indians, which is a responsibility of the federal government. Nevertheless, many Indigenous people attend provincial schools, either because they are not status Indians, because they do not live on reserves, or because their reserve has ceded responsibility for education to the province. For a discussion of the financial factors that may inform such decisions, see Drummond and Rosenbluth (2013).

10. Ray is referring to a stretch of Winnipeg's Main Street that has frequently been regarded as that city's skid row.

11. On *bimaadizawin*, see Hallowell (1955, especially 104 and 269; 1992, 82–84), Gross (2003, 128–29), and L. Simpson (2008, 32–33).

12. This section discusses areas of deep disagreement; I hope I am able to convey a range of perspectives sympathetically.

13. For accounts of drummers' relationships to, respect for, and care of drums, see Diamond, Cronk, and Von Rosen (1994, 160–62); Browner (2002, 135); and Scales (2012, 49–50, 75, 123–24).

14. "Culture" has a number of senses in this chapter. Many Indigenous people use "the culture" to designate traditional cultural practices. Yúdice (2003) uses "expedient culture" to refer to practices (typically artistic ones) deployed in the hope of attaining social and economic results. Both of these senses are more circumscribed than is typical in anthropology and ethnomusicology.

15. The ceremonial protocols associated with the culture establish another kind of independence. While smudging and prayer at powwow club meetings and the complex sequences of opening events at powwows acknowledge and orient participants to the relations around them, they also do other kinds of work, including marking certain times and spaces as those in which Indigenous priorities and practices are sovereign.

10. Inuit Sound Worlding and Audioreelism in Flying Wild Alaska

1. "Alaska Native" is a designation for Indigenous people and original inhabitants of what is now known as Alaska. Although Alaska Natives have been understood historically as encompassing three equally broad subgroupings of "Indians," "Eskimos," and "Aleuts," they typically define themselves in the early twenty-first century in relation to cultural groupings distinguished along linguistic lines, such as Iñupiaq, Yup'ik, Unangan, Gwich'in,

and Tlingit. The term "native Alaskan" refers to non-Indigenous residents whose ancestors immigrated to Alaska. Whereas some have questioned the grammatical correctness of "Alaska Native" (instead of *Alaskan* Native), this designation has a very specific history and is indeed the correct term, evidenced by the naming of many prominent Indigenous organizations (e.g., Alaska Native Heritage Center, Alaska Native Justice Center, Alaska Native Medical Center).

2. There are twenty distinct Indigenous languages spoken in Alaska; two that are typically grouped under the term *Inuit* include Iñupiaq and Yupik, speakers of which come historically from the northern and western coastal regions, respectively. It is significant that the coastal village Unalakleet Northwestern sits at the historical boundary between Yupik- and Iñupiaq-speaking peoples, one of the many Alaskan locations where intertribalism and cultural mixing have been a way of life since time immemorial (see Holton and Parks 2011).

3. Paraphrasing a recent call by scholars to reinvigorate a sounded anthropology, my work aligns with those interested in the continued development of a sounded Native American studies to expand the field's tendency toward ocularcentrism (see Samuels et al. 2010).

4. This working list of nonfiction television projects filmed in Alaska includes shows that intended to run for one or more seasons and either were filmed solely in Alaska or regularly feature an Alaskan-based team (e.g., Papac Alaskan logging in the History Channel's *Ax Men*). Reruns and reality television specials (e.g., Discovery Channel's *The Klondike, Alaska Week*, or the *Deadliest Catch* spin-off *Hillstranded*) and one-shots (e.g., appearances on History Channel's *Top Gear*, Travel Channel's *Man v. Food*, or Discovery Channel's *Dirty Jobs*) are not included. It is worth noting here a few discrepancies from two multisited shows: seasons 1–2 (2007–8) and 7–8 (2013–17) of *Ice Road Truckers* featured drivers and routes based solely in Canada; seasons 3–6 (2009–12) alternated between drivers and routes in Alaska and Canada. *Ax Men* did not feature an Alaska-based logging operation until season 4 (2010–15), as seasons 1–3 (2008–10) followed logging operations based only in Oregon, Washington, Montana, Louisiana, and Florida.

5. According to a 1995 Inuit-language map published by the Alaska Native Language Center, twenty-four thousand Canadian Inuit people identified as speaking Inuktitun out of a total seventy-three thousand speakers across Alaska, Canada, and Greenland (see Holton and Parks 2011).

6. The ten tracks featuring Siberian-language songs (including Tunguisic, Chukotko-Kamchatkan, and Uralic) are from a ten-album series of ethnographic recordings by ethnomusicologist Henri LeComte and published by the Parisian Buda Musique label. Only the following four albums are featured in *FWA*: *Siberia 4. Korjak. Kamchatka: Drum Dance Far East Siberian* (1996); *Siberia 5. Nanaj. Oroc. Üdege. ULC: Shamanic and Daily Songs from the Amur Basin* (1998); *Siberia 7. Nenec. Sel'kup: Voice of the Artic Finisterre* (1999); and *Siberia 8. Evenk: Ritual Songs of the Nomads of the Taiga* (2003).

7. A detailed discussion of Pamyua appears in Bissett Perea (2012).

8. In this case, Pamyua's arrangement of "Reindeer Herding Song" was composed by Cecelia Foxie (Yup'ik) and was used by permission. The song is primarily vocables, with a few short Yugtun phrases, "All of us here have fun when we sing; All of us here have fun when we dance" (liner notes, Pamyua 1998).

9. For extensive accounts of these styles, see Grawunder (2009) and Levin and Süzükei (2006).

10. UNK is the three-letter identifier for the Unalakleet Airport.

11. Offscreen, Phillip Blanchett also wrote "Flying," an English-language pop-reggae song released as a single in 2012.

12. Bossi also notes BMI awards "go to the person or persons with the most cues on the show" (email corr., March 14, 2018).

13. Some of these videos are still available on YouTube (see *Discovery* 2012).

14. Bossi notes that the composition crew used a combination of samples performed on frame drums from Alaska and Lower 48 hand drums (email corr., March 14, 2018).

15. I maintain that some of the most well-known examples include composers of original cue sheets and restoration scores for Robert Flaherty's infamous film *Nanook of the North* (see Bissett Perea 2017). For discussions of European and North American settler-colonial representations of Inuit music, see Krejci (2010) and Van den Scott (2016).

16. Translations courtesy of Peand-eL (aka Peter Lyberth) (email corr., March 10, 2018).

17. The version of the main title song heard at the beginning of each show is further embellished with diegetic sounds of prop engines, radio chatter, bird strikes, and aircraft alarms, to name a few.

18. Original lyrics and English translation courtesy of Peand-eL (email corr., August 5, 2013).

19. The following shows also released soundtrack albums on iTunes: *Deadliest Catch* (September 25, 2007); *Ice Road Truckers*, for which volumes 1 and 2 are original compositions by Bruce Hanifan (May 20, 2008, and September 18, 2012) and vol. 3 (aka "Trucker Tracks") is a combination of licensed and third-party music and original compositions, all in the country-music genre (April 20, 2010); *Alaska: The Last Frontier* (October 5, 2014), the theme song for which features Jewel, a member of the show's Kilcher family and one of Alaska's most widely known pop-music stars; and *Alaskan Bush People* (April 25, 2016).

20. Interestingly, of these three shows only *Deadliest Catch* retained its original hard rock anthem throughout—most other shows rely on original compositions for their theme songs, perhaps because of the high cost of licensing popular hard rock anthems. In the case of *Alaska State Troopers* and *Gold Rush: Alaska*, they too opted for brief, instrumental drama underscores as their main titles.

21. Tweto's organization is called Popping Bubbles (2014).

11. Native Classical Music

1. For more information on Native Classical music, see Avery (2012, 2014), B. Diamond (2011a, 2011b, 2011c), Karantonis and Robinson (2011), and Levine (1998, 2002).

2. The Kanienkéha (Mohawk), along with the Oneida, Cayuga, Onondaga, Seneca, and Tuscarora, are the Six Nations that compose the Rotinonhsión:ni (Iroquois) Confederacy. The Six Nations Kanienkéha territory is located on the Grand River in Ontario, Canada.

3. Other Native Classical composers include Timothy Archambault (Kichespirini), Louis Ballard (Quapaw), Sadie Buck (Seneca), Barbara Croall (Anishinaabe), Brent Michael Davids (Mohican), Russell Goodluck (Navajo), R. Carlos Nakai (Navajo-Ute), George Quincy (Choctaw), Jerod Impichchaachaaha' Tate (Chickasaw), and Ron Warren (Echota Tsalagi).

4. Additional information on autoreflexivity as an Indigenous research method appears in Denzin (2003), Holman (2005), Stock (2001), Thomaselli, Dyll, and Francis (2008), and S. Wilson (2001). Information on Indigenous research methodologies appears in Battiste (2000), Chilisa (2012), Denzin, Lincoln, and Smith (2008), Gonzalez (2000), Kovach (2009), Mihesuah and Wilson (2004), Niezen (2003), and S. Wilson (2008).

5. Ethnomusicologists have only recently begun to explore classical music in relation to culture and ethnicity, largely because the focus of ethnomusicology was defined until somewhat recently as the study of non-Western and folk music (Nettl 2005, 4), whereas analytic and historical studies of classical music were the domain of musicology. Interest in Western classical music composed by members of diverse ethnic groups is relatively new (cf. Kingsbury 1988; Born 1995; Yoshihara 2007; Karantonis and Robinson 2011).

6. Kanatsioharé:ke is built on land in the Mohawk Valley, New York, that was repurchased by the Kanienkéha in 1993 "To promote the development of a community based on the traditions, philosophy, and governance of the Rotinonhsión:ni, and to contribute to the preservation of the culture of people as a framework for a blend of traditional native concerns with the best of the emerging new earth friendly, environmental ideologies that run parallel to these traditions. To conduct programs in the culture and traditions of the people; to foster an active accumulation of spoken Mohawk language by members of the community; and to continue oral traditions, stories, songs and dances in the unique spirit of the Mohawk path" (Kanatsioharé:ke Community 1993).

7. Additional information on traditional approaches to Native American musical creativity appears in Browner (2009b), Herndon (1982), Huang (1997), LaVigna (1980), and Nettl (1989).

8. For more on twinship or complementarity, see Avery (2014), Browner (2000, 2009a), and Diamond, Cronk, and Von Rosen (1994).

9. For more detailed information on graphic models for Native Classical composition that incorporate the medicine wheel and the turtle, see Avery (2014), Huber (1993), Lane et al. (1989), and Walker (2001).

10. The concepts of "cultural accents," described by Graf (1947) and Bennett (1976), as well as sonic and cultural borrowing, are worth exploring as part of both the product and process of composition by Native composers. A cultural flavor (indirect references) and direct cultural understanding may be expressed in music itself, in the explanation of particular pieces, or as a tool for preparing the performance of particular pieces. In terms of compositional creation, Gidal (2010) refers to this as "cross-cultural competence."

11. Reichard explains that the "swastika is a favorite Navaho design, probably because whirling log (*tsil noʼoli*) is a theme of the Night and Feather Chants. The chant symbol of the Hail Chant is a cross to the ends of which down feathers are fastened, giving it a swastika-like effect. It (*tónáxabil*) is the protective device of Winter Thunder's and Frog's home. . . . It is Thunder's whirling seat. When angry, Winter and Dark Thunder twirled their seats; when the gods were good-tempered, the seats became rainbows" (1983, 603–5).

12. *Yéʼi* are Navajo deities with spiritual powers; they include "Water Sprinkler, Fringed Mouth, Hunchback . . . Coyote, Big Snake Man, Crooked Snake People, Thunder People, and Wind People. . . . These beings and powers . . . are undependable, even though they may have given mankind many of their prized possessions. . . . [They are] forever present to Navaho consciousness as threats to prosperity" (Kluckholn and Leighton 1962, 182–83; see also Reichard 1983).

13. Further information on Southwest Indian concepts of time and pitch indeterminacy appears in Shapiro and Talamantez (1986), Givens (1977), and List (1985).

12. Speaking to Water, Singing to Stone

1. Defining Indigenous-centered methodologies and models of music analysis remains a challenge to be addressed in the field of Indigenous music and sound studies. Indigenous and Native American scholars here might look to the growing nation-specific forms of literary criticism, including Justice (2005) and Martin (2012). Debates on Native literary nationalism and resurgent theory are similarly useful in reflecting on nation-specific forms of criticism and interpretation.

2. The *Aesthetics of Reconciliation* project was funded by the Social Sciences and Humanities Research Council of Canada and led by Keavy Martin and Dylan Robinson. The project's aim was to understand the role of the arts in the Truth and Reconciliation Commission. Peter Morin was a participant in this project, and Martin and Robinson commissioned him to create a work that responded to events he attended (see Robinson and Keavy 2016).

3. Witnesses at this gathering included Keavy Martin, Sam McKegney, Elizabeth Kalbfleisch, Dylan Robinson, Helen Gilbert, Beverley Diamond, Niigaanwewidam James Sinclair, and Pauline Wakeham.

4. For a detailed examination of the discourse of witnessing at the TRC, see Gaertner (2016).

13. Purposefully Reflecting on Tradition and Modernity

1. Latour's analysis of the Western construction of the "modern"—a construction that relied on "separating the relations of political power from the relations of scientific reason while continuing to shore up power with reason and reason with power" (1993, 38) and the consequent situating of Indigenous cultures as "premodern"—is a thematic ground for many of the chapters in this volume. Since it is discussed elsewhere, I am not elaborating further in this chapter.

2. Some of these ideas were developed in Hovland (1996).

3. Their views resonate with others, since the relationship of Indigenous communities to development is contested worldwide. As Ravindran (2015) describes in relation to Indigenous groups in Bolivia, there are differences (and sometimes conflicts) between those who see Indigenous engagement with development as a means of benefiting the living conditions of their people and those who favor an "Indigenous cosmovision" that prioritizes ecological recovery. The divergent opinions reflect different concepts of well-being.

4. There are exceptions to this generalization, such as Judith Vander's *Songprints* (1988), which documents the changing repertories and broader social changes in the lives of five women across several generations.

5. See Dharwadker (2011) for an exploration of this problem in the theater history of India.

6. There were some notable Sámi writers in earlier eras, but the corpus of published literature expanded enormously in the late decades of the twentieth century.

7. Sapmi is Sámi land, spanning four nation-states.

8. Chakrabarty's "provincializing Europe" (2000) is a parallel conception.

9. This shift resonates with what Gaski describes as the necessary shift from "reactive politics" to "proactive praxis" (2013, 118).

10. See S. Wilson (2008), Kovach (2009), and L. Smith (2012) for Indigenous perspectives on purposeful research methodologies.

11. D. Robinson (2017) references the "hungry listening" of scholars, a concept drawn from the word *xwelitem*, translated as "settler" but more accurately meaning "starving person" in Halq'emeylem, the language spoken by Stó:ló people.

12. Théberge (2003) has demonstrated that the industry practice of selling "samples" of Indigenous and ethnic music for use in the movie industry or other artistic work has largely perpetuated elisions and stereotyping.

13. There are playful forms of mimesis in which the stakes may be low. The "zoom zoom" of cars or the "meow" of cats are familiar. Algonquian speakers connect morphemes

for sound to the motion from one vowel to another in the diphthongs "ue" or "ueue" that may indicate sound or motion of other types. The name of the Innu drum, *teueikan*, incorporates this diphthong and might be translated more literally as the "thing that vibrates." The syllables "ue" or "ueue" may be incorporated into words for other objects that move back and forth, such as flags or brooms.

14. Evidence of our growing concern includes frequent debates within the Society for Ethnomusicology about the problematic name of the discipline, which implies the priority and possibly the "purity" of ethnicity, as well as other discussions about such things as the imagery of the Indigenous "little man" that served as the logo for part of the society's history.

14. Pu' Itaaqatsit aw Tuuqayta *(Listening to Our Modern Lives)*

1. I thank Zoe Todd (2014, 2016) for exposing the ways Latour's work in the area of object-oriented ontology fails to fully acknowledge the intellectual labor of Indigenous peoples that preceded it. Here I hope to begin to offer an Indigenized approach to the kinds of theories Latour has advanced on the topic of modernity, which I think may be useful in reading the work of these exceptional Indigenous and non-Indigenous scholars.

REFERENCES

AANDC (Aboriginal Affairs and Northern Development Canada). 2011. "Registration Process." Last modified May 18, 2011. www.aadnc-aandc.gc.ca.

AED (Aboriginal Education Directorate). 2014a. "Aboriginal Education Directorate." Manitoba Department of Education and Advanced Learning. Accessed August 28, 2014. www.edu.gov.mb.ca.

———. 2014b. "Smudging Protocol and Guidelines for School Divisions." Manitoba Department of Education and Advanced Learning. Accessed September 20, 2014. www.edu.gov.mb.ca.

Agawu, Kofi. 2003. *Representing African Music: Postcolonial Notes, Queries, Positions*. New York: Routledge.

Agloinga, Roy, and Luann Harrelson. 2013. *Iġaḷuiŋmiutullu Qawiaraġmiutullu aglait nalaunaitkataat: Qawiaraq Iġaḷuik Inupiat dictionary*. Translated by Steven Agloinga and Agnes Komakhuk. Anchorage: Atuun.

"A.I.M. Song/B.I.A. Song." n.d. Smithsonian Folkways. Accessed July 11, 2018. https://folkways.si.edu.

Alaska Dispatch News. 2011. "Background Tunes in 'Flying Wild' Are Pamyua's." January 24, 2011.

Alfred, Taiaiake. 2005. *Wasáse: Indigenous Pathways of Action and Freedom*. Toronto: Broadview.

———. 2009. *Peace, Power, Righteousness: An Indigenous Manifesto*. Don Mills, ON: Oxford University Press.

Alim, H. Samy. 2004. "Hip Hop Nation Language." In *Language in the USA: Themes for the Twenty-First Century*, edited by Edward Finnegan and John R. Rickford, 387–409. New York: Cambridge University Press.

Allen, Paula Gunn. (1986) 1992. *The Sacred Hoop: Recovering the Feminine in American Indian Traditions*. Boston: Beacon.

Alstrup, Kevin. 2003. "'The Song, That's the Monument': Eskasoni Mi'kmaw Tribal Culture in the Music-Making of Rita Joe and Thomas George Poulette." PhD diss., Brown University.

Amadahy, Zainab. 2003. "The Healing Power of Women's Voices." In Anderson and Lawrence 2003, 144–55.

Amsterdam, Lauren Jessica. 2013. "All the Eagles and the Ravens in the House Say Yeah: (Ab)original Hip-Hop, Heritage, and Love." *American Indian Culture and Research Journal* 37 (2): 53–72.

Anawak, Jack. 1989. "Inuit Perceptions of the Past." In *Who Needs the Past: Indigenous Values and Archaeology*, Robert Hugh Layton, 45–50. London: Routledge.

Anaya, James. 2013. "Statement upon Conclusion of the Visit to Canada." Press conference video, 3:53. United Nations Special Rapporteur. October 15, 2013. http://unsr .jamesanaya.org.

Anderson, Kim. 2000. *A Recognition of Being: Reconstructing Native Womanhood.* Toronto: Second Story.

Anderson, Kim, and Bonita Lawrence, eds. 2003. *Strong Women Stories: Native Vision and Community Survival.* Toronto: Sumach.

"Angel Haze Talks with DJ Enuff and Spits a Freestyle." 2012. YouTube video. Interview with Angel Haze. Posted by Hot 97, July 23, 2012. www.youtube.com/watch?v=88RERY38P3c.

Anonymous. 1924. "Christmas Caroling in 1923: A Survey." *Music Supervisors' Journal* 11:26–28.

Aplin, T. Christopher. 2012. "Expectation, Anomaly, and Ownership in Indigenous Christian Hip-Hop." *MUSICultures* 39 (1): 42–69.

———. 2013. "Urban Beats, Religious Belief, and Interconnected Streets in Indigenous North American Hip-Hop: Native American Influences in African American Music." In *Sounds of Resistance: The Role of Music in Multicultural Activism*, ed. Eunice Rojas and Lindsay Michie Eades, 85–112. Santa Barbara: Praeger.

Appadurai, Arjun. 1996. *Modernity at Large: Cultural Dimensions of Globalization.* Minneapolis: University of Minnesota Press.

Appleton, Caroline D. 1919. "The American Indian in the War." *Outlook*, May 21, 1919, 110–11.

Arietta, Rose. 2004. "Nation Divided." *Global Policy Forum*. November 9, 2004. www .globalpolicy.org.

Armitage, Peter. 2011. "From Uapamekushtu to Tshakashue-matshiteuieau: Place Names, History and the Labrador Innu." Lecture for the Newfoundland Historical Society, Saint John's, April 28, 2011.

Asani. 2004. *Rattle & Drum.* Arbor Records AR12282, compact disc.

———. 2007. *Asani Electronic Press Kit.* Accessed May 28, 2013. www.sonicbids.com/2 /EPK/?epk_id=89323.

———. 2009a. *Listen*. Meta Music MM-1001, compact disc.

———. 2009b. "Listen." Microdocumentary series. Accessed November 26, 2009. http://asparagusgreen.ca.

———. 2013. "Asani." Summer Sisters. Accessed May 28, 2013. Asani.org.

Asch, Michael. 2007–8. "Folkways Records and the Ethics of Collecting: Some Personal Reflections." *MUSICultures* 34–35:111–27.

Augoyard, Jean-François, and Henry Torgue. 2005. *Sonic Experience: A Guide to Everyday Sounds*. Ithaca, NY: McGill-Queen's University Press.

Austin, John Langshaw. 1962. *How to Do Things with Words*, edited by J. O. Urmson and Marina Sbisà. 2nd ed. Cambridge: Harvard University Press.

Avery, Dawn. 2007. "Program Notes from the Maryland Tour of the North American Indian Cello Project, National Museum of the American Indian." Unpublished manuscript.

———. 2012. "*Tékani*, Two Worlds Many Borders: Classical Music through Indigenous Eyes." *MUSICultures* 39 (1): 129–68.

———. 2014. "Native Classical: Musical Modernities, Indigenous Research Methodologies, and a Kanienkéha (Mohawk) Concept of Non:Wa (Now)." PhD diss., University of Maryland.

Babcock, Barbara A., and Nancy J. Parezo. 1988. *Daughters of the Desert: Women Anthropologists and the Native American Southwest, 1880–1980*. Albuquerque: University of New Mexico Press.

"Babette Sandman Jingle Dress Dance Duluth, MN, 1/11/13." 2013. YouTube video, 8:13. Posted by J. P. Rennquist, WGZS-FM 89.1 Radio Service of Fond du Lac Band of Lake Superior Chippewa, February 4, 2013. www.youtube.com.

Bahle, Julius. 1938. "Arbeitstypus und Inspirationstypus im Schaffen der Komponisten." *Zeitschrift für Psychologie* 142:313–22.

Bailey, Peter. 1996. "Breaking the Sound Barrier: A Historian Listens to Noise." *Body and Society* 2 (49): 49–66.

Bailey, Walter. B. 2008. "Will Schoenberg Be a New York Fad? The 1914 American Premiere of Schoenberg's String Quartet in D Minor." *American Music* 26 (1): 37–73.

Bakhtin, Mikhail. 1981. *The Dialogic Imagination: 4 Essays*. Edited by Michael Holquist. Translated by Caryl Emerson and Michael Holquist. Austin: University of Texas Press.

———. 1986. *Speech Genres and Other Late Essays*. Edited by Caryl Emerson and Michael Holquist. Translated by Vern W. McGee. Austin: University of Texas Press.

Bal, Mieke. 2004. "Zwarte Piet's *Bal Masqué*." In Phillips and Schochet 2004, 110–51.

Banwell, Allie. 2017. "Ariel Tweto, Former Star of 'Flying Wild Alaska,' Lands New Show on Travel Channel." *Arctic Sounder*, November 13.

Barker, Adam J. 2015. "'A Direct Act of Resurgence, and Direct Act of Sovereignty': Reflections on Idle No More, Indigenous Activism, and Canadian Settler Colonialism." *Globalizations* 12 (1): 43–65.

Barker, Joanne, ed. 2017. *Critically Sovereign: Indigenous Gender, Sexuality, and Feminist Studies*. Durham: Duke University Press.

Barz, Gregory, and Timothy J. Cooley, eds. 2008. *Shadows in the Field: New Perspectives for Fieldwork in Ethnomusicology*. 2nd. ed. New York: Oxford University Press.

Basso, Keith H. 1988. "'Speaking with Names': Language and Landscape among the Western Apache." *Cultural Anthropology* 3 (2): 99–130.

———. 1996. *Wisdom Sits in Places: Landscape and Language among the Western Apache*. Albuquerque: University of New Mexico Press.

Battiste, Marie. 1984. "An Historical Investigation of the Social and Cultural Consequences of Micmac Literacy." EdD diss., Stanford University.

———. 1988. "Different Worlds of Work: The Mi'kmaq Experience." In *Work, Ethnicity, and Oral History*, edited by Dorothy E. Moore and James H. Harrison, 63–70. Issues in Ethnicity and Multiculturalism Series 1. Halifax: International Education Centre.

———, ed. 2000. *Reclaiming Indigenous Voice and Vision*. Vancouver: University of British Columbia Press.

Bauman, Richard, and Charles L. Briggs. 2003. *Voices of Modernity: Language Ideologies and the Politics of Inequality*. New York: Cambridge University Press.

Beaucage, Marjorie. 1992. *Speaking to Their Mother: Ayumee-Aawach Oomama-Mowan*. Video. Toronto: V Tape. DVD.

Beaudry, Nicole. 2008. "The Challenges of Human Relations in Ethnographic Inquiry: Examples from Arctic and Subarctic Fieldwork." In Barz and Cooley 2008, 224–45.

Becenti, Juantio. 2015. *Squash Blossom*. Unpublished composition.

Becker, Jane S. 1998. *Selling Tradition: Appalachia and the Construction of an American Folk, 1930–1940*. Chapel Hill: University of North Carolina Press.

Belmore, Rebecca, and Wanda Nanibush. 2014. "An Interview with Rebecca Belmore." *Decolonization: Indigeneity, Education and Society* 3 (1): 213–17.

Bennett, Stan. 1976. "The Process of Musical Creation: Interviews with Eight Composers." *Journal of Research in Music Education* 24 (1): 3–13.

Berger, Harris M. 2003. "Introduction: The Politics and Aesthetics of Language Choice and Dialect in Popular Music." In *Global Pop, Local Language*, edited by Harris M. Berger and Michael T. Carroll, ix–xxvi. Jackson: University of Mississippi Press.

Bigenho, Michelle. 2002. *Sounding Indigenous: Authenticity in Bolivian Music Performance*. New York: Palgrave.

———. 2011. "The Intimate Distance of Indigenous Modernity." Paper presented at the World Conference of the International Council for Traditional Music, St. John's, Newfoundland, Canada, July 18.

Big River Cree. 2011. *Stand by Me*. Turtle Island Music, B0059CMT51, digital album.

Bijsterveld, Karin. 2008. *Mechanical Sound: Technology, Culture, and Public Problems of Noise in the Twentieth Century*. Cambridge, MA: MIT Press.

Bissett Perea, Jessica. 2012. "Pamyua's *Akutaq*. Traditions of Inuit Musical Modernities in Alaska." *MUSICultures* 39 (1): 7–41.

———. 2017. "Audiovisualizing Iñupiaq Men and Masculinities *On the Ice*." In Barker 2017, 127–68.

Bohlman, Philip V. 1991. "Representation and Cultural Critique in the History of Ethnomusicology." In *Comparative Musicology and Anthropology of Music: Essays on the History of Ethnomusicology*, edited by Bruno Nettl and Philip V. Bohlman, 131–51. Chicago: University of Chicago Press.

———. 2002. *World Music: A Very Short Introduction*. New York: Oxford University Press.

Born, Georgina. 1995. *Rationalizing Culture: IRCAM, Boulez, and the Institutionalization of the Musical Avant-Garde*. Berkeley: University of California Press.

Boston Globe. 1916. "Indian Music: Miss Densmore 'Cans' Ancient Songs; How She Collects and Records Them on Phonograph: Red Men Claim Some Songs Taught by Animals." April 2, 1916, SM15.

Brady, Erika. 1999. *A Spiral Way: How the Phonograph Changed Ethnography*. Jackson: University Press of Mississippi.

———. 2002. "Save, Save the Lore!" In *The Anthropology of Media: A Reader*, edited by Kelly Askew and Richard R. Wilk, 56–72. Hoboken: Wiley-Blackwell.

Brean, Joseph. 2014. "The Ambassador: Wab Kinew Is an Aboriginal Leader Seeking to Engage with Canadians at Large." *National Post*, June 20, 2014. http://news.national post.com.

Bristow, Nancy K. 1996. *Making Men Moral: Social Engineering during the Great War*. New York: New York University Press.

Brooks, James. 2002. *Captives and Cousins: Slavery, Kinship, and Community in the Southwest Borderlands*. Chapel Hill: University of North Carolina Press.

Brown, Michael F. 2004. *Who Owns Native Culture?* Cambridge: Harvard University Press.

Browner, Tara. 1995. "Transposing Cultures: The Appropriation of Native North American Musics, 1890–1990." PhD diss., University of Michigan.

———. 1997. "'Breathing the Indian Spirit': Thoughts in Musical Borrowing and the Indianist Movement in American Music." *American Music* 15 (3): 265–84.

———. 2000. "Making and Singing Pow-Wow Songs: Text, Form and the Significance of Culture-Based Analysis." *Ethnomusicology* 44 (2): 214–33.

———. 2002. *Heartbeat of the People: Music and Dance of the Northern Pow-Wow*. Urbana: University of Illinois Press.

———. 2009a. "An Acoustical Geography of Intertribal Pow-wow Songs." In Browner 2009b, 131–40.

————, ed. 2009b. *Music of the First Nations: Tradition and Innovation in Native North America*. Urbana: University of Illinois Press.

Bruce, Elyse. 2013. "Idle No More: Spin Doctors Need Not Apply." August 30, 2013. http://elysebruce.wordpress.com/.

Buford, Kate. 2010. *Native American Son: The Life and Sporting Legend of Jim Thorpe*. New York: Knopf.

"Building the 8th Fire Panel." 2013. Vancouver Public Library. Pts. 1–3. May 29, 2013. http://towardsdecolonization.wordpress.com/.

Burton, Antoinette. 2012. "Introduction: Travelling Criticism? On the Dynamic Histories of Indigenous Modernity." *Cultural and Social History* 9 (4): 491–96.

Bynner, Witter. 1923. "New Mexico Aflame against Two Bills." *Outlook*, January 17, 1923, 125–27.

Byrd, Jodi. 2011. *The Transit of Empire: Indigenous Critiques of Colonialism*. Minneapolis: University of Minnesota Press.

Cain, Celia. 2003. "Songbirds: Representation, Meaning, and Indigenous Public Culture in Native American Women's Popular Musics." PhD diss., University of Chicago.

Canada. 2011. "Reforming First Nations Education: From Crisis to Hope: Report of the Standing Senate Committee on Aboriginal Peoples." Standing Senate Committee on Aboriginal Peoples. Accessed August 28, 2014. www.edu.gov.mb.ca.

Carter, Huntly. 1910. "The Coming of Beautiful Cities." *New Age* 8 (1): 6–8.

Carter, Paul. 2004. "Ambiguous Traces, Mishearing, and Auditory Space." In *Hearing Cultures: Essays on Sound, Listening and Modernity*, edited by Veit Erlmann, 43–64. Oxford: Berg.

Castellano, Marlene Brandt. 2009. "Heart of the Nations: Women's Contribution to Community Healing." In Valaskakis, Stout, and Guimond 2009, 203–35.

Caven, Febna. 2013. "Being Idle No More: The Women behind the Movement." *Cultural Survival Quarterly* 37 (1): www.culturalsurvival.org.

Chacon, Raven. n.d. "Postcommodity Collective." Accessed October 10, 2013. www.imginenative.org.

Chakrabarty, Dipesh. 2000. *Provincializing Europe: Postcolonial Thought and Historical Difference*. Princeton: Princeton University Press.

Chase, Stuart. 1925. *The Tragedy of Waste*. New York: Macmillan.

Chávez, John R. 1984. *The Lost Land: The Chicano Image of the Southwest*. Albuquerque: University of New Mexico Press.

Chilisa, Bagele. 2012. *Indigenous Research Methodologies*. Los Angeles: Sage.

Chuh, Candice. 2003. *Imagine Otherwise: On Asian Americanist Critique*. Durham: Duke University Press.

Clemens, Justin. 2003. *The Romanticism of Contemporary Theory: Institutions, Aesthetics, Nihilism*. Farnham, Surrey, UK: Ashgate.

Clements, William M. 1996. *Native American Verbal Art: Texts and Contexts.* Tucson: University of Arizona Press.

Clifford, James. 1988. *The Predicament of Culture: Twentieth-Century Ethnography, Literature, and Art.* Cambridge: Harvard University Press.

————. 1997. *Routes: Travel and Translation in the Late Twentieth Century.* Cambridge: Harvard University Press.

Cline, John. 2014. Review of *Recording Culture: Powwow Music and the Aboriginal Recording Industry on the Northern Plains,* by Christopher A. Scales. *American Indian Quarterly* 38 (2): 271–74.

CMEC (Council of Ministers of Education). 2008. "Learn Canada 2020." Accessed September 9, 2014. www.cmec.ca.

Coleman, Elizabeth Burns, and Rosemary J. Coombe. 2009. "A Broken Record: Subjecting 'Music' to Cultural Rights." With Fiona MacArailt. In *The Ethics of Cultural Appropriation,* edited by James Young, xxx. Chichester: Wiley-Blackwell.

Cooley, Timothy J., Katherine Meizel, and Nasir Syed. 2008. "Virtual Fieldwork: Three Case Studies." In Barz and Cooley 2008, 90–107.

Corntassel, Jeff. 2012. "Re-envisioning Resurgence: Indigenous Pathways to Decolonization and Sustainable Self-Determination." *Decolonization: Indigeneity, Education, and Society* 1 (1): 86–101.

Coulthard, Glen. 2014. *Red Skin, White Masks: Rejecting the Colonial Politics of Recognition.* Minneapolis: University of Minnesota Press.

Creighton, Helen. (1956) 2004. *Folk Music from Nova Scotia.* Smithsonian Folkways Recordings, Folkways Records.

Croall, Barbara. 2010. "Native Drum." *Wholenote.* Accessed March 3, 2010. www.thewhole note.com.

Cruikshank, Julie. 1998. *The Social Life of Stories: Narrative and Knowledge in the Yukon Territory.* Lincoln: University of Nebraska Press.

Curtis, Natalie. 1913. "The Perpetuating of Indian Art." *Outlook,* November 22, 1913, 623–31.

Cusick, Suzanne. 2006. "Music as Torture/Music as Weapon." *Trans: Revista Transcultural de Música* 10. www.sibetrans.com.

Cyr, Alicia Kozlowski. 2018. Instagram photo, Renee Van Nett and Jingle Dress dancers. Posted January 8, 2018. www.thepictaram.club

Daughtry, Martin. 2015. *Listening to War: Sound, Music, Trauma, and Survival in Wartime Iraq.* New York: Oxford University Press.

Dave, Nomi. 2014. "The Politics of Silence: Music, Violence, and Protest in Guinea." *Ethnomusicology* 58 (1): 1–29.

Deerchild, Rosanna. 2003. "Tribal Feminism Is a Drum Song." In Anderson and Lawrence 2003, 97–105.

Defoe, Michelle (@MorningStar_ikwe). 2012. "Drum Circle at Miller Hill Mall Raises Concerns." Twitter, December 22, 2012, 5:56 p.m. twitter.com/morningstar_kwe.

Deger, Jennifer. 2006. *Shimmering Screens: Making Media in an Aboriginal Community.* Minneapolis: University of Minnesota Press.

De la Cadena, Marisol and Orin Starn. 2007. *Indigenous Experience Today.* Berg: Oxford.

De la Torre, Renee, and Christina Gutiérrez Zúñiga. 2013. "Chicano Spirituality in the Construction of an Imagined Nation: Aztlán." *Social Compass* 60 (2): 218–35.

Deloria, Philip. 2004. *Indians in Unexpected Places.* Lawrence: University Press of Kansas.

———. 2011. Afterword to *Native Acts: Indian Performance, 1603-1832,* edited by Joshua D. Bellin and Laura L. Mielke, 309–16. Lincoln: University of Nebraska Press.

Denny, Walter Jr. 2012. "Music, Religion, and Healing in a Mi'kmaw Community." With Gordon E. Smith. In Hoefnagels and Diamond 2012, 281–99.

Densmore, Frances. 1915. "The Study of Indian Music." *Musical Quarterly* 1 (2): 187–97.

———. 1918. *Teton Sioux Music and Culture.* Bureau of American Ethnology, Bulletin 61. Washington, DC: Government Printing Office.

———. 1927. "Musical Composition among the American Indians." *American Speech* 2 (9): 393–94.

———. 1934. "The Songs of Indian Soldiers during the World War." *Musical Quarterly* 20 (4): 419–25.

———. 1938. "The Influence of Hymns on the Form of Indian Songs." *American Anthropologist* 40 (1): 175–77.

———. 1941. "Native Songs of Two Hybrid Ceremonies among American Indians." *American Anthropologist* 43 (1): 77–82.

———. 1943. "The Use of Meaningless Syllables in Indian Songs." *American Anthropologist* 45 (1): 160–62.

———. 1944. "Traces of Foreign Influences in the Music of the American Indians." *American Anthropologist* 46:106–12.

———. 1945. "The Importance of Recordings of Indian Songs." *American Anthropologist* 47 (4): 637–39.

Denzin, Norman K. 2003. *Performance Ethnography: Critical Pedagogy and the Politics of Culture.* Thousand Oaks, CA: Sage.

Denzin, Norman K., Yvonna S. Lincoln, and Linda Tuhiwai Smith, eds. 2008. *Handbook of Critical Indigenous Methodologies.* Los Angeles: Sage.

Dharwadker, Aparna. 2011. "Special Book Review Essay: India's Theatrical Modernity: Re-theorizing Colonial, Postcolonial, and Diasporic Formations." *Theatre Journal* 63:425–37.

Diamond, Beverley. 1992. "Christian Hymns in Eastern Woodlands Communities: Performance Contexts." In *Musical Repercussions of 1492: Explorations, Encounters, and Identities,* edited by Carol E. Robertson, 381–94. Washington, DC: Smithsonian Institution.

————. 2002. "Native American Contemporary Music: The Women." *World of Music* 44 (1): 11–40.

————.2005. "Media as Social Action: Native American Musicians in the Recording Studio." In *Wired for Sound: Engineering and Technologies in Sonic Cultures*, edited by Paul D. Green and Thomas Porcello, 118–37. Middletown: Wesleyan University Press.

————. 2007a. "'Allowing the Listener to Fly as They Want to': Sámi Perspectives on Indigenous CD Production in Northern Europe." *Worlds of Music* 49 (1): 23–49.

————. 2007b. "The Music of Modern Indigeneity: From Identity to Alliance Studies." *European Meetings in Ethnomusicology* 12 (22):169–90.

————. 2011a. "Decentering Opera: Early 21st-Century Indigenous Production." In Karantonis and Robinson 2010, 31–56.

————. 2011b. "Music of Modern Indigeneity: From Identity to Alliance Studies." *Yoik: Aspects of Performing, Collecting, Interpreting*, edited by Dan Lundberg and Gunnar Ternhag, 9–36. Stockholm: Skrifter Utgivna av Avenskt Visarkiv.

————. 2011c. "'Re' Thinking: Revitalization, Return, and Reconciliation in Contemporary Indigenous Expressive Culture." Trudeau Lecture, Canadian Federation for the Humanities and Social Sciences and Congress. St. Thomas University, University of New Brunswick, June 1, 2011.

————. 2013. "Native American Ways of (Music) History." In *The Cambridge History of World Music*, edited by Philip V. Bohlman, 155–80. Cambridge: Cambridge University Press.

————. 2015a. "The Doubleness of Sound in Canada's Indian Residential Schools." In Levine and Bohlman 2015, 267–79.

————. 2015b. "Patriarchs at Work." *SEM Music Matters: An Online Forum.* Accessed June 21, 2018. https://soundmattersthesemblog.wordpress.com/.

————. 2015c. "The Power of Stories: Canadian Music Scholarship's Narratives and Counter-Narratives." *Intersections* 33 (2): 155–65.

————. 2016. "Resisting Containment: The Long Reach of Song at TRC National Events." In Robinson and Martin 2016, 239–66.

Diamond, Beverley, M. Sam Cronk, and Franziska von Rosen. 1994. *Visions of Sound: Musical Instruments of First Nations Communities in Northeastern America.* Chicago: University of Chicago Press.

Diamond, Beverley, Kati Szego, and Heather Sparling. 2012. "Indigenous Modernities: Introduction." *MUSICultures* 39:1–6.

Diamond, Neil, Catherine Bainbridge, and Jeremiah Hayes. 2010. *Reel Injun: On the Trail of the Hollywood Indian.* Montreal: Rezolution Pictures / National Film Board of Canada.

Diamond, Stanley. (1974) 2018. *In Search of the Primitive: A Critique of Civilization.* New York: Routledge.

Discovery. 2012. "The Flying Wild Alaska Soundtrack: Available on iTunes." July 5, 2012. https://youtu.be/pm9gbnpUoKc.

Draisey-Collishaw, Rebecca. 2010. "Encountering Culture, Inscribed and Ascribed: Meanings in Dawn Avery's *Fringe*." Unpublished manuscript.

Drezus. 2013. *Red Winter*. Drezus Music, B00B64J88E, digital album.

———. 2013. "Red Winter." YouTube video, 3:51. Posted by IamDrezus, January 11, 2013. www.youtube.com.

Drummond, Don, and Ellen Kachuk Rosenbluth. 2013. "The Debate on First Nations Education Funding: Mind the Gap." Queen's University, Policy Studies. December 2013. Accessed September 14, 2014. www.queensu.ca.

Dueck, Byron. 2013. *Musical Intimacies and Indigenous Imaginaries: Aboriginal Music and Dance in Public Performance*. New York: Oxford University Press.

Dunham, Mike. 1998. "CD Transplants Native Music to World Setting." *Anchorage Daily News*, April 21, 1998.

Ellis, Clyde. 2003. *A Dancing People: Powwow Culture on the Southern Plains*. Lawrence: University Press of Kansas.

Ellis, Clyde, and Luke Eric Lassiter. 2005. Introduction to *Powwow*, edited by Clyde Ellis, Luke Eric Lassiter, and Gary H. Dunham, vii–xv. Lincoln: University of Nebraska Press.

Ellis, Clyde, Luke Eric Lassiter, and Gary H. Dunham, eds. 2005. *Powwow*. Lincoln: University of Nebraska Press.

Emcee One (Marcus Guinn). 2004. *A Collection of Demos*. One Innertainment, compact disc.

———. 2007. *Somebody's Gotta Tell 'Em*. One Innertainment, online stream.

———. 2012. *Introducing for Again for the First Time: Emcee One*. One Innertainment, online stream.

Erickson, Winston P. 1994. *Sharing the Desert: The Tohono O'odham in History*. Tucson: University of Arizona Press.

Eskasoni Mi'kmaw Nation. n.d. Website. Accessed June 25, 2018. www.eskasoni.ca.

Farley, Melissa, Nicole Matthews, Sarah Deer, Guadalupe Lopez, Christine Stark, and Eileen Hudon. 2011. *Garden of Truth: The Prostitution and Trafficking of Native Women in Minnesota*. Saint Paul: Minnesota Indian Women's Sexual Assault Coalition, William Mitchell College of Law.

Feld, Steven. 1976. "Ethnomusicology and Visual Communication." *Ethnomusicology* 20 (2): 293–325.

Fienup-Riordan, Ann. 1990. *Eskimo Essays: Yup'ik Lives and How We See Them*. New Brunswick: Rutgers University Press.

Filene, Benjamin. 2008. *Romancing the Folk: Public Memory and American Roots Music*. Chapel Hill: University of North Carolina Press.

Fiske, Jo-Anne. 1996. "The Womb Is to the Nation as the Heart Is to the Body: Ethnopolitical Discourses of the Canadian Indigenous Women's Movement." *Studies in Political Economy* 51 (Fall): 65–95.

Flahive, Ryan S., ed. 2012. *Celebrating Difference: Fifty Years of Contemporary Native Arts at IAIA, 1962–2012.* Santa Fe, NM: Sunstone.

Fletcher, Alice C. (1893) 1994. *A Study of Omaha Indian Music.* Lincoln: University of Nebraska Press.

"Flying Wild Alaska Soundtrack on iTunes, July 6, 2012." 2012. *Discovery Music Source,* July 5, 2012.

FNNMCFS (First Nations of Northern Manitoba Child and Family Services Authority). 2013. "First Nations of Northern Manitoba Child and Family Services Authority: History." Accessed September 25, 2013. www.northernauthority.ca.

Forgey, Pat. 2015. "Gov. Walker Signs Bill Ending Alaska Film Incentive Program." *Alaska Dispatch News,* June 16, 2015.

Foucault, Michel. 1995. *Discipline and Punish: The Birth of the Prison.* 2nd ed. New York: Vintage Books.

Fox, Aaron A. 2007. *Real Country: Music and Language in Working-Class Culture.* Durham: Duke University Press.

Fox, Frank H. 1919. "The Modern American Indian." *Outlook,* December 10, 1919, 475–77.

Free Dictionary. 2013. s.v. "modernity." Accessed April 15, 2013. www.freedictionary.com.

Friesen, Andrew. 2013. "Dancer Shares the Healing Power of the Jingle Dress: Hundreds Expected to Converge on Portage and Main to Greet UN Special Rapporteur James Anaya." Canadian Broadcasting Company. October 11, 2013. www.cbc.ca.

Frisbie, Charlotte. 1967. *Kinaaldá: A Study of the Navaho Girl's Puberty Ceremony.* Middletown, CT: Wesleyan University Press.

———, ed. 1978. "Special Symposium Issue on Navajo Mortuary Practices and Beliefs." Special issue, *American Indian Quarterly* 4 (4): 303–410.

Frozen Whitefish. 2012. *Wiinga Ellpet'llu.* Yuk Media, digital album.

Gaertner, David. 2016. "Sehtoskakew: 'Aboriginal Principles of Witnessing' and the Canadian Truth and Reconciliation Commission." In Robinson and Martin 2016, 135–56.

Ganster, Paul, and David E. Lorey. 2008. *The U.S.-Mexico Border into the Twenty-First Century.* Lanham, MD: Rowman and Littlefield.

Gaonkar, Dilip Parameshwar. 1999. "On Alternative Modernities." *Public Culture* 11 (1): 1–18.

Garrett, Charles Hiroshi, Carol J. Oja, George E. Lewis, Gayle Sherwood Magee, Alejandro L. Madrid, Sherrie Tucker, and Robert Fink. 2011. "Studying U.S. Music in the Twenty-First Century." *Journal of the American Musicological Society* 64 (3): 689–719.

Gaski, Harald. 2000. "The Secretive Text: Yoik Lyrics as Literature and Tradition." In *Sami Folkloristics,* edited by Juha Pentikäinen, 191–214. Turku: NNF.

———. 2013. "Indigenism and Cosmopolitanism: A Pan-Sami View of the Indigenous

Perspective in Sami Culture and Research." *AlterNative: An International Journal of Indigenous Peoples* 9 (2): 113–24.

Gehl, Lynn. n.d. "Ally Bill of Responsibilities." Accessed June 10, 2014. www.lynngehl.com.

George Stroumboulopoulos Tonight. 2013. Season 3, episode 84, "Wab Kinew." Aired January 18, 2013, on Canadian Broadcasting Company (CBC).

Gidal, Marc. 2010. "Contemporary 'Latin American' Composers of Art Music in the United States: Cosmopolitans Navigating Multiculturalism and Universalism." *Latin American Music Review* 31 (1): 40–78.

Giddens, Anthony. 1991. *Modernity and Self-Identity: Self and Society in the Late Modern Age.* Stanford: Stanford University Press.

Gilbert, Helen. 2013. "'Let the Games Begin': Pageants, Protests, Indigeneity (1968–2010)." Conference paper, November 13, 2013.

Givens, Douglas. 1977. *An Analysis of Navajo Temporality.* Lanham, MD: University Press of America.

Goertzen, Chris. 2001. "Powwows and Identity on the Piedmont and Coastal Plains of North Carolina." *Ethnomusicology* 45 (1): 58–88.

Gonzalez, Marie C. 2000. "The Four Seasons of Ethnography: A Creation-Centered Ontology for Ethnography." *International Journal of Intercultural Relations* 24:623–50.

Goodman, Steve. 2012. *Sonic Warfare: Sound, Affect, and the Ecology of Fear.* Cambridge, MA: MIT Press.

Gordon, Colin. 2000. Introduction to *Power,* by Michel Foucault, edited by James D. Faubion, translated by Robert Hurley and others, xi–xli. Vol. 3 of *Essential Works of Foucault, 1954–1984.* London: Penguin Books.

Gordon, Jessica, and the Founders of Idle No More. 2014. "The Idle No More Manifesto." In Kino-nda-Niimi Collective 2014, 71–73.

Gould, Elizabeth S., and Carol L. Matthews. 1999. "Weavings: Aboriginal Women's Music, Poetry, and Performance as Resistance." *Women and Music* 3:70–78.

Gow, David D. 2008. *Countering Development. Indigenous Modernity and the Moral Imagination.* Durham: Duke University Press.

Graf, Max. 1947. *From Beethoven to Shostakovich: The Psychology of the Composing Process.* New York: Philosophical Library.

Grant, John W. 1980. "Missionaries and Messiahs in the Northwest." *Studies in Religion* 9 (2): 125–35.

Grawunder, Sven. 2009. *On the Physiology of Voice Production in South-Siberian Throat Singing Analysis of Acoustic and Electrophysiological Evidences.* Berlin: Frank and Timme.

Green, Joyce, ed. 2007. *Making Space for Indigenous Feminism.* Black Point, NS: Fernwood.

Green, Rayna. 1992. "Cherokee Stomp Dance: Laughter Rises Up." In Heth 1992, 177.

Greene, Crystal D. 2013. "#JingleDress Healing Dance a Call to Action: Welcoming the UN Special Rapporteur on the Rights of Indigenous Peoples to Winnipeg." Vimeo video. October 7, 2013. https://vimeo.com/.

Greenwood, Margo, Sarah de Leeuw, and Nicole Marie Lindsay, eds. 2015. *Determinants of Indigenous Peoples' Health in Canada.* Toronto: Canadian Scholars Press.

Griffen, Joyce. 1980. "Navajo Funerals, Anglo-Style." Museum of Norther Arizona Research Paper 18. Flagstaff: Museum of Northern Arizona.

Griffin-Pierce, Trudy. 2000. *Native Peoples of the Southwest.* Albuquerque: University of New Mexico Press.

Griffith, James S. 1992. *Beliefs and Holy Places: A Spiritual Geography of the Pimeria Alta.* Tucson: University of Arizona Press.

Gross, Lawrence W. 2003. "Cultural Sovereignty and Native American Hermeneutics in the Interpretation of the Sacred Stories of the Anishinaabe." *Wicazo Sa Review* 18 (2): 127–34.

Guilford, Andrew. 2000. *Sacred Objects and Sacred Places: Preserving Tribal Traditions.* Boulder: University Press of Colorado.

Gutierrez, Jose Angel. 2011. "The Chicano Movement: Paths to Power." *Social Studies* 102 (1): 25–32.

Habermas, Jürgen. 1981. "Modernity versus Postmodernity." *New German Critique* 22:3–14.

Hallowell, A. Irving. 1955. *Culture and Experience.* Philadelphia: Pennsylvania University Press.

————. 1992. *The Ojibwa of Berens River: Ethnography into History.* Edited by Jennifer S. H. Brown. Fort Worth: Harcourt Bruce Jovanovich College.

Hamalainen, Pekka. 2008. *The Comanche Empire.* New Haven: Yale University Press.

Hamill, Chad. 2012. *Songs of Power and Prayer in the Columbia Plateau.* Corvallis: Oregon State University Press.

Hart, Mickey. 2003. *Songcatchers: In Search of the World's Music.* Washington, DC: National Geographic Press.

Hartt, Mary Bronson. 1912. "The Skansen Idea." *Century Magazine,* April 1912, 916–20.

Hatton, Orin T. 1990. *Power and Performance in Gros Ventre War Expedition Songs.* Canadian Ethnology Service Mercury Series Paper 114. Hull, Quebec: Canadian Museum of Civilization.

Haycox, Stephen W. 2002. *Alaska: An American Colony.* Seattle: University of Washington Press.

Healing Songs of the American Indians. 1965. Folkways Records FE 4251.

Heartbeat: More Voices of First Nations Women. 1998. Smithsonian Folkways SD 40455, compact disc.

Heartbeat: Voices of First Nations Women. 1995. Smithsonian Folkways SF 40415, compact disc.

Hearts of the Nations: Aboriginal Women's Voices in the Studio. 1997. Banff, AB: Banff Centre for the Arts.

Hedican, Edward J. 2008. "The Ipperwash Inquiry and the Tragic Death of Dudley George." *Canadian Journal of Native Studies* 28 (1): 159–73.

Hegeman, Susan. 1999. *Patterns for America: Modernism and the Concept of Culture.* Princeton: Princeton University Press.

Heidegger, Martin. (1927) 2008. *Being and Time.* New York: HarperCollins.

Henderson, Archibald. 1925. "Civilization and Progress: An Inquiry." *Virginia Quarterly Review* 1 (1): 19–35.

Hermes, Mary. 2005. "'Ma'iingan Is Just a Misspelling of the Word Wolf': A Case for Teaching Culture through Language." *Anthropology and Education Quarterly* 36 (1): 43–56.

Herndon, Marcia. 1982. *Native American Music.* Darby, PA: Norwood.

Heth, Charlotte, ed. 1992. *Native American Dance: Ceremonies and Social Traditions.* Washington, DC: National Museum of the American Indian, Smithsonian Institution.

Hilder, Thomas R. 2015. *Sámi Musical Performance and the Politics of Indigeneity in Northern Europe.* Lanham, MD: Rowman and Littlefield.

Hobsbawm, Eric, and Terence O. Ranger. 1983. *The Invention of Tradition.* Cambridge: Cambridge University Press.

Hodges, William Robert. 2009. "*Ganti Andung, Gabe Ende* (Replacing Laments, Becoming Hymns): The Changing Voice of Grief in the Pre-funeral Wakes of Protestant Toba Batak (North Sumatra, Indonesia)." PhD diss., University of California, Santa Barbara.

Hoefnagels, Anna. 2002. "Powwow Songs: Traveling Songs and Changing Protocol." *World of Music* 44 (1): 127–36.

———. 2007a. "Renewal and Adaptation: Cree Round Dances." Department of Canadian Heritage through Canadian Culture Online. Carleton University. Accessed June 25, 2015. www.native-dance.ca.

———. 2007b. "'What Is Tradition if We Keep Changing It to Suit Our Needs?' 'Tradition' and Gender Politics at Powwows in Southwestern Ontario." In *Folk Music, Traditional Music, Ethnomusicology: Canadian Perspectives, Past and Present*, edited by Anna Hoefnagels and Gordon E. Smith, 187–200. Newcastle upon Tyne: Cambridge Scholars' Press.

———. 2012. "Aboriginal Women and the Powwow Drum: Restrictions, Teachings, and Challenges." In Hoefnagels and Diamond 2012, 109–30.

Hoefnagels, Anna, and Beverley Diamond, eds. 2012. *Aboriginal Music in Contemporary Canada: Echoes and Exchanges.* Montreal: McGill-Queen's University Press.

Hoehner, Bernard. n.d. *Hymns in Lakota.* Walnut Creek, CA. Audiocassette.

Hofmann, Charles, ed. 1968. *Frances Densmore and American Indian Music: A Memorial Volume.* New York: Museum of the American Indian/Heye Foundation.

Holm, Tom, J. Diane Pearson, and Ben Chavis. 2003. "Peoplehood: A Model for the Extension of Sovereignty in American Indian Studies." *Wicazo Sa Review* 18 (1): 7–24.

Holman, Jones S. 2005. "Autoethnography: Making the Personal Political." In *The SAGE Handbook of Qualitative Research*, edited by Norman K. Denzin and Yvonna S. Lincoln, 763–91. 3rd ed. Thousand Oaks, CA: Sage.

Holton, Gary and Brett Parks. 2011. *Indigenous Peoples and Languages of Alaska*. Fairbanks: Alaska Native Language Center/University of Alaska, Anchorage/ Institute of Social Economic Research.

Hopi Tribe. 1994. *Hopi Tribal Council Resolution No. H-70-94*.

Hopkins, Kyle. 2011. "Reality TV Invades Alaska." *Anchorage Daily News*, February 14, 2011.

——. 2014. "As Films Disappear, State Subsidies Explode for Alaska-Based Reality Shows." *Alaska Dispatch News*, August 4, 2014.

Hovland, Arild. 1996. *Moderne urfolk: Samisk ungdom i bevegelse*. Oslo: UNGforsk/NOVA.

Huang, Hao. 1997. "The 1992 Turtle Dance (Oekuu Shadeh) of San Juan Pueblo: Lessons with the Composer, Peter Garcia." *American Indian Culture and Research Journal* 21 (4): 171–215.

Huber, M. 1993. "Mediation around the Medicine Wheel." *Medicine Quarterly* 10 (4): 355–65.

Huhndorf, Shari. 2003. "*Atanarjuat, the Fast Runner*: Culture, History, and Politics in Inuit Media." *American Anthropologist* 105 (4): 822–26.

Huhndorf, Shari M., and Cheryl Suzack. 2010. "Indigenous Feminism: Theorizing the Issues." In *Indigenous Women and Feminism: Politics, Activism, Culture*, edited by Cheryl Suzack, Shari M. Huhndorf, Jeanne Perreault, and Jean Barman, 1–17. Vancouver: University of British Columbia Press.

Hurley, Mary C., and Tonina Simeone. 2010. "Legislative Summary of Bill C-3: Gender Equity in Indian Registration Act, Status of the Bill." Library of Parliament Research Publications, Social Affairs Division. March 18, 2010. Revised November 15, 2010. www2.parl.gc.ca.

Husslein, Joseph. 1940. Preface to *Rural Roads to Security: America's Third Struggle for Freedom*, edited by Luigi G. Ligutti and John C. Rawe, vii–ix. Milwaukee: Bruce.

"Idle No More Duluth." 2012. YouTube video, 3:48. Posted by "proudfather," December 22, 2012. www.youtube.com.

"Idle No More: Priscilla Settee and Sheelah McLean." 2013. YouTube video, 10:27. Published by Don Kossick, January 9, 2013. www.youtube.com.

Idlout, Lucie. 2003. *E5-770: My Mother's Name*. Arbor Records AR-12002, compact disc.

Institute of American Indian Arts. 1972. *Future Directions in Native American Art*. Santa Fe, NM: Institute of American Indian Arts.

International Cry. 2008. "Tohono O'odham Demand Halt to Construction of Border Wall." July 18, 2008. https://internationalcry.org/.

Ireland, Michael. 2014. "60s 'Scoop Kids' Bear Emotional Scars and Want Apology." *Indian Life*, May–June 2014. Academic OneFile. www.newspaper.indianlife.org.

Jaakola, Lyz. 2011. Opening Statement at "A Native American Musical Showcase," Duluth MN, September 22, 2011.

Jensen, Joan M., and Michelle W. Patterson. 2015. "Conclusion: A Picture Is Worth Deconstructing." In *Travels with Frances Densmore: Her Life, Work, and Legacy in Native American Studies*, edited by Joan M. Jensen and Michelle W. Patterson, 409–20. Lincoln: University of Nebraska Press.

"Jingle Dress Healing Dance: Portage and Main, Saturday Oct 12, 2013, 10am." Facebook, October 13, 2013. www.facebook.com.

Joe, Rita. 1978. *Poems of Rita Joe*. Halifax, NS: Abanaki.

———. 1996. *Song of Rita Joe: Autobiography of a Mi'mkaq Poet*. Charlottetown, Prince Edward Island: Ragweed.

Johnson, Birgitta. 2011. "Back to the Heart of Worship: Praise and Worship Music in One African American Megachurch in Los Angeles." *Black Music Research Journal* 31 (1): 105–29.

Johnston, Patrick. 1983. *Native Children and the Child Welfare System*. Toronto: Canadian Council on Social Development/Lorimer.

Jones-Bamman, Richard. 2006. "From 'I'm a Lapp' to 'I am Saami': Popular Music and Changing Images of Indigenous Ethnicity in Scandinavia." In *Ethnomusicology: A Contemporary Reader*, edited by Jennifer Post, 351–68. New York: Routledge.

Jonez, Lakota, and DJ Creeasian. 2011. "Native Hip-Hop." Interview with Ostwelve, on RPM Podcast #007. September 22, 2011. http://rpm.fm/.

Justice, Daniel Heath. 2005. *Our Fire Survives the Storm: A Cherokee Literary History*. Minneapolis: University of Minnesota Press.

———. 2014. "Indigenous Writing." In *The World of Indigenous North America*, edited by Robert Warrior, 291–307. New York: Oxford University Press.

Kammen, Michael. 1993. *Mystic Chords of Memory: The Transformation of Tradition in American Culture*. New York: Vintage.

Kanatsioh**:**ke Community. 1993. "Mission Statement." Accessed July 10, 2013 www.mohawkcommunity.com.

Karantonis, Pamela, and Dylan Robinson, eds. 2011. *Opera Indigene: Re/presenting First Nations and Indigenous Cultures*. Farnham: Ashgate.

Kawagley, Angayuqaq Oscar. 1995. *A Yupiaq Worldview: A Pathway to Ecology and Spirit*. Long Grove, IL: Waveland.

———. 2006. *A Yupiaq Worldview: A Pathway to Ecology and Spirit*. 2nd ed. Long Grove, IL: Waveland.

Keightly, Keir. 1996. "'Turn It Down!' She Shrieked: Gender, Domestic Space, and High Fidelity, 1948–59." *Popular Music* 15 (2): 149–77.

Keillor, Elaine. 1987. "Hymn Singing among the Dogrib Indians." In *Sing Out the Glad News: Hymn Tunes in Canada*, edited by John Beckwith, 33–44. Toronto: Institute for Canadian Music.

Kemnitzer, Luis S. 1997. "Personal Memories of Alcatraz, 1969." In *American Indian Activism: Alcatraz to the Longest Walk*, edited by Troy R. Johnson, Joane Nagel, and Duane Champagne. 113–18. Chicago: University of Illinois Press.

Kenworthy, Mary Anne, Eleanor M. King, Mary E. Ruwell, and Trudy Van Houten. 1985. *Preserving Field Records: Archival Techniques for Archaeologists and Anthropologists*. Philadelphia: University Museum, University of Pennsylvania.

Keyes, Cheryl. 1991. "Rappin' to the Beat: Rap Music as Street Culture among African Americans." PhD diss., Indiana University.

Kheshti, Roshanak. 2015. *Modernity's Ear: Listening to Race and Gender in World Music*. New York: New York University Press.

Kingsbury, Henry. 1988. *Music, Talent, and Performance: A Conservatory Cultural System*. Philadelphia: Temple University Press.

Kino-nda-Niimi Collective, ed. 2014. *The Winter We Danced: Voices from the Past, the Future, and the Idle No More Movement*. Winnipeg: ARP Books.

Kisliuk, Michelle. 1998. *Seize the Dance: BaAka Musical Life and the Ethnography of Performance*. Oxford: Oxford University Press.

Klein, Laura A, and Lillian A. Ackerman, eds. 1995. *Women and Power in Native North America*. Norman: University of Oklahoma Press.

Kluckholn, Clyde, and Dorothea Leighton. 1962. *The Navaho*. New York: American Museum of Natural History and Anchor Books.

Knauft, Bruce M. 2002. "Critically Modern: An Introduction." In *Critically Modern: Alternatives, Alterities, Anthropologies*, edited by Bruce M. Knauft, 1–56. Bloomington: Indiana University Press.

Koepplinger, Suzanne, Mark Rubin, and Christine Stark. 2013. "Native Sex Trade Crossing International Borders through Lake Superior." With Tom Weber. Minnesota Public Radio. *Daily Circuit*, August 28, 2013.

Korry, Keeker, and Empire Juneau. 2005. "Yup'ik Encore: Six-Member Anchorage Group to Perform Free Show Saturday at Juneau-Douglas High School." *Juneau Empire*. October 13, 2005.

Kovach, Margaret. 2009. *Indigenous Methodologies: Characteristics, Conversations, and Contexts*. Toronto: University of Toronto Press.

Kozlowski, Anna, Vandna Sinha, Tara Petti, and Elsie Flette. 2012. "First Nations Child Welfare in Manitoba (2011)." CWRP Information Sheet #97E. Montreal: Centre for Research on Children and Families, McGill University. Accessed September 27, 2013. http://cwrp.ca.

Krehbiel, Henry E. 1910a. "Mme. Sembrich's Concert of Folksongs; Some Remarks on a Musical Type." *New York Tribune*, December 7, 1910, 7.

——. 1910b. *Program Notes: Marcella Sembrich, Soprano; Frank LaForge, Piano*. Carnegie Hall, December 6, 1910. N.p.

Krejci, Paul. 2010. "Skin Drums, Squeeze Boxes, Fiddles, and Phonographs: Musical Interaction in the Western Arctic, Late 18th through Early 20th Centuries." PhD diss., University of Alaska Fairbanks.

Kroeber, Alfred L. 1912. "Ishi, the Last Aborigine." *World's Work*, July 1912, 304–8.

Krouse, Susan Applegate, and Heather A. Howard, eds. 2009. *Keeping the Campfires Going: Native Women's Activism in Urban Communities*. Lincoln: University of Nebraska Press.

Krueger, Andrew. 2012. "Drum Circle at Miller Hill Mall Raises Concerns." *Duluth News Tribune*, December 22, 2012. www.duluthnewstribune.com.

Kuper, Adam. 1988. *The Invention of Primitive Society: Transformations of an Illusion*. New York: Routledge.

Kurath, Gertrude. 1957. "Catholic Hymns of Michigan Indians." *Anthropological Quarterly* 30 (2): 31–44.

——. 1959. "Blackrobe and Shaman: The Christianization of the Michigan Algonquians." *Papers of the Michigan Academy of Sciences, Arts, and Letters* 44:209–15.

LaBelle, Brandon. 2010. *Acoustic Territories: Sound Culture and Everyday Life*. New York: Continuum.

Lane, Phil Jr., Judie Bopp, Michael Bopp, Lee Brown, and Elders. 1984. *The Sacred Tree*. Twin Lakes, WI: Lotus.

Lassiter, Luke E., and Clyde Ellis. 2002. *The Jesus Road*. Lincoln: University of Nebraska Press.

Latour, Bruno. 1993. *We Have Never Been Modern*. Cambridge, MA: Harvard University Press.

——. 2013. *An Inquiry into Modes of Existence: An Anthropology of the Moderns*. Translated by Catherine Porter. Cambridge: Harvard University Press.

Lauzon, Jani. 2007. *Mixed Blessings: Hand Drum and Flute Songs*. Ra Records RR 0017, compact disc.

LaVigna, Maria. 1980. "Okushare, Music for a Winter Ceremony: The Turtle Dance Songs of San Juan Pueblo." *Selected Reports in Ethnomusicology* 3 (2): 77–99.

Leach, James. 2007. "Creativity, Subjectivity and the Dynamic of Possessive Individualism." In *Creativity and Cultural Improvisation*, edited by Elizabeth Hallam and Tim Ingold, 99–116. New York: Bloomsbury Academic.

Levin, Theodore Craig, and Valentina Süzükei. 2006. *Where Rivers and Mountains Sing: Sound, Music, and Nomadism in Tuva and Beyond*. Bloomington: Indiana University Press.

Levine, Victoria Lindsay. 1998. "American Indian Musics, Past and Present." In *The Cam-

bridge History of American Music, edited by David Nicholls, 1–29. Cambridge: Cambridge University Press.

———. 2002. *Writing American Indian Music: Historic Transcriptions, Notations, and Arrangements.* Middleton, WI: AR-Editions for the American Musicological Society.

———. 2004. "Music." In *The Southeast.* Vol. 14 of *Handbook of North American Indians,* edited by Raymond D. Fogelson, 720–33. Washington, DC: Smithsonian Institution.

———. 2013. "Stomp Dance." In *The Grove Dictionary of American Music,* edited by Charles Hiroshi Garrett, 33–34. 2nd ed. New York: Oxford University Press.

———. 2014a. "Daksi Dinasatdi (Cherokee Leg Rattles)." In *The Grove Dictionary of Musical Instruments,* edited by Laurence Libin, 2:7. 2nd ed. New York: Oxford University Press.

———. 2014b. "Reclaiming Choctaw and Chickasaw Cultural Identity through Music Revival." In *The Oxford Handbook of Music Revival,* edited by Caroline Bithell and Juniper Hill, 300–322. New York: Oxford University Press.

———. 2015. "Regional Songs in Local and Translocal Spaces: The Duck Dance Revisited." In Levine and Bohlman 2015, 458–70.

Levine, Victoria Lindsay, and Philip V. Bohlman. 2015. *This Thing Called Music: Essays in Honor of Bruno Nettl.* Lanham, MD: Rowman and Littlefield.

Levine, Victoria Lindsay, and Bruno Nettl. 2011. "Strophic Form and Asymmetrical Repetition in Four American Indian Songs." In *Analytical and Cross-Cultural Studies in World Music,* edited by Michael Tenzer and John Roeder, 288–315. New York: Oxford University Press.

Lewis, Orlando F. 1919. "The Work of the War Camp Community Service in Community Singing." In *Proceedings of the Twelfth Annual Meeting of the Music Supervisors' National Conference,* 117–22. Pittsburgh: McIlroy.

Lincoln, Jackson Steward. (1935) 2003. *The Dream in Native American and Other Primitive Cultures.* New York: Dover.

List, George. 1985. "Stability and Variation in a Hopi Lullaby." *Ethnomusicology* 31 (1): 18–34.

Little Bear, Leroy. 2000. "Jagged Worldviews Colliding." In Battiste 2000, 77–85.

Locke, Deborah. 2012. "A Ballroom Full of Promise." *Mille Lacs Band of Ojibwe District News,* April 7, 2012. http://millelacsband.com.

Lomawaima, K. Tsianina, and Teresa L. McCarty. 2006. *"To Remain an Indian": Lessons in Democracy from a Century of Native American Education.* Multicultural Education Series. New York: Teachers College Press.

Los Angeles Times. 2012. "Chalk Protests Draw Defiant Lines: Occupy LA Members Clash with Police as They Use ArtWalk as Canvas for Their Anti-Gentrification Theme." *Los Angeles Times,* July 14, 2012.

Luna-Firebaugh. 2005. "'Att Hascu 'Am O'I-oi? What Direction Should We Take? The

Desert People's Approach to the Militarization of the Border." *Journal of Law and Policy* 19:339–63.

MacIntyre, Brenda (Medicine Song Woman). 2005. *Thunder Mountain Healing Songs.* Indian Urban Productions, compact disc.

———. 2007. *Spirit Connection.* Imaginit Music Studio, compact disc.

———. 2009. *Medicine Song.* Imaginit Music Studio, compact disc.

MacLean, Edna Ahgeak. 2014. *Iñupiatun Uqaluit Taniktun Sivuniŋit: Iñupiaq to English Dictionary.* Fairbanks: University of Alaska Press.

Makagon, Daniel, and Mark Neumann. 2009. *Recording Culture: Audio Documentary and the Ethnographic Experience.* Los Angeles: Sage.

Maracle, Lee. 1996. *I Am Woman: A Native Perspective on Sociology and Feminism.* Vancouver: Press Gang.

Maracle, Sylvia. 2003. "The Eagle Has Landed: Native Women, Leadership and Community Development." In Anderson and Lawrence 2003, 70–80.

Marchant, Beth. 2011. "Sonixsphere and iSpy Music Find a Sonic Soul for *Flying Wild Alaska.*" *Studio Daily*, December 14, 2011.

Marsh, Charity. 2012. "Bits and Pieces of Truth: Storytelling, Identity and Hip Hop in Saskatchewan." In Hoefnagels and Diamond 2012, 346–71.

Marshall, Kimberly Jenkins. 2016. *Upward, Not Sunwise: Resonant Rupture in Navajo Neo-Pentecostalism.* Lincoln: University of Nevada Press.

Martin, Keavy. 2012. *Stories in a New Skin: Approaches to Inuit Literature.* Winnipeg: University of Manitoba Press.

Marx, Karl. (1906) 2011. *A Critique of Political Economy.* Vol. 2 of *Capital.* Edited by Friedrich Engels. Translated by Samuel Moore and Edward Aveling. Mineola, NY: Dover.

McAdam, Sylvia. 2014. "Armed with Nothing More Than a Song and a Drum." In Kinonda-Niimi Collective 2014, 65–67.

McAllester, David. 1952. "Menomini Peyote Music." *Menomini Peyotism* 42 (4): 681–700.

———. (1954) 1973. *Enemy Way Music.* Milwood, NY: Kraus Reprint.

McCartney, Andra. 2013. "Ecotonality and Listening Praxis in Sound Ecology, Ambiences, and Popular Music." *Wi: Journal of Mobile Culture* 7 (1). Accessed June 24, 2018. http://wi.mobilities.ca.

McCormick, Charlie T. and Kim K. White, eds. 2011. *Folklore: An Encyclopedia of Customs, Tales, Music, and Art.* 2nd ed. Santa Barbara: ABC-CLIO.

McCoy, Kathleen. 2014. "Hometown U: Atwood Chair Aims to Develop Native Journalists." *Alaska Dispatch News*, August 9, 2014.

McFadden, David Revere, and Ellen Napiura Taubman. 2005. *Changing Hands: Art without Reservation 2; Contemporary Native North American Art from the West, Northwest and Pacific.* New York: Museum of Arts and Design.

McKinnon, Crystal. 2010. "Indigenous Music as a Space of Resistance." In *Making Settler*

Colonial Space: Perspectives on Race, Place and Identity, edited by Tracey Banivanua Mar and Penelope Edmonds, 255–72. New York: Palgrave Macmillan.

McLean, Sheelah. 2014. "Idle No More; Re-storying Canada." In Kino-nda-Niimi Collective 2014, 92–95.

McMahon, Ryan. 2012. "The Round Dance Revolution: Idle No More." *RPM (Revolutions Per Minute): Indigenous Music Culture*, December 20, 2012. http://rpm.fm.

MDEAL (Manitoba Department of Education and Advanced Learning). 2004. "Aboriginal Education Action Plan, 2004–2007." Accessed September 9, 2014. www.edu.gov.mb.ca.

———. 2008. "Bridging Two Worlds: Aboriginal Education and Employment Action Plan 2008–2011." Accessed September 9, 2014. www.edu.gov.mb.ca.

———. 2013. "Aboriginal Academic Achievement Grant (AAA)." Accessed October 2, 2013. www.edu.gov.mb.ca.

———. 2014a. "Aboriginal Education: Incorporating Aboriginal Perspectives; A Theme-Based Curricular Approach." Accessed August 28, 2014. www.edu.gov.mb.ca.

———. 2014b. Letter to Superintendents/CEOs of School Divisions. March 2014. Accessed September 20, 2014. www.edu.gov.mb.ca.

Meigs, Doug. 2011. "Native Hip-Hop Wraps Alaska Reality TV Show." *Indian Country Today Media Network*, January 28, 2011.

Mendoza, S. Lily. 2013. "Savage Representations in the Discourse of Modernity: Liberal Ideology and the Impossibility of Nativist Longing." *Decolonization: Indigeneity, Education and Society* 2 (1): 1–19.

MFNERC (Manitoba First Nations Education Resource Centre). 2013. "First Nations Operated Schools Directory: 2013–2014." October 2013. Accessed August 28, 2014. www.mfnerc.org.

Miami Herald. 1917. "Indian Melody Collected by Smithsonian Sung by Sembrich." January 28, 1917, 2.

Mihesuah, Devon Abbott. 2003. *Indigenous American Women: Decolonization, Empowerment, Activism*. Lincoln: University of Nebraska Press.

Mihesuah, Devon Abbott, and Angela Cavender Wilson, eds. 2004. *Indigenizing the Academy: Transforming Scholarship and Empowering Communities*. Lincoln: University of Nebraska Press.

Millard, Andre. 2005. *America on Record: A History of Recorded Sound*. New York: Cambridge University Press.

Miller, Christine, and Patricia Chuchryk, eds. 1996. *Women of the First Nations: Power, Wisdom, and Strength*. Winnipeg: University of Manitoba Press.

Miller, James. R. 1996. *Shingwauk's Vision: A History of Native Residential Schools*. Toronto: University of Toronto Press.

Minwaashin Lodge. 2006. *Our Songs Are Our Prayers*. Mach One Music Studio. compact disc.

Mishler, Craig. 1993. *The Crooked Stovepipe: Athapaskan Fiddle Music and Square Dancing in Northeast Alaska and Northwest Canada.* Urbana: University of Illinois Press.

Mitchell, Frank. 1978. *Navajo Blessingway Singer: The Autobiography of Frank Mitchell, 1881–1967.* Edited by Charlotte J. Frisbie and David P. McAllester. Tucson: University of Arizona Press.

Mithlo, Nancy Marie. 2009. "A Real Feminine Journey": Locating Indigenous Feminisms in the Arts." *Meridians: Feminism, Race, Transnationalism* 9 (2): 1–30.

Moffat, Alfred. 1907. *The Minstrelsy of the Scottish Highlands: A Collection of Highland Melodies, with Gaelic and English Words.* London: Bayley and Ferguson.

Morin, Peter. 2016. *this is what happens when we perform the memory of the land.* In Robinson and Martin 2016, 67–91.

Morse, Ann. 2011. "Arizona's Immigration Enforcement Laws." National Congress of State Legislatures. Accessed June 30, 2014. www.ncsl.org.

Muñoz, Carlos. 2007. *Youth, Identity, Power: The Chicano Movement.* New York: Verso.

Myers, Helen, ed. 1993. *Ethnomusicology: Historical and Regional Studies.* New York: Norton.

Nabokov, Peter. 2002. *A Forest of Time: American Indian Ways of History.* Cambridge: Cambridge University Press.

Nannyonga-Tamusuza, Sylvia. 2005. *Baakisimba: Gender in the Music and Dance of the Baganda People of Uganda.* New York: Routledge.

Navarro, Armando. 2005. *Mexicano Political Experience in Occupied Aztlán: Struggles and Change.* Walnut Creek: Altamira.

Nettl, Bruno. 1989. *Blackfoot Musical Thought: Comparative Perspectives.* Kent, OH: Kent State University Press.

———. 1995. *Heartland Excursions: Ethnomusicological Reflections of Schools of Music.* Urbana: University of Illinois Press.

———. 2005. *The Study of Ethnomusicology: Thirty-One Issues and Concepts.* Champaign: University of Illinois Press.

Newkirk, Pamela. 2015. *Spectacle: The Astonishing Life of Ota Benga.* New York: Amistad/HarperCollins.

New York Times. 1917. "Mme. Sembrich Sings: The First of Her Four Historical Song Recitals in Aeolian Hall." January 5, 1917, 7.

NIB (National Indian Brotherhood). (1972) 2014. "Indian Control of Indian Education: Policy Paper Presented to the Minister of Indian Affairs and Northern Development by the National Indian Brotherhood/Assembly of First Nations." Accessed September 20, 2014. http://64.26.129.156/calltoaction/Documents.

Niezen, Ronald. 2003. *The Origins of Indigenism: Human Rights and the Politics of Identity.* Berkeley: University of California Press.

Niles, John D. 1999. *Homo Narrans: The Poetics and Anthropology of Oral Literature.* Philadelphia: University of Pennsylvania Press.

Nordstrom, Carolyn. 2008. "Prelude: *An Accountability,* Written in the Year 2108." *Social Analysis* 52 (2): 1–11.

Norrell, Brenda. 2006. "Indigenous Border Summit Opposes Border Wall and Militarization." *Americas Policy Program.* October 31, 2006. http://americas.irc-online.org.

Nuckolls, Janis B. 2004. "Language and Nature in Sound Alignment." In Erlmann 2004, 65–86.

NUIFC (National Urban Indian Family Coalition). 2008. "Urban Indian America: The Status of American Indian and Alaska Native Children and Families Today." Accessed May 23, 2017. http://caseygrants.org.

O'Connell, Cathleen. 2012. *Sousa on the Rez: Marching to the Beat of a Different Drum.* Lincoln: Visionmaker Media. DVD.

Obamsowin, Alanis. 1993. *Kanehsatake: 270 Years of Resistance.* Ottawa: National Film Board of Canada.

Ochoa Gautier, Ana María. 2006. "Sonic Transculturation, Epistemologies of Purification and the Aural Public Sphere in Latin America." *Social Identities: Journal for the Study of Race, Nation and Culture* 12 (6): 803–25.

———. 2014. *Aurality. Listening and Knowledge in Nineteenth-Century Colombia.* Raleigh: Duke University Press.

———. 2016. "Acoustic Multinaturalism, the Value of Nature, and the Nature of Music in Ecomusicology." *Boundary* 2 (43): 107–41.

Ontiveros, Randy J. 2014. *In the Spirit of a New People: the Cultural Politics of the Chicano Movement.* New York: New York University Press.

Oropeza, Lorena. 2006. "Viviendo y Luchando: The Life and Times of Enriqueta Vásquez." In *Enriqueta Vásquez and the Chicano Movement: Writings from El Grito del Norte,* edited by Lorena Oropeza and Dionne Espinoza, xxvi–liii. Houston: Arte Público.

Orozco, Richard A. 2012. "Racism and Power: Arizona Politicians' Use of the Discourse of Anti-Americanism against Mexican American Studies." *Hispanic Journal of Behavioral Sciences* 34 (1): 43–60.

Pamyua. 1998. *Mengluni* [The beginning]. Ellavut Records 1109801, compact disc.

———. 2001. *Apallut* [Verses]. Ellavut Records 1100002, compact disc.

———. 2003. *Caught in the Act.* Arctic Voice Records 11000301, compact disc.

———. 2012. *Side A / Side B.* Arctic Voice Records 884501688383, compact disc.

Pardes, Joan. 1999. "'Yup'ik Doo-wop' Band Mingles Jazzy Scats, Chants." *Juneau Empire.* August 5, 1999.

Patterson, Michelle Wick. 2010. *Natalie Curtis Burlin: A Life in Native and African American Music.* Omaha: University of Nebraska Press.

Pearce, Roy H. (1953) 1988. *Savagism and Civilization: A Study of the Indian and the American Mind*. Berkeley: University of California Press.

Perea, Jacob Evanjelisto. 1985. "Ethnic Studies in Transition: A Case Study." EdD diss., University of California, Berkeley.

Perea, John-Carlos. 2012a. "The Unexpectedness of Jim Pepper." *MUSICultures* 39 (1): 70–82.

———. 2012b. *Waking from the Roots*. Phoenix, AZ: Canyon Records.

———. 2014. *Intertribal Native American Music in the United States: Experiencing Music, Expressing Culture*. New York: Oxford University Press.

Phillips, Mark Salber, and Gordon Schochet, eds. 2004. *Questions of Tradition*. Toronto: University of Toronto Press.

Picq, Manuela Lavinas. 2018. *Vernacular Sovereignties Indigenous Women Challenging World Politics*. Tucson: University of Arizona Press.

Pisani, Michael V. 2005. *Imagining Native America in Music*. New Haven: Yale University Press.

Pompana, Yvonne. 2009. "Tracing the Evolution of First Nations Child Welfare in Manitoba: A Case Study Examining the Historical Periods 1979–2006 and 2000–2006." PhD diss., Trent University.

Popping Bubbles. 2014. "Popping Bubbles." Accessed June 22, 2018. www.poppingbubbles. org.

Povinelli, Elizabeth. 1999. "Settler Modernity and the Quest for an Indigenous Tradition." *Public Culture* 11 (1): 19–48.

———. 2002. *The Cunning of Recognition: Indigenous Alterities and the Making of Australian Multiculturalism*. Durham: Duke University Press.

Powers, William K. 1986. *Sacred Language: The Nature of Supernatural Discourse in Lakota*. Norman: University of Oklahoma Press.

———. 1990. *War Dance: Plains Indian Musical Performance*. Tucson: University of Arizona Press.

Preston, Richard. 1985. "Transformations musicales et culturelles chez les Cris de l'est." *Recherches Amérindiennes au Québec* 15 (4): 19–29.

Prins, Harold. 1996. *The Mi'kmaq: Resistance, Accommodation and Cultural Survival*. New York: Harcourt Brace College.

Qashu, Leila. 2016. "Toward an Understanding of Justice, Belief, and Women's Rights: Ateetee, an Arsi Oromo Women's Sung Dispute Resolution Process in Ethiopia." PhD diss., Memorial University.

Quese Imc (Marcus Frejo). 2006. *The Betty Lena Project*. Makvsee Music, online stream.

———. 2008. *Bluelight*. Makvsee Music, online stream.

———. 2011. *Hand Drums for Whiskey Bottles*. Makvsee Music, online stream.

Rae, Heather, dir. 2007. *Trudell*. Warren, NJ: Passion River.

Raheja, Michelle H. 2007. "Reading Nanook's Smile: Visual Sovereignty, Indigenous Revisions of Ethnography, and Atanarjuat (the Fast Runner)." *American Quarterly* 59 (4): 1159–85.

———. 2010. *Reservation Reelism: Redfacing, Visual Sovereignty, and Representations of Native Americans in Film*. Lincoln: University of Nebraska Press.

Raibmon, Paige. 2005. *Authentic Indians: Episodes of Encounter from the Late-Nineteenth-Century Northwest Coast*. Durham: Duke University Press.

Ramirez, Michael. 2012. "Performing Gender by Performing Music: Constructions of Masculinities in a College Music Scene." *Journal of Men's Studies* 20 (2): 108–24.

Rampton, Ben. 1995. "Language Crossing and the Problematisation of Ethnicity and Socialisation." *Pragmatics* 5 (4): 485–513.

Rath, Richard Cullen. 2003. *How Early America Sounded*. Ithaca, NY: Cornell University Press.

Ravindran, Tathagatan. 2015. "Beyond the Pure and the Authentic: Indigenous Modernity in Andean Bolivia." *AlterNative* 11 (4): 321–33.

Reichard, Gladys A. 1983. *Navaho Religion: A Study of Symbolism*. Tucson: University of Arizona Press.

RedCloud. 2007. *Hawthorne's Most Wanted*. Syntax Records, online stream.

———. 2011. *1491 Nation Presents: MC RedCloud*. 1491 Nation Records, online stream.

———. 2012. *LightningCloud*. 1491 Nations Records, online stream.

Rellik. 2013. "Idle No More (feat. Nathan Cunningham)." YouTube video, 3:59. Posted by Rellik, February 17, 2013. www.youtube.com.

RETSD (River East Transcona School Division). 2014. "Aboriginal Academic Achievement." Accessed July 26, 2016. www.retsd.mb.ca.

Rhodes, Willard. 1952a. "Acculturation in North American Indian Music." In *Acculturation in the Americas: Proceedings and Selected Papers of the 24th International Congress of Americanists*, edited by Sol Tax, 127–32. Chicago: University of Chicago Press.

———. 1952b. "Songs of American Indian Still Live." *New York Times*, November 23, 1952, X7.

———. 1954. *Music of the American Indian: Indian Songs of Today from the Archive of Folk Culture*. Washington, DC: Library of Congress, AFS L36.

———. 1960. "The Christian Hymnology of North American Indians." In *Proceedings of the 5th International Congress of Anthropological and Ethnological Sciences in Philadelphia*, 324–31. Philadelphia: University of Pennsylvania Press.

———. 1963. "North American Indian Music in Transition: A Study of Songs with English Words as an Index of Acculturation." *Journal of the International Folk Music Council* 15:9–14.

Richardson, Troy. 2011. "Navigating the Problem of Inclusion as Enclosure in Native Culture-Based Education: Theorizing Shadow Curriculum." *Curriculum Inquiry* 41 (3): 332–49.

Richland, Justin B. 2008. *Arguing with Tradition: The Language of Law in Hopi Tribal Court*. Chicago: University of Chicago Press.

———. 2011. "Hopi Tradition as Jurisdiction: On the Potentializing Limits of Hopi Sovereignty." *Law and Social Inquiry* 36 (1): 201–34.

Ridington, Robin. 2006. *When You Sing It Now, Just Like New: First Nations Poetics, Voices, and Representations*. Lincoln: University of Nebraska Press.

Riney, Scott. 1997. "Review Essay: Education by Hardship; Native American Boarding Schools in the U.S. and Canada." *Oral History Review* 24 (2): 117–23.

Robinson, Angela. 2005. *Ta'n Teli-Ktlamsitasit (Ways of Believing): Mi'kmaw Religion in Eskasoni, Nova Scotia*. Canadian Ethnography. Vol. 3. Toronto: Pearson Education Canada.

Robinson, Dylan. 2012. "Listening to the Politics of Aesthetics: Contemporary Encounters between First Nations/Inuit and Early Music Traditions." In Hoefnagels and Diamond 2012, 222–48.

———. 2016a. "Intergenerational Sense, Intergenerational Responsibility." In Robinson and Martin 2016, 43–66.

———. 2016b. "Welcoming Sovereignty." In *Performing Indigeneity*, edited by Yvette Nolan and Ric Knowles, 5–32. Toronto: Playwrights Canada Press.

———. 2017. "Public Writing, Sovereign Reading: Indigenous Language Art in Public Space." *Art Journal*. Indigenous Futures Special Issue (Summer 2017): 81–99.

———. n.d. "Subject-Subject Relations: Apposite and Arts-based Practices of Music Scholarship." In *Intensities: Toward Non-exceptionalist Experiences of Music in Canada*, edited by Dylan Robinson and Mary Ingraham, eds., n.p. Waterloo, ON: Wilfrid Laurier University Press. Forthcoming.

Robinson, Dylan, and Keavy Martin, eds. 2016. *Arts of Engagement: Taking Aesthetic Action in and beyond the Truth and Reconciliation Commission of Canada*. Waterloo, ON: Wilfrid Laurier University Press.

Robinson, Jennifer. 2013. "The Urban Now: Theorising Cities beyond the New." *European Journal of Cultural Studies* 16 (6): 659–77.

Rochberg, George. 1973. *Caprice Variations for Unaccompanied Violin*. New York: Galaxy Music.

"Rolfe Kent Receives Richard Kirk Award at BMI Film and TV Awards." 2012. *BMI.com*. May 17. www.bmmi.com.

Rubio-Goldsmith, Raquel, M. Melissa McCormick, Daniel Martinez, and Inez Magdalena Duarte. 2006. *The "Funnel Effect" and Recovered Bodies of Unauthorized Migrants Processed by the Pima County Office of the Medical Examiner, 1990–2005*. Tucson: Binational Migration Institute.

Sainte-Marie, Buffy. 1996. *Up Where We Belong*. Angel 724383505920, compact disc.

Samuels, David W. 2004. *Putting a Song on Top of It: Expression and Identity on the San Carlos Apache Reservation*. Tucson: University of Arizona Press.

Samuels, David W., Louise Meintjes, Ana Maria Ochoa, and Thomas Porcello. 2010. "Soundscapes: Toward a Sounded Anthropology." *Annual Review of Anthropology* 39:329–45.

Sand, Shara, and Ross Levin. 1992. "Music and Its Relationship to Dreams and the Self." *Psychoanalysis and Contemporary Thought* 15 (2): 161–97.

Sandweiss, Martha A. 2002. *Print the Legend: Photography and the American West*. New Haven: Yale University Press.

San Francisco Chronicle. "Contact with Civilization Proved Fatal." 1916, 31.

San Francisco State University. 2013. "'We Are Still Here' Exhibit Opening Celebration." YouTube video. Accessed June 24, 2018. http://youtu.be3bkGt3ALNIQ. Site now discontinued.

Scales, Chris. 2007. "Powwows, Intertribalism, and the Value of Competition." *Ethnomusicology* 51 (1): 1–29.

———. 2012. *Recording Culture: Powwow Music and the Aboriginal Recording Industry on the Northern Plains*. Durham: Duke University Press.

Schafer, R. Murray. 1994. *The Soundscape: Our Sonic Environment and the Tuning of the World*. Rochester, NY: Destiny Books.

Schertow, John Ahni. 2008. "Tohono O'odham Demand Halt to Construction of Border Wall." *International Cry Magazine*, July 18, 2008. https://intercontinentalcry.org.

Schneider, Lucien. 1985. *Ulirnaisigutiit: An Inuktitut-English Dictionary of Northern Quebec, Labrador and Eastern Arctic Dialects*. Quebec: Les Presses de l'Université Laval.

Schwager, Laura. 2003. "The Drum Keeps Beating: Recovering a Mohawk Identity." In Anderson and Lawrence 2003, 37–53.

Seeger, Anthony. (1987) 2004. *Why Suyá Sing: A Musical Anthropology of an Amazonian People*. Urbana: University of Illinois Press.

———. 1996. "Ethnomusicologists, Archives, Professional Organizations, and the Shifting Ethics of Intellectual Property." *Yearbook for Traditional Music* 28:87–105.

Shapiro, Anne Dhu, and Inés Talamantez. 1986. "The Mescalero Apache Girls' Puberty Ceremony: The Role of Music in Structuring Ritual Time." *Yearbook for Traditional Music* 18:77–90.

Shepherd, Patricia. 2013. "Idle No More Indigenous Report." Progressive Radio Network. September 4, 2013. http://prn.fm.

Shining Soul. 2011a. "Papers by Shining Soul (Extended Version)." YouTube video. Posted by Shining Soul, July 24, 2011. www.youtube.com/watch?v=x79mpAj84ww.

———. 2011b. *We Got This*. Whobiz Production/Sound Wave Recordings, compact disc.

———. 2013. *Sonic Smash*. Whobiz Pros, digital album.

———. 2016. *Politics Aside.* Folded Arms Studios, digital album.

Shore, Fred J. 1994. "The Lubicon Nation in Canada: Long Conflict and Elusive Peace." *Peace Research* 26 (3): 41–53.

Silman, Janet. 1987. *Enough Is Enough: Aboriginal Women Speak Out.* Toronto: Women's Press.

Simpson, Audra. 2014. *Mohawk Interruptus: Political Life across the Borders of Settler States.* Durham: Duke University Press.

Simpson, Audra, and Andrea Smith, eds. 2014. *Theorizing Native Studies.* Durham: Duke University Press.

Simpson, Leanne. 2008. "Looking after Gdoo-naaganinaa: Precolonial Nishnaabeg Diplomatic and Treaty Relationships." *Wicazo Sa Review* 23 (2): 29–42.

———. 2011. *Dancing on Our Turtle's Back: Stories of Nishnaabeg Re-creation, Resurgence and a New Emergence.* Winnipeg: Arbeiter Ring.

Simpson, Leanne, and Kiera L. Ladner, eds. 2010. *This Is an Honour Song: Twenty Years since the Blockades.* Winnipeg: Arbeiter Ring.

Sinclair, Niigaanwewidam James. 2014. "Dancing in a Mall." In Kino-nda-Niimi Collective 2014, 148–49.

Sissons, Jeffrey. 2005. *First Peoples: Indigenous Cultures and Their Futures.* London: Reaktion Books.

"Skip Sandman at Lake Avenue Idle No More Duluth, MN January 11th, 2013." 2013. YouTube video, 4:58. Posted by JP Rennquist, WGZS-FM 89.1 Radio Service of Fond du Lac Band of Lake Superior Chippewa, February 6, 2013. www.youtube.com.

Small, Christopher. 1998. *Musicking: The Meanings of Performing and Listening.* Hanover, NH: Wesleyan University Press.

Smith, Linda Tuhiwai. 2012. *Decolonizing Methodologies: Research and Indigenous Peoples.* 2nd ed. London: Zed Books.

Smith, Paul Chaat. 2009. *Everything You Know about Indians Is Wrong.* Minneapolis: University of Minnesota Press.

Solis, Gabriel. 2012. "Thoughts on an Interdiscipline: Music Theory, Analysis, and Social Theory in Ethnomusicology." *Ethnomusicology* 56 (3): 530–54.

Spady, James, Charles Lee, and H. Samy Alim. 1999. *Street Conscious Rap.* Philadelphia: Black History Museum.

Spady, James, and Joseph Eure. 1991. *Nation Conscious Rap: The Hip Hop Vision.* Philadelphia: PC International Press.

Spears, Shandra. 2003. "Strong Spirit, Fractured Identity: An Ojibway Adoptee's Journey to Wholeness." In Anderson and Lawrence 2003, 81–96.

Spinney, Ann Morrison. 2006. "Medeolinuwok, Music, and Missionaries in Maine." In *Music in American Religious Experience,* edited by Philip V. Bohlman, 57–82. New York: Oxford University Press.

Spirit Wind Singers. 2001. *Breathing the Wind*, compact disc.

———. 2003. *Soul Talkin'*, compact disc.

———. 2004. *Awakening*, compact disc.

Statistics Canada. 2017. *Aboriginal Ancestry (6), Single and Multiple Aboriginal Ancestry Responses (3), Age Groups (6) and Sex (3) for the Population in Private Households of Canada, Provinces, Territories, Census Metropolitan Areas and Census Agglomerations, 2011 National Household Survey.* Catalogue no. 99-011-X2011029. Accessed May 23, 2017. www12.statcan.gc.ca.

Stevenson, Robert. 1973. "Written Sources for Indian Music until 1882." *Ethnomusicology* 17 (1): 1–40.

Stock, Jonathan P. 2001. "Toward an Ethnomusicology of the Individual, or Biographical Writing in Ethnomusicology." *World of Music* 43 (1): 5–19.

Stolze Lima, Tania. 1999. "The Two and Its Many: Reflections on Perspectivism in a Tupi Cosmology." *Ethnos* 64 (1): 107–31.

Sullivan, Michael. 2006. "WOJB's Hand Drum Contest: History and Tradition Is Important." *News from Indian Country: The Independent Native Journal*, January 2006.

Sullivan and Day. 2009. *Love, Lies, and Lullabies: Round Dance Songs.* Canyon Records B00B7U6UWO, digital album.

Swain, Rachel. 2014. "Dance, History and Country: An Uneasy Ecology in Australia." In *Enacting Nature: Ecocritical Perspectives on Indigenous Performance*, edited by Birgit Däwes and Marc Maufort, 165–82. Brussels: Lang.

Swift, Tom. 2008. *Chief Bender's Burden: The Silent Struggle of a Baseball Star.* Omaha: University of Nebraska Press.

Szwed, John. 2011. *Alan Lomax: The Man Who Recorded the World.* New York: Penguin.

Tailfeathers, Olivia. 2005. *Ninihkssin ("Song").* Arbor Records AR12152, compact disc.

Taussig, Michael. 1993. *Mimesis and Alterity: A Particular History of the Senses.* New York: Routledge.

Taylor, Donald, Martha Crago, and Lynn McAlpine. 2001. "Toward Full Empowerment in Native Education: Unanticipated Challenges." *Canadian Journal of Native Studies* 21 (1): 45–56.

Taylor, Michael P. 2016. "Not Primitive Enough to Be Considered Modern: Ethnographers, Editors, and the Indigenous Poets of the *American Indian Magazine*." *Studies in American Indian Literatures* 28 (1): 45–72.

Tedford, Deborah. 2002. "Mexican Migrants Risk Death to Cross U.S.-Mexico Border." Reuters. August 6, 2002. http://legacy.utsandiego.com.

Tenzer, Michael. 2006. *Analytical Studies in World Music.* New York: Oxford University Press.

Théberge, Paul. 2003. "'Ethnic Sounds': The Economy and Discourse of World Music

Sampling." In *Music and Technoculture*, edited by René T. A. Lysloff and Leslie C. Gay Jr., 93–108. Middletown, CT: Wesleyan University Press.

Thomaselli, Keyan G., Lauren Dyll, and Michael Francis. 2008. "'Self' and 'Other': Auto-Reflexive and Indigenous Ethnography." In *The Handbook of Critical and Indigenous Methodologies*, edited by Norman K. Denzin, Yvonna S. Lincoln, and Linda Tuhiwai Smith, 347–72. Los Angeles: Sage.

Thompson, Oscar. 1937. "An American School of Criticism: The Legacy Left by W. J. Henderson, Richard Aldrich, and Their Colleagues of the Old Guard." *Musical Quarterly* 23 (4): 428–39.

Thrush, Coll. 2016. *Indigenous London: Native Travelers at the Heart of Empire*. New Haven and London: Yale University Press.

Tick, Judith, ed. 2008. *Music in the U.S.A.: A Documentary Companion*. New York: Oxford University Press.

Todd, Zoe. 2014. "An Indigenous Feminist's Take on the Ontological Turn: 'Ontology' Is Just Another Word for Colonialism." *Uma (in)certa antropologia*. Accessed on June 26, 2018. https://umaincertaantropologia.org.

———. 2016. "An Indigenous Feminist's Take on the Ontological Turn: 'Ontology' Is Just Another Word for Colonialism." *Journal of Historical Sociology* 29 (1): 4–22.

Tomlinson, Gary. 2009. *The Singing of the New World: Indigenous Voice in the Era of European Contact*. Cambridge: Cambridge University Press.

Toner, Peter. 2007. "Sing a Country of the Mind: The Articulation of Place in Dhalwangu Song." In *The Soundscapes of Australia: Music, Place and Spirituality*, edited by Fiona Richards, 165–84. London: Ashgate.

Torgovnick, Marianna. 1990. *Gone Primitive: Savage Intellects, Modern Lives*. Chicago: University of Chicago Press.

Tortorici, Dayna. 2011. "The Q&A: Dayna Tortorici, Hipster Taxonomist." *Economist*, January 12.

Toulmin, Stephen. 1992. *Cosmopolis: The Hidden Agenda of Modernity*. Chicago: University of Chicago Press.

TRC (Truth and Reconciliation Commission). 2015a. *Calls to Action*. Winnipeg: Truth and Reconciliation Commission.

———. 2015b. *The Final Report of the Truth and Reconciliation Commission of Canada*. 5 vols. Montreal: McGill-Queen's University Press. Accessed June 27, 2018. http://nctr.ca/reports.php.

———. 2015c. "TRC Findings." Accessed August 12, 2015. www.trc.ca.

Troutman, John W. 2009. *Indian Blues: American Indians and the Politics of Music, 1890–1934*. Norman: University of Oklahoma Press.

Truax, Barry, ed. 1978. *The World Soundscape Project's Handbook for Acoustic Ecology*. Vancouver, BC: ARC.

———. 2001. *Acoustic Communication*. 2nd ed. Westport, CT: Ablex.

Tulk, Janice Esther. 2008. "Our Strength Is Ourselves": Identity, Status, and Cultural Revitalization among the Mi'kmaq in Newfoundland." PhD diss., Memorial University.

———. 2009a. "Postdoctoral Pathways: From Powwow to Gregorian Chant." *Canadian Folk Music* 43 (1): 15–19.

———. 2009b. *Welta'q — "It Sounds Good": Historic Recordings of the Mi'kmaq*. St John's, Newfoundland: Research Centre for Music, Media and Place, Memorial University, compact disc and booklet.

Ulali. 1994. *Mahk Jchi*. Thrush Records B000050O6EH, compact disc.

Ulali Project. 2014. "Idle No More." YouTube video, 3:22. Posted by "clockle," May 13, 2014. www.youtube.com/watch?v=jlBwE77Pkoc&index=1&list=RDjlBwE77Pkoc.

"Ulali Project: Idle No More; Official Music Video." 2014. YouTube video, 3:23. Official video of the Ulali Project's song "Idle No More," first performed at the Givens Performing Arts Center–UNC Pembroke in April 2014 for the Fourth Annual River People Music and Culture Fest. Posted by Tapwe Production Projects, June 18, 2014. www.youtube.com/watch?v=YuHqtOdqBuc.

United Nations. 2007. *United Nations Declaration on the Rights of Indigenous Peoples*. Articles 11, 32. New York: United Nations. Accessed June 30, 2015. www.refworld.org.

U.S. Census Bureau. 2012. *The American Indian and Alaska Native Population: 2010*. C2010BR-10. Accessed May 23, 2017. www.census.gov.

Valaskakis, Gail Guthrie. 2005. *Indian Country: Essays on Contemporary Native Culture*. Waterloo, ON: Wilfred Laurier University Press.

Valaskakis, Gail Guthrie, Madeleine Dion Stout, and Eric Guimond, eds. 2009. *Restoring the Balance: First Nations Women, Community, and Culture*. Winnipeg: University of Manitoba Press.

Van den Scott, Jeffery. 2016. "Music of the 'True North': A Study of the Interaction of Canadian Music and an Inuit Community." PhD diss., Northwestern University.

Vander, Judith. 1988. *Songprints: The Musical Experience of Five Shoshone Women*. Urbana: University of Illinois Press.

Van Vechten, Carl. 1918. *The New Art of the Singer: In the Merry-Go-Round*. New York: Knopf.

Various Artists. 2012. *Flying Wild Alaska: The Soundtrack*. Los Angeles: Discovery Studio Tracks.

Vestal, Stanley. 1928. "The Wooden Indian." *American Mercury*, January 1928, 81–86.

"Video Excerpt 1: Fiddlers; My Home." 2015. YouTube video, 2:52. Fiddlers from the Cape Breton Fiddlers' Association playing during the Mass for Wilfred Prosper's funeral in 2005. Posted by Gordon Smith, July 15, 2015. www.youtube.com/watch?v=36JDEe Sxo-I.

"Video Excerpt 2: Fiddle Solo; Bovaglie's Plaid." 2015. YouTube video, 2:27. Fiddle solo played by Carl MacKenzie during the Mass at Wilfred Prosper's funeral in 2005. Posted by Gordon Smith, July 15, 2015. https://youtu.be/fA1SVK2XmpM.

"Video Excerpt 3: Ikwanuté; At the House." 2015. YouTube video, 2:06. Mi'kmaw Round Dance song sung by a group of women singers as the casket is removed from the family home prior to Sarah Denny's funeral in 2002. Posted by Gordon Smith, July 15, 2015. https://youtu.be/si2norpvkJM.

"Video Excerpt 4: Honour Song Procession; On the Road." 2015. YouTube video, 2:04. Mi'kmaw Honor Song sung during the procession of the casket from the house to the church at Sarah Denny's funeral in 2002. Posted by Gordon Smith, July 15, 2015. https://youtu.be/XDPDcQ4yu84.

"Video Excerpt 5: Honour Song Procession; On the Hill." 2015. YouTube video, 1:48. Mi'kmaw Honor Song sung during the procession of the casket mounting the hill leading to the church at Sarah Denny's funeral in 2002. Posted by Gordon Smith, July 15, 2015. https://youtu.be/ptr9vmL_WxQ.

"Video Excerpt 6: Ikwanuté; At the Church." 2015. YouTube video, 2:10. Mi'kmaw Round Dance song sung by a group of women singers as the casket is carried up the steps and into the church at Sarah Denny's funeral in 2002. Posted by Gordon Smith, July 15, 2015. https://youtu.be/nRs-tHimjTE.

"Video Excerpt 7: Glorious Mysteries; In the Church." 2015. YouTube video, 1:50. Processional song sung by choir members at the beginning of Sarah Denny's funeral in 2002. Posted by Gordon Smith, July 15, 2015. https://youtu.be/Ap34JMesyOo.

Viola, Herman J. 1981. *Diplomats in Buckskins: A History of Indian Delegations in Washington City*. Washington, DC: Smithsonian Institution Press.

Viveiros de Castro, Eduardo. 1992. *From the Enemy's Point of View: Humanity and Divinity in an Amazonian Society*. Translated by Catherine V. Howard. Chicago: University of Chicago Press.

Vizenor, Gerald, ed. 2008. *Survivance: Narratives of Native Presence*. Lincoln: University of Nebraska Press.

Volcler, Juliette. 2013. *Extremely Loud: Sound as a Weapon*. New York: New Press.

Von Rosen, Franziska. 1990. "Not Knowing: Dilemmas in Musical Ethnography." In *Ethnomusicology in Canada*, edited by Robert Witmer, 62–69. Toronto: CanMus Documents, Institute for Canadian Music, University of Toronto.

——. 1998. "Music, Visual Art, Stories: Conversations with a Community of Micmac Artists." PhD diss., Brown University.

Vosen, Elyse Carter. 2013a. "The Round Dance as Spiritual and Political Vortex." Paper presented at the annual meeting of the Society for Ethnomusicology, Indianapolis, November 15, 2013.

——. 2013b. "'We Need More Than Love': Three Generations of North American Indigenous Protest Singers." In *The Routledge History of Social Protest in Popular Music*, edited by Jonathan Friedman, 263–78. New York: Routledge.

"Wab Kinew Surprises the George Tonight Audience with a Flash Mob Round Dance." 2013. YouTube video, 3:14. Posted by Strombo, January 18, 2013. www.youtube.com.

Wakeham, Pauline. 2012. "Reconciling 'Terror': Managing Indigenous Resistance in the Age of Apology." *American Indian Quarterly* 36 (1): 1–33.

Waksman, Steve. 2001. *Instruments of Desire: The Electric Guitar and the Shaping of Musical Experience*. Cambridge: Harvard University Press.

Walia, Harsha. 2014. "Decolonizing Together: Moving beyond a Politics of Solidarity toward a Practice of Decolonization." In Kino-nda-Niimi Collective 2014, 44–50.

Walker, Polly. 2001. "Journeys around the Medicine Wheel: A Story of Indigenous Research in a Western University." *Australian Journal of Indigenous Education* 29 (2): 18–21.

Wallace, Anthony F. C. 1993. *The Long Bitter Trail: Andrew Jackson and the Indians*. New York: Hill and Wang.

Wallace, Russell. 2012. "Intercultural Collaboration." In Hoefnagels and Diamond 2012, 218–21.

Walser, Robert. 1993. *Running with the Devil: Power, Gender, and Madness in Heavy Metal Music*. Middletown, CT: Wesleyan University Press.

War Camp Community Service. *A Singing Nation Welcomes a Singing Army*. Milwaukee Unit, Plankinton Arcade. 1918. Accessed July 12, 2018. www.wisconsinhistory.org.

Waziyatawin. 2012. "Towards a Turtle Island without the U.S. and Canada, with Waziyatawin." In *Tangled Roots: Dialogues Exploring Ecological Justice, Healing, and Decolonization*, edited by Matt Soltys, 140–58. Guelph, Ontario: Healing the Earth.

Waziyatawin and Michael Yellow Bird. 2012. "Introduction: Decolonizing our Minds and Actions." In *For Indigenous Minds Only: A Decolonization Handbook*, edited by Waziyatawin and Michael Yellow Bird, 1–14. Santa Fe, NM: SAR Press.

We Are Full Circle: An Aboriginal Women's Voice Concert. 2003. Banff Centre Records CW BANFF, compact disc.

Weigle, Marta, and Barbara A. Babcock, eds. 1996. *The Great Southwest of the Fred Harvey Company and the Santa Fe Railway*. Tucson: University of Arizona Press.

Werry, Margaret. 2011. *The Tourist State: Performing Leisure, Liberalism, and Race in New Zealand*. Minneapolis: University of Minnesota Press.

Whidden, Lynn. 1984. "How Can You Dance to Beethoven? Native People and Country Music." *Canadian University Music Review* 5:87–103.

———. 2007. *Essential Song: Three Decades of Northern Cree Music*. Aboriginal Studies. Waterloo, ON: Wilfrid Laurier University Press.

Whitson, Helene. 1999. *On Strike! Shut It Down! A Revolution at San Francisco State: Elements for Change*. San Francisco: Leonard Library, San Francisco State University.

Whyte, Henry. 1883. *The Celtic Lyre: A Collection of Gaelic Songs with English Translations.* Edinburgh: Maclachlan and Stewart.

Williams, Maria Shaa Tláa, ed. 2009. *The Alaska Native Reader: History, Culture, Politics.* Durham: Duke University Press.

Wilson, Nina. 2014. "Kisikew Iskwew, the Woman Spirit." In Kino-nda-Niimi Collective 2014, 102–7.

Wilson, Shawn. 2001. "Self-as-Relationship in Indigenous Research." *Canadian Journal of Native Education* 25:91–92.

———. 2008. *Research Is Ceremony: Indigenous Research Methods.* Halifax: Fernwood.

Wissler, Holly. 2009. "Grief Singing and the Camera: The Challenges and Ethics of Documentary Production in an Indigenous Andean Community." *Ethnomusicology Forum* 18 (1): 37–53.

Witness, Bear. 2013. Interview with Jian Gomeshi. *Q with Jian Gomeshi*, June 20, 2013. www.cbc.ca/q.

Womack, Craig S., Daniel Heath Justice, and Christopher B. Teuton, eds. 2008. *Reasoning Together: The Native Critics Collective.* Norman: University of Oklahoma Press.

Women of Wabano. 2006. *Voices.* Bartmart Audio and Wabano Centre for Aboriginal Health, OCN317667838, compact disc.

Wood, Fawn. 2012. *Iskwewak: Songs of Indigenous Womanhood.* Canyon Records CR-6494, compact disc.

Woolard, Kathryn A. 2006. "Codeswitching." In *A Companion to Linguistic Anthropology,* edited by Alessandro Duranti, 73–94. Malden, MA: Blackwell.

WSD (Winnipeg School Division). 2013. "Winnipeg School Division." Accessed September 30, 2013. www.winnipegsd.ca.

Yoshihara, Mari. 2007. *Musicians from a Different Shore: Asians and Asian Americans in Classical Music.* Philadelphia: Temple University Press.

Young, James E. 1993. *The Texture of Memory: Holocaust Memorials and Meaning.* New Haven: Yale University Press.

Young Bear, Severt, and R. D. Theisz. 1994. *Standing in the Light: A Lakota Way of Seeing.* Lincoln: University of Nebraska Press.

Yúdice, George. 2003. *The Expediency of Culture: Uses of Culture in the Global Era.* Durham: Duke University Press.

Zamir, Shamoon. 2014. *The Gift of the Face: Portraiture and Time in Edward S. Curtis's "The North American Indian."* Chapel Hill: University of North Carolina Press.

ABOUT THE EDITORS AND CONTRIBUTORS

VICTORIA LINDSAY LEVINE is a professor of music at Colorado College, located on traditional lands of Ute, Cheyenne, and Arapaho peoples. She is the author of *Writing American Indian Music: Historic Transcriptions, Notations, and Arrangements* (2002); coauthor of *Choctaw Music and Dance* (1990); and coeditor of *This Thing Called Music: Essays in Honor of Bruno Nettl* (2015), among other publications. Her research interests include musical revitalization, historical ethnomusicology, music in Indigenous ceremonial life, and the circulation of music along trade routes.

DYLAN ROBINSON (Stó:lō) is the Canada research chair in Indigenous arts at Queen's University, located on traditional lands of the Haudenosaunee and Anishinaabe peoples. He researches Indigenous composition, the politics of Indigenous inclusion and recognition in classical music, Indigenous ontologies of music, sound art, and interarts collaboration. He is the coeditor of *Opera Indigene: Re/presenting First Nations and Indigenous Cultures* (2011) and *Arts of Engagement: Taking Aesthetic Action in and beyond the Truth and Reconciliation Commission of Canada* (2016).

———

T. CHRISTOPHER APLIN is an independent scholar who earned a PhD at the University of California, Los Angeles. With this chapter he concludes a three-part series of articles on Indigenous North American hip-hop, addressing Afro-Indian histories, Christianity, and the cosmopolitanism of Indigenous peoples both past and present. He is currently preparing a book about the music of the Apache prisoners of war taken with Geronimo in 1886 and exploring related research projects in the Los Angeles area that emphasize connections among music, violence, militarism, and imprisonment.

DAWN IERIHÓ:KWATS AVERY is of Mohawk (Kanienkéha) descent and wears the turtle clan. Committed to Indigenous language and cultural preservation as a musician, educator, writer, and participant in longhouse ceremonies, Avery is also a professor of music at Montgomery College and has published cultural-revitalization projects in various media. She is a Grammy-nominated performer, and her music features in many films and recordings, including the North American Indian Cello Project. She won Global Music Awards for *50 Shades of Red* (2014) and her soundtrack for *Ajijaak on Turtle Island* (2018).

JESSICA BISSETT PEREA (Dena'ina) was born in Anchorage, Alaska, and is an enrolled member of the Knik Tribe and a shareholder in Cook Inlet Region (an Alaska Native corporation). Her research projects juxtapose the priorities and processes of two broad areas—music and sound studies with Native American and Indigenous studies—to cultivate a more *Indigenized* sound studies and a more *sounded* Indigenous studies. She is an assistant professor in the Department of Native American Studies at the University of California, Davis.

BEVERLEY DIAMOND is an honorary research professor at Memorial University of Newfoundland. Her publications have addressed Canadian cultural historiography, feminist music research, and Indigenous studies. Her research on Indigenous expressive culture has explored constructs of technological mediation, transnationalism, and concepts of reconciliation and healing. Her publications include *Native American Music in Eastern North America* (2008) and two coedited anthologies: *Aboriginal Music in Contemporary Canada: Echoes and Exchanges* (2012) and *Music and Gender* (2000).

BYRON DUECK is a senior lecturer and the head of music at the Open University. His research interests include North American Indigenous music and dance, musical publics, and rhythm and meter. He is the author of *Musical Intimacies and Indigenous Imaginaries: Aboriginal Music and Dance in Public Performance* (2013) and the coeditor of *Experience and Meaning in Music Performance* (2013) and *Migrating Music* (2011).

ANNA HOEFNAGELS is an associate professor of music in the School for Studies in Art and Culture at Carleton University. She specializes in First Nations music, the music of Canada, and music and gender. Her current research explores urban Aboriginal music making in the context of cultural reclamation and recovery, primarily focusing on the intergenerational effects of colonialism on First Nations women in Canada and the use of music and music-making activities in women's personal journeys of cultural recovery.

CHRISTINA LEZA (Yoeme-Chicana) is an associate professor of anthropology at Colorado College. She is a cultural and linguistic anthropologist, and her research interests include Indigenous peoples of the Americas, discourse and identity, racial and ethnic discourses, grassroots activism, verbal art, and cognitive anthropology. Her recent research focuses on Indigenous activist responses to U.S.-Mexico border policy, which she conducts in collaboration with grassroots Indigenous organizers on the U.S. southern border.

JOHN-CARLOS PEREA (Mescalero Apache–German-Irish-Chicano) is an associate professor of American Indian studies in the College of Ethnic Studies at San Francisco State University. He is the author of *Intertribal Native American Music in the United States* (2014). Perea maintains an active career as a multi-instrumentalist and Grammy award–winning recording artist. His composition *Improvising Home*, for Native American flute and jazz ensemble, was premiered in 2017 with the support of the San Francisco Arts Commission and San Francisco State University.

TREVOR REED (Hopi) is an associate professor of law at Arizona State University's Sandra Day O'Connor College of Law. Reed's research focuses on Native American intellectual and cultural property principles and theory, and he directs the Hopi Music Repatriation Project. He holds a JD and a PhD in ethnomusicology from Columbia University and an MA in arts administration from Teachers College, Columbia University.

DAVID W. SAMUELS is an associate professor of music at New York University and the former director of the Native Studies Forum. He is the author of *Putting a Song on Top of It: Expression and Identity on the San Carlos Apache Reservation* (2004), and his essays have appeared in leading folklore and anthropology journals. He specializes in the relationship between music and language and the ethics of vernacular modernities.

HEIDI AKLASEAQ SENUNGETUK (Inupiaq) is a postdoctoral fellow in Indigenous studies at McGill University, where she studies music of northern regions. She earned a PhD in ethnomusicology at Wesleyan University, an MMus in violin performance at the University of Michigan, and a BMus at Oberlin Conservatory. Senungetuk is an active member of the Kingikmiut Dancers and Singers of Anchorage, a traditional dance group with ancestral ties to the Native Village of Wales, Alaska. Oxford Bibliographies published her article "Indigenous Musics of the Arctic" (2017).

GORDON E. SMITH is a professor of ethnomusicology in the Dan School of Drama and Music at Queen's University, where he is also vice-dean in the Faculty of Arts and Science. Among his publications are the coedited anthologies *Marius Barbeau: Modelling Twentieth-Century Culture* (2008) and *Music Traditions, Cultures and Contexts* (2010). His current research explores themes of reconciliation through musical and social frameworks in the Mi'kmaq community of Eskasoni on Cape Breton Island, part of the eastern Canadian province of Nova Scotia.

ELYSE CARTER VOSEN is an associate professor of global, cultural, and language studies at the College of St. Scholastica. For twenty years she has worked with Anishinaabe community members in northern Minnesota on language revitalization as well as antiracism efforts through the Cross-Cultural Alliance of Duluth. Her doctoral dissertation, "Seventh Fire Children," explores drum and dance performance as decolonizing forces in the lives of Anishinaabe youth. Her publications have appeared in *The Grove Dictionary of American Music* (2013) and *The Routledge History of Social Protest in Popular Music* (2013).

INDEX

NOTE: Page numbers in *italics* indicate illustrations, figures, or tables. Page numbers with "n" indicate notes.

centralization programs, 34

Chacon, Raven, 202–6, *205*, 210, 212–15, *214*, 217

Changing Hands: Art without Reservation exhibition (2005), xiv

Chase, Stuart, 14

Chavis, Ben, 82

Chicano movement, 74, 81, 82, 269n3

Chicanos/Chicanas: Aztlán in ideology of, 82–84; border activism of, 71; colonial oppression of identity, 81–82; hip-hop music and, 74; Indigenous identity claims of, 73, 83–84; nation building among, 269n8; origins of term, 74

child-welfare agencies, 161–64, 167–69, 171, 172

Choko, Martha Lena, 124

Christianity: imagery and metaphors related to, 122; Indigenization of, 123; in Mi'kmaw funeral rituals, 39, 42, 45–47; musical borrowing of hymns from, 251–52; on place of culture in education, 172; powwow music as viewed in, 167–68; in Residential Schools, 271n5; traditional adaptations of music from, 40

civilizational violence, 101, 103

civil rights, 5–6, 70, 74, 84, 269n3

classical music. *See* Native Classical music

Clements, William, 26

Clifford, James, 48

Cline, John, 16

code mixing, 6, 72, 85, 87–88

code switching, 6, 7, 72, 85, 87

Collier, John, Sr., 154

colonialism: activism against, 52; in Alaska, 177–78, 181; aural regimes of, 256; in ethnomusicology, 243; Eurocentric justifications for, 1; land dispossession during, 19; legacy of, 200–201; modes of resistance to, 243; oppression of Indigenous identity during, 81–82; paradigms for transformation of, 103–4; perpetuation of, 83; settler-arrivant narrative in, 176–77, 181, 196–97; site singing at monuments of, 229;

231; sound worlding and, 176, 192; strategic relationships during, 117; urban areas as sites of, 128–29; violence and, 116. *See also* decolonization

Columbia Glacier (Senungetuk), xiv

communication markers, 117–18, 122–23, 135, 141

community-based music, 23, 24, 30, 265–66n7

Composer Apprentice National Outreach Endeavor, 205

conflict resolution, 11, 247

consumerism, 91, 128

Corntassel, Jeff, 112

correctional facilities, availability of cultural activities in, 249, 271n6

corridos (Mexican narrative ballads), 74, 269n5

cosmopolitanism, 117, 118, 139, 140–41, 167

country music, 126–27, 238

Cremo, Elizabeth, 39

Cremo, Lee, 31

Croall, Barbara, 204

cross-cultural competency, 9, 209, 210, 217, 276n10

cross-cultural musical collaborations, 6, 72, 85, 253

cultural accents, 208, 276n10

cultural efficacy, 170–73

cultural expediency, 169–70, 172, 272n14

Cultural Graffiti (Morin), 224, 229

cultural resilience, 104, 231

cultural revitalization, 4–5, 22, 44, 48, 205

culture vultures, 82, 83

Curry, Leo, 38

Curtis, Edward S., 18

Cusick, Suzanne, 254

Cyr, Alicia Kozlowski, 112

"Dancing in a Mall" (Sinclair), 94–95

Daughtry, Martin, 254

Dave, Nomi, 156

Davids, Brent Michael, 205

Deadliest Catch (television program), 178, 181, 192, 274nn19–20

by, 223, 239; nation-to-nation context in work of, 233, 238; public expression of First Nations traditions by, 10; silent ceremony conducted by, 231–32; site singing by, 228–31, *230*; on Truth and Reconciliation Commission, 224–28

Morse, Mat, 188

Mountain Chief, 4, 15–19, *17*, 21–28

music: as change-resistant, 22; community-based, 23, 24, 30, 265–66n7; cross-cultural collaborations, 6, 72, 85, 253; dreams as inspiration for, 13, 201–2; efficacy of, 172; fear as affective factor in reception of, 154, 155; listening to learn, 248–49; at Mi'kmaw funerals, 39–46; solidarity through, xiv, 50, 131; song translation in recovery of language, 40. *See also* ethnomusicology; Indigenous music; *specific artists and genres*

musical borrowing, 202–4, 216, 251–52

musical markers, 208–9

music education programs, 143, 271n3

musicking, defined, 144–45

music therapy, 258

Myers, Helen, 26

"My Home" (Gaelic song), 42, 267n14

NAICP (North American Indian Cello Project), 218–19

National Bureau for the Advancement of Music, 265–66n7

National Indian Brotherhood (NIB), 162

Native American Church, 22, 251

Native American Composer Apprenticeship Program, 205, 206

Native Americans: Aztlán as viewed by, 82–84; border-related issues for, 71, 76, 79–80; ethnic solidarity and, 70; Indigenous identity claims of, 83–84; misrepresentations of, 175, 176; organization into tribes, 116; in peoplehood matrix, 82; in rural areas, 126–27; strategic relationships formed by, 117; in urban areas, 127–31. *See also* tribes; *specific peoples*

Native Classical music, 198–219; audience participation in, 216–17; characteristics of, 198–99; continuum of style in, 204, *205*; cultural metaphors in, 208–10; cultural revitalization projects for, 205; decolonization and, 218; decolonization as embodied through, 9–10; dreams as inspiration for, 201–2; in ethnomusicology, 275n5; Indigenous creative processes in, 201–6, 212–13, 215; Indigenous theory in analysis of, 9, 10; modernity processes in, 198, 200, 201; musical borrowing in, 202–4, 216; self-determination as applied to, 205–6, *207*, 210

"Native Threats" (RedCloud), 119–20, *121*, 139

Native Women's Association of Canada, 54

Navajo concepts and mythology, 203, 207–9, 213, 215, 276nn11–12

Nettl, Bruno, 271n3

neutral markers of communication, 118, 135, 141

NIB (National Indian Brotherhood), 162

"Niche" (Shining Soul), 85–86

Niles, John, 28

noise: categorization of, 149, 150, 154; community emergence through, 150; contextualization of, 150, 154–55; cultural hierarchies and, 154; disciplining of, 152; physiological and psychological experience of, 151; powwow music perceived as, 7–8, 142, 145–46, 149–53

noise music, 206, 221, 238

"No Mercy" (Shining Soul), 79–80, 87–88

Nordstrom, Carolyn, 256

The North American Indian (Curtis), 18

North American Indian Cello Project (NAICP), 218–19

Northern Plains music, 147–48, 154–56

Nuckolls, Janis B., 255

Nurre, D. J., 183, 186, 188, 191

Oakes, Richard, 151

Occupy LA protests, 130

visual sovereignty, 176

Vosen, Elyse Carter, 6, 91, 202

Wakeham, Pauline, 70

"War Chant" (Wright), 118, *119*

Waziyatawin, 103, 112

"Welcome All" (RedCloud), 131

welfare agencies. *See* child-welfare agencies

Werry, Margaret, 93

"Whiskey Bottles" (Quese Imc), 132, 138

Wilson, Nina, 53, 91

women: activism of, 5, 50–59; discrimination against, 55; empowerment of, 5, 51, 56, 61, 65, 205; exploitation of, 6, 103; gender inequalities and, 5, 55; marginalization of, 54, 56, 61; in matriarchal communities, 56; murdered and missing, 53, 55–56; music for social change by, 57–68; nurturing role of, 56–57, 68; in powwow groups, 148, 249; in reserve versus urban life, 63, 65; sexual abuse of, 103. *See also* gender inequalities

Women of Wabano, 58

Wood, Fawn, 58

Wood, Matthew (DJ Creeasian), 96

worlding. *See* sound worlding

Wounded Knee massacre (1890), 122

Yellowface (Chacon), 215

ye-ye music, 137, 270n6

Young Bear, Severt, 147–49

Yúdice, George, 170, 272n14

"Zoom" (LightningCloud), 137

Robert Walser
Running with the Devil: Power, Gender,
and Madness in Heavy Metal Music

Dennis Waring
Manufacturing the Muse: Estey Organs
and Consumer Culture in Victorian
America

Lise A. Waxer
The City of Musical Memory:
Salsa, Record Grooves, and Popular
Culture in Cali, Colombia

Mina Yang
Planet Beethoven: Classical Music at the
Turn of the Millennium

Library of Congress Cataloging-in-Publication Data

Names: Levine, Victoria Lindsay, 1954– | Robinson, Dylan.
Title: Music and modernity among first peoples of North America /
edited by Victoria Lindsay Levine and Dylan Robinson.
Description: Middletown, Connecticut : Wesleyan University Press,
[2019] | Series: Music/culture | Includes bibliographical references and
index.
Identifiers: LCCN 2018046946| ISBN 9780819578624 (hardcover : alk.
paper) | ISBN 9780819578631 (pbk.)
Subjects: LCSH: Indians of North America—Music—History and
criticism. | Music—North America—History and criticism. | Indians
of North America—Social life and customs. | Ethnomusicology—
North America.
Classification: LCC ML3550 .M88 2019 | DDC 780.89/97—dc23
LC record available at https://lccn.loc.gov/2018046946